HR Pioneers:

A History of Human Resource Innovations at Control Data Corporation

HR Pioneers:

A History of Human Resource Innovations at Control Data Corporation

By Mark Jensen

With Norb Berg, Frank Dawe, Jim Morris, and Gene Baker

NORTH STAR PRESS OF ST. CLOUD, INC.
St. Cloud, Minnesota

ISBN 978-0-87839-653-5

First edition: September 2013

Printed in the United States of America

Published by
North Star Press of St. Cloud, Inc.
P.O. Box 451
St. Cloud, MN 56302

www.northstarpress.com

North Star Press – Facebook

North Star Press – Twitter

This book is dedicated to the CDC human resources function, whose efforts improved the lives of the people who came to work for Control Data Corporation.

Acknowledgements

This book would not exist without the support and guidance of several people. First, I need to thank Jim Morris for proposing this project and then acting as both mentor and manager throughout our work together. Next, I need to acknowledge the rest of the Control Data advisory team—Norb Berg, Frank Dawe, and Eugene Baker—all of whom answered my persistent questions and provided their historical insights and personal source material. These four initiated the project shortly after Control Data's fiftieth anniversary, agreeing a history should be written about CDC's human resources function. A special thank you also goes to Robert Price, whose guidance and knowledge fine-tuned the history of Control Data Corporation.

Several individuals were interviewed for this book. I thank you all for taking the time to share your memories and perspectives of the company with me. Additionally, I need to acknowledge the Charles Babbage Institute, who provided yet another treasure trove of original source documents and photographs. I must also thank my wife Jill and our two children; all three endured many quiet evenings with me sequestered in front of my computer.

Lastly, I wish to acknowledge all of the individuals who spent much of their careers shaping Control Data Corporation. They built a dynamic company that advanced humanity through cutting edge computer technologies, pioneering human resource activities, and groundbreaking social responsibility ventures. Unfortunately this book does not have room to acknowledge all their specific contributions. However, these pages are truly intended to be about the careers they built and the lives they touched during their years within the Control Data idea factory. You are about to read their story.

Table of Contents

Introduction

*H*R PIONEERS IS A BOOK that delivers exactly what its title implies. This book describes an HR function at Control Data Corporation (CDC) that created a number of HR initiatives that were ahead of their times. The book also describes a unique company and some exceptional leaders who made these and other business initiatives happen.

The institution of CDC was clearly the product of William Norris, the founder and CEO for most of Control Data's existence. He developed a number of business ideas that were very forward thinking for the time. CDC was also ahead of its time in social responsibility. Norris pursued social projects on a scale that is probably unmatched even today. These social projects attracted a lot of criticism from Wall Street financial types, and led to a history of mutual animosity between CDC and Wall Street. As a result, the CFO never attained the level of influence that we find at other companies. Instead, Bill Norris formed a partnership with Norb Berg, his head of HR. The partnership gave HR a status and influence I have never seen at any other company. The partnership also led to CDC's third area of uniqueness: the programs initiated by HR. Many of these programs still exist today as profit-making enterprises. Let us look at each of these four unique contributions.

Control Data's core business was mainframe computers. It fell victim to the waves of creative destruction that wash over the computer industry every decade or so. CDC joins other mainframe manufacturers (Honeywell, Burroughs, NCR), mini-computer makers (DEC, Wang, Data General), workstation designers (Sun Microsystems) and maybe even the PC makers (HP, Dell) in being diminished by the next wave after a period of temporary success. But during this period, Bill Norris foresaw the rise of computer services to go along with selling the computers. Many of these service businesses are what survive from the Control Data mothership. One service that was particularly well known was the computer education services.

Control Data and its HR group were very interested in keeping their employees, in general, and their engineers, in specific, up-to-date and well informed. Like all of the HR programs and services for CDC employees, the purpose was to create effective and productive talent. But as the program became successful, it became the Control Data Institutes, and its services were sold to the general public. As part of its social responsibility pursuits, the educational program was made available to the inner city and rural poor, and then to prison populations. This progression from HR program to profit-seeking business to social good was mirrored in many subsequent HR initiatives.

In another example, CDC's educational software program, PLATO, enhanced the computer education services. The PLATO business received a great deal of effort. It was probably too far ahead of its time, but it still exists, like the Control Data Institutes. One only has to look at the enthusiasm for online courses today to realize the insights that Bill Norris and Control Data HR had some thirty to forty years ago.

A second area where Control Data and its HR group were ahead of the times was in the pursuit of the social good. Today, companies in good standing are expected to be socially responsible. Young people want to join companies that pursue a purpose and not just make money. My colleagues at TruePoint, Mike Beer, Nathanial Foote and Russ Eisenstat, wrote a book about this higher ambition. They have established a leadership institute to train and follow leaders who want to do well by doing good. But this was not the view at the time when Control Data introduced its social initiatives. Instead, they earned the criticism of Wall Street and paid the pioneer's tax. But CDC persisted in its programs. They never saw these programs as charity. They were intended to be profit-making endeavors that would support the effectiveness of the company. For example, CDC needed to build plants. So why not build them where people needed jobs, like the inner city and at prisons? There were handicapped people who could not travel. So why not give them computers and let them work from home?

The HR department was an integral part of these initiatives. The hiring, recruiting, training and managing of these people were a challenge. Today all companies have diversity programs of some sort. By placing plants in the places where they were needed, CDC had a diversity program where they took the work to diverse populations. Once again, CDC was ahead of its time.

The third area where Control Data played a pioneering role was in HR itself, hence, the title of this book. The HR contributions began with Bill Norris's desire to have a caring company. And once again, the purpose was to attract, develop and retain talented people, especially the engineers. The HR people started with the Employee Advisory Resource (EAR), which was a twenty-four-hour, seven-day per week hotline to help with all kinds of personal issues. CDC also created StayWell, which informed and encouraged healthy habits. How many companies have this health orientation today? For those that do, reducing health care costs is the primary motivation. At CDC, cost reduction was desirable, but the primary purpose of the HR programs was to attract and retain healthy and trained people. These programs followed CDC's typical pattern of internal success, and were later marketed externally to make them available to all companies, and then to underserved populations in the community.

The HR function was also influential in the business decision-making process. Today there are many companies with poor track records of acquiring and integrating other companies. One of the issues is that HR is not part of the due diligence process. The acquisition is made and then the company discovers a cultural mismatch. At CDC, HR was part of the due diligence team and could prevent a mismatch before it happened. They had a voice in important decisions. Today many HR functions at other companies are still hoping for a "seat at the table" where business decisions are made. Forty years ago, the HR group had one at CDC.

The fourth unique aspect of HR at CDC was its influence throughout the company. They not only had a seat at the table, but they used it. This authority was played out in the succession decision to replace Bill Norris when he retired. Norb Berg, the head of HR, was considered to succeed Norris for the chairman position. Norb Berg would then share executive roles with Bob Price, a CEO candidate who rose through the ranks by running businesses and had P+L experience. Due to the difficult times Control Data experienced in 1985, the board decided not to split the executive roles, selecting Bob Price as CEO and Chairman. However, Norb Berg retained the title of Deputy Chairman, demonstrating how highly CDC valued its HR group.

In summary, this is a book about a unique and unusual company. One of the singular aspects of the company is its HR group. It was ahead of its time with HR programs. It was uncommon in that era to make them available in the market and to offer them to deserving groups in the community. For those readers who want to understand the origins and pure contributions of some of today's more forward thinking initiatives, this book is both a history lesson and instruction manual for today's leaders. The leaders at CDC were truly HR pioneers.

Dr. Jay Galbraith
Galbraith Management Consultants
Breckenridge, Colorado
June 5, 2013

Chapter One

Of Transistors and Transitions

"We were up against entrenched competitors with vastly superior resources. Yet there was in Control Data both optimism and fierce determination . . . We succeeded to a remarkable degree."
—*William C. Norris*

"What I think and do matters; I can make a difference!"
—*Control Data Human Resources Philosophy*

THE PRESS ANNOUNCEMENT IN 1992 WAS, for many who admired the company, a solemn moment. Control Data Corporation (CDC), the once titan forefather of the supercomputer hardware industry, would formally cease operations under the Control Data banner. Its remaining business units were split into two organizations. The company's legacy computer hardware product line and related businesses became Control Data Systems, Inc. This company would operate as a separate organization, providing support services for users of the parent corporation's mainframe computers and integration services for government and business interests. The remaining Control Data units specialized in services: business management offerings like payroll processing, benefits administration, and employee assistance. This company was renamed as Ceridian Corporation. The name change effectively turned the organization into a new company, cutting it away from Control Data's identity and past history. Customers would then only think of Ceridian as a business management services provider.

The Control Data Corporation brand immediately disappeared from the worldwide business landscape (Control Data Systems, Inc. eventually would as well; the company was acquired by Syntegra in 1999). It was a difficult outcome for the many individuals who had spent over thirty years building this globally recognizable company. At its height, Control Data Corporation manufactured the fastest mainframe computers in the world, had an international workforce of over 60,000 employees, and was frequently ranked as one of the best and most admired companies in the United States. While many of its product lines and business units survived within the child companies and acquired business units that spun away, the Control Data brand name did not.

Corporations come and go, of course, but Control Data Corporation was truly unique. The company had been a place of innovative, maverick thinking and groundbreaking new technologies and services. Control Data frequently explored ways technology and business ideas could be paired to address a social need to improve the lives of their employees and the economic viability of communities. During the days when this company built geo-ballistic computers for the Navy's Polaris submarine, CDC expanded its assembler workforce by hiring women in rural Minnesota, Wyoming, South Dakota, and Kentucky. Control Data's many customers included NASA, where CDC computers were used during the Apollo moon program, and the Rosebud Indian Reservation, where CDC computers were used to track the health records of Native Americans. Instead of fleeing urban centers for safer ground after the riots of the late 1960s, Control Data built a series of poverty-area plants. These plants hired unskilled, predominately minority workers, many of whom became long-term CDC employees. While company engineers created amazing devices, direct predecessors of today's electronic marvels, the company also launched the first 24/7 employee counseling service to support the workers who manufactured these devices. Today employee assistance providers, or EAPs, are standard services provided by corporations—and all are modeled after Control Data's original concept.

These diverse products, services, and employee programs may seem a strange mix for a mainframe computer and peripheral manufacturer, but notice the connection all of these initiatives share. Many were value-added services that could be better provided by controlling data through CDC computers. The name of the organization even emphasizes this focus—the company wanted to control data, not control hardware. This services business strategy was not always clear to the public, however, as Control Data was associated more with hardware development than the services CDC hardware could provide. The strategy behind these service business concepts was to improve the company's bottom line. By creating a healthy work environment, Control Data would have a stable, experienced employee base to ensure the long-term profitability of the organization. Then by supporting educational and economic ventures within developing communities, Control Data would reduce the demand for welfare and other government services, and so likewise reduce their tax burden in these communities. It was a holistic approach to business that would make the company an innovator in both computer technology and human relations. When Control Data faded and transformed, the loss of this company's approach to business was acutely felt by all the communities and organizations Control Data's efforts had touched.

Reasons for the company's dissipation were attributed to several sources. Control Data Corporation had four main areas of business activity: computer mainframe manufacturing, computer peripheral equipment manufacturing, data processing services, and financial services. Advances in personal computer technology throughout the 1980s had slowly eroded the demand for its mainframe hardware and data processing service centers. At the same time, several companies in Japan emerged as key competitors in the peripheral market and undermined CDC's ability to compete in this once secure product area. Control Data also had made substantial, long-term investments in the ETA-10 mainframe computer. Despite the exciting promise of this new product, Control Data no longer had the research capital, or the potential market, to justify continuing the ETA-10 system. Critics argued, though, that company leaders should have moved ahead of the technological curve to develop a personal computer product line and other related technologies. Supporters countered this argument by stating Control Data leadership did indeed move in the best direction for the organization, guiding the company to its logical evolution into Ceridian, Control Data Systems, and its many spinoff entities.

Just as the classic parable, however, about how blind men can touch various parts of an elephant and come to different conclusions about the shape of the animal, the analysis about Control Data's decline or transformation is often told more in part than in whole. CDC faced the same difficulties which competing mainframe computer manufacturers wrestled with at the time. RCA, Honeywell, Burroughs, Bendix, Zenith, IBM, General Electric, and others all had mainframe manufacturing divisions, and, like Control Data, most of these manufacturing centers no longer exist today. These giant competitors, however, had other product lines it could fall back on. Unlike them, Control Data derived much of its income from its mainframe and peripheral manufacturing, and when these once profitable product lines declined, Control Data found itself in a precarious position. Company leaders were also well aware about the growing personal computer market, and the company had the engineering talent to design these increasingly popular devices. CDC's manufacturing facilities, however, were not set up to handle the mass assemblies required for personal computer production. A transition into this type of commodity manufacturing would have been extremely costly and difficult. CDC was gradually moving more and more toward a service-based strategy, but the volatility of the industry did not give the company enough time to completely target its energies into this growing market space. All these issues were contributing factors in the company's challenges.

Another criticism articulated at the time was that Control Data Corporation's diverse social ventures had doomed the organization. Some business commentators and Wall Street investors asserted CDC's adventures in welfare capitalism had diverted focus and drained vital resources away from its core businesses. With its leaders' investing resources into social responsibility ventures, they concluded CDC had lost direction. Control Data's founder and CEO, William Norris, received harsh criticism in the media. *Fortune* magazine called him "a business genius who unfortunately thinks he's social philosopher," and *Inc.* magazine concluded Norris was an "eccentric corporate do-gooder." In the growing free market of the early 1990s, Control Data's transformation was held up as an example that corporations should focus on selling products and making money (Peters and Waterman's "stick to the knitting" principle), and leave society's ills to non-profit organizations and government agencies better equipped to handle such activities. This diagnosis made hot press, and was fueled in part by several years of heated antagonism between Wall Street investors and the media on one side, and maverick Control Data Corporation on the other. Norris and other company leaders had constantly explained they were attempting to address society's unmet needs as profitable business opportunities, but this rationale was lost amid cries against the amount invested and the growing decrease in shareholder value in the mid-1980s. A new direction was put in motion that eventually led to the organization's final transformation into Control Data Systems and Ceridian Corporation.

Regardless of the causes, the breakup of Control Data Corporation marked the end of one of most dynamic and innovative companies in the corporate history of the United States. This company opened new doors of technology that led to the ever-expanding role computers and other electronic devices now play in commerce, government, and everyday life. The philosophy of its leaders fostered a climate of innovation within the company, and this corporate culture continues to be an admired example of how encouraging employees to bring forward innovative ideas can also encourage the development of new businesses for emerging markets. Its emphasis on creating value-added services from its hardware products has become the business model for many technology companies since Control Data first launched this strategy. And some of Control Data's social enterprise endeavors did become profitable businesses; these ventures demonstrate how corporations can be a powerful agent for advancing the welfare and prosperity of disadvantaged populations.

This chapter contains the historical background about Control Data Corporation. Its purpose is to illustrate the CDC approach to innovation through its groundbreaking technologies and services. This background is important to understanding how the company later approached its human resources function, eventually turning the corporate-level HR functions into a separate services organization as well. This chapter also illustrates how Control Data's social responsibility ventures were not an experiment in civic responsibility, but were actually in tune with the overall strategic direction of the company. The middle sections of this book then explore the history behind many of Control Data's social responsibility ventures—and their influence today on both corporate culture and global business practices. The book concludes with a chapter on what has happened to several of the business concepts and child companies that were originally launched within the Control Data idea factory.

Beginnings

CONTROL DATA CORPORATION WAS BORN amid the battles of World War II. The individuals who would later become the founding members of the company were almost all engineers and scientists from the Communications Intelligence (COM INT) unit within the Navy. This group was charged with gathering enemy radio communications and decoding them. Founder and CEO of Control Data, William C. Norris (or, as he didn't mind being called, "Bill"), ran the Atlantic radio fingerprinting process, which was more commonly known by its abbreviation, RFP. This group's mission was to identify German U-boats by the unique characteristics of their radio transmissions. They used early electronic devices to capture Nazi U-boat transmissions and roughly calculate the location of each submarine. Navy bombers were then dispatched to the location in an attempt to destroy the vessel. When radio operations received these transmissions, they were also simultaneously sent to COM INT cryptologists in order to decode their messages. While British Intelligence had broken the German enigma code, their analysis process took far too long. By the time the message could be deciphered, the U-boat was gone. Due to the massive supply ship losses that occurred during this period of the war, the Navy initiated a large-scale research effort to improve the effectiveness of this technology and speed up the decoding process. At its peak, over 1,000 mathematicians, physicists, engineers, and social scientists were put to this task, and their efforts were highly successful. Due to the improved decoding process, many German U-boats were either sunk or disabled. The German U-boats' threat to shipping greatly diminished, giving the Allies much-improved access to the supplies needed in the European theater of the war.

With this success achieved in the Atlantic seas, a similar breakthrough was needed for the war waging in the Pacific. Navy commanders decided this radio technology and decoding process had to be immediately applied against the Japanese armada, so a new RFP Center was built at the Naval Radio Intercept Station in Hawaii on the island of Oahu. As before with the German code, this group was tasked with the responsibility of breaking the Japanese code. Through both determination and serendipity, the COM INT cryptologists were finally able to crack the Japanese code. This breakthrough was one of the major factors that helped America and its allies win the Battle of Midway, which ultimately turned the tide of the war against Axis Japan. It was a remarkable achievement, and Navy commanders did not forget about the agile young minds who had managed this feat.

At the end of World War II, the military began the rapid and necessary demobilization of its forces. Not only were the armed forces reducing their number of enlistees, the government was also scaling back and eliminating defense contracts that were no longer necessary. William Norris and his staff officers, however, wanted to continue their work in communications intelligence by starting a new company. They presented this idea to a high ranking commander, Admiral Wenger, and he gave them permission to develop a business plan. Admiral Wenger and the rest of the Navy brass did not want their core group of code-breaking technologists to disband, as they hoped to benefit from future technological innovations. Ultimately, Defense Secretary James V. Forrestal approved the plan as the best way to keep this group of technologists together.

Norris and his staff officers began presenting their business plan to several companies, but despite some solid interest, had no success in securing a backer for the venture. With demobilization happening rapidly, Norris and his group were running out of time. Luckily, they found a key partner in John Parker, president of Northwest Aeronautical Corporation, a Twin Cities firm that had manufactured troop gliders for the war effort. With the glider defense contract now expired, John Parker had an empty manufacturing facility. Admiral Chester Nimitz, former commander of the Pacific Fleet, personally met with Parker in order to gain his financial support for the start-up business. As Admiral Nimitz told Parker, "It may be more important in peacetime than it is in wartime." Supported by the encouragement of the Navy, John Parker invested both capital and the empty facility into creating a new company within the Northwest organization. Because of this decision, the Minneapolis-St. Paul area became one of the major hotbeds for early computer research immediately at the end of World War II.

The new company was named Engineering Research Associates, or ERA, and it opened its doors in 1946. (Originally the company was going to be called Research and Development Associates, but the group realized this name could be abbreviated by competitors as RED ASS.) Its first employees were twenty-five newly discharged Navy cryptographers, scientists, and engineers who had been members of the COM INT team. Led by Bill Norris, this dynamic laboratory fast became an exciting place of discovery, and the growing business organization developed several early computing devices. The company's close association with the Navy helped spur its financial growth, as this military branch had a constant demand for improved technology due to mounting Cold War tensions with the Soviet Union. The key customer for ERA products within the Navy was the Naval Computing Machine Laboratory, which meant much of ERA's work was done under very tight security, but this relationship also gave the ERA engineers access to other computer research being done across the country. Free from much corporate intervention and burdensome oversight, the ERA lab was a bastion for research and development into an uncharted world of technological possibilities. The ERA team designed large-scale vacuum tube digital computers and a variety of peripheral devices. Several of these early machines are the predecessors for much of the digital equipment commonly used today.

Eventually the company needed additional funding to leverage the commercial potential beginning to open up for its products. John Parker sold Engineering Research Associates to the Remington Rand Corporation in 1951, at nearly eighty-five times what the original founders had paid to start it up just five years before. Remington Rand Corporation had its own computer research and manufacturing division, Eckert-Mauchly, a firm originally started by two scientists in Philadelphia who had built the world's first digital computer, the UNIVAC-T. When the sale to Remington Rand was complete, the ERA and Eckert-Mauchly divisions were merged to form the UNIVAC division. Now almost all significant computer research and development in the United States was being carried out through the same corporation, Remington Rand. This merged division, 1,500 employees strong, was led by the former World War II commander of the cryptographers—now Vice President William Norris.

Norris, born in 1911, was a Nebraska farm boy used to long hours and hard work. As part of the independent rural work ethic impressed upon him during his childhood, he had an intense desire to improve both himself and the people around him. He attended the University of Nebraska and received a degree in electrical engineering. However, when his father died in 1932, he returned home to run the family farm. With the Great Depression in full swing, it was a difficult time. During one summer, a long dry spell decimated pastures and the hay crop, and thistles sprouted everywhere in the alfalfa ground. The cattle herd would soon face starvation. Norris, however, was resourceful. He noticed some of the cattle eating the young thistle plants that had not yet grown sharp barbs. He hired some neighbors to harvest the thistles before they matured and used them for hay. They thought he was crazy, but some agreed to try it. While not great hay, the young thistles worked well enough to keep the herd alive until the rains came and better hay was available.

Farming was not for Bill Norris though, mainly because these long, prolonged periods of drought caused him, as he stated, "to develop a desire to not be subject to something so much beyond my control." He soon sold off the entire cattle herd in Omaha and looked for another direction for his career. Thanks to his college degree, he got a job at Westinghouse in Chicago engineering and selling x-ray equipment, where he was introduced to corporate business and culture. During this time, he learned a valuable lesson about technology: eventually new hardware becomes a cheap commodity, and only value-added services provided by this hardware stay profitable in the long term. Norris applied this principle to his business strategy throughout his career. He stayed at Westinghouse until World War II broke out. Then as a member of Naval Intelligence, he was part of a team dedicated to finding innovative solutions to complex communication and intelligence decoding problems. This background made him an ideal leader for the new UNIVAC division. He had a joint desire to maintain high morale in the engineers working for him, while at the same time producing technological innovations that would propel the division forward. Although his demeanor could be sometimes gruff and salty, Bill Norris was highly regarded and well respected throughout the emerging national computer industry.

During these early years, the division also hired an intense young engineer, Seymour Cray, whose genius for engineering was only matched by his passion for solitude. Born in Chippewa Falls, Wisconsin, in 1925, he earned a Bachelor of Science degree in electrical engineering from the University of Minnesota in 1950, and a Master of Science degree in applied mathematics in 1951. Hired by ERA immediately after graduation, he soon became one of the major engineering masters of the research facility, and his growing talents were a part of ERA and later UNIVAC's technological breakthroughs. Key to that success, however, was the innovative and entrepreneurial spirit that existed in the original small, nimble ERA lab. As the demand for computers grew beyond the military into the scientific and university sectors, it became more important to deliver products quickly enough to satisfy the market than to design new and better computers. The merger with Eckert-Mauchly also caused a clash of cultures and project strategies, ultimately resulting in a competition for resources. Cray and the other engineers began to long for a return to the days of the smaller ERA research center at the old glider factory.

Then in 1955, the Remington Rand Corporation merged with the Sperry Gyroscope Company to form the Sperry Rand Corporation. Under even more corporate oversight and demands than ever before, former ERA members were no longer secretly longing for the recent past—they were fervently discussing it. Seymour Cray and several other engineers approached

Bill Norris, expressing a desire to "become an ERA again." Norris shared this desire as well, as he had been quietly opposed to the first sale of the company to Remington Rand, but ultimately decided he could not do anything about it. Now under Sperry Rand, he felt this merged corporation had wasted its opportunity to become the dominant world leader in computer hardware. Despite having massed together tremendous talent, Sperry Rand decided against making the investments and taking the risks it needed, and soon IBM became the industry leader. "We sat there," as Norris remembered, "with a tremendous technological and sales lead and watched IBM pass us as if we were standing still." Sperry Rand was not empowering its technologists to pursue their full creative potential. Chafing under the restrictions placed upon the UNIVAC division, Norris "had a belly full" and began seriously exploring how he could create a new company that would have the innovative and entrepreneurial culture which matched the business philosophy that had worked so well at ERA.

He and his associates pursued this end under some secrecy. As the head of UNIVAC, Norris had a stable position, and he and his associates were gambling it all away in a risky start-up venture. His decision would also attract a lot of attention in the press if his exit was prematurely made public, and Norris needed everything tightly in place for investment in the new company to begin. On July 8, 1957, Control Data Corporation was incorporated in Minnesota, and it offered 600,000 shares at a dollar apiece. It was the first computer company to be publically traded. With Norris involved, investors eagerly infused the start-up with this capital, and the venture began its operations. Interestingly, the first public inkling that a new computer corporation was being formed was hinted at by Sid Hartman, a well-known Minneapolis *Tribune* sportswriter, on July 30, 1957. Hartman wrote, "Have several former UNIVAC people resigned from the St. Paul Sperry Rand branch to form a firm called Control Data that will deal in electronic research?" Hartman continued, "If Norris was resigning and will join the new firm, the development is even larger than anyone has realized." It was now official: William Norris and a small group of associates from UNIVAC had broken away to create their own company. As a former founder of the new corporation stated, "We knew that Norris was the key to getting the idea off the ground, and if he hadn't come, Control Data wouldn't have happened." William Norris was selected unanimously as the CEO, and the formal split from Sperry Rand was essentially complete. On September 1, 1957, CDC started operations with four employees.

Their first office was in the McGill Building at 501 Park Avenue in Minneapolis. The prospectus of the newborn company stated their purpose was focused on ". . . the design, development, manufacture, and sales of systems, equipment, and components used in electronic data processing and automatic control for industrial, scientific, and military uses." Research began in earnest. The start-up was now either on the road to success or oblivion.

Norris fostered an entrepreneurial environment within the new workspace, making sure the founding team had a ground floor, "everyone is in this together," atmosphere. Norris wanted to maintain as flat a management organizational structure as possible, to reduce the

The first office of Control Data Corporation at the McGill Building in 1958. Notice the company's placard on the entrance. (Photo courtesy of the Charles Babbage Institute.)

frustrating chain of command that had hampered progress at Sperry Rand. The new company was to be a joint effort, and he was no better than anyone else in working toward the success of the company. The accommodations themselves were slightly crude, as this office space was an unadorned warehouse with concrete floors and portable dividers. The location also had no air conditioning or screens on the windows, which meant a lot of flies buzzed around the place. It became quite a pastime to kill the insects during the summer; some of the staff kept scorecards to compare their kill numbers. And although Norris did have a better office than the rest of the group, he did not have a separate bathroom or air conditioning unit. Because of this, he occasionally visited with the staff when he needed some fresh air or the use of the facilities, which kept him in contact with these first employees.

Seymour Cray immediately wanted to resign from Sperry Rand and join the new ERA-styled endeavor, now officially launched at 501 Park Avenue. To his frustration, though, he was still working on a key project for UNIVAC, and Norris refused to hire him until that project was finished. This demonstrated a pattern of leadership Norris would follow his entire career, making sure that while changes in business would happen and cause companies and individuals to go their different ways, the divergent parties could separate on as amicable terms as possible. Norris had no desire to hurt Sperry Rand, so he refused to hire Cray until he was able to leave at what would be a good point for UNIVAC. Cray finished his last project as quickly as he could, and soon led the engineering talent at the tiny Control Data lab. When Cray officially joined CDC, the new business grew to thirteen employees.

Seymour Cray and his team threw away many of the rules and assumptions of computer design up to that point and started with a clean slate. Cray approached all projects through this method, which when it worked, created brilliant results. For his first series of projects at Control Data, Cray developed the CDC Little Character, a totally transistorized machine, and other early software tools. These small "bootstrapped" tools were used to make the larger tools that, in turn, would eventually make mainframe computers. Specifically, Cray used the CDC Little Character for testing to see if it was feasible to create a larger system made up only of transistors. Up until that time, computers used either vacuum tubes or a combination of vacuum tubes and transistors. The CDC Little Character ran successfully only on transistors, and Cray and his team gathered the base research they needed to embark on their next full project. The importance of these early tools cannot be overstated. Control Data was only running on venture capital and some income from small government contracts. If these test machines had failed, the survival of CDC would have been much less certain.

With proof-of-concept in hand, Cray now took on the main project. Leveraging the power of transistors and abandoning vacuum tubes, his engineering team created the 1604 computer. This groundbreaking creation was the largest machine of its time and was the first fully transistorized computer manufactured anywhere in the world, with over twenty-five miles of wiring tightly looped inside each computer. They also decided to use an expanded 48-bit word length instead of the common 36-bit word length used in other computers. While this expanded word length gave the 1604 a competitive advantage, it also added more overall hardware costs to the machine. But ultimately the expanded word length made the 1604 faster, more precise, and easier to program than competing machines. In many surprising ways, the 1604 design ran

Bill Norris shaking the hand of Bill Hyland, agent from North American Van Lines. North American Van Lines delivered the 1604 computers to Control Data's first customers. (Photo courtesy of the Charles Babbage Institute.)

against the original strategy of CDC's development plan of creating a more conventionally designed computer system for its first product, but the independent approach encouraged by Norris had yielded an impressive result.

Competitors certainly took notice of CDC when the company released its 1604 mainframe computer, but several industry leaders predicted Control Data would run out of venture capital and quickly disappear from the scene. This dire prediction was not to be. The 1604 turned into a goldmine for the new company. During its first year of sales in 1959, the company had a gross income of $786,000. During the next fiscal year, gross sales reached $10 million. By the close of the next fiscal year in 1961, gross product sales doubled to over $20 million in revenue. Norris and his associates' connections with the military were a major factor in the incredible sales of the new company, with seventy-five percent of its income gained through defense contracts and the remaining percentage from commercial organizations. Between outright sales of the 1604 at its $1.5 million price tag and its rental service rate of $300 per hour, Control Data Corporation's growth exploded in ways that probably surpassed even the original hopes of Bill Norris.

Sperry Rand did not take the brain drain from its UNIVAC talent pool lightly. Upon the release of the 1604, Sperry Rand immediately initiated a lawsuit against CDC claiming the new company had copied computer designs originally developed at UNIVAC, and so was entitled to copyright infringement compensation. Accusations were made that Control Data's 1604 was the same as UNIVAC's 1103, claiming all CDC did was add the number of their new address (501 Park Avenue) to UNIVAC's 1103 to come up with the name for the CDC 1604. The lawsuit dogged the first few years of the new company. However, Cray's design was significantly different from what he had developed at UNIVAC, and the lawsuit was settled out of court in 1962. Control Data Corporation was now totally free and clear of the past, and could follow a path that would lead to the many and large dreams of Norris—and the talented team he had inspired to join him.

New Products, New Frontiers

WHILE THE 1604 WAS THE MARQUEE PRODUCT that brought CDC into prominence, it was not the only device released by the company in the early 1960s. Other teams besides the Cray group created a significant series of computers that increased the customer base for the company and ensured a steady stream of income. One of these important keystone products was the 3600, a large, general purpose computer system. These high-performance machines had a flexible assembly system that helped speed up its manufacturing process and also reduced its costs. The testing and maintenance requirements of the 3600 were also reduced, making it an easier machine for customers to maintain. In 1962 alone, fifty CDC 3600 machines were installed. This product became part of the base design for the 3000 series of smaller computer systems, and these more affordable mainframe machines fit the needs of smaller scientific and commercial customers.

Besides broadening CDC's market presence, it also generated much-needed cash flow while the Cray team worked on their next product, the 6600 mainframe.

Another early, interesting product was the 160 and 160A mini-computer. These machines were the first computers small enough to fit within an office desktop. Originally the 160 mini-computer was simply created as a device used to test the circuitry within the 1604. The engineering team soon realized this test device was actually a computer as well, and best of all, it could be totally housed inside a desk, making it one of the first "desktop" computers. Released in 1960, this product proved this size computer could be made and that customers were willing to buy them. Because of this, the 160A was developed, a more successful computer that improved and expanded on the original ideas of the 160. Many 160A computers were sold through a major original equipment manufacturer (OEM) contract with NCR. The 160 line of computers were versatile machines, as they could either connect to a 1604 to expand the main frame system into a network or be used as an independent computer system. A successor to the 160A, originally dubbed the 160Z, was also put into development. This computer was soon renamed the 3200, and its technology was incorporated into the base design for Control Data's popular 3300 line of smaller mainframe computers sold throughout the 1960s.

After the 160A, future mini-computer CDC products were limited to specific military applications. In the early 1980s, Control Data's most likely candidate for a personal computing device was a small machine called the 469, manufactured exclusively as a flight computer for fighter planes. Due to the nature of this sensitive defense contract, CDC could not repurpose this mini-computer into a commercial product. So while Control Data did have experience designing smaller computers, these devices were always created for very specific purposes and were produced through a limited manufacturing cycle. They were never designed for widespread commercial use.

During the company's early years, Control Data also made its first acquisition. CDC acquired Cedar Engineering, a business that manufactured servos and gyroscopes. Control Data's main interest in the acquisition was the firm's manufacturing center. Cedar Engineering had a nice, clean facility that CDC could use as a marketing tool to show prospective military customers they owned a facility that could potentially be used for some development or assembly work. Cedar Engineering was run by Thomas Kamp, a man who would soon become the leader of an extremely profitable product line for the fledgling company.

Early computers were often called the "electronic brains" that ran calculations against the data entered into them. But additional outside devices, termed peripheral devices, were required to both push the data into these electronic brains and then pull the calculated data out of them. While Control Data created impressive, competitive, and fast computers, the company relied on outside vendors to supply these tape drives, tape transports, and other crucial peripheral devices. When archrival IBM bought out the supply of a small, but key, peripheral device, sales of the 3600 and other computers were placed in serious jeopardy. Control Data needed to make

The CDC 160, the first desktop computer, built in the early 1960s. (Photo courtesy of the Charles Babbage Institute.)

their own peripheral devices (and fast!) or face the demise grimly predicted by its competitors. To solve this problem, Norris asked Thomas Kamp to lead a huge expansion into peripheral electromechanical manufacturing. Kamp formed a design team consisting primarily of the engineers he had worked with at Cedar Engineering, and the development effort began.

The gamble paid off, as sales of the 3600, 3300, and the 1604 helped boost purchases of the new peripheral devices, while the availability of these peripheral devices likewise encouraged sales of these mainframe products. The Peripheral Products operation became a major profit center for CDC, as competitors enlisted CDC as an OEM supplier for the peripherals they needed for their own mainframe computer products. Through this strategic move, Control Data increased sales for its original product offerings and gained new income from an additional hardware line.

Control Data received much of its early income through various high end government contracts. Not surprisingly, the company had a close association with the Navy; during 1963, the company built eleven advanced geo-ballistic computers for the Polaris submarine fire control system. This multi-million-dollar contract was one of several major contracts the company negotiated with the Defense Department—and one of the few it could publicly disclose. Many of these Department of Defense contracts were for classified computer system projects the company could not reveal, but these top secret projects were very profitable. Control Data Corporation also contributed a significant device that advanced NASA's effort to put a man on the moon before the Soviet Union. The 924 Control Computer was a small, dependable machine that successfully integrated throughout the NASA launch and support functions. NASA needed this machine quickly, and the 924 development team flawlessly delivered this computer on time, within budget, and on target with its design. This computing device was one of the forerunners to "reduced instruction set" (RISC) computers—high performance, lean machines designed specifically for technological solutions. The 924 machines, however, were not the only CDC computers used by NASA, as two CDC 3600s were later installed at Cape Kennedy in 1966, for use on the Apollo moon flight program. Thereafter, NASA continued to be a key customer.

A new business also grew along with the mainframe computer and peripheral sales. As Norris learned at Westinghouse, eventually hardware becomes a low profit commodity. Despite the huge splash of its first mainframe computers, the future of Control Data's business would eventually lie in the services the company could provide through the use of its technology. From the moment the company released the 1604, Control Data immediately began exploring computing services the company could market. Control Data started renting computer processing time to customers who either did not need a mainframe or could not afford the hefty price tag of one. The Control Data Services organization built several data services centers, each of which housed a mainframe computer. Customers could schedule processing time with this mainframe machine, receiving the data input and generating the requested data output. One of the services these centers could provide was payroll checking, processing, and printing, and this soon became a popular offering. The services product line would eventually add a third major area of income for CDC. As Robert Price, a former Control Data CEO relates, "Where computers could provide the services, that was the direction where Bill Norris wanted to take the company." This success validated his approach to technology, and so Norris actively encouraged his teams to explore other innovative services they could provide through Control Data hardware.

With this top down support, Control Data developed a culture of imagination and energy. All kinds of human activity could be improved through the use of computer technology. As an example during this early period, the company began exploring what it termed as the "industrial use of computers." William Keye was the vice president of this development group. During the 1963 annual shareholder's meeting, he explained the various ways computer technology could be leveraged for industrial purposes. "In some companies," he said, "this will mean the use of computers in the control of a pipeline or in the control of a chemical plant or oil refinery; in others, it will mean the control of a power plant; in others the collection of data in computer language from the production floor; while in still other companies, it will be the computer control of communications between plants." He then described a system being built for the Duncan Meter Company that would test and adjust electric watt hour meters at the end of a production line. Computers were rapidly becoming much more than simply a military tool of the Cold War; they had exciting applications for manufacturing, monitoring systems, and beyond.

Besides expanding the product line, Control Data was also keenly active in opening new markets overseas for its products and services. In the fall of 1962, a group of five Control Data employees, all young U.S. citizens, started an international office in Lucerne, Switzerland. They hired three Swiss administrative and clerical people, and the international arm of Control Data Corporation began. The office's first sale was for a 1604 computer, the mainframe computer purchased by Regencentralen, a Danish research organization. However, computers were not the main technology products in demand. European businesses were particularly excited about CDC's tape transport and other peripheral devices, and within a few short months Control Data received major purchases from international customers. Sales offices were rapidly set up in Switzerland, Germany, Sweden, Holland, England, and France to take advantage of this demand. All of these opportunities further fueled the CDC explosion.

During this time, another individual entered the company who would first help lead this international effort and then later become the guiding force behind CDC's technological innovations. Joining the company as a programmer in Palo Alto in 1961, Robert M. Price was the collaborator William Norris needed, and would eventually be the catalyst behind Norris's technology and services direction. Price graduated magna cum laude from Duke University, and his first job out of college was as a mathematician at the Lawrence Livermore Laboratory. While employed at Lawrence Livermore and later at Convair (General Dynamics), Robert Price worked on the largest, most powerful Control Data computers available. He was instrumental in developing applications for physics, aircraft design, and many other engineering projects. He gained a solid reputation for expertly leading and completing impressive large scale application projects.

In 1963, William Norris was looking for someone who could handle the complexity of CDC's introduction into international markets. Frank Mullaney, a co-founder of Control Data with Norris and a member of the board of directors, suggested he consider Robert Price as a candidate to lead this effort. Norris flew out to Palo Alto to interview Price, who was at this point working at a CDC facility. The two technologists shared a common bond. Norris, in his preface to Robert Price's book, *The Eye for Innovation*, described their first interview: "We were on the same wavelength from the very beginning. He was intelligent and had all the necessary technical knowledge, his integrity was the highest, and I could count on him to give me the facts no matter how painful they might be. You can't ask for more than that." Robert Price became the director of international operations in late 1963, and advanced as one of Norris's most influential advisors.

Price embraced William Norris's approach to fostering innovation within the company. Despite all the challenges that lay in the years while he was CEO, Price embodied one of the defining mottos of the company, which was, "there must always be a better way." In his book about innovation, Price describes Control Data's model of approach, writing, "The correct definition of innovation is problem solving. It is the ability to see a need and to think creatively how that need might be met in a better way. That is how we apply technology—maybe new technology, maybe old technology—in novel ways to fashion a better way." Throughout the early 1960s, Control Data made incredible strides in technology that caused the entire industry to advance the power and importance of the computer. But the computer is ultimately a tool like any other—a tool with a variety of uses. With a solid base of cutting edge products and a culture of innovation thoroughly instilled in the company, employees at CDC continuously explored ways their amazing tools could open up imaginative possibilities for larger and larger markets. Everybody at the company wanted to become the next Seymour Cray, and all were empowered by CDC's leadership to pursue this ambition. Control Data was the ERA lab again, but this time the company was creating more than top secret innovations for the military, it was creating very public innovations for the entire world.

In 1967, Control Data Corporation was ten years old. CDC now employed over 15,000 people worldwide and had sales running at over $200 million per year. During that ten-year span the company had installed over 2,000 computer systems in the United States and internationally, and the total value of all of the computer hardware was valued at over $700 million. The peripheral line of products was quite a broad offering as well, so much so that eight of the world's ten largest computer manufacturers regularly purchased CDC peripheral equipment. Control Data had also been listed on the New York Stock Exchange starting in 1963. To illustrate the company's explosive growth, one statistic explains this expansion the best. If an investor had purchased $10,000 in CDC stock in 1957, this investment would have been worth $6.8 million by 1968. The exit from Sperry Rand had been a good move. As William Norris would later humbly state, "We succeeded to a remarkable degree."

The Human Resources Explosion

WHILE DESIGNING THE 1604, 3300, 3600, and the peripheral equipment were key to the company's success, these products would do very little for the company if they were not manufactured and fully marketed. All of this effort required renting, building, or buying shop floor equipment and space—and then hiring the workforce needed to design, produce, sell, and support these product lines. Hiring qualified employees was the responsibility of the personnel department (later on, this CDC function was called human resources). The rapid expansion of the company required that job recruiters aggressively target college campuses and job fairs to look for the talented engineers needed to give the company its technological edge. New manufacturing facilities had to be built and then quickly filled with assemblers and managers. Then to complete the company, all these individuals needed to be supported by payroll, clerical, and custodial staffs. As the company expanded its operations and acquired new companies, a personnel office was needed within each new area of the company—which meant the personnel department itself had to rapidly expand and change as well. It was a daunting, never-ending task.

During these early years, Control Data hired a tireless HR professional who would quickly become one of the primary leaders who shared in William Norris's utilitarian vision—Norbert (Norb) Berg. A Korean War veteran, Berg had earned a Bachelor's degree in social science in 1955, from St. John's University, and a Master's degree in industrial relations in 1957, from the University of Minnesota. After graduation, Berg worked for the Standard Oil Company of New Jersey in their personnel department. But this job was on the East coast, far from his Wisconsin hometown and family. Berg heard about the growing little company in Minneapolis and, even though there was no job opening, sent a cold call letter to the company. Berg was hired as the company's first personnel supervisor in 1959, and the personnel department was organized around this same time. CDC was just two years old and, by this point, had grown to a workforce of 180 employees. Norb Berg's time at the company was nearly short-lived, however, as within just a few years of working for Control Data he contracted tuberculosis. Though Berg was unable to work for six months, Norris demanded that the company keep Berg employed until he was able to return to work. This act of compassion deeply affected Berg. When he recovered, Berg was understandably one of Norris's major supporters within the organization.

Berg eventually became the leader of the personnel department, assuming the title of corporate director of administration and personnel in 1962. During Berg's tenure, the department enjoyed an extraordinary and unusual amount of input in corporate decisions. Good use of human resources was seen as vitally important to the health of the ballooning organization, for without a satisfied, well-educated, and highly trained workforce, the present and future of CDC's prospects would be in jeopardy. In Berg, William Norris had found a partner for his vision of a caring corporation, so he gave Berg increasing autonomy to carry out this vision as the years went on. While Seymour Cray, Thomas Kamp, and Robert Price were the leaders driving the company's technology efforts, Norb Berg and his personnel department started an equally innovative, leading edge foray into the company's employee and social business initiatives.

An example of an early success was the expansion of CDC manufacturing plants into rural Minnesota. The personnel department concluded that farmwives were an untapped labor force who would benefit from better job opportunities, so Control Data placed these new plants in rural Minnesota towns such as Cambridge, Redwood Falls, Faribault, Montevideo, and Spring Grove—areas where these individuals could be more easily hired. This approach turned out to be extremely beneficial for both CDC and the rural communities where they built the plants. This project also gave the personnel team the experience and confidence needed to build plants in the economically depressed areas of inner cities, a project that would pitch Control Data into a popular spotlight during the civil rights era of the late 1960s.

But that was all yet to come. The main issue for Control Data at the start of the 1960s was where to put everyone. The company had expanded so much, the accommodations at 501 Park Avenue no longer had the floor space to handle the burgeoning demands the main office now required. In 1962, the company moved its headquarters to a new 103,000-square-foot building in suburban Bloomington, Minnesota, a location at which the expanding corporate headquarters would remain for the rest of Control Data's history.

Enter the 6600

Seymour Cray was growing restless again. To his frustration and dismay, an all-too-familiar growth pattern was beginning to happen at CDC. Within just a few short years (and thanks to the success of his 1604 design), the small-team culture that was similar to the ERA environment was being replaced with one which reminded him of the relentlessly busy conditions that had driven him to near distraction at Sperry Rand. He felt like he was constantly on demand, and became notorious for his ability to avoid meetings and work in seclusion. He longed to be constantly on task for his next generation mainframe computer design, but the distracting environment in Minneapolis was pushing him to the edge of his patience. He decided if he was to complete this design, he had to initiate a change.

Like he had done at Sperry Rand just a few years before, Cray made his frustrations known to William Norris. And as before, Norris was sympathetic to Cray's concerns and wanted to arrive at an agreeable solution with him. This time, of course, starting a new company was not an option. But in addition to hating the growing mass of humanity at CDC headquarters, Cray also hated the growing mass of humanity in the Twin Cities. He longed for quiet. The solution he presented Norris was to create a permanent ERA-style lab, a secluded cocoon, where he and his engineering team could focus. He wanted Control Data to build a new laboratory outside of the metropolitan area, in the quiet countryside of Chippewa Falls, Wisconsin, his hometown. Norris and the rest of the CDC management team were eager for Cray to be focused and productive, as his upcoming creation was of critical importance. It was an easy decision to make. The lab would be a solid, relatively inexpensive investment for Control Data, so Norris agreed. A new state of the art facility was built at Chippewa Falls, and Seymour Cray relocated his small team to this laboratory as soon as it was ready.

Cray controlled total access to the Chippewa Falls laboratory. Nobody could visit the facility without an appointment—and this rule even extended to William Norris. Free of essentially all the aspects of corporate life which were an intense burden to him, Cray could completely focus on creating the successor of the 1604 mainframe. And if the 1604 computer system was a groundbreaking innovation, the new design that emerged from the Chippewa Falls laboratory was legendary.

Often called the first successful supercomputer, the CDC 6600 mainframe was the fastest computer in the world throughout most of the 1960s. (It only lost that title when Seymour Cray's next design, the CDC 7600, entered the market.) Upon its release in 1963, the 6600 had three times the performance of its closest rival, the IBM 7030 Stretch. To achieve this speed, Cray and his engineering team incorporated new silicon-based transistors into the design. These

The CDC 6600 mainframe computer, complete with the CPU, tape storage drives, card reader, desk interface, and other peripheral devices. Twenty years later, some personal computers would have the same data processing power. (Photo courtesy of the Charles Babbage Institute.)

new transistors offered improved switching performance, resulting in speeds never seen before in a computer. Its blazing performance made it the most powerful computer of its day. An article in *Fortune* magazine had this to say about the 6600: "It has a voracious appetite for raw material, and users are hard put to keep it fully occupied. It performs at speeds of more than three million instructions a second and can, for example, multiply every telephone number in both the 1,524-page Brooklyn and 1,830-page Manhattan telephone directories by the number that follows it, add the product of each of these multiplications, divide the total by any number and print out the answer in less than two seconds." With the United States at the height of the Cold War, the speedy 6600 was the right machine at the right time. Its rapid computing power was a major asset for the military and scientific tasks assigned to it.

Lawrence Livermore Radiation Lab was the first organization to order a CDC 6600, and from this first sale, purchases boomed. Control Data Corporation had created a supercomputer juggernaut. The company arrived as a major technology player and was featured in leading industry and news magazines. The release of the 6600 also started an intense rivalry with IBM, which now saw its dominance in this market sector severely challenged. The giant corporation, despite its massive resources, did not have a computer with equal speed or memory. Their CEO, T.J. Watson, wrote in a memo dated on August 18, 1963, "Last week CDC had a press conference during which they officially announced their 6600 system. I understand that in the laboratory developing this system there are only thirty-four people, including the janitor. Contrasting this modest effort with our own vast development activities, I fail to understand why we have lost our industry leadership position by letting someone else offer the world's most powerful computer." The sting caused by the CDC 6600 caused much pain and handwringing at IBM, and executives at this company now looked at CDC as their prime target. Somehow, some way, the IBM leadership would figure out a way to best Control Data in the mainframe game. And a marketing choice IBM made later on in the decade would eventually have serious consequences.

The move to Chippewa Falls had pushed back the release of the 6600, but Cray's often-delayed successor to the 1604 was clearly worth the wait. Cray's independent project took longer than scheduled, but Norris was patient and the company reaped the benefits. Cray had once again come through for CDC. As William Norris wrote in the 1964 annual report,

> Our CD 1604, when it was introduced in 1958, set a new standard and Control Data has been setting the pace since then. This year it was again possible for Control Data to take the lead in offering computer customers the most computing per dollar. Our 6600 is the undisputed world leader in the computer industry. It is not only the largest computer, but also the most efficient. This year it became evident that there was widespread demand, so we have started substantial production of 6600's.

Control Data was no longer a small start-up company; it was now a substantial provider of computer hardware, and sales orders were placed for its products from throughout the United States and the world.

And Seymour Cray now had a little more time to spend on his favorite Wisconsin lakes, using the new sailboat he had built. But in typical Cray fashion, when the lakes froze over that fall, he burnt up the sailboat so he could build a new one over the winter, to have it ready in time for next spring.

A Gnat That Swallowed a Whale

ALTOGETHER, CONTROL DATA COMPLETED over a hundred acquisitions during its thirty-five years of operations. Each acquisition provided the company with strategic resources that enhanced or supplemented other areas of CDC business ventures. The company made acquisitions that solved a vital need for its manufacturing process or added another product CDC could bring to market. While the company grew by expanding facilities, strategic acquisitions were by far the main reason the company grew so quickly in such a short span of time. The Control Corporation acquisition (1960) provided much-needed knowledge of gas, oil, and water distribution systems that helped CDC develop technologies for industrial markets. The Holley acquisition (1961) added capabilities in the design and manufacture of printers. The Meiscon acquisition (1963) gave CDC additional engineering competence. The individuals who joined the company through these acquisitions, like Thomas Kamp, often brought significant expertise and creativity which proved crucial to the company, and in turn fueled more growth. Many of these acquisitions were large purchases. The largest acquisition ever made by CDC, however, was the unconventional, unique purchase of the Commercial Credit Company in 1968.

The Commercial Credit Company (CCC) was a major financial services institution. It was one of the oldest financial organizations in Canada, but they conducted much business within the United States. Through the company's 700+ offices, the Commercial Credit Company financed loans for many product lines—mortgages, car purchases, businesses, and other products. The organization financed large business ventures, as well; one company Commercial Credit supported through a major business loan was a fledging start-up called FedEx. It also had credit insurance and vehicle leasing services in its portfolio.

Now Commercial Credit was in a difficult spot. CCC executives were fighting a hostile takeover by Loew's, a competing financial firm. To counter this takeover, they approached Control Data with the proposal they join CDC to strategically provide the benefits of both alleviating CDC's frequent cash shortages and financing the computer system and peripheral leases piling up against the company's balance sheet. It was a strange, intriguing proposition. The Commercial Credit Company, in size and capital, was much, much larger than Control Data. But the acquisition would give Control Data a different income stream, an income stream removed from the ups and downs of the computer hardware development cycle. For what benefit it received from the proposal, Commercial Credit would essentially remain a separate entity with a separate board, as CDC did not have financial product operations it could merge with it.

The merger appealed to Norris, as it provided a major inroad into another potential services sector for mainframe technology—financial services. He agreed to the deal. Publicly it was announced Control Data had acquired Commercial Credit. As John Fossum, a former CDC employee and retired professor of human resources at the Carlson School of Management at the University of Minnesota describes, "The Commercial Credit acquisition was basically a case of a gnat swallowing a whale." The details of the agreement were actually more complex than what was publicly disclosed, however. On paper, it was Commercial Credit which technically "acquired" Control Data. Commercial Credit became the financial arm within the Control Data organization, keeping its name to maintain itself as a separate business identity. The surprising acquisition was complete.

To complete the transaction, several CDC executives moved to Commercial Credit and, vice versa, several CCC executives moved to Control Data. One Control Data executive, Bill Rowe, led the human resources transition at Commercial Credit. Bill Rowe had similar responsibilities as Berg had at Control Data. Berg and Rowe, kindred spirits, worked closely together. During Rowe's tenure at Commercial Credit Corporation, their human resources function adopted many of the same practices used at Control Data. Another key Control Data executive who eventually moved to Commercial Credit was Paul Miller, the president of Control Data's marketing function. A well-regarded and respected executive who led the early, successful efforts selling computers to industry, government, education, and other sectors, Paul Miller became the chief executive officer at Commercial Credit. Several past employees of the company, including George Klaus, a former Control Data sales manager and former CEO of Epicor Software Corporation and Frank Dawe, Control Data's Senior vice president of administration in the late 1980s, credit Miller's approach to business and customer relations as one of the key factors for Control Data's consistently profitable years in the early 1970s. Now placed in charge of Commercial Credit Corporation in the mid-1970s, Miller held his executive position with this organization for well over a decade, ensuring Control Data's long-term relationship with Commercial Credit.

So did the computer hardware manufacturer benefit from purchasing this financial services company? It turned out to be a strategically shrewd move. Control Data was often short on cash, investing much of its earnings into research and development for the next product. Commercial Credit provided CDC with a much more consistent revenue stream to smooth out earnings during fiscal periods that had heavy research and development expenses. In fact, Commercial Credit profits were sufficient enough during a number of tough quarters to keep Control Data in the black. A 1972 article in *Forbes* magazine describes one such situation: "It was the Commercial Credit stock that saved CD last year when its loans fell due. And it was Credit's rising earnings that kept CD's head above water during the excruciating days of 1970 and 1971. For all of 1970, Control Data lost $37 million after taxes, but Commercial Credit's profits, $38 million, made up the loss." Designing and manufacturing a mainframe computer line was always a high-wire tightrope walk, and the acquisition provided much-needed stability. As Frank Dawe, former senior vice president of administration, describes, "Commercial Credit saved our bacon numerous times."

These financial services were also a strategic benefit to the core business. Through Commercial Credit, CDC gained an easier way to help customers finance major purchases and leases of its mainframe computer equipment. Now when a customer purchased or leased a CDC 6600, the million-dollar-plus loan could be processed through Control Data's financial business. It was a convenient service, and many customers took advantage of Commercial Credit's financing program, using it to finance leasing or outright purchase of mainframe computers, peripherals, and data services. The benefit to Commercial Credit was immediately apparent as well, as this financial institution now had access to Control Data's customer base, many of whom were stable, large organizations that took out substantial loans. So the increased revenue helped increase this financial services business as well, as Commercial Credit now had additional capital available to back up the loans it could provide through its other financial services.

In a short period of time, the acquisition proved to be the fourth major product area for Control Data Corporation. Now along with computer hardware, peripherals, and computer services, CDC added financial services to its main offerings. Although Norris would continue to seek out other business ventures throughout the 1970s, these four product areas ultimately defined the company's primary sources of income until its decline and transformation began in the middle of the 1980s.

Cray Departs

ALSO IN 1968, THE CHIPPEWA FALLS lab completed work on what turned out to be Seymour Cray's last major product design for Control Data, the CDC 7600 mainframe. His goal in the 7600 design was to create a machine faster than the 6600, and the 7600 did not disappoint. It was about ten times faster than the 6600. The original plan for the product was that it would be highly compatible with the 6600, so it was originally called the 6800. But when Cray decided he could not make the design completely compatible in order to gain the performance he wanted, the name of the new mainframe was changed to the 7600 to emphasize it was the next generation CDC computer. The 7600 had similar features to the 6600, as it had identical instructions and a 64-bit word size. It was not completely source-code compatible with its formidable predecessor, though. Operators could, however, link compilers and operating systems between the 6600 and the 7600 without too many issues, but this was the only compatibility between the two mainframe systems.

The eagerly awaited CDC 7600 was extremely successful and continued Control Data's dominance in the mainframe sector throughout the early 1970s, as it was the fastest general purpose mainframe system on the market—only losing this distinction in 1975. The machines had lasting power, though, as some CDC 7600s were still in use up until the early 1980s. However, this design is generally considered not as elegant as the 6600, as this mainframe device was victim to frequent breakdowns. In order to achieve the performance results, Cray designed the 7600 so each circuit module was densely packed with resistors, diodes, and transistors; the close proximity of the components meant that when working together they would generate a lot of heat in a small space. So much heat was generated from the 7600, in fact, that in some installations the hot air output was circulated through the building as a heat source. The back of each side of the computer also had Freon-cooled aluminum plates installed to provide cooling for the circuitry. Unfortunately, this cooling system was vulnerable to breakdowns, so Cray designed the 7600 into a huge "C" shape to give a maintenance team access to the modules by walking inside this "C" shape and opening the cabinet that contained the problem unit. Despite this drawback, the 7600 was dependable enough, and the increased processing power more than made up for the additional maintenance required to run the machine.

The relationship between Cray and Norris had not been very smooth during the development of the 7600. Cray, along with a founding member of the company, Frank Mullaney, did not like how fast the company was expanding. Both men and their supporters wanted to keep the company a smaller business and only focus on mainframe computer development and manufacturing. Norris, however, believed the company could not survive on just mainframe income alone and argued that expansion, particularly with value-added peripherals and services, was necessary for the future health of the organization. For a while this dispute festered privately within the CDC board room, but in 1966, the argument became public when both Mullaney and Cray resigned from the board of directors. Mullaney left the company, but Cray stayed on as a director of research at the Chippewa Falls lab. He stated, however, that this decision was made more out of devotion to his work than out of loyalty to Control Data. As he was quoted in a *Wall Street Journal* article at the time about his decision, "I resigned from the board because my objectives are more limited than the board's; my interest lies in large computers, and the company is getting into a lot of areas I'm simply not interested in. Years ago, when the company launched its expansion program, I felt kind of sorry."

This incident was behind Seymour now, however, and the 7600 was a significant success. Ever focused on improving performance and computing power, Cray and his Chippewa Falls team immediately started work on their next generation mainframe—the 8600. Cray's goals were, not surprisingly, to design a machine ten times as fast as its 7600 predecessor. If he could achieve this goal, Control Data would ensure their dominance in the mainframe market throughout the 1970s. With Cray leading this design effort, 7600 sales and his reputation both huge, the company and the market anticipated CDC's crown as the king of mainframe performance would not be toppled anytime soon.

It was not to be. William Norris and Seymour Cray soon found themselves in a difficult situation that caused Cray to leave the company and start his own rival venture. Problems began when the world economy experienced a significant downturn in 1971, and Control Data was hit hard with unexpected losses (which it survived thanks in part to the Commercial Credit acquisition, as previously described). A mandatory ten percent pay cut was instigated across the company. Resources were inevitably pulled back for the Cray team, and consequently, development on the 8600 slowed down. Now two and a half years into the development cycle, the 8600 design was still not coming together, and company leaders were anxiously pressuring Cray to get the 8600 out to the market. Cray, only concerned about design and engineering, did not want the continuing success of the company and its growing number of employees resting so squarely on his creations. His focused passion was to create experimental, cutting edge computers. Having so much of the company's fortunes placed on his work was both stressful and distracting. Even though the dark cloud of the financial crisis eventually passed, Cray resented the outside pressure the crisis had placed on his secluded Chippewa Falls lab.

Meanwhile, the state of things was no less stressful inside the lab. Cray came to the conclusion he had selected the wrong technology for the design, as the 8600 prototypes were constantly breaking down. It was nearly impossible to get all the modules in the entire machine to run at the same time. Cray had to totally abandon the current 8600 design and start over. What he ultimately needed to do was to get away from the lab for a while and think about how exactly he would redesign the 8600. But would that help? Cray was becoming increasingly depressed and worried. So much of the company's well-being depended on his designs, and the stress of this responsibility was often more than he wanted to handle. Worst of all, if the 8600 failed, as he was totally convinced it would, his failure would be on national public display. He felt that he simply could not do his best work under these limitations and pressures. In 1972, Seymour Cray resigned from Control Data.

The announcement was shocking, and it came at a time when CDC was extremely vulnerable. The bad economy, the ten percent cut in pay, and now Cray's departure totaled a string of hard events for the company to work itself through. Wall Street responded negatively to the news, and the value of Control Data stock fell sharply. The future of Control Data suddenly looked very bleak. Luckily the situation was temporary, as the economy recovered quickly enough to avert larger financial fallout, and Control Data survived the crisis. The parting of ways between William Norris and Seymour Cray was also surprisingly amicable. As Norris stated in a *Forbes* magazine article at the time, "It was inevitable. You can't keep an individualist like Seymour working for a giant corporation. He won't be confined by organizations. Look at it this way: How many companies have managed to secure the services of a brilliant innovator like Seymour Cray for more than a decade? I think we got more than we ever had the right to expect."

Cray decided he would found his own company, Cray Research, and Norris had Control Data invest $300,000 in Cray's new venture. Norris, as was his approach to business, was not vindictive and did not want to end the relationship with his former megastar engineer. Norris also strongly believed that by fostering competition, companies are forced to improve their products and customers ultimately receive more benefit at lower price points. Prudent businesses practices followed the split, however, as Cray did sign a covenant not to compete directly with Control Data for the first few years. Seymour Cray and Control Data were now, however, on separate paths. Despite the failure of the 8600, Cray's reputation was impressive, and soon he was able to receive additional investment capital from Wall Street speculators. Once again he created an ERA-style laboratory and was able to focus full-time, creative energy on his next mainframe design, the CRAY-1. And Control Data's investment in Cray Research proved to be a smart choice, as this company's stock did very well, returning a respectable profit for Control Data.

As for the 8600, the remaining members of Cray's team felt they could complete and deliver the 8600. Norris gave them his support, and work continued on the project at the Chippewa Falls lab. But Cray's predictions would prove true, as by 1974, the 8600 still could not

The Control Data World Headquarters building during the 1970s. (Photo courtesy of the Charles Babbage Institute.)

run without frequently breaking down. Meanwhile, another engineering team within the company (led by former Cray collaborator Jim Thornton) completed the design on the STAR computer system, so this new mainframe computer line could now go into production. The 8600 project was canceled. The STAR mainframe computer was released in 1974 and was positioned to be the successor to the 7600. Unfortunately, the STAR did not have the performance it needed to keep Control Data at the forefront of the supercomputer market. When Cray Research began selling the much faster CRAY-1 later in the decade in direct competition with the STAR (the duration of the non-competition covenant had expired), Control Data suddenly found it difficult to compete as successfully in this sector. William Norris, Robert Price, and the rest of the leadership team hoped this situation would be short-lived and CDC could again return to mainframe dominance. But the loss of Seymour Cray would ultimately signal Control Data's end as the premiere, dominant player in the design and development of mainframe supercomputers.

The executive community in 1975. From left to right—Marv Rogers, Tom Kamp, Bob Price, John Lacey, Paul Miller, John Sheehan, and Norbert Berg. (Photo courtesy of the Charles Babbage Institute.)

Full Steam Ahead

ONCE CONTROL DATA GOT PAST the shakeup caused by Cray's exit and the turbulence of 1970-1971, the company entered what can be categorized as a golden decade. The company basically took stock of its assets and re-organized into five major operations—Commercial Credit, Systems, Services, Products, and Marketing. It was a massive project. Control Data Corporation had grown so quickly that the lines of reporting between the various business areas had become overly complicated. This new organizational plan proved to be an advantageous move, as it helped streamline its operations and focus its efforts. The corporate headquarters reflected this growth, as a tall, gold-and-green-colored skyscraper was built on the CDC campus in 1972. Aside from Commercial Credit Corporation headquarters located in Baltimore, the main office for each major CDC operation was moved into this large new building. Control Data emerged from its 1970-1971 crisis as a stable company with a solid catalog of products and value-added services upon which it could build. Services, while a main offering since the company began, gained even more emphasis throughout the 1970s. And thanks to the diversity of acquisitions and the talent pool CDC added through them, the mainframe computer was not the only area of innovation Control Data could pursue. Norris and his primary advisor in this aspect of the business, Robert Price, continued to green-light several projects which resulted in exemplary breakthrough products.

Many of these innovations were in the peripherals organization. Under Thomas Kamp's direction, this line of products had grown steadily in demand, with their primary customers continuing to be other computer equipment manufacturers who purchased these peripherals through OEM contracts. The 800 series of disk drives were one of the standout products, as these devices represented a next step in both mass storage magnetic densities and speed of data retrieval. All disk drives today use a similar design, as they do the same concurrent read-write data processing developed for the 800 disk drives. The company was one of the first to develop flat panel displays, an innovation that would later achieve widespread popular use for computer monitors and televisions. CDC hardware engineers also developed harsh environment exterior packaging for several devices. The various branches of the military were the early customers for this technology, and used several CDC devices housed in this packaging in difficult field conditions. Later generations of this technology were refined for use in small electronics like cell phones, personal digital assistants (PDAs), and other handheld devices.

Although the STAR mainframe did not deliver competitive performance and had limited success in the marketplace, the Cyber series of mainframe computers, developed through a joint venture with the Canadian government, achieved solid business results throughout the 1970s. This computer family became Control Data's primary mainframe product line, as the Cyber 200/205 machines were able to hold their own against the CRAY-1. These computers were loosely based on 6600 and 7600 architecture, and were reconfigured in a variety of price and performance power options in order to widen the customer base. The company also built several customized computers for individual clients in order to match a computer with an organization's specific data processing needs.

The last major hardware design direction for the company in the 1970s was the Cyber 80 project. This mainframe design ran old 6600 programs, so the target market for this developing platform was existing 6600 customers. The goal of this project was that these customers would eventually migrate from the 6600 to this new system. The prototype models, however, ran into difficulties and ended up being redesigned and debugged past the originally planned 1980 release. Eventually though, the product line was released under a series of different names throughout the 1980s.

During this period, Control Data also worked with a number of companies and countries by creating a series of joint ventures. Through these business agreements, the participating parties shared resources and knowledge to develop products and services beneficial to both parties. Some of these joint ventures were between Control Data and other international organizations like the C. Itoh (now ITOCHU Corporation), a major trading company from Japan. Control Data also partnered with foreign governments, like Romania and Israel, to help create technologies these countries needed. During the joint venture with Romania, the company developed a series of new peripheral products. Control Data also partnered with Iskra, a major electronic equipment manufacturer in the former Yugoslavia (this company is now divided into Iskratel, Fotona, and other organizations). As described previously, Control Data also had a joint venture with Canada. This government worked with Control Data to develop technology applicable for government use, and this joint venture resulted in the Cyber series of computers. Through these partnerships, Control Data gained vital knowledge and new products the company could not have developed on its own, while in the meantime the partnering organization received products and services beneficial to its needs. The joint ventures with these organizations and countries were frequently successful and productive.

The company crisis of the early 1970s also caused William Norris to place even more emphasis on the growing services market. As Norris had predicted since the beginning of Control Data, increased competition and better technology meant that mainframe hardware was slowly becoming a less profitable commodity business. Computer services, however, were a growing sector as more and more customers wanted to leverage computer processing. One offering of the service business, for example, was Control Data could rent time on its 6600 machines to organizations that only needed to run a specific project through the mainframe calculations. Another large market for the services business was running payroll; companies could deliver their punch card and magnetic data to a services center and payroll checks would be processed and printed quickly and efficiently. As Robert Price relates, the challenge was how a corporation primarily focused on manufacturing electronic hardware could generate enough services income to financially balance the research and development required to design and build more advanced computers. If CDC could make this strategy work, the financial health of the company would be much more stable, and it could then pursue more innovations in mainframe development. Business practice differences exist, however, between a more service-based company and a more product manufacturing-based company. Some CDC products did not mesh as well with this strategy than others, and could not be incorporated into the services financing model. But the steady growth of the company throughout the 1970s demonstrates that overall, the value-added services strategy which Control Data pursued did succeed quite well.

Norris also worked hard to protect the business interests of the company. After the release of the 7600, arch-rival IBM decided on a duplicitous marketing strategy, at least from the perspective of Control Data management. IBM would market a computer that existed in blueprint form only, with the goal of eroding future sales of the already released CDC 7600. The nonexistent machine would supposedly be faster than the 7600, and customers were advised by IBM to wait until the release of the more powerful IBM machine. The strategy worked. IBM convinced several customers who already held contracts with Control Data that it made more sense to hold off on a 7600 purchase and invest in the larger, currently fictitious (now called vaporware) machine promised by Big Blue.

Norris was enraged by the tactic, and in 1968, launched an anti-trust suit against IBM. Norris argued that by marketing a product before it actually existed, IBM was in effect acting as a monopoly in an effort to eliminate competition. The day the lawsuit was announced to CDC employees, quite a few product line managers throughout the organization asked, "What in the hell is he doing now?" The financial community was also not supportive of the move, and felt the lawsuit would put the company into serious jeopardy. Norris, never much of a fan of Wall Street advice anyway, pressed on with the lawsuit. Norris argued IBM was "abusing its

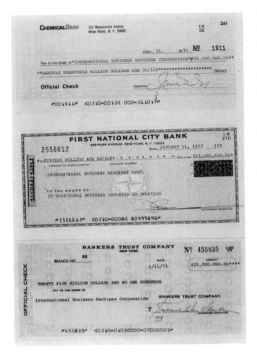

The checks Control Data received as part of its settlement with IBM. (Photo courtesy of the Charles Babbage Institute.)

monopolistic power" by marketing a product it could not deliver yet.

The gamble worked. In 1973, the case was settled out of court in CDC's favor. Control Data received roughly $200 million in damages from IBM. In order to satisfy a major part of the $200 million anti-trust settlement, IBM gave away a sizeable division of its business to Control Data, the Service Bureau Corporation, or SBC. This large time-sharing, domestic data service operation was a wonderful fit with Control Data Services; it was an impressive business that focused on the domestic market. The IBM settlement was a significant victory against the nemesis corporation that had so often positioned itself against CDC (plus, to Norris's ire, IBM had once eclipsed the Sperry Rand computer division back in the 1950s), so the settlement was a welcome development after the loss of Seymour Cray.

The lawsuit brought about another interesting benefit as well. In order for Control Data's attorneys to bring the claims against IBM, they examined over twenty million pages of IBM documents, photocopied over one million pages, and in the process had added some 150,000 documents to the company's legal database. Control Data had the computer hardware it needed to handle this mass of data, but not the software to sort through all of this information. So CDC programmers developed a file management system referenced by a keyword search program. The Control Data lawyers could then quickly find documents they needed by entering various search terms. This enormous mass of documents was now both organized and searchable electronically. It marked the first time high-speed computer technology was leveraged in a major legal case, and this technology was a major factor in causing the out-of-court settlement. Naturally enough, a new business, Litigation Services, sprang up because of this technology. With proof-of-concept in hand, Litigation Services emerged as a new business within Control Data, eventually changing its name to Quorum in the 1980s.

William Norris, with his unorthodox approach for running the corporation, was now beyond a doubt considered a maverick CEO by the investment community. This label brought with it both fans and detractors, and the negative criticism was not ignored by Norris. As Albert Eisele, a former executive of Control Data relates, "Bill Norris would frequently say, 'Most of those Wall Street analysts don't know their butts from third base about our company." Only, he didn't say butts." However, if analysts were not supportive of the IBM lawsuit and other un-orthodox moves made by Norris, his next direction for the company would have them vigorously shaking their heads for years to come. For soon, William Norris would direct his company to address social needs by creating profitable business opportunities. It was during the stable ex-pansion era of the 1970s that Norris would task his partner in vision, Norb Berg, to move CDC into the unusual directions of social ventures for which it became known after the Cray years—and for which the company would be vigorously criticized in the mid 1980s, during its next substantial crisis.

A Society That's Burning

THE SUMMER OF 1967 WAS LONG and unusually hot in Minneapolis. It also turned violent, as riots broke out in the Minneapolis Northside community, burning large sections of this eco-nomically depressed neighborhood. The National Guard had to be called out to restore the peace. However, this event was not an isolated incident but one of many riots, like those in Newark, Detroit, and Milwaukee, which broke out in cities across the country in protest and frustration over the conditions facing minority Americans. The violence continued throughout 1968, following the assassinations of Robert Kennedy and Dr. Martin Luther King, Jr., and the country was alarmingly on the edge of large-scale, violent unrest. William Norris was shocked by the disturbing side of America these events revealed. He wanted to do something, but what? During this period he attended a speech given by Whitney Young, the executive director of the National Urban League. Young spoke about the social and economic injustices faced by African-Americans, and the importance of providing equality to all members of American society. Norris later asked Young what a corporation could do to help. Young replied that what young African-Americans needed was jobs. Stable employment would give prosperity to this popula-tion and to their neighborhoods as well. It was an epiphany for Norris.

Before the explosive years of 1967-1968, William Norris had never shown any interest in societal needs. He was always focused on new technology and the service applications he could leverage from this technology, and he was a significant driving force behind the explosion of computer hardware and services that were now a permanent part of the world landscape. But Norris saw major populations within America did not enjoy the same level of prosperity and freedom experienced by the majority of white Americans. As a major taxpayer, Control Data Corporation was ultimately paying for the high costs of this poverty—whether through govern-ment welfare programs or increased law enforcement. If these pressures on government organ-izations could ease, it would likewise follow that taxes would decrease, providing businesses with more capital to expand and ultimately increase prosperity for all. Norris felt Control Data should be a corporate leader in this effort. As Whitney Young advised, addressing joblessness

35

would be the place to begin—and Norris decided joblessness was an issue Control Data could do something about. He called his staff together and explained that as a major employer, Control Data had a moral and ethical obligation to hire African-Americans in significant numbers throughout the organization. His reasoning was both blunt and effective. "My God," he said, "you can't do business in a society that's burning." Norris had started on a new journey that would define the rest of his career and the future trajectory of Control Data Corporation.

Could CDC flex its corporate might to help combat the war on poverty? And could efforts to address this social ill result in opening up new, profitable markets for the company? How could the well-being of all people—specifically minorities, women, and the handicapped—be improved? Norris tasked the personnel function with leading this effort. Rather than approach these issues through charitable giving, however, Control Data Corporation took the unique approach that these represented potential untapped markets for new products and services—particularly services provided in part or in whole through computer technology. As Berg described in press releases at the time, "Society's problems—education, poverty, crime, and criminal justice, affordable housing, energy, health—represented multi-billion dollar markets to be addressed as profitable business opportunities by our computer, financial, and managerial expertise." Control Data could, and would, use company resources to do its part to tackle poverty and hopefully find new markets into which the organization could expand sales of its products and value-added services.

This effort began when Control Data launched a concerted initiative to hire minority workers from the inner cities in the Minneapolis/St. Paul region. The main issue in hiring these workers was transportation. Control Data's local manufacturing facilities were all built in the suburbs, and the majority of these new workers lived in poverty and could not afford a car. To make it possible for these workers to come to work, Control Data set up a busing system to transport inner city employees to the suburban manufacturing facilities. This concept achieved limited success. The distance and time it took for these workers to arrive at the plants proved to be a difficult hurdle. Because these workers did not have their own transportation, they were basically stuck at the manufacturing facility until the next bus arrived. If a situation happened at home, school, or a nursing home, it was hard for these workers to respond quickly.

Plus for many minority workers, these suburban facilities were intimidating places. Predominately staffed by Caucasian workers, it was difficult for minority individuals not to feel like they were trespassing into a foreign territory. While some inner-city workers continued their employment with Control Data, several found the employment situation less than ideal and left the company. This was a good faith initiative by the corporation, but it did not gain the level of long-term success Control Data was hoping to achieve. Obviously the company could not bring inner-city workers to the jobs they desperately needed. Learning from this result, a new concept emerged in response; perhaps Control Data could instead bring the jobs directly to these workers.

Starting with manufacturing expansions which became known as the inner-city, or poverty-area plants (one plant was located at Campton, Kentucky, a town located in the second poorest rural county in the United States), CDC launched a series of external and internal initiatives to improve the welfare of its employees and the communities in which they lived. Control Data purposefully placed each poverty-area plant within an area particularly hard hit by low income and crime. To answer charges that these plants were nothing more than charity projects, Norris also placed the manufacture of significant products within the walls of these plants. These manufacturing expansions would then have to be financially successful, or else the company's performance would also be severely compromised.

The same standards of quality and profitability expected at these plants' sister operations were also expected in the poverty-area facilities. All the managers involved were keen to ensure the full realization of these plants, as their livelihoods were also at stake. To staff the assembly lines at these plants, Control Data employed a group of people many other companies would categorize as not hirable. To help these previously unemployed people adjust to the responsibilities of a regular job, the company created a work orientation program. And even when some of these employees ended up in trouble with the law for minor violations, CDC established a bail program to get these individuals released from jail so they could come back to work. Instead of being failures, the poverty-area plants thrived and remained in active production throughout the 1980s, until new technologies resulted in far less labor intensive manufacturing and assembly processes, ending the viability of these facilities.

Norris also believed that key to the prosperity of the company was the well-being of each and every CDC employee. Norris expressed this belief in a memorandum he wrote to the entire company in August 1966: "Everybody should have a personal project of improving himself. We are continually assisting our employees to improve and acquire new skills. Everyone can rise, not only in pay but in ability, and the more you rise the more the company rises." Employee turnover cost the company a great deal in the hiring and training of new employees, so programs were launched to reduce turnover and make Control Data a supportive and exciting place to work. These were not "Nice to Do" programs; rather they were programs designed to realize the human potential of each employee.

A major program that emerged from this effort was the aptly named Employee Advisory Resource (EAR) service. This twenty-four-hour, seven-day a week hotline eventually helped employees with all kinds of personal issues—money troubles, marital issues, employment concerns, chemical addictions, alcohol addiction, and more. Other related initiatives followed, including StayWell, a program geared toward encouraging exercise and better health habits among CDC employees. The company also put the Peer Review system in place to resolve conflicts between managers and employees. And to keep employees up to date with technology and other practices, learning centers, using computer education technology, were established so employees could take classes on subjects pertinent to their roles within the company. The initiatives supported by management were very innovative, developed in the same spirit as Cray's massive supercomputer projects. The driving goal behind all of these initiatives was to increase productivity, reduce absenteeism and turnover, and cut health care costs. CDC won several awards for their groundbreaking affirmative action initiatives that improved the livelihood of minorities, women, and the handicapped. Later chapters of this book detail the history of each of these initiatives, many of which exist today as standard best practices across corporate America.

For Norris, social responsibility also meant more than creating programs to benefit employees. He was convinced technology could be applied to several untapped areas of human need that could radically improve society and become profitable. These ventures would not be charity projects; Control Data's leaders did not believe directly giving away money was the most effective way to help the disadvantaged in the long term. For example, Control Data was never a member of the 5% Club (today known as the Minnesota Keystone Program), an organization of Minneapolis corporations which pledged five percent of their pre-tax profits to charities like the United Way and similar organizations. Instead, CDC leaders wanted to help society directly by creating a business which both addressed a social need and would eventually become profitable.

To do this, the personnel function was allied with the Committee for Social Responsibility, a twenty-member group of CDC leaders, managers, and employees charged with a broad base of responsibilities. These responsibilities included researching and proposing plans for businesses that would target an unmet social need. This committee was also charged with creating recommendations on how CDC should allocate financial resources toward pursuing social responsibility opportunities and other more traditional charitable contributions. As Norris would frequently state after his retirement, "We never had social programs. We had programs that addressed society's unmet needs as profitable business opportunities." These were not "do-gooder" endeavors, because Norris had a practical objective in mind, and tasked the Committee for Social Responsibility to evaluate potential opportunities and define the resources the company could provide in support of them.

For years, Control Data had managed to maintain its high-wire act of advanced electronic hardware manufacturing, but as previously described, it had come close to falling off this wire. For example, a major part of CDC's income came from government contracts which stipulated hard deadlines. If the company didn't release the product in time by or on the deadline, it would be penalized for each day it was overdue—sometimes by as much as a million dollars per day. Norb Berg describes Norris by saying, "He could see into the future better than anyone, he knew what was going to happen, but not precisely how or when." And Norris was sure of one thing: mainframe computer manufacturing would not last forever. While attending an opening ceremony when a new plant began production in Bemidji, Minnesota, Norris privately told Berg, "Take a good look around, because you're going to close this plant someday." All of these social enterprise endeavors were pursued in an attitude of "enlightened self-interest" that tied in with Norris's overall service strategy concept. While the mainframe and its derivative products continued to generate income, the company would begin a series of start-up ventures, many of which were service-based, all of which would hopefully become profitable before the mainframe devolved into yesterday's technology.

Throughout the 1970s and 1980s, Norb Berg led, with Norris's blessing, a talented team that embarked upon several community outreach initiatives, mostly targeted as expanding opportunities for marginalized people. Some, like the poverty-area plants, were directly related to the company's business needs. Others were a way to apply CDC technology and services to improve conditions for a specific community. An example of this effort was the development of a better health care system for the Rosebud Indian Reservation in South Dakota. This initiative, proposed by the Committee for Social Responsibility, provided computers to store patient medical records; the company also financed a much-needed mobile clinic to directly bring health care to remote areas of the reservation. It was a business venture in its own right, thoroughly calculated, with the hope the Rosebud Health Care project would either evolve into a profit center or give CDC the knowledge it needed to expand this business into other domestic and international regions lacking sufficient access to quality health care.

Educational businesses were also created to benefit individuals both inside and outside the company. One of its first educational ventures was the company's chain of Control Data Institutes. What started as an internal training program in the early 1960s for employees became an educational business that fueled popular interest in computer technologies. These highly profitable schools were created across the United States and internationally with the hope of teaching technology to customers, engineers, and programmers who would later be hired by CDC and other organizations. The Control Data Institutes steadily grew in number; at their peak, about fifty Control Data Institutes were in operation worldwide. Similar to the Control Data Institutes, the learning centers were built in company locations to train employees, but were also used as a venue to teach individuals deemed by many as not teachable. FAIR-BREAK was an educational business created to teach the chronically unemployed in the hopes of providing skills for these people to gain successful work; in some locations this venture was also run through learning centers. The company also launched a major community initiative to work with prison inmates. CDC contracted with the Department of Corrections for inmates to build computer equipment, providing them with new employment possibilities both during the term of their sentences as well as after their release from prison. CDC created another innovative educational business, HOMEWORK, to provide training to CDC employees who found themselves unable to return to regular work due to health problems. The HOMEWORK curriculum emphasized programming skills, with the expectation that upon completion of the training, the employees could be regularly employed by Control Data again—even working from home if necessary. All these social business ventures will be explored in later chapters.

Norris was also keenly aware of the energy crisis of the early 1970s. Control Data Corporation became one of the first companies to look for and invest in "green" technologies. It purchased majority ownership in Jacob's Wind Energy, a wind technology and manufacturing company. This company developed the three-blade wind turbine, an efficient design commonly seen today on many wind farms. One of Control Data's largest warehouses, the World Distribution Center, was partially powered by solar energy through a massive series of panels installed on its roof. The costs to heat and cool the building typically were about sixty-five percent less than buildings of a similar size. CDC also invested in a St. Paul laboratory that experimented with growing vegetables without soil through hydroponic nutrients. The company even experimented with "green" office and residential buildings. The Terratech Center, built in 1979, was an earth-sheltered office and residential building. By being partially buried underground, the energy required for heating and cooling the facility was minimized, plus some of the building's heat was supplied by solar panels.

This partial list represents just a sample of the experimental technologies CDC invested in during this era. Norris's office regularly received proposals from professors, inventors, and employees. If Norris was intrigued by the idea, he frequently passed it along to Norb Berg. Berg would then make it happen either by leveraging internal resources in personnel or by finding these resources elsewhere—within the company, externally, or both—who were interested in pursuing the opportunity. This team diligently and passionately provided key support to make many of these ideas become realities—for better, for worse, and for every result in between.

With all of these initiatives in play, Control Data Corporation was an exciting place to work during the socially conscious 1970s. College graduates and other individuals admired the company's initiatives in these areas, and Control Data's personnel representatives at job fairs and other recruitment events always received a steady pile of applications. As Norris would state after his retirement in 1986, ". . . I received a continuous stream of letters from all categories of employees expressing great pride in the opportunity to work for a company that was willing to address social needs. . . . Our recruiting sessions on college campuses were always jammed with young people eager to join our company, they said, because of our corporate social responsibility activities." Far from distracting the main pursuits of the company, the foregoing initiatives made the company one of the most well-respected organizations, frequently listed as one of the top 100 corporations to work for within the United States. Berg, now senior vice president of the administration, was rewarded for the benefit these services gave the corporation, as he was elected to the CDC board of directors in 1977, becoming the board's youngest director. It was highly unusual for a human resources professional to become a member of the board. His inclusion was significant, highlighting the emphasis Control Data placed on employee development and relations.

The golden decade rolled on. The personnel department changed its name to human resources to reflect the expanded role this department played within the company and the overall change this function was performing in American corporate culture. And Control Data itself continued to grow. In 1976, the corporation now had a worldwide employee force of 42,000 employees and conducted business in over thirty countries. A summary of the company's income for the 1976 fiscal year stated the following: "Revenues from computer activities reached $1.25

An engineer learning through PLATO courseware. Notice he is manipulating the course by touching the screen, one of the first applications of touch screen technology. (Photo courtesy of the Charles Babbage Institute.)

billion. Financial services reached $675 million. Profits reach $41.5 million at $2.44 per share." It was during these impressive years of the 1970s for which Control Data would forever be remembered, dismissed by some, and admired by many others.

Bytes of Education

NORRIS FELT STRONGLY THAT PROVIDING EVERYONE with a good education was one of the best ways to combat poverty. He envisioned that computer technology could be the perfect avenue through which knowledge and training could be made more easily accessible and affordable to those who needed it the most. Unlike a flesh-and-blood teacher, a computer terminal could always be available to provide instruction twenty-four hours each day, seven days a week, so scheduling classroom time would be extremely flexible. Those who needed education the most could receive it on a schedule best suited to their needs. And unlike the time limitations of a class, a computer-based course could move along at the student's own pace of learning. If a computer system could be designed totally for educational purposes, it would be a tremendous advance into a large, new, untapped business market.

During the late 1960s, William Norris became aware of an engineering project developing exactly the electronic educational tool he envisioned. The University of Illinois, through a series of grants, was developing the Programmed Logic for Automated Teaching Operations

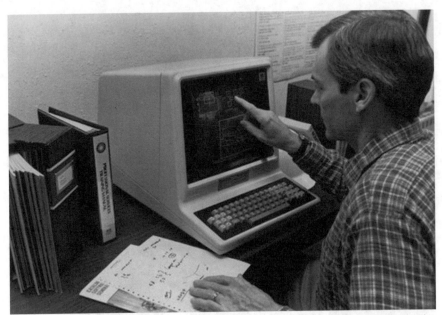

Management training through PLATO technology. (Photo courtesy of the Charles Babbage Institute.)

system, more commonly known as PLATO. The system was being designed by Dr. Donald Bitzer, a professor at the university. It was a perfect match for CDC hardware technology, as it consisted of using a dedicated mainframe for both receiving and transmitting data through a series of display and input terminals. The courses offered through PLATO were housed on the mainframe and were activated by users on the terminals, and these programs both received input from the students and then displayed the results on the terminals. The terminal network was also not limited to a specific location, as these terminals could be installed wherever needed, and the data passed back and forth through cables or remotely through telephone lines.

The PLATO system was an early application that pioneered many features now commonly found on the Internet. It was one of the first computer networks to feature online forums, message boards, email, chat rooms, instant messaging, and remote screen sharing. It even developed the functionality for users to play some of the first multi-player computer games—one of the original games being a multi-user flight simulator. Some developers from the PLATO development team continued their careers at Microsoft, so many of these concepts were reused when this company (and others) began developing Internet applications. So in many tangible ways, the current Internet experience owes a great deal to the first experiments explored by the PLATO development team in the 1960s and 1970s.

As part of a joint development agreement, William Norris donated a CDC Cyber 73 to the University of Illinois to develop the PLATO system. The computer was installed rent-free for the PLATO team. This launched another joint venture, this time between the University of Illinois and Control Data, with both organizations contributing financial and other resources to the project. By 1975, the PLATO III network contained nearly one-hundred-fifty locations that included elementary schools, high schools, and higher learning institutions. Users could also access the system from various military installations. The PLATO IV upgrade was released later that year, and this version featured text, state of the art graphics capability, and embedded animation in course content. William Norris strongly felt that the PLATO system could now be released as a major CDC product.

PLATO was also a match for Norris's overall strategies of evolving Control Data into a predominantly service-based company as well as turning societal needs into business opportunities. Computer-based education had a seemingly endless market. He set up a new business to develop "courseware" for PLATO, and this venture began creating an ambitious slate of subject matter offerings. As a first step toward implementation and proof of the concept, PLATO terminals were set up in all Control Data learning centers. New and existing employees received much of their job training through these terminals. And in 1976, Control Data formally announced the acquisition of PLATO. As was stated in a corporate review at this time, ". . . we introduced Control Data PLATO, a comprehensive computer-based approach to education. We believe it is the answer to the pressing material and international need to improve the productivity and quality of training in industry, government, and in general education, from basic learning skills to post graduate instruction." The excitement the technology generated within the company at the time was enormous, and Control Data predicted that by 1985, half of the company's income would come from PLATO services. To help advance the product, the technology was used as the backbone tool for several human resource initiatives, including both FAIRBREAK and HOMEWORK. The gamble was on and the dice were thrown. For better or worse, the PLATO system would figure prominently in CDC's future.

At the Peak

CONTROL DATA CORPORATION ENTERED the first years of the 1980s as a very large organization that seemed to have survived it all. It had created a series of dazzling products in the 1960s that pushed the shaky start-up venture against the largest competitors in the industry, and won the battle. Through its controversial IBM lawsuit, it had fought off a malicious effort by a gigantic competitor to seriously weaken sales of a significant new product. The company had also survived the resignation of its chief mainframe designer by diversifying its product lines into peripherals, services, and financial offerings. During this time, the company recognized it had an ethical responsibility to address social needs, and in response, launched several unique business ventures in response to these needs. As James J. Bowe wrote in an article about the company in 1982, "It has grown into a four billion dollar computer and financial service company, sixty thousand employees doing business in forty-seven countries." Twenty-five years before, Control Data had

Robert Price, Norbert Berg, and William Norris—members of the corporate executive office (1980). (Photo courtesy of the Charles Babbage Institute.)

four employees and some initial investment capital. Now CDC was in the stratosphere, as the early years of the 1980s were some of the most profitable in company history, achieving sales of five billion and an employee population of over 60,000. Control Data employees looked to the rest of the new decade to be more of the same.

William Norris was in his early seventies, so he began to formulate a strategy for his retirement. His main desire was to pass the leadership onto successors who would continue his utilitarian vision for the corporation. He had two individuals in mind—Robert Price and Norbert Berg. Both men had run their areas of the company with distinction, and Norris envisioned that a two-member executive team could guide the company through its next great era. Norris began seeding the idea for this transition in the first CDC annual report of the decade by writing, "In July 1980, Robert M. Price and Norbert R. Berg joined me as members of a newly created corporate executive office. At the same time, Mr. Price was elected president and chief operating officer of the company and Mr. Berg was elected deputy chairman of the board." Both men shared Norris's vision of innovation and they worked well together. Price would handle all technological interests, while Berg would lead the more administrative areas of the company. Both men had great respect for each other, so Norris thought this arrangement would be a smooth transition. The hardships of the near future would prove otherwise. All three men would eventually retire from the company before the close of the decade.

One of Norris's last major achievements as head of Control Data Corporation was the founding of the Microelectronics and Computer Technology Corporation, or MCC. Created in response to rising competition from abroad, particularly Japan, this organization was a first-of-its-kind research collective headquartered in Austin, Texas. To create the MCC, Norris successfully lobbied Washington to pass the National Cooperative Research Act. This law gave participating companies a legal safe harbor from anti-trust regulations in order to work together, with the goal of providing its members with a means for creating new technologies—which would in turn help participating companies compete against the world market. Now free to create such a consortium,

Bob Price and leaders from several other computer hardware companies began meeting regularly to form the organization. Under the MCC umbrella organization, research and development resources from participating companies would combine to create breakthrough computer technologies. These technologies would then be brought back to the labs of the member companies and integrated into their product lines.

Twelve companies—including DEC, Harris, Control Data, Sperry-Univac, RCA, NCR, Honeywell, National Semiconductor, Advanced Micro Devices, and Motorola—initially contributed both money and personnel to the project. Each member company had to commit to MCC for a minimum of three years. Control Data held a major leadership role in the early days of the organization, as Bob Price was elected chairman of the board. The first president of MCC was Admiral Bobby Ray Inman, a former director of the National Security Agency and former deputy director of the Central Intelligence Agency. Experienced in leading large, complex projects, Inman began assembling the MCC research teams. The participating companies contributed engineers and other personnel, and the think tank began its work.

Microelectronics and Computer Technology Corporation was a successful organization throughout the 1980s, employing nearly 400 workers at its high point, providing a secure place for joint research. As Bob Price relates, one of the central issues of the organization was ownership. Not every company wanted to participate equally in each MCC project, yet did that mean all the parent companies still had access to new technologies they had not supported? These legal questions were very interesting, but the participating organizations eventually resolved many of these ownership issues. The MCC could now begin developing new technologies.

The concept gradually worked as expected, and throughout MCC's existence, several innovations were launched and brought back to the parent organizations. Some of these innovations included system architecture improvements that optimized the relationship between hardware and software design, advanced microelectronics packaging, and environmentally conscious technologies. Control Data specifically made use of the packaging technology, but ultimately as CDC moved away from hardware design and development in the late 1980s, the company received fewer new technologies than Norris and Price had originally hoped. However, other corporations greatly benefited from the collaboration and the organization achieved much of its original purpose. Spin-off companies, like Evolutionary Technologies, resulted from the collaboration, and the MCC helped American technology corporations remain competitive during the massive upheaval in the computer industry during the 1980s. MCC continued for many years until advances in personal computers and the Internet made its purpose obsolete in 2000. However, the Microelectronics and Computer Technology Corporation became the model for many collaborative initiatives created to support other industries, and these organizations are now a permanent fixture of corporate research and development activity in the United States.

Norris also wanted to end his career at a high point by restoring CDC's dominance in the supercomputer sector. Once again using a strategy that had worked so well for the original

ERA lab, the original CDC lab, and the Chippewa Falls lab, William Norris decided to create a research and development center outside of the corporation. This new organization, ETA Systems, would operate as a separate company run by employees. Free from what Norris reasoned would be excessive corporate meddling but financed by both outside capital from strategic partners as well as Control Data, ETA Systems would be an innovative, independent branch of the company. The similarities in concept to the old Chippewa Falls lab were apparent. A team of engineers was selected, and the design process began for the upcoming ETA product line. The future of Control Data seemed as solid and promising as ever.

Decline of the Dream

ONE BY ONE THE STRINGS OF CONTROL DATA'S harmonious violin began to snap, pushing the company into a financial freefall. The reversal of the company's profitability came fast. The first major issue erupted in the peripherals market, as competitors from Japan began flooding this sector with devices they could produce at a much lower price. Similar to what happened in the automobile industry during the early 1980s, peripheral manufacturers were viciously undercut by more efficient Japanese production methods and reduced labor costs. As Bob Price relates, Control Data came to the strategic decision that the company should get out of the peripherals market, as these devices had become low-cost commodity products. The return on investment for these products had been growing increasingly marginal, but the peripheral product line had always been a cutting edge, impressive sector of the company. Times had changed. By the early 1980s, the engineering costs alone were more than the total prices of competing Japanese products.

The peripherals manufacturing business was clearly in tough straits. This situation complicated Control Data's desire to sell it, as the company could not find a buyer willing to take on the improvements needed to make peripherals profitable again. CDC began a massive retooling and restructuring of its peripherals organization to reduce overhead and restore profitability. This process took a significant period of time and the downturn in peripherals income contributed to the company's massive losses in 1985. During this time, Thomas Kamp moved out of the peripherals group and eventually decided it was time to retire from Control Data, starting a floppy disk repair company with his son. Lawrence (Larry) Perlman, the president and chief operating officer of the Commercial Credit Company at the time, assumed the leadership of the peripherals organization. This division was tasked to change their manufacturing processes to make them more efficient and cost effective. By the end of the decade this painful process was successful, and Control Data once again became one of the top disk drive manufacturers in the industry. Company leaders, though, assumed this situation would not last and began actively seeking a buyer for the much-improved peripherals organization.

While the peripheral shake-up was difficult, the rise of the personal computer cut even more deeply into the company's health. Control Data's leaders were keenly aware of the increasing popularity of this technology throughout the 1970s, and had significant discussions about how to go about building a personal computer product line. The problem was not design and engineering. Twenty years before the company had made the desktop-sized 160 and 160A, but successors to these early machines evolved into the 3300 line of small mainframe computers. CDC did have one mini-computer during this era that would have been relatively easy to retool as a personal computer. However, this machine, the 469, a computer four inches by six inches by nine inches in size, was manufactured under a Department of Defense contract for the sole purpose as a flight computer in fighter jets. This computer was a very effective military device (these computers and their immediate successors were still in use on some jets until the 2000s). However, CDC could not legally repurpose this computer for the commercial market, so a completely new design would have to be developed. While this was doable, the key problem was manufacturing expertise. The method of manufacturing for a mainframe computer was a significantly different process from the mass manufacturing productions required for a personal computer. Control Data had neither the skill set nor the robotic facilities required to produce small computers on the scale required to be competitive and profitable in this market space.

Some past and present CDC leaders at the time also believed personal computers were not powerful enough to become a serious threat to the supercomputer market. As Seymour Cray once joked about the power of personal computer processing, "If you were plowing a field, which would you rather use: Two strong oxen or 1024 chickens?" In the 1970s, these machines were primarily the tool of hobbyists, so it was hard for some CDC product line managers to predict these tiny devices would eclipse the demand for their more powerful supercomputer machines and services. They were basically viewed as a form of high-tech popcorn, and nothing more. In some cases, a few executives vehemently lobbied against any ventures into personal computers at all. So in addition to the daunting hurdle of mastering a new manufacturing process, some high level CDC professionals were solidly against pursuing a small computer initiative anyway. Control Data was at a major disadvantage, lacking both the intellectual capital and the manufacturing facilities to create a viable, successful personal computer.

However, the most compelling reason why a personal computer project did not launch was that Control Data had a firm belief in and commitment to investing in services. Company leaders came to the conclusion that the ultimate evolutions for computer hardware, large and small, was these devices would eventually also become a low cost, low margin commodity business. Because of this, Control Data leaders formulated a business strategy geared to provide customers services on Control Data hardware.

The outside pressure for the company to launch a personal computer line was enormous. During this time period, Bill Gates, the young CEO and founder of Microsoft Software Corporation, met with Bob Price to actively encourage Control Data to launch a personal computer hardware line. Investors also were dismayed that Control Data was keeping away from personal computer manufacturing, as it seemed obvious the company was missing out on a major bonanza. But the company chose instead to bet its future on computer services, not hardware. As the small computer began to take increasing market share away from the mainframe computer, Norris and his management team chose instead to focus company effort on developing service offerings, an area of the industry the company had much more intellectual capital to build upon. Given the corporation's history of mainframe and peripheral manufacturing, it was difficult for many at Control Data to see and support this business trajectory.

Likewise, raising the capital required for personal computer manufacturing was problematic. ETA Systems, hard at work on the ETA-10 mainframe supercomputer, had an annual investment cost of $50 to $70 million per year, so realistically, CDC could not launch another computer product. Control Data was no longer a nimble company that could easily switch directions to capitalize on a new technology—too many jobs, expertise, and hardware tools were in play (their rival, IBM, was also in a similar position). It would instead take a start-up company formed in a garage, Apple Computer, to rise to become the dominant designer and manufacturer of personal computers—particularly upon release of its Macintosh computer. Other personal computer companies, like Dell, Compaq, and Hewlett-Packard, would soon spring up after Apple, developing rival Microsoft DOS-based machines; mini-computers were soon on desks in offices, schools, and homes throughout the country and the world. When it became clear in the mid-1980s that Control Data was way behind the curve on the PC market and was in serious trouble because of this new technology, it was too difficult to change the direction of CDC product development. As Norbert Berg vividly describes, "It was like trying to turn around a yacht in a creek."

The personal computer seriously hurt the company in nearly every aspect of its business. CDC's time-sharing services organization found itself in escalating trouble. Much of the tasks smaller companies had hired CDC services to do on a per hour basis, like payroll processing and engineering calculations through Data Services, could now be performed cheaply on a personal computer. Demand for renting mainframe computer time quickly fell. Then as network technology improved, a string of interconnected PCs could together handle the needs of most small to large businesses. The flexibility of these smaller machines, and their higher return on investment, gave them an attractive advantage over mainframes, and the demand for supercomputer hardware dropped steadily throughout the 1980s.

Massive geometrics of technology scale and economics were at play. In 1960, Control Data's 1604 had a five times performance advantage over anything available at the time, and each computer cost $1.5 million to purchase. In 1985, the performance of a 1604 mainframe was available in the IBM Z-150 personal computer, and each Z-150 cost $6,000. Because of this technological commodity shockwave, three of CDC's core areas of business—peripherals, computer manufacturing, and computer services—were rapidly hemorrhaging money. As was summarized by James Worthy in his article about William Norris, "The difficulties lay in the company's bread and butter businesses: in its supercomputer and big mainframes where the competition is brutal; in its data storage products where swift advancements in technology con-verted a once-secure business niche into a dog-eat-dog commodity market; and in data services where the desktop computer radically and practically overnight changed the structure of the timesharing industry." In 1985, Control Data lost $568 million.

Regardless of the causes, the turnaround in the company's fortunes was fast, and public opinion of the company fell even faster. CDC was ranked as one of the most admired companies in 1983 (one of its most profitable years), but two years later the company became one of the least admired. Surprisingly however, Control Data's troubles were not blamed on the seismic revolutions occurring in electronic technology. Rather it was the social business ventures that became the target of the most widespread criticism. Norris was charged with neglecting the business to pursue social causes, and Wall Street investment bankers wanted all of these programs (or "garbage," as some characterized them) eliminated so the company could get back to what it did best: computer mainframe hardware. Much of this ire at least partially originated from Norris's public disdain for Wall Street, and now with the corporation in serious trouble, the in-vestors he regularly dismissed struck back hard at him. Investors increasingly demanded a change in leadership at CDC, and Norris complied. In January 1986, William Norris, now seventy-four years old, resigned as chairman of Control Data Corporation.

The board was no longer supportive of William Norris's plan to split his leadership duties between both Robert Price and Norbert Berg. The main reason was the board believed Wall Street would be happier to see a single person in charge and responsible for the results of the company. Also, because of the close association Berg had with Norris, board members and investors were concerned Norris would continue to influence the direction of the organization. Instead, Robert Price was named sole chairman and CEO, honoring at least part of Norris's wishes. Worried Berg would resign over this change in plans, however, members of the board, including Robert Price, agreed that Berg was key to helping the company move through this major transition. Berg and Price got along very well and considered each other as allies. Berg's loyalty to the company was both deep and fierce, so he stayed on to help oversee the transition. By 1988, the company was once again profitable and the worst appeared to be over (1987 revenues were $3.66 billion and profits were $25 million), so Berg decided his career at the corporation was complete. In his resignation speech, he said, "The ship is in good hands with its captain and crew." In June of 1988, two years after Norris left the company, Norbert Berg followed his longtime boss into retirement.

News of Berg's retirement was greeted with affirmation among a few national investors. Ulric Weil, of Weil and Associates, had this to say about Norbert Berg: "If you go by results, the social ventures he managed or was in charge of didn't do much, did they? Whether they were windmills or farms, they didn't pan out or do anything for the company, and I'm not sure they did anything for anybody else." (Berg actually had no connection with the windmill and farm business ventures.) Weil concluded, "Berg's departure is good news, because it gives Bob Price an even stronger and freer hand to do what has to be done. It removes the last representative from the Norris school." The hostility in the media against Berg—and in proxy, Norris—was unfortunate, as it painted both Norris and Berg as dreamers who put their social agenda ahead of the best interests of the company. Despite their many statements that these ventures were not social programs but business endeavors calculated and designed to be profitable, many commentators in the press castigated both men. Control Data's foray into unmet social needs was over, publically branded as good intentions gone wrong.

In reality, the social business ventures had little to do with the diminishing returns of the company. The so-called unconventional programs used only a small fraction of the company's total assets. Some sources estimate these ventures used around five percent of total assets, but even this percentage is dubious and too high, as these ventures were fully supported at the height of the company's profitability in the 1970s and early 1980s. During many of these years, the company was worth between four to five billion dollars, and so CDC's total investment in these ventures during each year was clearly far less than five percent of the total value of the company. A similar figure frequently cited in various articles is a cost of $200 million. Interestingly, the origin of this figure comes from a surprising source—Bill Norris. After the PLATO acquisition, Norris frequently spoke to various organizations about the benefits of computer-based education. As part of these talks, he often mentioned that PLATO cost $200 million to develop. This figure was the total investment cost of developing PLATO by the University of Illinois, Control Data, and other partnering organizations over a period of several years. Norris was emphasizing the total value of the PLATO technology which Control Data now owned and supported, but this cost amount was later cited in the business media as the investment CDC had poured into its social ventures. Because of this, the actual cost was greatly distorted and exaggerated during the company's major troubles during 1985. Former Control Data executives, including Bob Price, estimate the actual budget for the social ventures at their peak was less than $5 million per year. This amount was often less than the contribution budget for similar-sized companies.

One additional factor not described by the media at the time was that many of these ventures were profitable. The Employee Advisory Resource (EAR) program was now a solid business making money each quarter, as CDC sold these services to outside companies. The StayWell health program was a profit-making venture being sold externally to other companies as an HR service. The investment in these programs had also paid off internally in substantial ways, as EAR, StayWell, and other human resource programs were credited with reducing insurance costs and maintaining a stable workforce. And as described previously, these programs helped the company recruit employees and improve overall goodwill with the communities in which CDC conducted business.

Of course, it is also true that not every venture was in the profit category; Control Data Business Advisors, a consulting venture created to stimulate and encourage small business entrepreneurs, was losing money. And ventures in energy conservation technologies like solar and wind energy also become poor investments in the mid-1980s, as the Reagan administration eliminated the Carter-era tax credits for developing these technologies. Placing most of the blame for the company's faltering on these "off target" social ventures was not accurate, but it made for good commentary in an era favoring less social consciousness and more corporate bottom-line success. The unconventional company with its maverick leader was in serious trouble, and these radical "do-gooder" business ventures were clearly the cause—both in the minds of some Wall Street investors and a few media commentators. Berg and Norris repeated over and over the company's problems ran much, much deeper, as mainframe divisions of larger corporations like Honeywell were also in serious trouble. The accusation was made, though, and the public verdict was in—the social agenda had seriously harmed the company.

Despite all of this bad press, Berg predicted, "I have confidence . . . that the ideas are intrinsically sound, that the Control Data experience in implementing them represents a valuable body of learning and that concepts introduced into practice by Norris will be familiar features of the economic and social landscape of the years ahead." As the years after Control Data's transformation would prove, this viewpoint was frequently correct, as many of these ideas have become well-established, viable business concepts. Subsequent chapters describe how many of these concepts have evolved today into profitable businesses and ethical practices.

In 1987, William Norris did not attend the Control Data annual company meeting; it was the first meeting he had missed in thirty years. Robert Price, now CEO, stood before a giant screen that displayed two key words—"Shareholder Value." During the five remaining years CDC would officially be in business, first Price, then his successor Larry Perlman, found themselves in a focused and frantic search for a way to satisfy the immediate demands of profitability and, in turn, keep the Wall Street investment dollars flowing into the company. By 1987, overall staff of Control Data had been cut by twenty-five percent. Part of this huge reduction was due to the divesture during the previous year of the Commercial Credit Company. CDC took this action to infuse much-needed capital into the organization. The original purpose of the acquisition was to finance the customer purchases and leases of mainframe computers, but this business was no longer as significant as it once had been. And unlike the rest of the company, Commercial Credit was not suffering financially. This organization had consistently been profitable, so it was an attractive business to sell off and, in turn, use the capital to build up the rest of the company. And so this important strategic acquisition came to an end. As a spun-off business, Commercial Credit became the first of the primary corporate building blocks that would eventually become Citigroup, Inc.

A key technology product that rapidly diminished after Norris retired was the PLATO educational system. By the early 1980s, the cost for this project had grown and there were internal debates about shutting PLATO down. Norris vigorously opposed the move, and instead committed more resources for courseware development. Many of these classes were basic education courses developed for the FAIRBREAK program, but others were surprising—including a class on steam power concepts for M.I.T. and a firearms training course for police force training in

California. A massive advertising campaign was launched in the early 1980s, and this helped increase market interest in the PLATO system.

The system turned out to generate much less income than predicted, though, and PLATO never made much money for CDC. It was just too expensive, as installing one terminal cost thousands of dollars. And this cost did not take into account the enormous price tag for developing each courseware program. CDC attempted to recoup these massive expenditures through the service rate it charged for use of the PLATO terminals. This service rate, however, at fifty dollars per hour per student, was much more than it cost to hire an actual flesh-and-blood person to teach the same subject. PLATO was the right idea housed on a technology that was too expensive to achieve significant sales. After Norris left the company, PLATO was sold and became an independent business. The new owners of PLATO decided to drop the link to the mainframe platform, as personal computers became a cheaper, effective distribution technology for the original concept. This improved technology resource, of course, was not available when PLATO was launched, so the concept ultimately was simply just ahead of its time. The courseware and teaching methods created for the original system became the design base for computer-based education. The company that emerged from the former CDC venture, Plato Learning, Inc., successfully continues operations today. As Norris predicted, computer-based education became a profitable industry—but it instead uses personal computers as its technology platform.

In an effort to focus the company, businesses considered outside of the scope for the computer hardware and services focus were sold off in order to please Wall Street investors. These decisions were controversial and hotly debated, but ultimately, many businesses were sold. In some cases, these sales were made to former CDC employees. One of these former employees, Nasser Kazeminy, purchased several CDC businesses, some of them already profitable. Under his leadership, these businesses became even more profitable, which gave him the capital to acquire other companies outside of the Control Data corporate sphere. From these acquisitions, he formed NJK Holding Corporation. Likewise, Larry Jodsaas, a senior vice president, and his partner Gregory Peterson, acquired Control Data's microcircuit organization, known as VTC. The company became a major developer of pre-amplifier microchip technology. Employees Gail Gantz and Jack Wiley purchased the Survey Research Unit, an employee research service within the HR function. Together they formed Gantz Wiley Research, a firm that conducted employee research for corporate clients. And StayWell, the health management program, was sold to three former employees, David Anderson, G.L. (Bud) Anderson, and John Tarbuck, who turned it into a successful, independent business. Like grown children moving out of their parents' house, these spin-off companies left the fold, where they grew up, matured, and became important entities by themselves—validating the ideas these businesses were built upon. As for Control Data, though, these divestures solved short-term needs and contributed cash to the organization, but did little in the long term to stabilize the overall company.

Possibly the most publically surprising move during these last years was when Control Data spun off of its profitable peripherals business. This manufacturing business had successfully retooled and reorganized from the near-catastrophe of the early 1980s to become a leading builder of high end hard drive devices. As described previously, however, the motivation behind this massive restructuring was to make this organization an attractive business to potential buyers. Control Data wanted to get out of the peripherals market, as these increasingly smaller devices (like the 5.25" floppy disk drives of the time) had also increasingly smaller profit margins. To that end, Control Data separated the Peripheral Products organization from the company, spinning it into an independent organization and renaming it as Imprimis Technology, Inc. As planned, the separate Imprimis brand was short-lived. Within a year, Seagate Technology purchased Imprimis for $450 million from Control Data, and this company completely absorbed the massive CDC peripherals organization. Now flush with a powerful hard drive product line and the former CDC facilities to manufacture these units, Seagate became the industry leader in peripherals technology. While this move was intended as part of the overall services strategy, from the public perspective it was clearly a major shock to see Control Data divest itself of its peripherals business, a product space where it had been a market leader for nearly thirty years.

Probably the event that sealed Control Data's inevitable, final transformation, though, was the closing of ETA Systems. The yearly $50 to $70 million investment made by CDC since 1983 was enormous, but the independent research and development unit in return had made significant strides. The laboratory had designed and released its first supercomputer, the ETA-10. This mainframe was essentially an update of the Cyber 205, and the engineering team deliberately did this to ensure compatibility with the older system. The ETA-10 was faster than the Cyber 205, and the foundation was laid for a product line that could place CDC on top once again in the supercomputer sector. The mainframe's key problem, however, was its software was severely limited, as it did not ship with an operating system. In the past, mainframe computers were frequently sold through this method, as customers would often develop their own operating system to meet their specific needs. However, with operating systems becoming more standard and the added time needed to implement the ETA-10, some customers refused to pay for the machines until they received a viable operating system as part of their purchase. Responding quickly in 1988, ETA Systems created an operating system based on UNIX System V. It looked like the ETA-10 was finally ready to vigorously attack the market. The ETA-10 had the best performance for its price against current, competing supercomputers, and it seemed poised to become a kingmaker.

One morning in 1989, ETA Systems held an unscheduled company meeting. Robert Price, in a decision he would later describe as one of the most difficult in his career, announced ETA Systems would shut down and all manufacturing on the ETA-10 would cease. The product had not failed; it was an issue of money. With its $400 million total investment so far, Control Data needed more financing, but the supercomputer was not an attractive investment for most potential strategic partners. Control Data no longer could find strategic partners to keep ETA going. The venture was over. Members of the stunned laboratory were now out of jobs, and six years of rigorous design and development came to a highly unsatisfactory and controversial end. Anger was high, but the decision was not debatable. The reason for closing was simple: the mainframe sector was proving less and less profitable, and the final numbers were not adding up. Despite the success of the ETA-10 system, it would never recoup its development costs. With the closing of ETA Systems, nearly all significant mainframe development also ceased within the company. Control Data Corporation had completely severed itself from the supercomputer, the very product through which it had built its reputation. CDC was rapidly becoming a vastly different kind of computer-based company, but exactly what that company would be nobody knew for certain.

All these closings and divestures were essentially strategies for a reorganization plan championed by CEO Robert Price. His goal for Control Data was to transform the computer hardware-based company into a more application services-based company. He pressed for this transformation through his "Levels of Service" speech, a speech he frequently gave at company and investor meetings. Price described the three levels of service a company could provide:

1. You sell a person a tool (like a hammer or a computer), and this person, in turn, sells the value-added services that can be provided using this tool (pounding nails or processing data). The company only receives income from selling the tool.

2. You sell a person several tools (multiple hammers or server/client machines), and this person, in turn, assembles these tools to create a complete product (a house or a computer network). The company receives more income from this approach, as it sells multiple tools to the same value-added service provider.

3. In addition to selling the customer several tools, you also sell the value-added services these tools provide. For example, you can sell the hammers and then provide the services (construction) derived from these tools. As another example, you can sell the server/client machines and then provide the services required to maintain the computer network. The company receives the most income from this level of service, as it sells both the tools and the value-added services directly to the customer.

As reasoned through this strategy, the company might not always have the most competitive hardware on the market, but it could always provide a service of some kind. So Price argued this level of service was a more stable, profitable direction for the company. Control Data would no longer manufacture hardware; it instead would develop and sell integration systems for gathering and using data through multiple databases. The plan was to give customers better, faster ways to gather and control the data they needed. It was, of course, essentially the same course of direction William Norris started from the company's beginning at 501 Park Avenue.

The difference was now Norris's gradual switch to services would be more vigorously and rapidly pursued. As Robert Price would later describe, the business model was in some ways similar in design and strategy to what a future company, Google, would later profitably execute.

Price had a difficult time, however, prodding the company into that direction. While services had always been one of the main profit centers, Control Data's history as a high end mainframe computer and peripheral device manufacturer proved hard to transcend. This background was a huge part of CDC culture, and so Price encountered some internal resistance to putting this services direction fully in motion. The strategy was further complicated as these plans failed to execute quickly, causing some areas of the corporation to not complete their transition process. Meanwhile, the losses continued to mount. Too many holes were popping up, and it became increasingly difficult for Price and his management team to plug enough fingers in all of them. The 1989 fiscal year became a repeat of the difficult days of 1985, and, as described previously, caused the closing of ETA Systems. Complaints about Price's leadership of the company grew stronger, and in response Robert Price decided it would be best for him to step down from the chief executive position in 1989. He also decided not to seek re-election as CDC chairman of the board. With this decision, Robert Price left the company he helped build for three decades. The final member of the ruling 1980 triumvirate was gone.

As the 1990s began, Control Data was a slowly fading ember of the organization it once had been. In the United States, CDC primarily became a computer services company. The company's mainframe computer hardware was still selling well overseas, and the company also had contracts with the military. It was a significant company, but the many years of selling off businesses and reformulating and re-reformulating the corporate strategy had largely pushed the company into a position without purpose. A new CEO, Larry Perlman, the former head of the peripherals organization, assumed management responsibilities from Price, and he set into motion the final, and for some, controversial transformation of the company. He sold off several businesses, even though several of them were highly promising. Perlman stated he did this "to focus the company" but many employees inside the organization complained he was trying too hard to please Wall Street. These individuals believed these businesses had great potential and their startup pains were behind them. Over time many of these businesses did turn out to be very profitable ventures, but as successful companies now independent from Control Data. It was a difficult, stressful turnaround for CDC employees who were used to so many years of groundbreaking, yet stable, expansion.

In most cases the employees in these spin-off businesses continued to work, so at least for these individuals, the transition was relatively painless. It was under Perlman's tenure that the remaining computer hardware and related maintenance services group splintered off as Control Data Systems—a name it held until a private investment firm purchased this company in 1999 and it became part of Syntegra. The last section that remained of Control Data, with its human resource service applications, focused on developing "soft" technology—applications designed for the employee service industry. Perlman described the transformation as, "We no longer make anything you can drop on your foot." The transformation into a service-based company was complete, but along the way, the Control Data brand was sacrificed to emphasize this new purpose of the organization. This reconfigured company became Ceridian Corporation, and currently continues operations as an employee service application provider.

While Price was criticized for the final outcome of the company, in many ways, his plan and Norris's original overall strategy ultimately worked. Ceridian Corporation can be viewed as the inevitable evolution Control Data Corporation had to undergo in order to survive. The original company had stood on a threshold just as the Internet burst onto the scene. Perhaps if CDC had more time and if the innovative verve the company enjoyed in the 1960s had been present in the 1990s, the corporation might have re-emerged as one of the first Internet-based companies. William Norris described what happened to the organization in a 1997 interview, saying, "The thing was that we were unable to move quickly enough in switching from manufacturing computers to providing computer services." Just as the company's expertise was not in personal computer manufacturing, the company was not as comfortable making the jump to primarily a services and software company.

Robert Price argues Control Data was innovative to its very last day. In a newspaper article commemorating CDC's fiftieth anniversary in 2007, he stated, "What seemed like management missteps were really bold, strategic moves to get out of the computer hardware business before it became a commodity (as it is today) and to concentrate instead on data services and software (now major markets). The strategy worked. . . ." For those who remember the computer hardware giant in its prime, however, the company's break-up and transformation is still a hard loss. Employees planned on working their entire careers at Control Data, but instead found themselves either re-employed in a spin-off company or an acquired business unit, or much worse, searching the job market for their next position. Careers and companies moved on, though. Companies like Apple Computer, Compaq, Dell, Hewlett-Packard, and Microsoft became the new, hot technology players, and as the era of the supercomputer wound down, the era of the personal computer erupted around the world.

Regardless of whether one views the last days of Control Data Corporation as a failure to execute or as a logical strategic evolution, a key aspect of the company's history cannot be debated. Control Data Corporation was a unique organization that came to apply its approach to innovation, its philosophy of entrepreneurship, and its technological know-how onto social problems—with the goal of evolving these social innovations into profitable business ventures. Its history serves as an example of how one company tried to be much more than a profit-making machine; it wanted to become a force for change within as many communities and disadvantaged populations as it could possibly touch. Perhaps the flaw in the CDC strategy is that Norris built his direction upon a computer hardware business, and this product base ultimately proved to be shifting sand instead of solid rock. Time, though, is a great tool for evaluating past endeavors. Did these ideas for social business ventures work? Could some of these ideas, even those that did not succeed as well, become models for future business possibilities? The rest of this book explores these questions.

Chapter Two

A Seat at the Table

"It's got to be day after day, year after year, we demonstrate we really do care about our people."
—*Norbert Berg*

FROM THE BEGINNINGS OF THE ORGANIZATION, Control Data Corporation took a unique approach to the human resource function (originally called the personnel and administration function until 1986), turning it into a proactive organization that believed advancing employee well-being would also advance the company. William Norris made it a core principle to ensure CDC employees felt they were key partners in the shared journey of the corporation, and articulated this business ethic frequently through memos and speeches. Traditionally, organizations consider HR mainly a payroll and hiring/termination function, but CDC made the unique choice of including human resources as an integral member of corporate management. Norris tasked this group with making many vital decisions for the company (so much so that company critics later argued the human resources function held too much power). Members of the HR function were included at all levels of Control Data's management organization, representing employee needs in an effort to curtail workplace issues before they became major problems. These individuals were encouraged to be unconventional thinkers, developing ideas for increasing productivity and improving the company's bottom line. Many of these ideas met this dual challenge, improving both the financial health of the company and the physical health of people these initiatives served.

Human resources was an extremely busy function. The challenges of an ever-expanding workforce throughout the 1960s to the mid-1980s required regional, national, and international efforts to attract, retain, and motivate qualified employees. Labor laws in different regions of the world had to be quickly understood and mastered. HR staff members were always on the front line as CDC opened new markets for its various electronic and financial products. Reflecting the civil rights movement of the era, Control Data launched several affirmative action programs for minority, female, and handicapped individuals. Control Data was in the forefront of this national effort, receiving several awards, like the National Award for Progress and Equal Opportunity Employment given to the company by the *Business and Society Review*. The Department of Labor also recognized Control Data in 1983 through its Department of Labor

Recognition Award for Achievement in Affirmative Action. Control Data was one of the first companies to receive this award. Over the years, Control Data received many similar awards in appreciation of their equal opportunity efforts.

As the company gained creditability by employing individuals viewed by many as un-hirable, government agencies sought out Control Data professionals for advice and resources— particularly in the area of criminal corrections. Ventures were launched in conjunction with the Minnesota prison system and other correctional facilities. Internally, the HR function developed several programs to improve the employee experience at Control Data. Among these many ven-tures was Employee Advisory Resource, a twenty-four-hour hotline established to help employees with a variety of personal problems. Even as the company fortunes became less stable, the HR function developed an approach to downsizing called "Rings of Defense," through which em-ployee layoffs would occur in a calculated manner to protect as many employees as possible with the hope of returning the organization to profitability as quickly as possible. Control Data HR professionals were closely involved with every change in the company, and strived to innovate in both the flush and the lean times.

Many former human resources employees speak warmly of their years of service within this CDC function; they were not only working to improve the company, they were working to improve all lives touched by the company. Both goals walked side by side at Control Data. The human resources function truly had a seat at the CDC management table.

HR in America—A Brief History

The human resources function at Control Data Corporation reflected an employee relations philosophy that had slowly evolved over the history of American corporate growth and development in the United States. Throughout much of this history, managers and laborers were often at odds, and these confrontations would occasionally even have tragic consequences. However, as the Amer-ican free enterprise experiment continued to develop and expand during the second half of the twentieth century, more constructive labor relationship principles were embraced by many organ-izations. Control Data's leaders understood these principles. The HR function worked hard at find-ing a middle ground to address both the needs of company management and the needs of the workforce, creating a relationship that was, more often than not, mutually beneficial to both groups.

This employee relationship philosophy was based on a human relations movement that was, through a series of fits and starts, slowly gaining acceptance by corporate management. The philosophy had taken nearly a century to evolve. At the end of the Reconstruction period following the Civil War, the structure of the modern American corporation began to take shape. Railroads were built at a breakneck pace, canvassing the country, delivering goods and people across the vast continental United States at a rate never seen before in human history. These railroad companies became tremendously wealthy, and their owners—Carnegie, Vanderbilt, Hill, and others—were the ruthless, yet benevolent heroes of the age. With the railroads, other large companies emerged to supply the increasingly prosperous United States with the lumber, steel, glass, and many, many other products needed for the rapidly developing large and small communities that sprang up across the continent. The industrial age was in full bloom, and millions of workers, recent immigrants and natural born citizens, were employed by these powerful companies. A similar revolution was occurring in Europe, as technology replaced the craftsman's shop on both sides of the Atlantic, and large factories produced goods and services at a feverish rate. It had taken two hundred years for European-style communities to thoroughly populate the eastern lands of North America, but after the Civil War, much of the western half of the continent was largely populated in about thirty years.

During this time period, seeds were planted for the ideological struggle that would eventually dominate the world stage throughout the twentieth century. On one side, laissez-faire capitalism, with the philosophy that the less fetters placed on commerce, the better wealth for companies and, in turn, the better wealth for humanity. On the other side, socialism, a reaction against the Industrial Revolution, with the belief that exploitation of workers by the bourgeoisie would eventually lead to a revolt against the establishment (a peaceful overthrow for the socialists, a violent overthrow for the communists), the result of which would mean the equal distribution of wealth among citizens. Both belief systems have individual prosperity as their outcomes, but the means by which individuals gain this prosperity are radically different. The relationship between labor and management, in several occasions in American history, became a violent crucible for testing these emerging ideologies.

Both sides found vindication for their beliefs, particularly in industries where companies expanded quickly and employed hundreds of workers, while simultaneously these same workers often found themselves barely able to pay for basic necessities. Before the rise of the labor movements in the early part of the twentieth century, most large organizations viewed employees as simply a resource with which they could do whatever they pleased. The American style was essentially "at will" employment whereby companies could hire, fire, and reduce pay with little if any repercussions to the overall business. Labor was a commodity like any other, and the needs of the individuals who toiled in these factories were supposed to be obedient and grateful they received at least some income. However, as the labor movement grew increasingly strong and eventually unionized, corporations soon found themselves fighting these labor unions, in many cases violently, in order to maintain control over the individuals who manufactured their products and provided their services.

Between the 1890s and 1920s, a series of violent altercations between workers and company owners resulted in Congress passing some of the first major labor laws in the United States. Many conflicts led to these early labor laws, and one of the most significant was the gold miners' strike at Cripple Creek, Colorado, in 1894. This five-month, often violent strike began when J.J. Hagerman, David Moffat, and Eben Smith, major industrialists and owners of several Cripple

Creek goldmines, decided in order to satisfy growing demand for their gold, they would lengthen the work day from eight hours to ten hours without an increase in the three-dollar daily wage. When the mine workers protested, the owners agreed to restore the eight-hour workday but at a pay reduction at two dollars and fifty cents per day. The miners balked at this counteroffer as well. They had recently joined a new, fledging union, the Western Federation of Miners (WFM). John Calderwood, the president of this new union, demanded the mine owners restore both the three dollars per day wage and the eight-hour work day. When the owners of the goldmine did not respond and began enforcing the ten-hour per day schedule, the Western Federation of Miners organized a strike on February 7, 1894, and the five month ordeal began. The conflict nearly escalated into an armed battle between the mine owner's private army and the striking workers.

Sympathetic toward the miners' cause, Colorado Governor Davis Waite organized meetings with the mine owners and WFM President Caldwell, and an agreement was finally reached on June 4, 1894 restoring the three-dollar per day wage and the eight-hour per day work schedule. The mine owners agreed not to prosecute any miner who had joined the strike and the union agreed not to harass any nonunion worker who remained employed in the mines.

While at the time it was a significant victory for the Western Federation of Miners, the union now had a reputation of being a violent organization, and never enjoyed as much popular support afterwards. Members of the WFM, however, were some of the founding members of the Industrial Workers of the World (IWW), a socialist-leaning organization prominently involved in the growing labor movement in the early twentieth century. Meanwhile, company owners were alarmed by how effective the strike had been, and initiated steps to prevent such a situation from occurring again within their various industries. The battle lines between the socialist and capitalist ideologies were sharply drawn.

Various unions sprang up in the 1910s and 1920s. Unions for unskilled employees tended to follow more communist philosophies, while unions for skilled employees tended to pursue a more balanced position between labor and management. However, corporate owners felt they knew better about how to manage their employee interests, and they resented the interdiction of union leaders into corporate affairs. Because of this, corporate owners often did whatever they could to break up the unions, and these unions responded in turn with work slowdowns and strikes. The more radical union organizers, like members of the IWW, were frequently arrested and vilified. The U.S. Congress eventually responded to the labor movement by creating laws to regulate employment practices in the United States. One of the most significant laws was for worker compensation, whereby workers who were injured on the job had the right to receive insurance compensation. Unfortunately, the Great Depression of the 1930s caused many of these labor laws to go unenforced, resulting in little legal progress for labor until after the end of World War II.

During this same time period, academic interest in labor issues also began to emerge. One of the first pioneers in this field of study was Mary Parker Follett (1868-1933), who through numerous books, articles, and speeches, began linking organizational behavior patterns with human psychology. She developed several management theories. One of her prominent ideas was the concept of micromanaging employees, or as she called it, "bossism," that served to stifle the ability of employees to work effectively. She also advocated the idea of "reciprocal relationships," whereby individuals responded more favorably to one another through power sharing and mutual participation within an enterprise. Her ideas, as well as those advocated by Lillian Gibreth and Max Weber, led to the eventual establishment of the human relations movement of the 1930s. Founded by Australian psychologist George Elton Mayo (1880-1949), this academic movement examined the effects of social relations, motivation, and employee satisfaction on manufacturing productivity. Instead of viewing workers as replaceable machines, these academic theories emphasized the importance of workers as integral to the overall corporation, an organization that ultimately benefited through more cooperative human relationships. Through both his research, known as the Hawthorne Studies, and his book, *The Human Problems of an Industrialized Civilization* (1933), he concluded social behavior had a huge effect on job satisfaction. He developed many management principles, some of these including:

1. Natural social groups between people take precedence over the functional organizational structures within companies.
2. Effective upward and downward communication, from worker to chief executive and vice versa, is an effective tool in preventing disputes.
3. Cohesive, fair leadership is required to articulate organizational goals and ensure effective decision making from all levels of an organization.

Mayo concluded that employee work performance depended both on social issues and job content. He said there existed a natural tension between workers' feelings toward their work and contribution and managers' feelings toward controlling cost and increasing efficiency. A good organization needed to balance these needs effectively in order to prevent conflicts from disrupting the workplace and destroying organizations. In reaction to the labor struggles and in support of some of these labor relations theories, a new philosophy emerged that stated the needs of workers and managers could be addressed by leveraging the tools of capitalism. This philosophy eventually became called welfare capitalism, and it stressed that by providing vital services for employees and society at large, corporations actually would benefit through a more stable, healthy, satisfied workforce. By improving the welfare of employees, companies could reduce expenses caused by employee turnover, poverty, drug abuse, and other problems.

One of the first industrialists to embrace an early form of welfare capitalism as a business strategy was Milton Hershey, founder of the Hershey Chocolate Company. He incorporated this strategy when he needed to build a new chocolate factory in 1905. To make sure he had a continuous supply of milk available to produce his chocolate candy bars, Milton Hershey built his factory in the heart of dairy country in rural Pennsylvania. Then to attract employees and make his factory an inviting place to work, he also built a village near the factory, envisioning this village would be a working class utopia. Up until that point, most company-built towns were quickly and cheaply constructed communities with shoddy designs. Hershey took the opposite approach. He ordered the construction of affordable two-story homes with yards and inviting, tree-lined streets. This village also had recreational facilities which included a park with baseball fields, an amphitheater for music performances, bowling alleys, a swimming pool, and an amusement park. A trolley system was also built for workers to go from their homes to work in the factory, making the commute to and from work a pleasant experience. This trolley system also connected the village to the surrounding communities, so people from outside of the new village, appropriately named Hershey, could enjoy the amenities of the chocolate factory town.

While this was a wonderful, beneficial way to support his employees, Milton Hershey's motives were focused on his balance sheet. The nearly perfect town ensured he would maintain a dedicated, stable workforce within his chocolate factory. Plus his altruistic, perfect-as-possible town gave his business free national publicity, so customers were more aware of Hershey chocolate products. By improving the lives of employees, the Hershey Chocolate Company became an American institution. Milton Hershey's experiment demonstrated that creating an environment where employees can lead happy, stable lives was also a method for building a profit-making, stable company. The town of Hershey, Pennsylvania, is an example of how a corporation can be a mechanism for social change while, at the same time, grow hugely profitable in the process.

The Ford Motor Company also embraced an early form of welfare capitalism that proved to be a masterstroke of business strategy. Sales of its popular and affordable Model T had made the automobile maker a vastly successful organization. Unfortunately, work on Henry Ford's revolutionary assembly line was also dull and repetitive, so the employee turnover rate at the manufacturing plants was quite high. Much effort was required to continually hire and train new assembly line workers. Henry Ford also felt he had a moral obligation to his employees. He had grown up on a farm in rural Michigan, and he understood how difficult it could be at times for working class families to pay their bills. In 1914, he made the surprising decision to institute a five-dollar a day pay rate for his automobile workers, a pay rate that was nearly twice as much as workers could receive in rival automobile factories. (In 2008 dollars, this rate is the equivalent of around $111 per day.) Ford also launched a reduced work week. Although sources on this adjusted schedule vary, this reduced work week was either five or six eight-hour days per week. He called this strategy the "wage motive" for his workforce. He believed that by raising his workers' pay and reducing their work schedule, his employees would be much happier and so would stay employed longer with the company. This would lead to less training costs, as the turnover rate would be reduced. And always a firm supporter of traditional family life, Ford believed that with the men employed at his factory receiving higher pay, fewer of their wives would be forced to work outside the home, leading to more family stability. Perhaps Ford's biggest motivation was that by making the Ford Motor Company an attractive place to work, the company could attract a talented, dedicated, and productive work force.

He was strongly criticized by Wall Street and other industrialists for these changes, and so investor confidence in the Ford Motor Company stumbled. However, Ford's "wage motive" quickly gave the automobile maker a major advantage over his competition. Because Ford was paying the highest salary available at that time, the best mechanics in Michigan did indeed come to work—and stay at work—for the Ford Motor Company. The knowledge and skills expertise within the company grew tremendously, and this combined with the high retention rate (Ford claimed he no longer needed to track employee turnover at his factories) dramatically improved the efficiency of the Ford automotive plants. This increased efficiency, combined with more improvements to assembly line technology, reduced the cost of a new Model T from $850 in 1914 to $290 in 1915. Likewise, the increased stability in his workforce caused a huge reduction in his operating costs. Company profits went from $30 million in 1914 to $60 million in 1916. And as a side benefit, the employees' increased wages also meant they could afford to buy their own Model T cars, and soon Model T's were cruising around Detroit and the surrounding Michigan countryside—further promoting the Ford brand across the region.

However, Ford's plan had its controversial side. He called the increased wages profit sharing, and employees had to meet several requirements in order to receive it. The five-dollar per day wage was only offered to employees who had worked for the company for six months or more. They also needed to live their lives in a moral manner—specifically, no heavy drinking or gambling. To enforce this policy, Henry Ford created what he called a social department to monitor these lifestyle standards. The social department employed fifty investigators and additional support staff to make sure employees lived responsible, moral lives. The motive behind the Social Department was an example of an early form of paternalism, as Henry Ford wanted to improve the health and well-being of his employees. It turned out to be the wrong approach, as the company tried to exert way too much dictatorial control over its workforce. Interestingly, the more fascist leanings of the social department didn't stop there either, as this organization was also responsible for publishing the *Dearborn Independent*, an anti-Semitic newspaper, and other anti-Semitic literature (because of these publications, Hitler was a great admirer of Henry Ford). Needless to say, the social department's investigation into the private lives of his workers was very controversial. Ford soon abandoned the more intrusive aspects of the social department initiative; by 1922, the Ford Motor Company no longer pursued this program. Publication of the anti-Semitic *Dearborn Independent* finally stopped in 1927.

Henry Ford also believed that he was the best advocate for his employees, and he bitterly opposed the unionization of the Ford Motor Company workforce. He felt unions, particularly those run by socialist-leaning leaders, caused more harm to workers than good, as these leaders maintained power by causing manufacturing slowdowns and strikes—hurting a corporation's ability to compete and reducing jobs in the long term. This led to the last major struggle of Henry Ford's career.

In 1935, the United States Congress passed the National Labor Relations Act, otherwise called the Wagner Act, which gave workers a right to collective bargaining and other protections from unfair employer practices. Empowered by this new law, union organizations were able to receive a permit to distribute union handbills at the gates of the Ford River Rouge Plant. What happened next became known as the "Battle of the Overpass," as several union organizers were savagely beaten by men tasked by Ford to prevent the union's activities. Newspaper reporters and photographers were on hand as well, recording the entire notorious incident. Photographs of the injured union organizers were published throughout the national press. The National Labor Relations Board ruled that Ford had violated the Wagner Act and ordered the company to stop interfering with union organizing.

Despite all of this bad publicity, Henry Ford still stubbornly refused to negotiate with the United Auto Workers union. The struggle boiled on during the next four years. Finally in April 1941, the UAW staged a sit-down strike at the River Rouge Plant, totally shutting down production at the plant. Henry Ford was so distraught he threatened to dissolve the entire company, and angst within the Ford family was huge. His wife Clara even threatened to divorce him unless he relented. Heeding his wife's threat and his own desire to continue the company, Henry Ford agreed to sign a contract with the United Auto Workers in June 1941. The Ford Motor Company went from being the most anti-union automaker to one with the most favorable union contract terms.

As Ford's fight against the unions demonstrates, the emphasis on management control continued to dominate the United States corporate culture, and the labor philosophies advocated by Mary Parker Follett and others were not pursued or taught on a widespread scale. Both Henry Ford and Milton Hershey developed ways to improve the lives of employees, but their emphasis was benevolent paternalism to improve the bottom line, as opposed to a means to build positive, constructive human relationships between management and labor. Then World War II broke out and dramatically, permanently altered American corporate culture. Because of the needs of the war effort, new employee relations practices developed in order to maintain stable workforces and ensure productivity. Control Data Corporation later embraced and improved upon these practices developed during World War II.

At the start of the war, virtually all major American industries became unionized as a way to help mobilize the workforce to facilitate the war effort. Union contracts were developed on a massive scale throughout the United States, determining wages, hours, and terms of employment. Because of the needs of wartime, laws were passed to restrict union activities and employment pressures. Strikes were declared illegal as the country needed to maintain an extremely high level of manufacturing productivity to defeat the Axis powers. Likewise, wages were frozen by law in order to keep production costs low. However, companies still needed to compete for skilled workers.

Because of the wage freezes, these companies could not lure skilled potential employees away from other companies through wages. However, they could offer competitive benefits like better health insurance. Unions would then negotiate for these benefits at other corporations, and a concept of providing welfare through employment emerged. John Fossum (retired professor of human resources at the Carlson School of Management, University of Minnesota) describes the evolution of employee benefits an "accident of history," as the employment directives put in place during World War II caused this practice to take root. Unions would ask for benefits from one company and receive them. Companies who wanted to retain their workforces and avoid labor unions would then quickly adopt these same benefits. Soon nearly every corporation had a benefits package of some kind, and employee benefits continue to be a standard method employers use to entice job seekers.

World War II caused significant social changes as well. Because of the massive number of men needed in the armed services, the United States experienced a significant labor shortage. Companies faced tremendous pressure to hire people, and so for the first time, huge numbers of young women joined the labor force. Personified by the various artistic and photographic incarnations of "Rosie the Riveter," a young woman who worked hard and looked glamorous under the grime to build war machines, these women worked on assembly plants throughout the United States. The presence of women changed the culture of many factories. Women had different needs than male workers, so new rules for workplace conduct emerged. Although many women left the workplace after the war to start families during the prosperous 1950s, the foundation for women becoming permanent members of the workforce was now laid in corporate culture. These female workers proved that women could handle nearly all jobs as capably as men, and the role of gender within manufacturing facilities was significantly blurred. When the daughters and granddaughters of "Rosie the Riveter" came of age, they would seek jobs in many areas of employment traditionally held by men.

After the end of the war, these workplace changes became permanent parts of the corporate landscape in the 1950s. Specialized individuals were now needed by corporations to administrate employee benefits, negotiate with unions, and facilitate employee compensation. To educate people with this set of skills, the industrial relations academic discipline developed in a few academic institutions. Young people were soon graduating with degrees in this discipline. While line managers still handled the needs of production with various factories, they increasingly relied upon members of this new group of professionals, industrial relations specialists, to administrate the various employment benefits and contract obligations. The people who took on this function were now considered a necessary part (in some viewpoints, a necessary evil) of doing business, but were not regarded as adding much benefit to the overall organization. As more colleges and universities began granting industrial relations degrees, however, the principles advocated by the human relations movement took on increasing prominence. The writings of Mary Parker Follett, George Elton Mayo, and other early pioneers were studied by students interested in the field, and many of these principles began to be put into practice in the workplace. The first members of Control Data's personnel had studied and understood several of these principles when they joined the company, and made these principles a core part of the company's approach to employee relations.

The rapid evolution of the industrial relations discipline into what is now called the human resources discipline occurred in the 1960s. Several laws passed by Congress permanently changed how companies hired and treated employees. Reflecting the increased role of women in the workplace, the Equal Pay Act of 1963 forbade employers from creating a wage disparity based on the sex of their workers. Then when Congress passed, and President Johnson signed, the Civil Rights Act of 1964, a seismic wave of labor force changes swept over the country. Companies were now required, by law, not to discriminate against workers based on race, gender, sexual orientation, or religion. This was followed by the Age Discrimination Act of 1967, a law that prohibited employers from not hiring able employees based on their age. These acts resulted in corporations facilitating various affirmative action programs in order to be in compliance with these series of fair labor acts. Industrial relations specialists were increasingly tasked to make sure their corporations met the requirements of these laws. Because these standards were not limited to industry positions, the discipline now encompassed all areas of employment, and the more accurate term, human resources, became the accepted name of the discipline.

A number of business schools built upon the early industrial relations curriculums now developed more fully realized human resources degrees. As an example, the University of Minnesota became a national leader in this discipline, and several Control Data HR professionals graduated from this department. Outside of academic institutions, two organizations, the American Society of Personnel Administration and the Society of Human Resource Management, emerged as venues for sharing principles and promoting HR as a discipline throughout North America. Most importantly, human resource professionals began to improve the profitability of American corporations. By having professionals work directly with employees, corporations became able to reduce employee turnover and absenteeism, restrict or even eliminate the need for union mediation, and successfully balance the interests of employees with the interests of organizations.

The central issues every human resource function struggles with today remain the same as they always have since the beginning of the Industrial Revolution. How do you attract and retain productive employees, not reward bad behavior, and tie income increases to good performance? Although labor disputes and strikes continue to this day, the development of human resources as a professional function was an important innovation that positively improved American free enterprise. Employee relations have come a long, long way from the bloody conflict of the Cripple Creek Miners' Strike.

The CDC Philosophy

As EXPLORED IN THE PREVIOUS SECTION, most nineteenth-century corporate leaders considered employees as a commodity, hired when needed and fired when not needed. Little consideration was given to their well-being during their term of service within the business. Cheap labor does not produce the best results, however, and poverty generates civil unrest that threatens to damage both work centers and the surrounding community. Because of these hard lessons of history, several business leaders came to believe an experienced, stable, well-paid workforce ultimately increases efficiency and productivity in the long run. William Norris embraced these principles, and a foundation of his management strategy was that corporations are not made up of buildings, but of people. He believed Control Data would save money by helping employees as much as was reasonably possible. With these business principles defined as a cornerstone of the young company's practices, he encouraged the human resources function to take the reins and explore the ways Control Data could find the best, most qualified people, and then retain them throughout their careers.

First and foremost, the purpose of the human resources (personnel) function was to help the corporation stay profitable. If the corporation failed to make money, it would no longer be a viable organization, so individuals in the HR function always had to keep that in mind as the end goal of their efforts. An internal memo from the early 1960s explains that the HR function helps the company make money through two key functions:

1. By getting the manpower the divisions need.
2. By developing and implementing whatever policies and practices are necessary to get the most productive use of the division's human resources.

The memo further describes how the company would carry out these functions: "To meet these objectives, the personnel department has several specific responsibilities—non-exempt employment, experienced exempt employment, college recruiting, salary administration, employee services and benefits, and training programs." What was fundamental to the company's financial statement, then, was that the HR function hired and facilitated the retention of qualified employees. To do that, each employee needed to be a satisfied, productive contributor within their area of responsibility. The human resource function approached this policy with a sense of "enlightened self-interest." If Control Data was able to improve the employee's skills and confidence, the company would also create better products and services. CDC management saw this goal as equally necessary to other management and technical goals required to maintain the continued viability and growth of the organization.

Because of this ethical standard, Control Data developed a corporate culture focused on maximizing the potential of every person. HR was not just a function that hired and trained people; it was a function responsible for the entire demographics of the company. The HR function encouraged creative approaches to improve employee abilities so that each person gained job satisfaction. The employee would, in turn, have to demonstrate initiative before Control Data would invest more resources in the employee. The company emphasized, "We'll help you reach your God-given potential. We want your loyalty so that you work for us." The members of the HR function were constantly on the lookout for any program or policy which would help improve employee satisfaction. It was a form of limited, pragmatic paternalism—look out for your employees and they will look out for you. Employment becomes a mutual commitment, a fair exchange between labor and management. A personnel goals document from 1961 contains these principles:

1. That our employees are this company's most valuable asset and their talents will be utilized in such a manner as to maintain and respect the dignity of the individual.

2. That we will recognize our employees as individuals, not averaging them, and not treating them alike without sufficiently relating their performance and conduct.

3. That we will spend as much or more time recognizing, developing, and rewarding the higher potential people, as we do in attempting to raise the substandard performer.

4. That we will not treat our employees like dependent children, but rather will help them be able to feel that they are earning their compensation.

5. That our employee services and benefits will create a climate that provides security without destroying incentive for good performance, a feeling of responsibility, and the obligation to earn a living.

6. That we will face uncomfortable decisions that must be made in the long-range interests of the company, the stockholders, and of the employees.

7. That our doors are always open for a fair hearing to the problems or questions of any employee.

All of this, from employee relations to community outreach to new businesses, was encouraged for one objective, the full utilization of employees. All boats—whether individual, community, or company—could rise together. This approach toward HR was continuously developed during CDC's existence. Ruth Rich, an employee who started as a secretary in the late 1960s and advanced through management to become an HR executive, gave a speech in 1981 where she described the goals ahead for HR during the company's next decade of operation. She said, "We will need innovative and unique implementation plans for job security, employee justice, flexible benefits, training programs and the many other elements of fair exchange. . . . Progressiveness, the ability to think to the future and do what's right for our employee has been a significant cornerstone. And what better example for the future than . . . the ability to plan and deal with tomorrow's problems." The company's focus on good employee relations was never lost through all its years.

After the riots of 1967-1968, Bill Norris directed the human resources function to take on an even larger role by developing ways to invest in social responsibility initiatives. Control Data could not only be an attractive employer, but could also apply its resources and know-how to ameliorate social ills. While the "War on Poverty" was launched by President Johnson's administration as a responsibility of the U.S. government, Control Data made a similar moral leap to be a private sector player in the same war. The root cause for crime, drug abuse, spouse abuse, and many other social ailments is poverty, and poverty is the result of unemployment and underemployment. If Control Data could create and maintain employment for the impoverished and underprivileged, the company would help reduce social problems by growing the local economies around their various facilities, wherever they were located. Rather than avoid hiring disadvantaged individuals, Control Data would instead give these individuals a solid chance either at jobs within the organization or at training which would lead to employment elsewhere. Just like the company's approach to employee relations, the HR leadership team did not view this commitment to community outreach as a charity mission. Yes, the company would help impoverished and disadvantaged populations, but CDC needed something back in return— productivity that would ultimately lead to return on company investment. A number of initiatives were explored and supported that matched the philosophy of addressing social needs as profitable business opportunities.

Control Data's leaders were willing to be patient while each new business opportunity took shape. A carefully planned series of targets were developed for each social business venture, and a significant amount of "greenhouse" time was granted in order for the growing initiative to recoup its costs. The approach assured that the company gave the project enough time to nurture by not demanding too much from it at the beginning of its existence. It also relieved the primary day-to-day organization from being distracted by a growing number of initiatives. As long as the initiative submitted regular reports and demonstrated some progress, the individuals in charge of the project worked independently from the rest of the organization. This management style was similar to the latitude given Seymour Cray, Thomas Kamp, and other project managers on various technological projects. So while the end products within the HR function were different from typical CDC endeavors, the approach to these projects was similar in strategy.

This patience had its limits, though. Control Data leadership insisted each program ultimately return a profit. Most social programs in other companies were a liability on the budget, but instead, these initiatives were viewed as entrepreneurial opportunities that, given enough time to develop, could evolve into profitability. Each program needed to find a way to become a growing business, another new product line just like a CDC mainframe computer. Once the program, such as Employee Advisory Resource (EAR), proved its viability, effort was eventually directed toward finding a way to sell the program to outside prospects and turn it into a business. Control Data's initial emergence as a developer of social services was met with some surprise and resistance, but gradually business leaders in other industries viewed Control Data as having expertise in this area. Some Control Data HR initiatives did evolve into services purchased by outside companies and, both during and after the transformation of the company, became businesses in their own right. Many other Control Data HR innovations, such as its practice of providing personal days off that combined sick leave and vacation, were emulated by other companies because they were solid business practices that helped reduce overall operating costs.

To make all of this happen, the Control Data HR function had to be an experimental organization with the same innovative spirit as the post-war Engineering Resource Associates lab. In fact, this approach to innovation was very similar to the "skunkworks" system developed at Lockheed Martin during World War II to support its intense effort developing superior fighter planes. By definition, a skunkworks is a small group of people dedicated to working on a project in an unconventional way with minimal management oversight. The term "skunkworks" apparently came about at Lockheed Martin as a reference to the moonshine factory in the *Li'l Abner* cartoon (although some sources jokingly claim it referred to the resulting personal hygiene of the participants in the skunkworks). As part of Norris's social responsibility direction for the organization, the HR function adopted this same strategy for its innovations. Proposals for new businesses and new ideas were encouraged and reviewed. Norb Berg expected ideas from his team, but these ideas had to pass a proof-of-concept stage before resources would be assigned to the project. It was a creative environment with a focus on viability. Not every idea, in fact far fewer than perhaps imagined by corporate watchers at the time, reached fruition. The environment was such, however, that a failed proposal was not viewed as a waste of effort. Even if an idea stumbled on its way through the hurdles, the primary objective was that the idea was discussed. In true skunkworks spirit, a rejected idea could become the spark for a better innovation.

Control Data pursued this course of action in the 1960s and 1970s, at a time when social justice was being advocated by many sectors of American society—particularly among youth who felt disenfranchised both by the government because of the Vietnam War and by society because of economic and legal inequalities felt by minorities and women. Rallies and protests were held on college campuses across the county as young Americans sought social justice and equality. CDC leaders watched all this activity with interest, but ultimately many felt these activities would lead to nothing which would last long term. In an interview with the St. John University alumni magazine in 1969, Norb Berg said this about the activism of the 1960s: ". . . The shouting on college and university campuses creates pressure, makes some people act, but I really think its void of practical accomplishment. Won't that be a fantastic reversal a few years from now to . . . find out that business is the place where the projects were quietly accomplished?" Members of the Control Data HR function believed they had the potential to touch and improve thousands of lives.

Leaders empower the people around them, and Berg embodied this principle through his personality and his job strategy. How his role evolved personifies the unique nature of CDC's human resources function. He went from being an HR manager to becoming one of the key architects of Control Data Corporation, primarily because he took on labor relations responsibilities which the more technologically focused leaders generally did not want, or could not do as successfully. His counseling skills were frequently called upon by senior executives throughout the company, helping them work through employee situations to arrive at an equitable solution. In an article about Berg, William Norris stated about the early years of Control Data, "In those days virtually everyone reported to me. Where there was a controversy that couldn't be settled, Norb Berg represented our employees, and he always seemed to have the right answers."

Berg constantly read and kept current with the changing needs of personnel, so he was always ready when called upon by his colleagues to resolve various employment issues. Frank Dawe, former senior vice president of administration during the 1980s, described Berg in this way: "Norb wins people over by proving the idea is right, by demonstrating it. He is a voracious reader. He becomes a student of the of the subject, and he puts people to work studying whether the idea is viable and can be implemented. No one welcomes failure, but Norb Berg abhors it, which is why he studies and prepares so diligently." Many of the social initiatives Control Data put into motion in the 1970s and 1980s began as memos on Berg's desk, which he then passed along to individuals he felt could best act on these ideas.

Berg was the ringmaster of an ever-evolving segment of the company which formed the backbone for the emerging computer technology and hardware company. Human resources drew expertise from all areas of the organization, domestic and international, from wherever the company conducted business. An example of an international employee who rose to become an HR executive is Frank Dawe. A native of Canada, Frank had worked as personnel manager for State Farm Insurance before joining Control Data in 1968. He moved to the United States, bringing his knowledge of relationships between United States and international organizations to the HR function. Dawe started as the director or personnel in the Computer Systems Group and then went on to hold many positions in HR, including senior vice president of human resources and senior vice president of administration. Dawe was instrumental in supporting and guiding many of the social business initiatives pursued by the HR function.

Another important innovator within the HR function during this time was Roger Wheeler, an executive who joined the organization in 1962. A Minnesota native, Wheeler left an HR position at the Northern Trust Company in Chicago to return to his hometown and work for Control Data. He began his CDC career as a manager for corporate personnel services, and gradually worked his way up through the HR function to become one of its primary executives, earning the title of vice president of personnel services. When Bill Norris began tasking human resources to pursue social business ventures in the early 1970s, Wheeler was typically the executive who made these initiatives reality. While Berg gathered and researched the ideas, Wheeler was the driving force behind implementing many of these activities. In a speech given during a Control Data HR conference in the early 1980s, Berg honored Wheeler by stating, "I once heard that to really know a man, you should observe his behavior with a woman, a child, and a flat tire. I know that Roger would react with the same compassion, decency, and caring that he holds for people . . . and which they hold for him." Wheeler would eventually hold the title of vice president for HR development and public affairs, reflecting his prominent role in developing the various groundbreaking social business initiatives that will be explored in later chapters.

However, these men were just three of the many, many HR professionals who embraced and enacted Control Data's approach to employee relations and corporate social responsibility. Some of these individuals and their roles within Control Data HR initiatives will be explored later. The incredible number and range of the HR initiatives is a real testament to the multitude of individuals who embodied the principles and business strategy established by Bill Norris. The HR function helped make employment at Control Data a partnership between workers and managers, finding ways to foster positive relationships and encouraging the development of skills and expertise at all levels within the organization. Then these same HR professionals took these principles outside of the company to create better relationships with society at large. The individuals who made up the HR function at Control Data had a shared vision that reflected many of the ideas put forward by the human relations movement of the 1930s, proving these ideas are sustainable methods that can result in good business practice.

In the Hot Seat

CORPORATIONS NEED TO BE CAREFUL about what organizational hierarchy is placed on top of their overall management structure, because it can adversely affect communication and task direction. This translates into reduced productivity and additional, unnecessary costs. The right organizational hierarchy has the opposite effect. When communication flows freely between the individuals who need it, a corporation is better equipped to react to the marketplace and resolve internal challenges. As described previously, the human resource function had an unusual amount of power and prestige, and participated in the leadership responsibilities in guiding the company. This power was reflected in how the organization was structured. For example, during much of the history of the company, Norbert Berg had a direct reporting line to William Norris, the CEO and chairman of the board, and high-level HR managers had a functional reporting relationship to Berg. This meant the human resource function was at the same level as the head of CDC finance, so human resource initiatives were thoroughly discussed and debated at the highest levels of Control Data management. The human resources function reported to the top person at every business unit within the company.

Robert Price describes his management style as being in tune with this approach—being anti-hierarchical, and despite his different focus at Control Data, of being in sympathy and support with the innovative human resource initiatives. "The human resources function,"

Price states, "had the ability to see actual problems instead of theoretical problems." He cites an example of how well HR was run from the very beginning of the organization. The average age of a CDC employee at the end of the 1950s was between twenty-five and twenty-seven years of age. One of the earliest benefits given to CDC employees was catastrophic illness insurance so if the unthinkable happened to a young employee, his or her family would be taken care of through this insurance policy. It was one of the best benefits a company could provide employees in this age group. The Control Data policy had an inherent logic and intelligence that fit well into Price's way of thinking about how a corporation should relate to its employees at this point in their careers. Human resource policies, procedures, programs, and issues were of vital importance to company affairs, as CDC wanted to know what the employees were feeling as much as was realistically possible.

The impact of this organizational structure was for the most part appreciated, championed, and ultimately leveraged throughout the company. Not every upper level manager at CDC felt that giving human resources so much authority was a good idea, however, and so there was some resistance. The conflicts that emerged could be intense and, of course, not everything was resolved in the HR function's favor. Plus, as Control Data opened up markets internationally, the HR function faced other struggles, as different laws and employment traditions in other countries made it more difficult for Control Data to follow all the "employee first" practices created in the United States. On balance, though, most of the company leadership liked the larger role human resources played, as HR managers would serve as support for resolving personnel issues—freeing up line managers to focus on engineering, manufacturing, and marketing tasks.

The HR responsibility was treated as a line management responsibility, and the HR manager provided support as a service to line managers for the various product lines. The actual organization nomenclature was that the lead human resources manager had a "solid line" reporting relationship to the division general manager while, at the same time, this person had a "dotted line" reporting relationship to a senior level HR manager. Each HR manager would discuss everything directly with the line manager that pertained to the administration of the line business, while the HR manager only discussed HR policy issues with the senior level HR manager. Likewise each line manager had one boss—the overall head of the business division which contained the product line. Because of this, the priority individual whom a line manager would always have to satisfy was the head of his or her business division.

A source of frequently used advice came from the HR manager assigned to the line business. Line managers typically did not want to handle human resource tasks, and because an HR manager was directly available within this area of the organization, line managers were not burdened to be both the employee resource person as well as the product manufacturing person. HR managers were thus equal members of the overall management team in each line organization. In many ways, this organizational structure made it easier for the line managers to do their jobs. The decisions line managers made about the products themselves were discussed with the head of the business division, while the line manager could then discuss employment situations with the HR manager. HR managers, in turn, had to wear a business hat to understand the situations confronted by the line managers and a labor relations hat to understand the needs of employees. Because of this strategy, the HR managers could arrive at a more balanced solution to a workplace problem. This dual relationship between HR and business improved production efficiency and also ensured the company kept its ethical bearings in its relationships with employees.

Line managers would involve the HR managers on evaluating promotions and performance reviews within their areas. In the case of deciding between competing promotions or internal disputes, line managers would also call on HR managers for their input. This structure was an integral part of the reporting hierarchy within each line organization. On organizational charts of the time, the general manager for the HR function was placed at the same level as the line function, enforcing the concept that these managers served as equals within the line organization. Not all line managers endorsed the active involvement HR had in their business area, but for the most part the human resources function was viewed as a helpful component in the line management process. Without this vital support from line managers, many innovations would not have been achieved. Jim Morris, the first general manager of EAR and president of the Control Data Business Advisors human resources consulting function, commented on this relationship,

> Human resource professionals had a great deal of support from the highest levels of the organization and were treated with respect by most line executives. I once heard one senior executive reference the human resource function and the finance function as the wings for the divisional airplane and key advisors to operating division or group executives. I believe that a much higher percentage of our line executives came to believe in the management principles in our human resource function than in almost all other companies.

During the height of the AIDS epidemic and hysteria of the 1980s, a situation arose where two homosexual employees tested positive for HIV during a routine physical exam. The line manager at the manufacturing facility wanted to fire the workers immediately, fearing the virus would spread to more workers at the facility. However, Control Data was one of the first companies to have an informed policy in place on how to deal with situations where employees had contracted AIDS. The policy was based on the knowledge that the disease was spread through direct blood interaction or other body fluids and not casual personal contact. The risk of infection to other workers at the plant was insignificant. Because of this policy, the HR manager instructed the line manager to keep these two workers employed. The line manager initially refused and planned on firing them anyway. However, after receiving a review of the policy and more education about the disease, the line manager finally relented and the two employees continued working at the plant. Pushing for the right decision was not always the popular decision. If it needed to use it, however, the human resource function had a lot of muscle to back up its decisions to get the desired result.

HR managers were also deeply involved during acquisition and merger processes. Control Data completed over a hundred acquisitions, and each had a unique set of issues to overcome if the acquisition or merger was to be successful. Before a merger would go forward, a social impact study was conducted to evaluate the culture of the incoming organization. This study evaluated how the people involved would be affected by the merger. The study's results were assembled into a report called the social impact statement. This statement was used as a template to examine areas within the incoming organization that were similar and also different to CDC corporate culture. Special emphasis was placed on reviewing what the impact would have on the acquired company's employees and the surrounding community. Another part of the acquisition equation was the employee values in place at the company. For example, what were the company's principles for employee relations? If these principles were quite different from Control Data's, this issue was weighed when evaluating whether the merger or acquisition should go forward. The impact of the local, state, and national government requirements reviewed through the merger process were also included as part of the social impact study.

This social impact statement was reviewed by Control Data's policy committee, a group that consisted of the top twenty-five executives within the organization. The board of directors was also required to review the social impact statement. If it was decided that the merger or acquisition would continue, the differences between the companies were often a shock for employees from the incoming organization. If the merger or acquisition was approved by CDC management, the HR function had guidelines of tasks to accomplish while the organization integrated with Control Data. For example, the new employees were required to review the employment benefits at CDC. Some benefits from the original company would end, new ones needed to be selected, and other existing benefits would transform into comparable packages at Control Data. HR managers would do their best to make sure these transitions went smoothly. International acquisitions and mergers added complexity. For example, many countries provided health and life insurance through government programs, so Control Data did not need to provide these services in these locations. Conversely, other aspects of the compensation package needed to be competitive with what potential employees would receive in these countries, so benefits packages were thoroughly examined before the merger could be complete. All these responsibilities put the HR function in the center of the action, helping CDC management decide if a proposed merger or acquisition would mesh well with CDC culture.

If Control Data's board of directors and managers decided, based on the social impact statement, that a subsidiary of the merged company did not fit Control Data's overall strategy, the subsidiary would be sold to another company. Before the sale of the subsidiary would be complete, the human resources function conducted another social impact study on the potential purchasing organization. The resulting social impact statement would then be used to evaluate whether the subsidiary would be a good fit with the potential buyer. If the conclusion of the social impact statement was that it would be a good merger, the subsidiary could be acquired by the new company. Control Data required protection for the subsidiary's employees, stipulating guarantees on maintaining jobs and pay levels. This process helped ensure acquisitions and "spin-offs" were handled through an ethical structure that protected employees as much as possible.

The base motivation for this structure was the principle that Control Data must attract, retain, and motivate talented employees. This motivation extended to the compensation packages which evolved, improving the offerings to help attract the talent the company needed. Fairness was a key ingredient. Managers and workers all had the same vacation and sickness policies, so no group of employees was treated with special privileges. Pay rates were also similar across the organization, as HR developed a series of compensation scale factors which were applied equally across all disciplines. Each employee received equal pay for equal contribution. These pay scales were clearly communicated, and these scales were one more example of how HR emphasized equality by fairly distributing benefits and compensation.

The successful results of a fully leveraged HR function were financially measurable, but also in many ways, these results were also immeasurable. Year after year, the Employee Advisory Resource, the twenty-four-hour helpline for employees, contributed significantly to health costs savings and reduced employee turnover. Control Data also had fewer lawsuits with current and former employees, as the Peer Review grievance system often resolved disputes in a manner respected by both employees and managers. And when Control Data began building manufacturing facilities near disadvantaged populations, the company gained recognition and positive publicity that helped catapult CDC in the spotlight—attracting employees who wanted to become part of a socially responsible company. Because of the combined aspects of the employee compensation packages and the social business initiatives, the HR function helped the company overall be more successful and financially viable year after year.

These positive outcomes gave the human resource function the respect and credibility it needed to be creative and risk taking. When one program or business venture was successful, another program would be built upon the knowledge gained from the previous program or business venture. The credibility factor also helped to determine if more capital would be allotted to a new HR business venture. As the years ticked on, the HR function developed a larger and larger array of seemingly disparate businesses, but they were all united by the common value of using Control Data know-how and technology to improve some targeted aspect of the human condition. Whether it was a health care initiative, language skills courseware, or a grievance system, the programs all had the common theme of improving individuals—making them employable, productive members within Control Data Corporation and within their surrounding communities.

The HR Culture Itself

THE HUMAN RESOURCES FUNCTION had its own unique sub-culture inside Control Data. The team was instructed to be non-conformists, to think differently about the normal way things should work (what would later be called in corporate parlance as thinking "outside the box") and come up with solutions to problems affecting the company. Risky solutions were encouraged, and so a maverick atmosphere permeated the function. Berg illustrates his relationship to many of the individuals who would work for the function through a story about General Eisenhower. The general once said to a paratrooper, "Young man, you must like to jump out of airplanes." The young man replied, "No, sir, I like being around guys who like to jump out of airplanes." Likewise, Berg often felt he was surrounded by human resources people who liked to take similar risks, and he relished their creativity and spunk. The staff was always encouraged to see what was going on in all areas of the company—picking up ideas both domestically and internationally, then coming up with ways these ideas could be applied to handle an employee need inside the company or address a social need outside of Control Data.

Ideas were frequently tossed back and forth between foreign offices and headquarters in Bloomington; for example, the idea for flexible hours originated from an employee practice common in Germany. Employees could work for German companies at times that better fit their personal schedules, as long as they worked during a common period of time to facilitate meetings. By becoming the first company to implement this work schedule policy within the United States, Control Data found a key way to make the company attractive to potential and existing employees. The mantra for the HR function was, "Reduce absenteeism, tardiness, and turnover. Attract, retain, and motivate." Optimizing the possibilities within the HR function was necessary and central for Control Data to achieve its strategic business objectives. An innovative, constantly evolving compensation package gave Control Data a distinct advantage over their competitors.

A good idea means nothing if that idea is not properly executed. Another set of leaders every organization needs are individuals who have the talent to organize and direct the development of the idea. William Norris described these different skill sets through an analogy that leaders were either pioneers or railroaders. The pioneers move out ahead of the rest of the group, exploring new areas and coming up with new ideas. The pioneers push through the wilderness. The railroaders then come along after the pioneers, building the infrastructure needed to grease the machines and keep things running—in other words, they implement these ideas and keep them running smoothly. He emphasized that both types of leaders were needed within any successful organization. For the HR function, the individual who led the efforts of the railroaders was Roger Wheeler. Wheeler's team implemented and expanded many of the ideas proposed through the HR function and figured out how these ideas could become reality. Because the HR function had people who were not afraid to come up with ideas and the people who could turn these ideas into new policies, programs, and businesses, the HR function was able to launch a number of initiatives and achieve successful results.

But how was Control Data able to gather this dynamic group of HR professionals? While the reputation of the HR function was obviously attractive, Control Data also had the additional incentive of paying salaries to human resource professionals that were always at least competitive with the market average. CDC did this because the company used its internal finance function as the market comparison for pay instead of the pay scale plan that human resource managers in other computer manufacturing companies received. With this financial incentive, Control Data attracted many impressive candidates to fill its positions. The HR function also used itself as the proving ground for affirmative action initiatives, encouraging women and minorities to apply for HR positions. Thus it had access to a diverse, talented group of employees, giving the function a wide range of background and perspectives. Perhaps the most important factor that attracted new employees, however, was the business Control Data Corporation was in. CDC was a major player during the birth of the computer and peripheral hardware industry—a fast-moving, ever-evolving sector of the national and international economy. The HR function could barely hire people fast enough to fill the needs of this rapidly growing company. The work was rarely dull.

Another interesting aspect of the culture was job positions within the HR function were fluid by design. HR managers rarely stayed at the same position very long, moving from supporting one area of the organization to another, often very different, area of the organization. The purpose for frequently moving the HR staff was to give the HR function a broader perspective of the entire company. As an example, Jim Morris was the first general manager of EAR, but then he was moved to Control Data Business Advisors, where Morris led the human resources service offerings sold to outside customers.

These frequent job transitions were expected to happen, because as team members moved through the ranks of the company, they saw and experienced more. HR professionals thus had a solid understanding of company matters across the product lines and, as Ruth Rich, a former HR executive, describes, gave the staff "a wise educational advantage." As individuals worked with diverse businesses, they encountered different kinds of employees with issues not shared by employees within other areas of the corporation. What worked well for one group of employees might not work as well for another group, so different approaches to employee issues could more successfully be developed. Because of these experiences, the HR staff responded to problems with effective, targeted solutions that matched the needs of the specific business. Thinking was tied to the full strategy of the company, to come up with answers that would help the overall bottom line.

The HR function was also a cooperative effort. Ruth Rich further describes the HR culture at Control Data as having "a company of fine mentors." As individuals moved to another area of the company, they were not required to go it alone. Instead, they were supported by insight from senior HR managers, and so, as Rich detailed, she "never felt on the outside looking in." Gene Baker, former vice president of human resource management services, echoed this observation, as CDC "had people who were charged with similar responsibilities, a family of professionals whom you could ask for help." With mentor advice and encouragement a major part of the culture, more junior HR professionals could explore ideas and initiate plans, knowing they would be supported in these endeavors.

Certainly not every project, program, or compensation package worked as planned. Along with innovation, the HR culture had to be flexible enough to correct a situation which was not working properly. A human resources procedure could be set up that was discovered to be unfair because the HR manager did not understand the full range of issues facing the affected employees. If a problem was discovered, steps were taken to correct the issue. But typically most mistakes were forgiven, and the HR team did not fear making mistakes. Company leadership wanted each HR manager to try new approaches, and if these approaches failed, to learn from the mistake and move on. Flexibility was a standard championed as much as innovation. Absenteeism and employee turnovers all cost Control Data money, so the HR managers worked hard to keep effective employees as long as possible. This philosophy guided the decision-making which went into new policies and programs. When a procedure was found to not be in tune with this philosophy, it was changed, and a better solution was implemented in its place.

To arrive at solutions and correct ineffective practices, the HR function governed its employment policies and initiatives through two committees—the Employee Relations Committee (ERC) and the Administration and Employee Relations Committee (AERC). These two committees had a two-tiered relationship they used to administrate human resource policies and initiatives across Control Data. The senior level group was the Administration and Employee Relations Committee. The AERC comprised six to eight human resource vice president-level individuals who were responsible for making final, critical decisions on the entire range of policy and procedures needed for the company. Monetary compensation plans, employee benefit issues, international considerations, and other central concerns were debated (sometimes hotly) within the AERC conference room. As an example, Pat Conway, the head of the CDC Real Estate and Facilities organization, would attend this meeting to discuss issues with manufacturing centers across the company. Whether a new facility was opening or an obsolete facility was shutting down, the AERC weighed in on the issues that affected the employees at these facilities. These regular meetings always had a set agenda, and they were the first event of the day—AERC meetings started promptly at 7:00 A.M.

The second-tier Employee Relations Committee served as both the gatherer of employment issues and then the executor of decisions made by the AERC. At any given time, the ERC was made up of between five to ten senior-level HR directors from all the operating units and corporate staff functions within Control Data. From a corporate culture perspective, these individuals were considered the number-two level managers within the HR function, just below the vice president level. Their primary role was to receive information about issues from the line organizations, handle as many of these issues as possible and come up with recommendations to present to the Administration and Employee Relations Committee. As an example, the ERC would be responsible for creating a plan, if needed, for employee layoffs. The recommendations made by the ERC were then passed along to the first-tier AERC. After the AERC made the final decision on an issue, the members of the ERC were then tasked with implementing this decision to the various line organizations they supported. This structural hierarchy helped the HR function enact and maintain consistent policies throughout the constantly growing corporation. The ERC and the AERC provided the guidance needed to administrate the entire HR function.

As for the hierarchical structure within the HR function, the HR managers were organized through six levels, reflecting how many employees the HR function was required to administrate throughout the organization. These HR managers were paired with an equivalent line organization manager. This dual ladder approach meant the HR function's rank of hierarchy matched the line operation hierarchy, and HR managers shared a similar classification and pay grade through this method. Another group of individuals were also involved with the leadership of the HR function—consultants. Consultants could serve on nearly every level within the HR function, including the executive level. However, these individuals did not have any direct reports, serving in an advisory role for the HR professionals at potentially each level of the business unit. The hierarchy for line organization managers, HR managers, and consultants was as follows:

1. Senior vice president/HR senior vice president/executive consultant
2. Vice president/HR vice president/executive consultant
3. General manager/HR general manager/executive consultant
4. Director/HR director/principle consultant
5. Manager/HR manager/consultant
6. Supervisor/HR supervisor/consultant

HR professionals at each level of this hierarchy were responsible for increasingly larger shares of the employee population, with supervisors being the immediate contact for specific departments contained within each line organization, and the director in charge of the overall HR function within an entire line organization. The vice president and senior vice president positions reviewed overall policy direction for the entire organization.

Another major component of the human resources culture was HR professionals from the various line organizations periodically got together for conferences. These conferences were typically called by the senior HR executive of each line organization, and these major gatherings often included as many as 150 people. Their main purpose was to share ideas, discuss the current state of the company, and establish relationships. Vice presidents and other HR leaders would give presentations on various initiatives and policies. Attendees would also have an opportunity to learn about these initiatives and directly ask questions from the presenters. These sessions helped ensure corporate personnel policies would be correctly and evenly implemented across the giant corporation. Perhaps most importantly, these regional conferences gave new human resource employees an opportunity to integrate with the human resources team. These employees could also put a "face" on an HR executive with whom they may need to interact with in the future.

Every two to three years, a worldwide conference of human resources professionals from across the corporation convened. Issues regarding HR policies that affected the entire organization were discussed, new technologies were taught, and people in related roles across the company would meet and share ideas. These conferences also served as a venue where HR executives could reinforce the business practices and corporate philosophy of the organization. Specifically, the concept of instilling a positive corporate environment was regularly emphasized. Frank Dawe, former senior vice president of administration, hit upon this theme on a speech he gave at the 1981 conference, when he said, "This whole spirit of the Control Data culture or personality directly touches each of us in personnel. It's at the very core of what we do, because at Control Data, we have the People Responsibility. . . . There is ample evidence that there is a strong correlation between a company's quality of work life and its competitive performance." These conferences were invaluable venues for the entire HR function to feel a part of something larger than their immediate job surroundings; they were the glue that greatly helped the company remain competitive and profitable. Being asked to attend any of these major conferences was a real honor, and past HR employees cite these conferences as major highlights in their Control Data careers.

Because of these meetings, connections were made which improved interaction among the worldwide HR division. These frequent gatherings assured that no one worked in a vacuum. As Jim Morris recalls, "I think the reason we were so innovative is that not only were people creative enough to come up with the innovative ideas, but humble enough to adapt the ideas of others to our own unique environment." With a group of senior managers open to new ideas, individuals were free to experiment in a secure, supportive, trusting environment. Control Data was not run by rules; it was run by collaboration created through personal relationships. Because of these frequent meetings, each employee had an opportunity to question every Control Data project and initiative. The structure of the function was not, however, a democracy. Ultimately the collaboration had to stop and a direction for the project or issue, for better or for worse, was decided upon by the ERC and/or the AERC. As the results of this decision were evaluated, the procedure was continued or a new series of approaches were proposed. The culture within the HR function was thus in a state of constant re-evaluation. By diligently reviewing the relationship between employees and the corporation and actively communicating ideas throughout the human resources function, HR professionals were better positioned to handle most difficult employment issues.

The Employee Equation

From the moment a newly hired individual walked through the doors of Control Data Corporation, the human resource function wanted that person truly excited about coming to work. They thought each new hire should immediately feel included as a vital member of an organization dedicated to a never-ending pursuit of professional improvement. To foster a spirit of belonging to CDC, each new employee received a tie pin or a bracelet as part of their orientation. This jewelry was designed by Jostens, Inc., the jewelry manufacturer who primarily specializes in class rings for students of educational institutions. Much like the class rings graduates received from Jostens to emphasize their membership with a school, this jewelry emphasized the new employee's membership within Control Data Corporation. Control Data was the first organization to offer orientation jewelry made by Jostens. This resulted in a whole new business for Jostens, as companies began requesting orientation jewelry to present to their new employees as well.

Every individual accepted for employment was hired for their potential to grow within the organization. Nobody knew what the future would hold for each new hire, of course, and certainly not everyone Control Data hired became an exemplary, dedicated employee. The corporate employment approach was that each person deserved the opportunity to succeed. While it was up to the employee to successfully execute and complete tasks, it was up to Control Data management to make new opportunities available for each motivated employee.

Control Data's philosophy was employment was a shared risk. If an employee got into difficult circumstances, the HR function would do what it could to help or find ways to assist employees into working out their own solutions. Two specific examples, among many, demonstrate this policy. Thie first is of a young man who was hired out of college and had a great deal of engineering ability. He was hired to work as a new engineer at the La Jolla facility. However, this young man had only worked for the company a few months when he ended up in a serious car accident. As a result of his injuries, he became a quadriplegic with significant brain injuries. The young man could no longer do what he was hired to do. Rather than let him go, however, the HR managers at this CDC facility kept him on by having him work the front door at the La Jolla plant, checking employee credentials as they entered the building and assisting outside people in finding the specific areas of the plant to which they needed to go. Another situation involved an engineer who had a vision problem. Although this engineer had failed the physical exam required for employment at the company, the HR manager handling his application was impressed with the young man's engineering ability. Despite his disability, he was hired and given an oversized television monitor so he could work on his engineering projects. He became one of the most respected engineers in his division. In both cases, these HR managers discovered ways the risks of employing these individuals could be overcome by finding suitable positions or technologies that compensated for their limitations and leveraged their skills.

Line managers throughout the organization were constantly instructed to keep these core values of shared responsibility and support in mind. Tom Kamp outlined these values in a document he wrote for the Peripheral Products operation in 1976. In the document, he writes, "Running down another person never accomplishes any good—and will destroy an organization from within. The more a company can help an employee's financial and physical health, the more productive the employee will be and the more contribution they will make to society." Kamp further states the drive for innovation within his organization: "We need creative designs, creative solutions to problems, not just to be told there's a problem. I really intend to constantly raise this point—creativity." The Control Data culture of innovation and support was an expected part of company culture—whether in the office cubicle or on the manufacturing floor.

As part of the ongoing commitment to employees, the HR function would be called upon to research and analyze workforce problems. The function did this through a variety of tools—attitude surveys, questionnaires, analyses of personnel records, interviews with employees, termination interviews, and so on. The results of these studies, interviews, and other projects were then turned into statistical reports for higher level management. In this way, line managers and every executive up to William Norris understood the challenges facing employees, as well as employee reactions toward various corporate policies. This reporting structure gave everyone from the board of directors down a vivid picture of the day-to-day situation within the corporation. These reports proved to be valuable tools, as they helped determine how to build the best employee relations package possible.

One interesting outcome of this HR approach was employees would request to decertify their union chapters within acquired companies. This procedure was only conducted within the United States. Because CDC offered the same or better compensation than what employees could receive through their union contract and had a reputation for fair treatment, employees within these acquired U.S. companies would eventually request to end their association with their unions. By law, Control Data could only help decertify the unions if a majority of the employees within the acquired organization request this change. Control Data could then legally send an HR representative to explain how the company handled the decertification process. When employees voted to this change, a decertification initiative was launched to make sure the process was conducted in a legal, public manner.

Control Data publicly stated it was "pro-employee, not anti-union." Of course, this approach was also part of the company's "enlightened self-interest" to be free from union intervention. So despite the rhetoric, at its heart Control Data was basically an anti-union corporation, typical of any large organization desiring to protect its business interests. As unions gained more benefits for employees at other competitive corporations, the HR leadership would adopt similar benefits package to alleviate union organizing within CDC factories. So while it is true that Control Data successfully kept unions out of their facilities in the United States, the company was also directly under their influence—as the HR function would rapidly implement competitive benefits at or above those recently negotiated by third party union mediators with other companies. The unions were justifiably quite frustrated with CDC, but they also grudgingly admired the progressive, employee-first philosophy that kept them out of the Control Data workforce.

But like any corporation, things did not always go so smoothly. As various business units evolved, the initial reason a specific employee was hired might change or even disappear. The person who was the perfect fit when hired may, just a few years or even months later, no longer be working in a position desirable for the company. And some new employees just plain did not work out. As Frank Dawe commented about the HR profession, "Lawyers meet their mistakes in jail, doctors when they're dead, but human resource managers meet their mistakes in the halls." As Control Data was chiefly in the computer hardware business, frequent and sudden advances in a technology could cause a product to lose its viability, which could lead to modifying or even shutting down an entire plant. And there was always the possibility that an economic recession or product line downturn would result in layoffs. To help the CDC workforce through these difficulties, the HR function created innovative solutions to help affected employees. If retraining was possible, the employees were given the opportunity to learn new skills and transfer to another area within the company. However, if future employment at CDC was not an option, employees were still not cast out into the cold. Control Data established an outplacement consultation service to help former employees. Individuals could use this service to develop professional résumés, work with a career counselor, and hopefully find a new job elsewhere.

Eventually the HR function was forced to put its activities toward initiating layoffs as the company struggled to stay solvent during the second half of the 1980s. Despite the challenges facing the company, the HR function still embraced and implemented the employee-first philosophy. In a document entitled "Ties That Bind," written in 1988, the authors define statements of intent for the HR function during these difficult times:

- Provide processes for reviewing business decisions that affect employees.
- Maintain a work force structure that minimizes loss by employees due to changing business conditions.
- Make employment changes based on business conditions or individual performance-related factors.
- Mitigate the effects of job loss on employees. Offer transition assistance in preparing for and finding new assignments within Control Data or employment outside the corporation.

Whether the employee was entering or exiting the corporation, Control Data's HR function sought to achieve an ethical, responsible relationship with each employee. The company dealt with very few employment lawsuits, and this fact reveals how favorably the CDC workforce viewed their relationship with the organization. Mary Parker Follett would have been proud.

ZZZ

Early Hurdles

THE FIRST YEARS OF THE HR FUNCTION (and at that time, it was still called the personnel function) at CDC was consumed by hiring engineers, assemblers, line managers, payroll managers, and a myriad of other positions needed to match the astonishing growth of the company. It was a daunting task, because as CDC took on more employees through recruitment and acquisitions, the human resource function needed to hire more HR managers to oversee the compensation packages and employee relations services for the expanding worker base. The success of the mainframe computers and the peripheral equipment of the 1960s ensured that job recruiters needed to aggressively pursue talented candidates throughout the decade. A human resources report from this time period states: "During the fiscal year which ended June 30, 1961, we hired 435 permanent and 106 temporary employees. Currently, we are hiring 50-80 people a month." The rate of new employees needed at the company was nonstop. One major obstacle at the time was computer science and manufacturing technology was barely ten years old. The pool of qualified graduates and available professionals to fill these positions was quite small. Other computer manufacturing companies were also seeking out new employees from the same limited pool of individuals, so it was in effect a war against other corporations to hire qualified people.

During this time within Control Data, Roger Wheeler was vice president of personnel development. He led the HR team that researched the compensation and benefits package available at rival organizations and created a competitive package to present to potential plant workers, new college graduates, and current professionals from other companies. Due to the success of the CDC 1604, printing and tape drive peripheral products, and then the CDC 6600, Control Data was in a fairly stable financial position to offer attractive compensation packages to the variety of individuals the company needed to increase production on their product lines. In terms of actual income, Control Data didn't pay starting salaries as low as those at banks nor as much as starting salaries at oil companies. So ultimately, Control Data could afford a reasonable amount of income for each employee, and this combined with other employee benefits always kept Control Data competitive in the effort to hire effective employees. Control Data also initiated a dual ladder for management and technical staff policy. Through this policy, individuals who wanted a technical career would enjoy the same compensation package as individuals who wished to pursue a management path. This policy motivated more technology-focused individuals to join the company, as there was an inherent fairness in how employees were paid.

The college recruitment program was one of the first initiatives set up by the HR function to market the company to graduates. Because Control Data had one of the best compensation packages available in the industry at the time, the HR function was able to draw many engineers, accountants, and other college-educated personnel for the available positions. A CDC employee benefits manual from this period states as the company objective for its package, "To contribute to corporate growth and profit through benefit program design and administration that strikes a proper balance between what the corporation can afford to provide in the way of benefits and what is needed to attract, retain, and motivate qualified personnel." The CDC benefits package worked well. In 1962, CDC had 2,273 employees. By 1967, ten years after the company was founded, total payroll numbered over 14,000 employees.

Creating a compensation package for domestic employees in the United States was one hurdle, but creating compensation packages for the international workforce was an even higher hurdle. When the first Control Data office in Europe was set up in Lucerne, Switzerland, the human resources function had to get up to speed quickly to understand the laws and compensation practices in a variety of locales in Europe. When manufacturing facilities were set up in South Korea, Hong Kong, and Mexico, the human resource staff had to do an identical task. HR was heavily involved in all of the early inroads for establishing businesses in these countries.

As the international HR function grew (at this time, called the international personnel organization), this function developed a charter statement which defined the personnel standards the company would follow. It read,

> Control Data Corporation, as a multinational company, will operate world-wide by organizing staff functions to recognize the legal, financial, psychological, and practical considerations that permit Control Data to operate and do business in any one country. The first method of operating assures the continuity of a product or service worldwide that only a single responsible management can achieve. The second assures the satisfaction of legal requirements within one political unit regardless of how the company organizes internally so that Control Data continues to be permitted to operate in that political unit. It also assures the consistency of those staff actions always necessary between geographically related Control Data operating units.

Negotiations with the countries and labor unions were often delicate. "One of the fundamental issues understood by someone from an international environment," Frank Dawe relates, "is that you should not superimpose United States values internationally, but rather work on integration." HR professionals found themselves in several unique parts of the world. In a couple situations, members of the HR team negotiated with the prime ministers' offices in both Portugal and Taiwan. When setting up facilities in France, the HR staff had to work with four or five different unions. One area of a new French manufacturing center had only three people, two of whom decided they didn't want to belong to the union, so the HR transition team worked out negotiations to dissolve the union representation. In other international situations, Control Data worked with unions to make sure the company complied with the foreign country's labor laws and regulations.

When Control Data established offices in foreign countries, the issues of income taxes frequently gave the HR office a fair share of headaches. Typically, taxes were much higher in these countries than in the United States, and new international employees hoped to be taxed using the income tax rate in the United States. Some international employees even tried to convince their HR managers they could legally establish offshore accounts to avoid paying income tax in their home country. But as Gene Baker, a former vice president for the first international HR office in Lucerne and other European offices (later vice president of human resource management services) describes, "Tax evasion was a no-go." All these attempts to create international accounts were ruled as tax avoidance, so the HR function established a standard policy whereby international employees had to be taxed using the rates required by their home countries. This became a good practice that prevented Control Data from getting into international complications or, worse yet, lawsuits. Doubtless the HR function saved the company a great deal of much-needed capital by making sure the compensation packages fulfilled the legal requirements established in foreign countries.

As the company expanded both domestically and overseas, the real estate and facilities function oversaw purchases of land, construction of new facilities, and design of manufacturing and office spaces. The human resources function was also included in this process, making sure the new plants and offices were in locations near a potential pool of employees. For example, the HR function made a suggestion to build plants where farm wives could be employed as a way to connect with this untapped labor force and improve the financial circumstances of farm families. The real estate and facilities function embraced this suggestion and built new factories in Cambridge, Redwood Falls, Faribault, Spring Grove, and other rural Minnesota communities. Later, when Bill Norris tasked the company to build plants in poverty-area communities, members of the HR function researched possible communities where these plants could be placed.

Workers at the Redwood Falls plant. Control Data hired primarily rural women to work in this plant. (Photo courtesy of the Charles Babbage Institute.)

A worker at the Faribault, Minnesota plant. (Photo courtesy of the Charles Babbage Institute.)

This unique relationship meant that the HR function essentially represented the needs of potential workers and the communities, while the real estate and facilities function matched these factors with the requirements of the new facilities. This relationship led to the creation of many successful plants that were both supported and respected in the communities in which they were built.

Because of Control Data's reputation for its employee-centric culture, the HR function had to be careful the company wasn't being manipulated by people looking to gain some extra money. One serious issue that emerged in the 1970s was that the HR function was giving in too easily on workers' compensation claims. These claims kept rising each year, despite the fact that the company's manufacturing facilities and office spaces were meeting or exceeding safety standards. After some research into these claims, members of the HR function discovered that a consistent group of Minneapolis lawyers, working in tandem with several doctors, had figured out it was easy to get about $3,000 per claim from CDC. These claims were small enough not to make a big impact, and they were a fast way to earn extra money.

HR managers across the region began carefully screening the workers' compensation cases that came across their desks. It was not long before another small claim from one of these lawyers crossed the desk of an HR manager. Control Data refused to pay the claim to the lawyer and the response was immediate. The number of minor workers compensation claims quite literally went down overnight. No longer able to pilfer the company, these unscrupulous lawyers and doctors quickly and quietly stopped placing frivolous claims against Control Data. The HR function, while benevolent, had a "tough as nails" side employees and outside individuals soon learned not to cross.

Because of its integration throughout the organization, the HR function was involved with nearly every major business decision the company made. HR managers and staff became a very experienced, competent group within Control Data, and the HR function established its credibility with most line managers. Members of the HR function were frequently leveraged for advice and decisions, ensuring the company made responsible choices in the policies and issues that arose from employee relations. The HR function soon took this know-how and applied it against many of the social challenges Control Data decided to take on.

Doors Wide Open

Dᴜʀɪɴɢ ᴛʜᴇ ᴇᴀʀʟʏ ᴅᴀʏꜱ ᴏꜰ CDC, the company mirrored the hiring practices common in the 1950s. When male college graduates came, they were given interviews by college relations. However, when female graduates came, they were interviewed by clerical recruiting. The company also had two job titles for manufacturing positions—the male assembler and the female assembler. The starting female assembler pay scale (Grade One) was always less than the starting male assembler pay scale (Grade Two). But by the end of the 1960s into the early 1970s, these hiring and compensation practices were ended in response to the fair labor laws enacted by the United States government. While other companies chafed at this equal opportunity and affirmative action legislation and resented being forced to hire women and minorities, Control Data made a concerted effort to jump ahead of the curve, creating a place where gender discrimination was reduced and eventually eliminated. As described previously, one of the company's first efforts to reduce discrimination in the workplace was to build manufacturing facilities in rural Minnesota communities, providing employment opportunities specifically targeted for women. And by the 1970s, women filled over half of the positions in the human resources function.

Minority employment effort at Control Data first focused on manufacturing positions. As the HR function developed, affirmative action practices were pursued in all areas of the corporation. Leading that effort was Bill English, a young African-American HR professional hired in 1969 to be the equal opportunity employment coordinator. Through his leadership, Bill English built bridges between CDC and minority communities. He launched several recruitment programs to convince young African-American men and women that they could work for Control Data and be treated fairly. To that end, he hired sports celebrities part-time during the off-season. These sports celebrities included Johnny Roseboro, a catcher for the Minnesota Twins and previously the Los Angeles Dodgers, and Alan Page of the Minnesota Vikings and later a Minnesota Supreme Court justice, to encourage young minorities to sign up for CDC interviews on college campuses. These popular sports figures also encouraged less-skilled minority candidates to apply for manufacturing jobs at Control Data plants, and many young minority individuals did apply for jobs. Affirmative action became the rule of the day, and the company reaped huge benefits from their open employment practices. The diversity in their workforce ensured there would always be a large and deep talent pool available to fill Control Data positions.

It was not always easy. Bill English's first major challenge happened when Control Data acquired a manufacturer which built water control systems. Control Data's interest in the plant was that it could integrate mainframe computers to work with these water control systems. However, as English discovered, this acquired plant was located within a heavily minority community within St. Paul, but it had no people of color working anywhere in the plant. English met with the plant manager to discuss ways the employee population could better reflect the minority makeup of the surrounding community. This turned into a difficult meeting, as the plant manager was also the former owner of the company and did not like the idea of this young black man telling him who he could and could not hire. The meeting ended, and Bill reported the result to his immediate supervisor, Tom Linklater, and, in turn, Norb Berg. These executives were not happy with the situation, and instructed English to return to the plant and have another meeting with the plant manager. Armed with the full support of both these HR executives, Bill English returned to the plant the next day stating the plant manager could either work with his HR representative to extend opportunities to minorities, or he could have a meeting with Berg. The plant manager soon met with HR and began improving his hiring practices.

Inequality in hiring and promotion was, however, done unintentionally as well as intentionally. In order to evaluate potential cases of discrimination throughout the corporation, a complaint function was set up wherein employees voiced concerns. This function was a rapid file system where employees could expect a response quickly—instead of waiting months for a tepid acknowledgement of the situation. In one case, an East Indian worker was passed over for promotion five times, and each promotion was a job for which he felt he was qualified. When the people receiving the promotions were reviewed, it was discovered in every case that these individuals were white males, indicating preferential treatment was involved in the selection process when the East Indian worker's application was in the mix. When the manager in charge was presented with these facts, the employee received his well-deserved promotion.

Despite all these strong actions taken by the HR function, as time went by it became clear line managers were still not achieving affirmative action goals. To provide motivation for line executives to meet these requirements, the human resources function came up with the idea of incorporating affirmative action goals in incentive plans. The human resource function was the scorekeeper, and if the goals were not met, the executives' compensation was negatively impacted. Needless to say, the line executives began focusing on their affirmative action goals. This policy was a significant factor in the increased performance in equal employment throughout the organization. Using this same approach, the executive incentive plan positively impacted training, quality, safety, and other important management areas.

While the company instituted these policies because it was the right thing to do, Control Data, like similar companies, was also encouraged to follow these policies through a carrot-and-stick relationship with the U.S. government. The HR function was required to report affirmative action progress in relation to all of Control Data's many government contracts. The company was required to have a compliance review through the Office of Federal Contracts Compliance, or OFCC. As long as Control Data demonstrated it was making a good faith effort to achieve these equal opportunity objectives, CDC did not incur any penalties. So between the internal pressure exerted by Control Data management and the external pressure required to satisfy government contracts, the company rapidly became one of the most aggressive companies to recruit minorities throughout the civil rights era and beyond. Control Data's progress drew national attention. Starting in 1971, William Norris was frequently invited to various conferences to speak about how to implement equal employment opportunities. And despite the difficulties the company faced during the early 1970s, CDC remained very aggressive in maintaining its efforts at minority employment. These statistics were included in a letter written to James D. Hodgson, the secretary of labor under the Nixon administration: "You may be interested in knowing about Control Data's efforts in affirmative action throughout the corporation. In 1971, despite a decline in total corporate population, sixteen and a half percent of all new hires were minorities. . . . In addition, nearly ten percent of all promotions in 1971 went to minorities."

During 1977, a similar initiative was launched to provide more job opportunities for women. The company set out to provide employment for women throughout the entire organization, from starting positions to the executive levels. Margo Hart became the first manager of Control Data's women's programs, and the company became very aggressive in promoting women to positions of high level responsibility. Ruth Rich, a former secretary hired in the late 1960s, advanced through the organization to become a human resources executive by the late 1970s. Lois Dixon-Rice, a leading member of the College Testing Board, ran the Washington office in charge of increasing employment opportunities for women. She also became the first African-American to serve on Control Data's board of directors. As the years went by, the employee population of the company became more and more diverse.

The HR function also launched a related fast track program designed for women and minorities to help them more rapidly advance to higher level positions. The concept was that Control Data could then build up a cadre of qualified women and minorities to fill executive-level positions throughout the organization. But the fast track program had little support from the employees it was created to assist, however, as most women and minority individuals did not want targeted help to advance through the company. The consensus among these employees was that they wanted to earn their positions like everybody else. Provided that the work environment was fair and that ability and talent would be considered before gender and ethnicity, these employees felt there was no need for them to receive special treatment. The fast track advanced program was soon shelved.

However, unscrupulous opportunists took advantage of Control Data's equal opportunity policy. In 1974, a person representing a minority newspaper in Los Angeles called William Norris, asking if CDC would like to place employment advertisements in the publication. Several ads were soon placed within this newspaper. Bill English later was in Los Angeles, so he decided to make a personal visit to the minority newspaper and introduce himself. When he attempted to locate their office, he instead found a P.O. drop box. The newspaper didn't actually exist; it was only a front to get Control Data and many other corporations to place ads in a nonexistent minority newspaper. Bill English alerted other companies about the scam, and soon publicity about the newspaper went national. Eventually Bill English had an interview with Mike Wallace from CBS's *60 Minutes* about the situation. At the same time, Mike Wallace asked questions about Control Data's affirmative action programs, and the company received national exposure for its achievements and efforts in hiring minority workers.

As HR managers worked with individuals from different circumstances, they gained new insights into how to recruit, develop, and maintain these employees. When the Northside manufacturing center opened, the first poverty-area plant, many of the employees were women. Surprisingly, after a short period of time, nearly fifty percent of this population group left their jobs. The HR staff conducted research to find out why, and they learned the primary reason minority women needed to quit their jobs was because they did not have sufficient daycare for their young children. To correct this situation, Control Data created one of the first corporate daycare facilities in the country. Working mothers could now bring their babies and toddlers to work with them, visit them on breaks, and pick them up after their shifts. By opening this center, CDC could tap into an underemployed segment of the population, and these individuals could maintain gainful employment at the facility.

This example is just one of many programs the HR function launched in order to hire the workforce in its poverty-area plants and elsewhere. Along the way, the HR function learned about the unique needs each new segment of the employee population brought to the workplace, from education on basic skills of money management to more serious needs requiring legal counseling. Conversely, Control Data managers throughout the company had to learn a new set of employee relationship skills. These managers were taught minority group dynamics, providing managers will the skills needed to interface effectively with all employees, regardless of ethnicity and gender. Control Data embraced these challenges, hiring and sustaining many people other corporations would not even consider for employment.

Political leaders in Minnesota took notice. In 1973, Minnesota Governor Wendell Anderson established a corrections ombudsman function for resolving inmate and staff problems within the prison system. Governor Anderson asked Norb Berg to serve as a member of the committee tasked with finding and hiring an individual to serve in the ombudsman office at the Stillwater Correctional Facility, a prison near the Twin Cities. Soon the ombudsman program began. Berg learned from an inmate who served on the committee the program was being overwhelmed by the demand placed against it by the inmates. Berg called Governor Anderson and asked if a member of the Control Data HR staff could assist this new office by acting in an advisory role. Governor Anderson felt that Control Data's experience with managing diversity issues would help make the ombudsman program more effective. Berg asked Richard Conner, an HR research manager, if he would be willing to help. Richard was willing, and this opportunity launched several prison programs, which are described in the next chapter.

Control Data won much recognition for its work with minorities, women, and other underemployed populations. One such national award, presented by *Business and Society Review*, acknowledged Control Data's efforts in the area of equal opportunity employment. The publication was impressed by CDC's success at creating and maintaining the poverty-area plants, prison work contracts, and other unique facilities. And in 1986, Bill Norris received the Employee Equal Opportunity Award from the Urban League in affirmation of the company's approach to affirmative action.

In an era where many individuals fought for equal rights, Control Data was consistently publicized as one of the top one hundred companies to work for in the United States. This helped the company draw skilled and talented individuals who wanted to become part of an organization that embraced equality. As Berg explained during an interview, "We have more know-how than any company in the United States in how to utilize employees others have shied away from—the so-called hard to employ, people out of prison, the handicapped, homebound, and unskilled. Those things don't bother us. We know how to attract, train, retain, and motivate disadvantaged people, and we've done it over and over again." As Control Data continued its equal employment policy throughout the years, the employee population in 1984 was made up by 16.9% minorities and 16.5% non-minority women, so nearly a third of CDC employees were made up of qualified people who most likely would not have achieved these same positions if Control Data's open employment policy was not put into place in the late 1960s. The net result is that, by becoming blind to gender and ethnicity, Control Data could hire the best and the brightest individuals it could find.

One key fact speaks to both the major achievement and the bottom line benefit CDC gained by opening employment up to as many individuals as possible. Despite the thousands of employees hired over the years, Control Data Corporation never had an equal opportunity lawsuit.

Growing in the Greenhouse

THE HUMAN RESOURCE FUNCTION embarked upon its most innovative period during the late 1960s, continuing until it had to eventually cut back its activities during Control Data's slow contraction during the late 1980s. Control Data's affirmative action initiatives, poverty-area plants, and international offices placed the HR function in a unique position to come up with solutions to answer the needs of the diverse population the company employed. Control Data did not want its hired, qualified workers to move in and out of the company through a revolving door. They wanted these individuals to stay within the company—hopefully for their entire careers. To achieve that goal, the HR function explored programs and policies that would make CDC a superior, attractive corporation, using its "enlightened self-interest" approach to employment so the more attractive the company was to a prospective employee, the more likely CDC would be able to hire and retain high quality, dynamic individuals who would ensure the future of the corporation.

These cutting edge programs and policies were explored in a greenhouse atmosphere: an enclosed development area where concepts were tested, reviewed and refined. If the program succeeded in its development, it was implemented in some capacity within the company. The innovative spirit was in high gear during all of these projects. The major initiatives, like Employee Advisory Resource and StayWell, resulted in real savings for Control Data, particularly in insurance costs. Following the concepts first proposed by human relations movement of the 1930s, what was good for the employee was good for the company, and there was a constant incentive to create new programs and improve the results gained from existing ones. However, rather than keep these programs as liabilities to the company's bottom line, Control Data also made a significant effort to later turn these programs into profit-making businesses.

The central group responsible for proposing the social business ventures was the Committee on Social Responsibility. This committee was formed in 1972. It had two main tasks. It was meant to identify areas where the company could use its knowledge, products, and services to alleviate social problems and then to come up with ways these areas could be addressed to utilize CDC's resources to support these social business opportunities. Each year the company reserved a set share of venture capital funds for developing and promoting social initiatives, and these funds were administrated by the Committee on Social Responsibility. Although these projects were not required to have commercial potential, the committee gave preference to the projects which had more business viability.

This committee was made up of fifteen people pulled from all levels of the corporation. This committee met regularly throughout the year and occasionally went on retreats to focus exclusively on generating program plans for the social initiatives the company would follow over the course of several years. The Committee on Social Responsibility proposed ways the company could improve the lives of economically depressed populations in both rural and urban communities. Several businesses were launched through proposals first presented and developed through this committee. Two of these businesses, Rural Ventures and City Ventures, were formed for the stated purpose of helping poor rural and urban areas develop economically. The plight of Native Americans on reservations was also examined, specifically in the Rosebud Indian Reservation in South Dakota. A health care initiative, in cooperation with tribal leaders, was launched to provide better health care services across the Native American reservation. The Committee on Social Responsibility became the source organization through which proposals—received both inside and outside the company—were evaluated. This committee planted the seeds of ideas that took root in the HR function's greenhouse.

Each HR innovation built on a previous innovation. Employees at poverty-area plants had unique needs which required different kinds of support than what employees at a more conventional plant required. For example, the HR managers developed a different employment application form which was less intimidating, based on the individual's goals for employment rather than past educational and occupational experience. The employees at the poverty-area plants also had a need for a variety of services like financial counseling, legal assistance, bail bonds, personal counseling, drug abuse counseling, classes on adapting to work, and so on. The experiences working with this employee base led to the realization that all CDC employees could benefit from similar services, and this discovery was one of the motivations for creating Employee Advisory Resource (EAR), a twenty-four-hour per day, seven-day per week counseling service eventually made available to the entire company. Experiences at the poverty-area plants also instigated another educational program for the disadvantaged, the FAIRBREAK program. The educational program was designed to give disadvantaged individuals the opportunity to receive a basic skills education. Each FAIRBREAK center leveraged PLATO terminals which contained basic skills courseware for reading, math, financial management, and similar offerings. While the company launched FAIRBREAK as part of its social responsibility initiatives, its goal was to turn FAIRBREAK into a new business as well.

In November of 1974, several HR services and initiatives became supported through a resource gathering organization—Human Resource Management Services (HRMS). This organization provided a central place to administrate some employee relations programs, social responsibility programs, and other initiatives. The HRMS organization leveraged the greenhouse method for developing business concepts which would allow Control Data to fund and manage new HR products and services apart from the standard product line. This unique organization was formed outside of the line organization and reported directly to Norb Berg. Human Resource Management Services could then run various services and initiatives in their early stages sheltered from the reporting structure that could potentially inhibit their outcomes.

The individual placed in charge of Human Resource Management Services was Eugene (Gene) Baker, a longtime HR professional with Control Data. Previous to heading Human Resource Management Services, Gene had been responsible for setting up human resource offices at Control Data facilities across Europe. Now he used his managerial experience to run HRMS, a position he held for the rest of his Control Data career. The primary service supported by HRMS was Employee Advisory Resource. Because EAR was placed outside of the line organization, it made it possible for counselors to intervene and resolve various issues. Often the counselors would serve as independent arbitrators to arrive at successful outcomes.

Throughout the years, various initiatives and services would be given to Human Resource Management Services to oversee. Some of these responsibilities were then moved outside of the HRMS umbrella to be run by other Control Data functions. In this way, HRMS evolved to become an internal greenhouse, or incubator, where a project outside of the main project or service lines could be explored and supported. For example, the public affairs function was placed under HRMS. This function focused on issues dealing with social concerns and managed the charitable contributions for Control Data. Public affairs directly communicated with a number of social support organizations within communities and the entire country, giving members of this function deep knowledge into issues affecting specific populations and communities within the United States. This knowledge greatly helped Control Data while the company explored business initiatives to improve the well-being of individuals and communities. Another initiative placed under HRMS was corporate security. A whole range of activities fit under this initiative, as team members worked to improve the integrity of protecting the company from theft at all levels of the organization.

As often eventually occurred, when HRMS was no longer needed to administrate the resources required for the service or initiative, it was moved outside of Human Resource Management Services. The service would then be reorganized to become part of another function or run itself as an independent entity. "This became a peculiarity of the organization," as Gene Baker describes. "Roles were very, very fluid. Nobody had an opportunity to become a dinosaur." Human Resource Management Services embodied that fluidity through the range of initiatives and services passed both in and out of its responsibility.

Frequently if the program or social responsibility venture proved viable, Human Resource Management Services explored ways the venture could be turned into profitable businesses. The advantages of this organizational structure was that now HR had a central place from which it could compete for service contracts within the public sector and seek out resources internally within Control Data. The Human Resource Management Services organization also served as a separate idea hothouse function, where it could methodically test programs before they were implemented across the company and eventually marketed externally. This internal organization became the backbone structure that facilitated many of the social business initiatives throughout the 1970s and 1980s.

The culture inside human resources made these achievements possible. The function had an idea-driven atmosphere which encouraged its staff to make a positive, lasting impact on improving the human condition. It was a remarkable period in the careers of all who worked for the HR function and for the many others who received benefits from its programs and services. Control Data's human resources function was a maverick place for imaginative hearts and minds, every bit as innovative as the CDC mainframe computer and peripheral device labs.

During a program celebrating the twenty-fifth anniversary of the company, Norb Berg gave out a plaque to his co-collaborators in the CDC human resources adventure. A quote from Martin Luther King, Jr. was inscribed on this plaque, reading, "Social change will not come overnight, yet the nonconformist works as though it is an imminent possibility . . . The saving of our world from pending doom will come, not through the complacent adjustment of the conforming majority, but through the creative maladjustment of a non-conforming minority." The next chapters of this book detail some of the programs, services, and businesses created during these amazing years of freedom and innovation within the Control Data HR function. The human resources team of maladjusted, nonconforming associates broke new ground that changed the culture of corporations forever.

Chapter Three

Business in a Burning Society

"You can't do business in a society that's burning."
—*William Norris*

THE RIOTS THAT EXPLODED ON THE STREETS of America in the late 1960s revealed holes in the fabric of the American dream. While the United States was enjoying a long period of economic prosperity, major segments of the population were not included in the growing wealth of these times. Racial attitudes toward employment, cultural traditions toward minorities, and laws which prohibited political equality had created impoverished communities in pockets throughout the country. Just after the midpoint of the twentieth century, situations in these various communities had reached a boiling point. With the ideological competition of communism threatening America from the outside and inequality in civil rights and economics threatening America from the inside, the country was on a dangerous precipice. Actions by the U.S. government, particularly the Civil Rights Act of 1964, helped ease these internal tensions. These changes proved slow in coming, however, and the open resistance against many of these changes was real. The assassinations of Robert Kennedy and Martin Luther King, Jr., dangerously fueled these tensions throughout the end of the decade.

However, progress was happening in several substantive ways, as actions were taken by both public and private sectors to correct, or at least lessen, the ills of discrimination. The issue of poverty loomed large, especially in regard to minorities, and a national debate about addressing this problem dominated public discussions. Two schools of thought emerged as to how to best improve the economic well-being of these individuals. On one side is the belief that government is the best catalyst for change, using government to enact laws requiring equality in the workplace. This approach is personified by President Johnson's War on Poverty, which led to the creation of the Office of Economic Opportunity, or OEO, a department that administered federal funds to reduce the effects of poverty. On the other side is the belief that the private sector should be the avenue for change by creating opportunities and growing the economy. Less government, through reduced regulation and spurring more business opportunities, would be the best tool to significantly reduce society's ills. This ideological struggle continues to dominate the politics of America to the present day.

Control Data Corporation embraced both sides of this debate first by rapidly implementing the affirmative action policies required by law, then by creating business ventures which targeted a specific social need. Many of these ventures were service-based businesses that leveraged CDC technology and/or business expertise in some way. As the years went on, William Norris articulated more and more strongly that private sector, service-based solutions were the answer, and directed corporate efforts to prudently explore this concept and prove it was both sound and profitable. The entrepreneurial philosophy which had worked so well for developing the CDC 6600 was now invoked to address many major problems facing American society. This effort began in earnest when CDC created plants within impoverished communities. The knowledge and experience the HR function gained though working with the employees at these facilities then led to the creation of other businesses which targeted populations in economic need. This chapter describes the beginnings of these groundbreaking social business ventures, how they evolved and changed, and their eventual outcomes.

A Plant Against Poverty

THE PRESS CONFERENCE WAS HELD on a chilly November day, the twenty-seventh, in 1967. Norbert Berg stood alongside officials from the Hennepin County Office of Economic Opportunity and announced that Control Data would build a manufacturing facility in one of the toughest, most deteriorating neighborhoods in Minneapolis, the Northside community. The population within this community was predominately African-American, and this demographic group had a very high unemployment rate. A quarter of the families in this neighborhood had annual incomes of only $3,000. Building a plant within Northside would provide much-needed jobs and help the economic viability of this poverty-stricken community.

In order to make sure Control Data's commitment to the new Northside facility was long term, Bill Norris identified three ground rules for the poverty area plant:

1. Make the plant new and modern.
2. Make it profitable.
3. Make us dependent on it, so we will have to make it work.

This new plant would build peripheral controllers, a major component required for Control Data's mainframe computers. These refrigerator-sized devices moved data from the mainframe computers out to line printers, card readers, magnetic tape handlers, and disc storage drives. Because of this product, the Northside plant had no choice but to succeed, because this device was a crucial part of CDC's product line. If the plant failed, it would be a major disaster for the company. Placing the manufacture of such an important piece of hardware clearly made the new plant a gamble. At the press conference, Berg emphasized Control Data's commitment to the plant. "Our move is motivated by economics," he insisted. "We have constantly sought out untapped sources of manpower in the firm's decisions on the locations of new plants. We think it's fortunate that this business decision helps us to contribute to solving society's problem of racial discontent and poverty."

Control Data was banking on its past success with placing manufacturing facilities in rural areas. Starting in 1965, the corporation had built such facilities in rural Minnesota communities like Redwood Falls, Cambridge, Spring Grove, and Montevideo. All these manufacturing facilities were successful operations, as CDC had been able to train this largely inexperienced workforce to assemble various components for its product line. The company discovered that after only a minimum amount of training, most employees at these facilities could become highly productive. Control Data felt confident it could do the same for workers within the Northside community and retain them as long-term employees. As Pat Conway, the head of the CDC real estate and facilities organization recalled, "We had a very fair environment, and our employees always appreciated it." The HR function had been highly involved in building these facilities and had gained much knowledge in helping untrained workers acclimate to the culture of a manufacturing facility. Members of the HR function felt confident they could have the same success within this inner-city neighborhood.

It was a bold proposal which received interest from the national press. Instead of waiting for a government mandate or regulated legal requirement to build such a facility, Control Data was taking the initiative to address inequality on its own. CDC was growing rapidly and needed to expand its manufacturing base, and the Northside community was in economic stress and needed jobs. Vice President Hubert H. Humphrey sent a telegram of congratulations, writing, "Your response to that community's effort to improve its employment opportunities is appreciated. It is my understanding that your company is undertaking this project as a part of your practice of placing new plants where manpower is available, and that you will recruit new employees from the immediate area, providing training where necessary. Control Data is to be congratulated for this endeavor and I wish you every success." The company was attempting to set an example for how corporate America should use affirmative action in a positive way, and the bold project was now on the national radar. If the plant succeeded, it would use the spirit of competitive enterprise to take action against a social ill. The immediate future would now determine if the new plant would succeed in its aims.

Getting the project to this point had not been easy. Some managers within Control Data were highly skeptical of Norris's proposal. They were particularly concerned the output at this plant would be too low because of poor work ethics, and that it would be hard to retain motivated employees. Some even went so far as to predict the plant would burn down. Likewise when Control Data representatives pitched their proposal to Northside community groups, these community leaders were equally skeptical of Control Data's intentions. The track record for corporations helping poverty area communities was dismal; it was common for companies to put a non-essential product within such plants and then shut down the facility after just a few short years of operation. Groups within the Northside community did not want charity work. They wanted real, long-term, substantial employment. During one meeting, the debate got so heated about CDC's intentions that it bordered on turning into a physical battle. But the Control Data representatives were persistent and kept coming back to meeting after meeting. Eventually enough members of the community became convinced that CDC intended to commit to the Northside facility for the long term.

Whitney Young, the executive director of the National Urban League, had asked William Norris to create jobs for poverty-area workers, and Norris directed the corporation to do just that. CDC had also embraced equal opportunity employment at all of its facilities, but, as CDC representatives explained to Northside community leaders, it was difficult to attract minority workers to apply for jobs at Control Data's mostly suburban plants. These plants were too far away, making the costs of transportation and time too much to handle for many potential inner-city workers. Since the company couldn't bring minority workers to the jobs, Control Data would bring the jobs closer to them.

Control Data also needed to rapidly expand its manufacturing capability, so the company had a justifiable need to expand its operations somewhere—why not Northside? Since peripheral controllers were of vital importance to the mainframe product line, it meant, as one newspaper described it, that "Norris had deliberately created a situation in which no retreat was possible." The Northside plant would satisfy two goals at the same time: it would expand much-needed manufacturing capacity and help satisfy Control Data's dedication to social responsibility. The new facility would have to be profitable in order to work. As Norris described at the time, "If all it does is makes jobs that keep people busy and gives them some income, it doesn't prove anything. It has to be a business success before it can be a social success." With backing from both Northside community leaders and from the Hennepin County Office of Economic Opportunity, work on the project began to move forward.

Financing for the Northside facility was primarily taken on by Control Data investment. The federal government also had funds available for creating and managing job training services in urban communities, so some financial support for training from public monies would be possible at a later time. However, Control Data was assuming nearly all of the start-up costs, assuming the plant would operate at a loss during its first years of operation. Because of the unique purpose of the plant, these losses were classified as social responsibility expenditures, similar to how corporations view contributions to non-profit organizations. Control Data essentially used venture capital in lieu of a more traditional social responsibility budget, applying its unique capabilities as a technology company to make a direct contribution against a social need.

With its internal funding in place, it could move forward with building the plant. Control Data would not have to go it alone very long. The day after CDC made the announcement, the U.S. Department of Commerce contacted the corporation, stating they would like to discuss ways the department could provide financial assistance. As William Norris stated, "This was rather pleasing because, while we did plan to contact Commerce later, Commerce took the initiative." The government would eventually subsidize the additional training required by these employees. With enough financial resources in place and assistance soon coming from the federal government, the Northside facility was in an excellent position to answer the goals defined for it by Norris.

The CDC real estate and facilities organization first negotiated a lease from the Inter-Chemical Corporation for a temporary plant that contained 17,000 square feet. Starting with this basic facility, Control Data began to accept job applications. Fifty to sixty individuals applied the first day. It was at this point that HR managers on the hiring team discovered their first major obstacle—the job application form. The form was too long and complex, making it difficult to fill out. It also contained a small box for the applicant to list previous arrests, and for some applicants, the space wasn't big enough to list each prior infraction. For many applicants, it was a very negative, discouraging experience. The HR staff realized they had a serious problem, and decided to toss out the standard employment form and created a much more open, simplified application form. This new form asked the applicants their name, address, emergency contacts, and desire for employment. "The solution was to greatly simplify the form," William Norris described, "by eliminating . . . requirements so that in essence we were saying 'we are more interested in your future than in your past.'" The one major requirement was each applicant had to read and write at a high school level. Other than that, no further requirements were needed to work at the Northside plant, as each worker would need "on the job" training anyway to master the tasks required on the assembly line. The new form was a major improvement, and soon CDC received 500 applications for the available positions in the new facility.

Because the human resources staff was now essentially accepting anyone who applied, selection for employment was based on different criteria. Each potential employee's family situation was evaluated and preference was given to applicants in the following ranking order:

1. Heads of household
2. Families with children
3. Single

Applicants who demonstrated they could read and write at a high school level and were the main breadwinners for their family were thus hired first, followed by applicants who had children. Aside from these general preferences, the hiring was basically first come, first serve. The workforce at the new plant would predominately be unskilled labor. For some new employees, their position at the Northside plant would be the first real, true experience they ever had with regular work. This situation would present another set of unique challenges. If Control Data was going to make the Northside plant a productive facility, the company would need to provide ways to support these highly inexperienced employees so they would stay motivated and remain at the facility.

The first Northside plant. Later, a larger facility was built in the Northside community. (Photo courtesy of the Charles Babbage Institute.)

In his annual "President's Newsletter," released just a few weeks after the announcement of the Northside facility, William Norris stated, "I believe the project will ultimately be successful in all respects. I think it will help the people employed to have a decent living, and I am confident that there will be no more loyal group than the people employed in that plant." Norris continued, "Despite some of the unique problems that we will have to work out, in the long run it will be a good investment for Control Data." The first challenge was one of work environment culture. The minority employees needed to work in an environment that did not seem adversarial, a place where they did not feel "watched" by the usual forces which had been so often been aligned against them. As Bill English, the coordinator for equal opportunity at the time, explains, "We didn't want a plantation with minority workers and a white overseer." To that end, the company searched for an African-American to manage the new facility. They didn't have to look very far. Amos Haynes, an assistant engineer at the Arden Hills facility, was offered the managerial position. He accepted, and the Northside plant now had its workforce. Amos Haynes would manage the plant, leading a complement of 430 workers who were a mix of fifty percent African-American, twenty percent Native American, and thirty percent white employees. Manufacturing on the peripheral controllers could now begin.

The first year of operations continued at the leased facility, and besides manufacturing the controllers, the plant also served as a sheet metal fabrication shop. Construction on a new plant near the temporary start-up facility began almost immediately. Within a year Control Data built a state of the art manufacturing facility on a nearby plot of land. The new plant was considerably larger than the temporary facility, as the 17,000 square feet of space was upgraded and replaced with 90,000 square feet of room. Control Data was now permanently embedded within the Northside community.

However, some unique problems did occur at the facility. The central issue for the Northside plant was whether it could maintain its workforce to ensure productivity. For many new employees, their assembler position was the first major job they had ever experienced, and they were not used to the requirements and rigors of everyday employment. The HR function took on this task as an education responsibility, and each new employee was taught the basics of the factory environment—getting to work on time, following the rules to ensure safety, feeling comfortable with asking questions when a task was not clearly understood, and learning why certain procedures were important and needed to be followed.

Each employee was then given the training they needed for assembling the peripheral controllers. Training sessions were also provided to give the Northside employees strategies for creating and maintaining a family budget from their regular income. Because some of these employees also suffered from alcohol and drug addictions, counseling services were provided to help these employees overcome their dependencies. Costs for some of this training were offset by funds from the Department of Labor, as Control Data received a $1 million reimbursement contract from the U.S. government. This contract only covered expenses above and beyond the normal expenses in training employees, but the added resources were a great help in developing and providing the additional services required at the plant.

Besides training, it also became apparent that legal counseling was needed for Northside employees. These individuals faced problems of divorce, child custody, and other legal challenges. One of the hardest challenges was the issue of late rent payments, as employees, despite their regular income, were often behind in the rent and forced to frequently move. To handle these issues, Gary Lohn, an HR professional (later an HR vice president) began work at the plant. His role was to find out what problems existed and come up with solutions to solve these difficult issues. Lohn would work together with the employees and help them settle issues with landlords, deadbeat spouses, and divorce needs.

Lohn received legal help from the outside law firm of Oppenheimer, Wolff, and Donnelly, a prominent law firm in the Twin Cities. The law firm offered their personnel on a pro bono basis—giving younger lawyers in the firm experience working on difficult cases. Through these pro bono legal services, Lohn and the attorneys would set up garnishments on employee wages, so these individuals could pay rent as well as cover larger purchases like televisions and refrigerators. A percentage of employees would also have difficulties with the law, particularly during the weekends, and as a result would end up in jail. In response, the company decided to direct the Oppenheimer law firm to post the bonds required for releasing these employees so they could return to work the following week. To streamline this process, Oppenheimer gave Gary Lohn a bail bond checkbook, complete with the Control Data Corporation logo. When needed, Lohn would drive out to the jail on Monday mornings and use the checkbook

Workers within the Northside plant. (Photos courtesy of the Charles Babbage Institute.)

to post the bond amount. The wayward employee was essentially released into Control Data's custody.

These legal services provided by the Oppenheimer law firm proved to be crucial for the success of the plant, as the services helped reduce the absenteeism these legal situations would typically cause, giving employees a better chance at staying employed at Northside. It was yet another aspect of working with this population, and the HR function adapted quickly to take on these unique issues. Several former human resources employees have remarked the problems some Northside employees faced were "a real eye opener." The challenges these employees had to endure in order to maintain a regular income—family problems, rent trouble, drug abuse, criminal history, and so on—were starkly different than those of the typical suburban employee. So in turn, Control Data HR managers learned as much about working with this population as the new employees learned about manufacturing computer hardware.

Even though support services helped keep many on the job, employee turnover still remained a problem. Solutions were tried to reduce the turnover rate. In many ways, the Northside plant became a test tube which the human resources function could use for both research and experimentation. A study was conducted in 1969 to discover the biographical factors which would cause new employees to leave the plant after just a few months of employment. The study, run by John Fossum, discovered, "For every 100 people hired, forty-four would stay longer than six months and fifty-six would terminate before completing three months of service." A weighted application blank was developed as a diagnostic tool to determine which new hires were most likely to leave early. Biographical values like financial stability, family situation, and so on, were used to evaluate an employee's chances for a short tenure at the facility. These individuals were then channeled into various programs to help them overcome risk factors in their lives—depending on the situation, the employee would be given counseling, special training, legal assistance, and so on. The stated goal was to retain fifteen more employees, so that out of every 100 employees hired, fifty-nine would remain at Control Data. This would significantly reduce the cost of training. As the HR function worked with this community, it tried to get better and better at responding to the needs of the at-risk individuals hired at the plant and, as a direct consequence, improve the lives of these employees.

One demographic group emerged as having the highest turnover rate—working mothers. Through exit interviews, the HR staff discovered about fifty percent of these individuals left their jobs because they did not have sufficient daycare to enable them to come to the plant every day. It was just too hard to juggle the responsibility of small children and the requirements of assembly line work. To answer this need, Control Data decided to open a daycare center near the plant. This was the first daycare center ever launched by a corporation in the United States. Called the Northside Child Development Center (NCDC), this center opened in August of 1970 under the leadership of Norma Anderson. An African-American who had trained to become a nurse, Norma Anderson was uniquely qualified for the position.

Employees could now drop off their children on the way to work and pick them up on the way home. Children who went home to an empty house after school (latch key kids) could also come to the center instead. If anything happened to the children during the shift, the proximity of the center to the plant made it easy for working parents to tend to their children. It became a popular service, greatly reducing the turnover rate at the plant for working mothers. The Northside Child Development Center became a national model for providing daycare support to employees. Soon it became clear the benefits the center could be brought to other residents of Northside, so the facility was expanded to provide child daycare to the entire community. In 1971, Northside Child Development Center became a non-profit organization. As of this writing nearly forty years later, the NCDC continues to operate as a childcare center for the Northside community. The center is now administered by Catholic Charities under the Archdiocese of Minneapolis-St. Paul.

In addition to providing the services needed for successful employment, the individuals working in the plant had to learn how to work together, and through this process they gained skills in mutual trust and respect. As work began within the Northside plant, line foremen started to notice they were missing scrapped circuit boards. Significant parts of these circuit boards could be salvaged and reused, so management immediately assumed theft was going on. When managers confronted employees with this issue, they received a surprising response. The employees had assumed the scrap circuit boards were junk, so had just brought them home to their families to show them the unique products they were working on. The circuit boards were immediately returned to the plant without a problem.

In another incident, a foreman walked through a break room while a couple African-American women were having their lunch break. He jokingly said, "Hey, you two look like the Gold Dust Twins," referring to two African-American children depicted on washing soap packages (Fairbank's Gold Dust Washing Powder) earlier in the twentieth century. The women took offense, feeling they had been racially insulted, and complained to the HR manager. The

Children at the Northside Daycare Center, and Bill Norris playing with children at the center. (Photos courtesy of the Charles Babbage Institute.)

foreman apologized and said he didn't realize he had said something offensive. From that incident, HR management decided line managers needed labor relations training as well, particularly in what they could and could not call minority workers. Sensitivity education began, and from these materials Control Data developed a new course called "minority group dynamics" which explored how to develop a workforce respectful of various cultures and set rules for conduct. The course was well regarded and was used throughout CDC. Eventually this course was also sold externally to other companies.

The Northside plant was a major success. It operated throughout much of CDC's existence, and average employment hovered between 200 and 300 people at any given time. The same standard for productivity required at other CDC plants was also put in force at Northside. Despite early concerns and dire predictions, productivitity was not a problem. As Fred Green, a former plant manager relates, "We ran at about 110% of standard efficiency and had minimal rejects." The plant grew profitable in just a few years because of the demand for peripheral controllers and because of the efficiency of its workforce. Other aspects of the plant, though, could not be measured by an income statement. Employees gained much self-confidence from working full-time. Because Control Data had made the effort to help them transition into the workforce, many were staying as long-term employees. The *Minneapolis Spokesman*, a prominent African-American newspaper in the Twin Cities, said about the plant, "First, it does something for and with people. It helps and inspires them to do things on their own, to earn the fruits and satisfactions of effort and accomplishment."

One story perhaps symbolizes the positive impact the Northside plant had on many people. As described previously, Bill English was a key leader in setting up the Northside facility. However, in a previous job, he had worked as a parole officer at a prison in Milan, Michigan. English had sternly disciplined an inmate nicknamed "Ghost" by placing him in isolation. As Bill English describes, he had to forcefully drag Ghost into the isolation "hole" for an infraction of some kind. Ghost was not happy and he made it known that because English had thrown him into isolation, "I'm going to mess you up when I get out." The years passed and Bill English eventually left corrections to work at Control Data. As English was walking through the Northside plant one day, he had quite a shock. There, working on the assembly line, was Ghost. The two men instantly recognized each other. English wondered if Ghost was going to make good on his threat, but the former inmate soon walked up to him and said, "I recognize you, but I got no beef with you." Ghost was in a new place and a better environment, and the past was forgiven.

Based on the experiences in working with the Northside community, Control Data developed a series of core guiding principles the company would follow for building more poverty-area plants:

1. Local community leaders would be relied upon for advice in eliminating barriers for employing the economically disadvantaged.
2. Real jobs should be provided. They should not just be vestibule training centers or back-up plants; the facility must be given sole source responsibility for a standard product or product line. No concessions could be made in the cost, quality, and schedule standards for the product assigned. This would signal that CDC was serious about the endeavor.
3. Credibility must be established and maintained in the community. The ideas of community leaders should be sought and implemented.
4. Past company procedures, particularly as they relate to selecting employees, should be questioned. Most people can be trained to perform entry-level jobs, so these jobs should be based on desire and need, not on past employment history.
5. Resources must focus on the retention of employees. Training programs and operating procedures must recognize the unique nature of the employee population and adapt accordingly. Wages and benefits must be competitive for others at this job level.

Plans were soon put in motion for the next poverty-area plants Control Data would build. The company had found a way to match manufacturing expansion with social responsibility.

Plants for Prosperity

ANOTHER DEPRESSED AREA was northwest Washington, D.C., a community which had endured a major riot after the assassination of Martin Luther King, Jr. The community was also a high crime neighborhood. A new organization, PRIDE, Inc., had formed for the purpose of creating jobs in this poverty area, and Control Data pitched building a factory to this advocacy group. PRIDE was led by Marion Barry, later mayor of Washington, D.C., and Rufus Mayfield, a young man from the neighborhood who had co-founded PRIDE with Barry. Rufus was Marion's guide to this part of the city, and Marion had the connections Mayfield needed for government action, so it was an ideal partnership for making meaningful change a reality. PRIDE had received funding from the Department of Labor to create jobs in the inner city, so this group was strategically important for developing a new poverty area plant.

Now that the Northside plant was a reality, pitching the Capitol plant to PRIDE was a much easier prospect. The main obstacle was acquiring a location. Finding a suitable site for a large assembly plant within the inner city was often a tricky task, as space requirements, availability of utilities, potential workforce population, and transportation access all had to factor in the final decision. Time was also a big issue. As Pat Conway, head of the CDC Real Estate and Facilities organization recalled, "The time table was always very short as the company grew so fast." Originally CDC located a large tract of land which housed a closed service station. This old service station sat on a large, open tract of land, so it was an ideal location for the new plant. PRIDE and members of the community, however, wanted to use the location for a future job training center. Discussions over the site grew heated, and eventually it was decided another location needed to be found. A desirable site was discovered relatively near the same area, and soon the Capitol facility came into existence, launching its operations in February of 1969. As it had done with the Northside plant, CDC initially leased a temporary 30,000-square-foot facility in the northeast section of Washington, D.C., but later built an entirely new facility at this location with 100,000 square feet of space.

The HR staff ran the job application process in the same way as the Northside plant, using the modified application form, and eventually 200 to 300 workers were hired, primarily African-Americans. These employees were initially trained to build a card reading device. Unfortunately this piece of equipment soon became obsolete, so the plant was modified for more short-term production needs. Complicating matters was that Control Data and the Washington Metropolitan Area Transit Authority became embroiled in a contract dispute over a product CDC had planned on building at the facility, and without this potential large customer, the original plan for the plant hit a serious snag. Because of this situation, employment had to be reduced to 100 employees, a population level which it maintained throughout the lifespan of the facility. The majority of these employees were always African-American; at one point, ninety-five of the employees were within this demographic group. As part of the short-term production cycle, the facility built a number of items, including card punch machines, cable sub-assemblies, credit card imprinters, and harness sub-assemblies. The Capitol plant also housed a printing operation that ran printing services for Control Data's nearby Washington locations as well as for the Commercial Credit Company subsidiary located in Baltimore.

Unfortunately, the Capitol plant was the least successful of the first series of poverty-area plants. Even as late as 1976, the plant had still not been profitable. This result was largely due to the constantly changing series of products, which caused the employee turnover rate to remain high as workers left when manufacturing on their specific product ended. Nevertheless, Control Data maintained the facility because it provided a good place to manufacture short-term items the company needed periodically. Control Data also gained much respect in the community. The workers felt ownership of the Capitol plant and ensured it was a place of integrity. As an example, one morning a new plant manager parked his Corvette in the lot. At the end of the day he left the facility, only to discover the Corvette had been stolen. However, the next day, the Corvette appeared again in the parking lot—and it had been washed.

Control Data continued to rapidly expand its workforce, and so the company decided to build another poverty-area plant in one of the poorest rural counties in the United States. Because of the company's success with starting plants in rural Minnesota and its growing knowledge of maintaining employment for poor and at-risk individuals, CDC leadership wanted to combine this expertise by improving economic opportunities in a rural community. After some research, the real estate and facilities organization targeted Wolfe County, Kentucky, as an ideal

Workers at the Capitol plant. (Photo courtesy of the Charles Babbage Institute.)

Workers at the Campton, Kentucky plant. (Photos courtesy of the Charles Babbage Institute.)

location for such a plant. The county's population had the second lowest per capita income in the United States. As Bill English remembers, he flew out to Kentucky as part of the team touring potential sites for the new plant. At first the state planners showed them a pristine location within an affluent community, which the CDC team immediately rejected. The Control Data representatives demanded to see potential locations in Wolfe County. Realizing the CDC team was determined to visit a poor community, state officials took them to Campton, the county seat of Wolfe County, a tiny Appalachian mountain town with fewer than a thousand residents. It was the first time Bill English had experienced white poverty on such a large scale. The area was exactly the type of economically challenged rural community in which Control Data wanted to build, and the company started formulating plans for the new facility.

A 30,000-square-foot plant was constructed in the hills of Campton. A much-needed device, a high speed printer, was selected as the major product to assemble at the facility. The workers CDC hired were very poor, predominantly married women, and many could just barely read or write. When the start-up process was complete, 168 low income individuals were hired and training for the high speed printer assembly began. As before in the Northside and Capitol plants, the employees really respected what Control Data was doing for their community. The high speed printer turned out to be a popular product, and the Campton plant became a profitable operation. Employment at the plant stayed around 180 workers during much of its operation history. Best of all, the annual payroll at the plant was $1.2 million, injecting much needed income into Wolfe County.

The fourth poverty-area plant, through a combination of bad luck and serendipity, became an unusual facility. This plant was built in an economically challenged neighborhood within St. Paul, Minnesota. The Selby-Dale plant (named for the streets it bordered) was built inside a converted bowling alley. The plant was planned to start operation in 1970, right when very tough economic times hit the computer hardware industry. Control Data no longer needed the part it originally planned to manufacture at Selby-Dale, and the whole venture was in serious trouble. Control Data had made promises to this community, however, and CDC really wanted to honor these promises; the company's creditability with minorities was a stake. Luckily Herb Trader, a young Control Data administrator, came up with a solution. He suggested the company

Norbert Berg with workers at the Selby-Dale Bindery. (Photo courtesy of the Charles Babbage Institute.)

move all the printing, binding, stitching, collating, punching, and drilling tasks for technical documentation within the new Selby-Dale plant. It was a terrific solution. Opening in March of 1970, this facility became the primary bindery for nearly all of Control Data's hardware and software technical manuals. The facility printed and assembled these manuals, and they were then sent to the company's various locations, both domestically and around the world. The new plant would centralize these activities for Control Data.

The Selby-Dale plant was also a unique experiment from the other poverty area plants, as its employees were made up entirely of part-time workers. The Urban Coalition for Employment, a group who worked with Control Data on developing this plant, surveyed the local population and concluded this model would serve the community best. This unique concept targeted two specific populations for employment. Half of the employees were mothers with school-age children; this demographic group would typically work the first shift from 8:30 A.M. to 2:30 P.M. (five hours). They would feed breakfast to their kids, get the kids off to school, and then often walk over to work at the bindery. These mothers would then be home before their children returned from school. The second shift was primarily young adult students, and they made up the other half of the employee population; these individuals were either working to supplement the family income or earning extra money to get themselves through college or tech school. This demographic group typically worked from 2:30 to 6:00 P.M. (three and a half hours) each night. An interesting aspect of the plant was that because most of the employees walked or biked to work, the Selby-Dale plant had a very small parking lot.

The plant employed 300 part-time workers, and ninety percent of these people were minorities. The plant manager, Richard Mangram, led production for many years. The human resources manager was Pat Collins, and she assisted the workers with all their needs. Both plant managers were African-American and a large percentage of the workforce originally was African-American, but as time and trends went on, more and more Hmong immigrants joined the workforce at Selby-Dale. Turnover within the bindery was at twenty percent, an extremely low rate. Although the bindery did not make a product from which CDC could earn a profit, the facility ended up saving Control Data considerable money, as previously the company had outsourced the printing and binding of its manuals at much expense. Over seven million pieces of paper were printed and bound at this plant per month.

Later in 1973, the Selby-Dale plant began selling its services to other businesses, which generated additional annual sales of $500,000 throughout the 1970s. One of the Selby-Dale plant's major customers was Lutheran Brotherhood, and this life insurance company had much of its materials printed at this facility. Production steadily increased throughout the next decade. Starting in 1982, the Selby-Dale bindery added a third late night shift to keep up with the growing demand. Many of the workers at this facility moved on from this experience to full-time employment either within Control Data itself or in companies elsewhere, working in similar occupations. Some government estimates concluded the Selby-Dale plant saved the local community nearly $225,000 each year in welfare costs.

This production center was a unique success in many ways. Control Data often showcased the Selby-Dale facility to visiting government and corporate officials in the hope other companies would follow this model and build similar plants. During this time, every Minnesota governor and executive of the chamber of commerce visited Selby-Dale. But as Pat Conway remarked, "We were trying to get companies to copy us, but very few ever would. I never understood why they didn't."

These four original poverty-area plants were proof jobs could be successfully placed in low-income areas. The economic boost to these communities was substantial, as in 1976 these four plants generated $5.2 million in payroll income. This injection helped other businesses within these communities as well, as CDC employees could afford cars, meals outside the home, and other products they previously were not able to purchase. The benefits for Control Data were quite significant, helping the company meet its affirmative action objectives required by state and federal agencies. During the years 1968-1976, the minority population of Control Data's employees grew from four percent to eleven percent of the company's total workforce. The Commercial Credit Company participated as well, as this subsidiary launched a loan program for employees at the poverty-area plants. This program only targeted employees who could not receive loans at other financial institutions. The loan program proved to be a solid business venture as well; a statistic in 1983 stated only four percent of these loans had defaulted.

Control Data continued to build more facilities in low income, inner-city areas. In 1977, the corporation built a large warehouse, the World Distribution Center, within the Summit University community of St. Paul, Minnesota. This facility housed the main headquarters for distributing computer hardware parts worldwide. Control Data specifically hired minorities from the local neighborhood to work at this warehouse facility. During its peak years of activity, the facility employed 500 workers. And as described in the first chapter, this facility also showcased "green" technology by having a series of solar panels on its roof used to help heat the building.

A peripheral products plant was later built in Toledo, Ohio, within the first floor of Control Data's Business and Technology Center in that city. The employee base at Toledo was made up of over ninety percent minorities. Lastly, in 1981, another poverty-area plant was built in San Antonio, Texas, within the Vista Verde community, a mostly Latino neighborhood. This plant built printed circuit board assemblies needed by other CDC manufacturing facilities. Eighty-five percent of this plant's workforce consisted of Latino employees.

At their peak years of operation, the five poverty-area plants employed about 1,600 people altogether. The new plants all fulfilled their original purposes, which was to add much-needed manufacturing capability to the company and address CDC's social responsibility objectives. However, company leaders still struggled against the public perception that the poverty-area plants were essentially good will projects. As Norb Berg explained in an interview, "The good will is a spin-off. We love it. But we aren't knocking our heads against the wall here trying to convince people we're only doing it to improve our public relations effort. Believe me, we're getting just as much out of social involvement as we're putting into it, or else we wouldn't touch it . . ." With each poverty-area plant Control Data built, the company gained more expertise at helping the communities in which they invested, and this expertise helped the company achieve the best economic impact from these facilities. More income for the CDC workers meant more income for local businesses, a reduction in crime and an improvment in the standard of living of the surrounding neighborhoods.

The additional services Control Data created for these plants would also spark more innovations later on. Employee Advisory Resource (EAR) and the FAIRBREAK educational service business, for example, were all ideas which sprang from working with poor, at-risk employees. Perhaps best of all, everyone at Control Data involved in the poverty-area plants, from the HR function to the production line to the real estate acquisitions function, felt satisfied they were helping solve some of the problems of racial discontent and poverty. Overall, the entire poverty area plant experience was a "win-win" for Control Data and the communities they supported.

All these facilities remained in operation well into the 1980s, until changes in electronic technology eventually made them obsolete as the industry became less labor intensive and fewer workers were needed. During their entire productive history, these plants (and the World Distribution Center) remained viable, vital, and well supported. One interesting aspect about these plants is that despite being located in some of the most poverty-ridden neighborhoods in the country, none of them were ever damaged by vandalism or graffiti. The lessons learned from these plants proved that, with enough patience and problem-solving, poverty-area plants can be profitable and sustainable.

Control Data hoped its experiences would inspire other large corporations to help revitalize low-income areas. As Bill Norris exclaimed in an interview about the poverty area plants, "Get involved in a job creating program in a community. Its good business, and you'll reach a higher plane. Plunge right in!" His rationale for creating these plants was (and is) an effective way at easing, and even ending, many of the primary issues facing society today. The more jobs available in a community, the less demand placed on government welfare agencies. Plus, when more economic stability exists in a community, less crime occurs—reducing the costs of law enforcement and legal services. This, in turn, places less demand on government budgets at all levels, resulting in less taxation. Control Data used this approach as the main justification for building these plants. As a major taxpayer, the company had a vested interest in finding ways to address these problems, as they would result in less taxes and more economic stability in the long run. The Control Data experience strongly shows that developing solutions to reduce poverty in a community can, at the same time, increase the bottom line for the companies conducting business in that community.

Minority Business Support

HIRING MINORITY WORKERS was one way to embrace affirmative action, and doing business with minority-controlled businesses was yet another way. Control Data, in 1973, established its affirmative action for purchases program. Through this program a certain percentage—two percent—of corporate supplies and services were required to be bought from businesses owned, or mostly controlled by, minority individuals. While this percentage sounds small, two percent of all of Control Data's purchases was a significant number. Through this program, many minority businesses received much-needed income, which in turn fueled their growth. During the construction of the World Distribution Center in St. Paul, a minority-owned business was hired to install all the electrical wiring. The program became an accepted element for the corporation's purchasing needs. Each year from the inception of the program, purchases from minority businesses continued to grow; in 1982, total purchases from minority small businesses totaled $14 million.

Control Data also initiated a minority banking program. Through this program, the company used minority-controlled banks to handle a number of tasks for the organization, including tax deposits, certificates of deposits, and operating accounts. The additional capital these banks received from Control Data translated into additional loans these banks could lend for inner city revitalization projects for education, business, and individuals. The immeasurable amount of good will Control Data received from these endeavors helped to solidify the admiration minority leaders had for the corporation. Both the affirmative action for purchases and the minority banking programs helped an increasing number of minorities receive their share of the American Dream.

To complete the investment CDC wanted to make in minority businesses, the company created the Control Data Community Ventures Fund, Inc. The fund was designed as source of loans to give socially and disadvantaged persons, specifically minorities, access to capital they needed to launch small businesses. Several banks assisted Control Data by helping with this fund. The First National Bank of St. Paul became an active participant, giving out several loans to minority entrepreneurs. Through this fund, several small minority-owned businesses were given a means to start operations with more success than they were having through the conventional banking system. This fund was a precursor to the concept of "microfinancing" small business loans to individuals. These small loans, typically for amounts as small as $300, help individuals launch a small business inside their homes. In yet another way, Control Data was ahead of the curve.

Education is Key

From the beginning years of the company, Control Data was interested in education. Starting as an internal training program for new employees, CDC launched its first Control Data Institute in 1965 for the purpose of increasing the pool of available computer technicians and programmers. The education program proved to be a viable, profitable business, and several Control Data Institutes were launched throughout the United States. The first international Control Data Institute was opened in Frankfurt, Germany. At their peak, Control Data Institutes were in operation throughout the entire United States and in several worldwide locations. It thrived as a standalone educational business. Graduates of the Control Data Institute were not expected to work for Control Data; they could apply for jobs with any company they wished. Every year, though, a percentage of Control Data Institute graduates became employees of Control Data. Between the income the company received from tuition and the strong possibility of gaining future employees, CDC considered the Control Data Institutes a good investment for both the company and the computer industry. Eventually colleges and universities began to create their own computer science departments, and several of these schools modeled their curriculum following the Control Data Institute educational plan.

When CDC started building plants within poverty area communities, the company needed to create educational centers for both the new employees and the managers. To deliver these services, learning centers were created so employees could receive valuable training on getting used to the workplace, assembling a particular device, and other work-related subjects. In the wake of the "Gold Dust" incident at the Northside plant, managers at these plants were likewise given instruction on affirmative action principles and sensitivity training. It was not long before Control Data found other uses for these learning centers, and they became a great outlet for training individuals on all kinds of educational topics. Subjects like comparison shopping, money management skills, insurance planning, and other practical life skills courses were taught. Soon PLATO terminals were installed in many of these facilities, which made them available for training throughout the entire work week. Employees could schedule time in the learning centers when it was most convenient for them to take the courses. Norris and other CDC leaders saw that having a series of internal educational facilities would be advantageous for the entire corporation, so an initiative was launched to build learning centers with PLATO terminals at many Control Data locations around the United States.

A graduating class at a Control Data Institute. (Photo courtesy of the Charles Babbage Institute.)

Managers were required to take at least forty hours of training a year, much of it through PLATO courseware. Of course, several managers did not like this requirement and protested vehemently, but this training was added as one of the requirements managers had to fulfill each year. To encourage completion of this training requirement, the PLATO courseware were included as part of the executive incentive plan. In addition to the cultural sensitivity courses, managers learned other useful employee relations concepts. The learning centers were also a great way to train managers on new technology, products, and manufacturing techniques. And as part of the services provided to poverty area plants, courses on life coping strategies were developed on alcoholism, drug use, living with a chemically dependent person, and so on. These classes were eventually made available at learning centers throughout the corporation. The courses were provided in the hope they would help employees tackle difficult problems that could hurt their continued employment and ultimately jeopardize their health. More than

559 separate courses were developed. In 1982, Control Data estimated employees had received approximately 1,000,000 hours of formal internal training. The Control Data learning centers operated in several locations across the country, including Dallas, Baltimore, Philadelphia, New York City, Washington, D.C., Minneapolis/St. Paul, and Cleveland.

Like many CDC projects though, the learning centers had other purposes besides internal training. As these centers used PLATO technology to deliver educational materials, Control Data also leveraged these facilities as a proving ground for PLATO hardware and courseware. Other businesses were set up within these centers to maximize their return on investment for the company. The FAIRBREAK remedial education program was implemented through the Control Data learning centers, and many classes for Control Data Business Advisors (a venture charged with helping start-up businesses, discussed in chapter five) were also conducted through these centers. And because of the use of PLATO technology, many of these initiatives inevitably ended up cross-pollinating each other. For example, Control Data created a joint venture with various non-profit organizations, including the United Way, to develop management training courseware for the non-profit sector. Control Data Business Advisors was also tasked with designing this courseware, as this group would provide guidance for helping non-profit organizations develop regenerative funding. Control Data would frequently try to spread the wealth among its multiple business ventures with tasks from a single business opportunity, and the United Way joint venture program is an example of this strategy.

The Two Ventures

During the mid-1970s, Control Data was instrumental in launching two companies dedicated to developing profitable ventures for revitalizing poor rural and urban areas. These companies were conceived by the company's Committee on Social Responsibility. Rural Venture Corporation was a consortium of agricultural science laboratories pulled together under the Rural Venture umbrella; this company administrated the research in a number of experimental studies launched through these laboratories. Meanwhile, the consortium of companies behind City Venture was impressive; Control Data Corporation, Dayton Hudson Corporation, First Bank System, Honeywell, Medtronic, Minneapolis *Star Tribune*, Reynolds Metals, the St. Paul Companies, and the United Church Board of World Ministries all had a stake in the start-up company. Funded by capital through this consortium, City Venture was dedicated to launching major projects to revitalize urban centers. City Venture Corporation's primary mission was to identify large-scale urban renewal projects, coordinate the funding and work with local governments to make these projects a reality. The company would gain income by charging a fee for these services.

Both companies came about because of Control Data's poverty-area plants. William Norris knew the poverty-area plants would only help as long as the technological devices they built were not obsolete. The viability of these technologies could change quickly, and just as quickly, this change could force these plants to shut down. The Rural Venture and City Venture corporations would instead provide more long-term economic solutions to rural and urban communities, and in the process, create long-term businesses for Control Data and the other participants in the venture as well. CDC was a key player, and a major stock holder, in both Rural Venture and City Venture.

Rural Venture was the smaller of the two corporations, but what it lacked in size it made up with activity. This company had a number of fascinating experiments going on simultaneously, all of which attempted to push agribusiness in new directions. One of these experimental ventures was a hydroponics lab in St. Paul where vegetables and fruit were grown without the use of soil. These plants were instead grown through a careful combination of nutrients and sodium lights. The original purpose for this technology was for a military application, as the goal was to develop methods for growing fresh fruit and vegetables on submarines to supplement the diets of sailors on long voyages. However, the possibilities for hydroponics were endless, as food could then be grown anywhere—whether in the desert regions of developing countries or on space stations orbiting the Earth.

Jim Morris, an executive with Control Data Business Advisors during this time, was in charge of helping this laboratory develop a marketing plan. As he recalls, "When you would open the door, there would be this explosion of color. Every cucumber was the same, the tomatoes were lush." Each plant would start at the base of a pole, and then the vines would wrap around pole. The lab was inside a sealed room, so electric lights were used to provide sunlight to these plants. The cucumbers, tomatoes, and other produce raised this way were always larger than produce raised the conventional way. Unfortunately, the cost of hydroponic tomatoes were three times the cost of conventional tomatoes, so produce raised this way could not compete economically on a large scale. This high cost continues to be a major impediment for this technology.

Another Rural Venture laboratory developed a way to clone strawberries. The concept was that a leaf could be clipped from a strawberry plant and then, using the plant's DNA, over 1,000 identical plants could be created from one strawberry plant. These cloned strawberry plants were being raised in a ninety-by-one-hundred-twenty-foot greenhouse on the roof of Control Data's corporate headquarters in Bloomington. The laboratory used an advanced propagation method for the purpose of cloning hundreds of disease-free plants from this single parent plant. The reproduced plants were then grown in aeroponic chambers, inside which the plant roots were misted with a nutrient solution on a regular schedule. Similar to the hydroponics lab, these plants did not need soil. The ultimate goal for this greenhouse was to reduce how long it took to deliver new plant varieties from the breeding state to the grower.

The greenhouse was a proof-of-concept experiment for another concept as well, as CDC used this laboratory to demonstrate that small-scale, profitable greenhouse businesses could be developed on rooftops, turning these under-utilized sections of urban real estate into places for both raising needed food and generating new sources of income. The company used waste heat generated by its computers to provide the heat needed to maintain the greenhouse in the winter. Urban rooftops were also utilized by other Rural Venture projects. Because rooftops were an excellent source of sunlight, one project placed experimental gardens on rooftops across the country to test which plants and bushes grew best in different climates. Gardening could then be brought back into the urban setting, and more food production would be possible throughout the world.

In Alaska, an attempt was made to grow vegetables in the winter. Through this experiment, plants were raised in plastic containers, insulated by snow, and the tops of the containers were opened during the day to let in sunlight and then closed at night to trap the heat. Control Data also had a contract with the Inuit Native American community of Selawik, Alaska. Through this joint experiment, the Inuits grew vegetables in the tundra above the Arctic Circle during the summer. Despite the occasional problem of moose and caribou wandering into these vegetable gardens, this project was a quiet success, producing a significant amount of vegetables for the town of Selawik.

Perhaps one of the most interesting Rural Venture projects was an experimental livestock farm which attempted to be a completely "closed loop" operation. The farm utilized every part of the crops and livestock it raised to generate the power and grow the food needed for the entire operation. Corn was grown to both produce ethanol for fuel and feed for the livestock. Methane from the cattle manure was captured to provide an additional source of gas. This manure was also used as fertilizer and spread over the fields to raise the corn. It was an "everything but the squeal" method of operation.

Control Data's approach to innovation was evident in all of these experiments. At one point, Rural Venture owned ten farms near Little Falls, Minnesota, where several of these innovations were actively tested. If an agribusiness idea seemed feasible, Rural Venture was the platform through which the company would pursue it. William Norris was occasionally contacted by professors and inventors across the country who proposed an agricultural experiment of some kind. If he felt it had potential, Norris would pass on this information to Norb Berg, who would in turn find the people and the means to launch the project. These agricultural experiments reflected Norris's farm background. As described in chapter one, Norris had once saved the family's starving cattle herd by harvesting thistles before they matured. Now Norris used Rural Venture as a way to support the same types of innovative ideas to create new opportunities for the agricultural industry, an industry he deeply wanted to support.

Rural Venture also embarked on a project that followed a much more typical Control Data social business model. The project focused on creating jobs through rural enterprises like small-scale food processing, small-scale agriculture, and other types of sustainable enterprises. Toward that end, CDC launched a project in 1980 with a target group of 500 low-income farmers in East Central Minnesota. Through a contract with the state of Minnesota, the project focused on six economically depressed counties near the town of Mora, Minnesota. The goal of the project was "to demonstrate that the small family farm . . . can be economically self-sustaining when sufficient technical knowledge, managerial skills, and financing are delivered in a coordinated manner." This service-focused project bundled a number of resources together to help this target group of farmers develop profitable businesses. Rural Venture would provide management advice, coordinate public and private financing, and, of course, provide computer-based training to help educate farmers on better business practices.

To ensure Rural Venture worked fairly with the farmers it was trying to help, Control Data also created a grievance system by which farmers could voice concerns and complaints about the company. Jim Morris, through his role at Control Data Business Advisors, often served as an ombudsman for the farmers involved with Rural Venture, resolving issues when the farmers did not feel they were "getting a fair shake" from Control Data. Through this structure, Control Data created an experimental business for pursuing possibilities for new industries and agriculture techniques in depressed rural areas.

Control Data also built a special learning center, the Agriculture and Business Services Center, near Princeton, Minnesota. To support this center, the company developed a series of agricultural education courses delivered through PLATO terminals. Some subjects for these courses included, "fundamentals of crop production," "starting to farm," "sheep production and management," "pepper production," "livestock guarding dog," and "introduction to specialty crops." In addition to these agricultural-based courses, the company made its basic educational courses available to teach poor rural individuals the basic skills they needed to get a job. These courses were the same ones used by CDC's FAIRBREAK program. Other courses explored how to use alternative sources of energy. Control Data built this program off its years of experience training computer technicians. As the proposal stated, "The individualized curriculum is patterned after the highly successful nine-month Control Data Institute courses for computer operators, technicians, and programmers." Through the computer-based education provided by the PLATO terminals, farmers could come to the Princeton learning center during a time that was most convenient and appropriate for them. And like the other learning centers, the building was a proving ground facility. CDC would use the Agriculture and Business Services Center as proof of concept to launch similar agricultural-based learning centers throughout the United States.

Besides the PLATO course package, Control Data searched for other technological ways to improve the economic plight of family farms. What most small farmers typically needed was a better way to control their budgets. CDC joined forces with Agro System Corporation out of Lubbock, Texas. This software developer had created AGPROS, the Agricultural Producers Accounting System. This specialized computer program, one of the first of its kind, was designed for use in managing a farm. This software package specialized in preparing credit documentation, tax information, and estate planning. Control Data also launched its own agricultural database service. Called AgServ, this application used "powerful simulation and statistical techniques to generate timely, accurate forecasts of wheat, corn, and soybean yields on any scale—global or by country." So while experimentation was part of Rural Venture, the company was also in step with Norris's services strategy, developing computer-based training courses, software applications, and computer education services for another potential base of new customers—the agricultural community.

In contrast, City Venture Corporation was charged with privatizing urban projects to carry out these projects more effectively and efficiently than government and charitable organizations. Herb Trader, the manager who had come up with bindery solution for the Selby-Dale plant, was now put in charge of City Venture. He and his staff administrated each urban renewal project, and these initiatives were on a much larger scale than the Rural Venture projects. Typically City Venture secured funding for a project through a government grant and then used this money to develop the project. City Venture then gained income by charging a fee for its services. As described in an advertisement about the company, "City Venture brings together the critical managerial expertise, public and private financing, and new (and emerging) technology, from both the physical and social sciences, for holistic solutions to urban problems." City Venture initiated projects in economically depressed neighborhoods in Minneapolis, Philadelphia, Toledo, St. Paul, and Baltimore. The goal for these projects was to encourage both the human and economic development of these communities. By providing for the growth of businesses and educating the people who would work in those businesses, City Venture was dedicated to improving the long term viability of an inner-city neighborhood in need. A typical City Venture project included the following components:

- A combination of new plants and new enterprises to produce jobs with a commitment to hire and train the unemployed.
- Programs geared to new entrepreneurs.
- New and rehabilitated housing, emphasizing energy efficiency and occupancy ownership.
- Priority on using emerging technologies to serve both the industrial and residential needs of the community in such areas as security, energy efficiency, inner and intra-neighborhood communication and transit, and housing design.

One large City Venture project was the Urban East project in Minneapolis. This project focused on a seventy-acre area encompassing a Minneapolis poverty area with high unemployment. One of the main keystones for this project was to create a Business and Technology Center to provide a resource for launching small businesses within the community. As a brochure describing the project stated, "Participation by inner-city residents in these small enterprises will give them control of their community and provide them with the long-absent economic opportunities and incentives for success." A learning center that would primarily house a FAIRBREAK learning center was also planned in order to help disadvantaged persons gain basic skills in reading, mathematics, and life management. The ultimate purpose of the Urban East project was to create at least 3,000 new jobs within the community and demonstrate how private enterprise could work effectively with government and community organizations.

Given Control Data's success in working with community groups to build the poverty-area plants, CDC leaders felt they had the knowledge and expertise to take the urban development model to a new, much more ambitious level. In the same brochure about City Venture, Control Data described how the company would pursue these projects, writing, "The approach mandates that any plan for building or restoring a community must be based on meeting resident needs for high quality, accessible and affordable education and training and, even more important, decent jobs." Despite this fundamental principle, City Venture projects had a hard time reaching completion. The politics within each neighborhood often proved to be the biggest obstacle. Ironically, the Urban East project in Minneapolis failed to be realized, as local community leaders were unsure about the company's motives and withdrew their support. Other City Venture projects faced similar political hurdles that proved extremely difficult to overcome. However, the Toledo project was successful, as the company developed a twenty-three-acre industrial park within a poor neighborhood. A similar project was completed in Baltimore's Park Height community. Both projects helped boost new small businesses and jobs for their communities. But because these projects were difficult to complete, the focus of City Venture changed over time as this urban consulting services business tried to find its way. Eventually, City Venture was put in charge of Control Data's various prison system initiatives, which will be explored later in this chapter.

During the transformation of Control Data during the late 1980s, components of Rural Venture and City Venture were either dissolved or sold, and they eventually ceased to be active organizations. However, the idea behind both companies, to create for-profit consulting businesses that would help build the economic infrastructure of depressed communities, was an interesting concept. All boats would rise, as while the company made money by bundling planning and management services, the cost of providing government services would go down, while the economic viability of struggling communities would improve.

Health Care on a Reservation

WHEN *BURY MY HEART AT WOUNDED KNEE* by Dee Brown was published in 1970, the book increased national awareness about the hardships faced by Native American populations on reservations. Control Data employed Native Americans, and so the Committee on Social Responsibility met with them to discuss the needs of this population. Meanwhile, Control Data had developed a system for inputting health care records into a mainframe computer and was selling this health care service to hospitals. The Committee on Social Responsibility decided that part of the company's social ventures capital should focus on improving the health and well-being of Native Americans. Perhaps Control Data could combine its technological know-how with other service offerings and affect positive health and well-being changes on reservations throughout North America. With that objective, a Control Data task team, led by Roger Wheeler, attended a meeting of state medical officials in South Dakota in 1974. Representatives of the health and welfare committee from the Rosebud Indian Reservation were also there to find out if the medical community was willing to help improve health care on their reservation.

The statistics from Rosebud were alarming. In the early 1970s this reservation had a population of between 9,000 and 10,000 Native Americans. Despite this relatively small population, one in three children on the reservation suffered hearing loss due to ear infections, and the infant mortality rate was over twice the national rate. Cases of diabetes were also high. Tuberculosis on the reservation was ten times the national average and hepatitis was eight times the national average. Chronic alcoholism was also a major health issue at Rosebud, causing injuries and death. Alcoholic cirrhosis of the liver was the third leading cause of death. Many of these illnesses could be easily prevented if this population had more frequent contact with professional doctors and nurses and other forms of institutional support. One of the reasons why these rates of illness were so high was primarily because many individuals had to travel over forty miles to reach a clinic. Few people had cars and there was no public transportation. The long distance and poor transportation meant some health conditions went untreated, and severe health emergencies often resulted in a loss of life. Rosebud had a population in need of assistance.

The Control Data HR team tasked with this project was also impressed with the Rosebud health and welfare committee, and decided to collaborate with them on discovering innovative ways health care could be delivered on the reservation. Working with Sunny Waln, a Native American who was chairman of the health and welfare committee of the Rosebud Reservation, the company created Indian Health Management, Incorporated (IHMI), assigning the venture an investment of about $300,000 a year from Control Data. Primarily, this was set aside to pay for staff costs during the early phases of the development period. The collaborative project with the Rosebud health and welfare committee would last three years. As a way to start the project, CDC purchased a used hearse which the company then converted into an ambulance. To make sure the vehicle was sound, the hearse was taken for a few test drives by Roger Wheeler from the corporate headquarters building in Bloomington. These trips became the topic of a few water cooler conversations, as the hearse was seen driving away from the main building. Some speculated whether Bill Norris had passed away in the building! The converted hearse ran fine, and it was soon sent to the reservation to become part of a much-needed ambulance service. The vehicle was also used for its original purpose as a hearse for funerals. Before the reservation received the converted hearse, the Rosebud residents had used the back of a pickup truck to bring caskets to the cemeteries.

It would take more than a refurbished ambulance to improve the long-term issues of the Lakota tribe. The health care institutions at the Rosebud Reservation had two immediate problems. The first was the main Indian Health Service hospital in the town of Rosebud. It had forty-one beds total for a reservation population of over 9,000. Surgery could often not be performed immediately, because the hospital lacked the money and space to effectively conduct surgical operations. Patients with critical illnesses needed to be sent to a different hospital in Rapid City, a location 230 miles away from Rosebud. The Rosebud hospital also had only five doctors on staff, most of whom worked at the hospital as part of their military service. Because the pay was so low, the doctors usually left after they completed their two-year military service obligation. Fifteen medical assistants also worked at the facility, and they were highly overworked and underpaid. The second major issue was the distance patients had to travel. Because many people did not have reliable transportation to get to the hospital in the first place, easily curable maladies, like infant ear infections, went untreated. To treat illnesses in remote locations, the medical assistants did house visits wherever they could. Altine Dubray, one of the medical assistants, had worn out four cars driving to remote homes to provide much needed health care. Strategies were required to resolve both situations.

The first phase of the joint project began. In order to alleviate the strain on the hospital staff, six additional medical assistants were hired and trained; these individuals would help the hospital with screenings, immunizations, and health education. These individuals went through training on a number of diseases, especially the six major diseases affecting the reservation. Indian Health Management developed a series of protocols on each disease, so these individuals could either help with the illness directly on site at the patient's home or recognize when the patient needed to visit the main Rosebud hospital. A large truck and trailer was also purchased to act as a mobile health care facility which the medical assistants, accompanied by a doctor, could drive wherever they needed to give immunizations and checkups. This vehicle, the Indian Health Mobile Clinic, made regular stops through all the major towns in the reservation on a yearly schedule. Meanwhile, members of the CDC professional services staff began converting the reservation's hospital records onto magnetic tape; these records could then be entered into a mainframe computer installed at the hospital. By placing all the records on a mainframe computer, medical staff personnel could spend less time creating and locating medical records, improving efficiency and service.

The next phase of the project was to eventually place community health representatives around the reservation in either mobile or stationary offices; each location would also be equipped with a computer terminal for entering medical information during a patient visit. The information would be evaluated by the mainframe computer, which would then send the medical assistants information on what tests to run next or which medicines to prescribe. The computer would also recommend whether the patient should be sent to the Indian Health Service hospital. Meanwhile, doctors at the main facility would know about situations as they were occurring throughout the

Children receiving medical care at the Rosebud Indian Reservation. (Photos courtesy of the Charles Babbage Institute.)

reservation. Because of this, hospital staff could be prepared for any patients arriving from the remote health care facility. Through this strategy, the plan melded Control Data technology with the needs of health services through a complementary method. Indian Health Care Management would also create jobs on the reservation for new health care workers, system analysts, and similar positions. If this service worked in Rosebud, the health care system could then be implemented in other locations with similar needs in the United States and internationally within developing countries. The potential market for such a system was huge, and the end result would be improved health care for at-risk populations around the world.

With this strategic initiative in place, the Indian Health Management Corporation first made a contract with the Rosebud tribal leadership to manage the women/infant/children program, a federally financed program to provide basic medical care for children five years of age or younger. A computerized health record was created for each child, and from the computer records, an immunization schedule was developed. Each month, the medical team generated a new immunization list, notifying the community health representatives which children needed to be given shots. By December 1975, immunizations were carried out against several childhood diseases, including rubella, diphtheria, and whooping cough—raising the immunization rate from twenty-one percent to thirty-five percent. The gain was modest, but it was a significant step toward protecting the youngest members of the reservation.

The next effort was to teach better health practices within reservation homes. Indian Health Management hired six Native Americans as additional medical assistants, individuals who were either registered nurses or at least qualified to administer first aid. After they completed their training, these medical assistants traveled across the reservation, making regular visits to homes in order to identify health problems, teach hygiene skills, and provide education on the ways communicable diseases were spread. If the assistant identified a person who needed to be

The Mobile Health Clinic used at the Indian Rosebud Reservation. (Photo courtesy of the Charles Babbage Institute.)

looked at by a physician, a visit was scheduled through the Indian Health Mobile Clinic. Selecting the Native Americans in these medical assistant roles was a key decision, because these individuals understood both the health problems and the cultural equation of each situation. These medical assistants could then find a solution that would work best for improving the health of the patient. As Anita Whipple, a medical trainer, described, "It does little good for one of our people to tell a patient to wash impetigo sores daily if that person has no running water." These Native American assistants helped doctors at the Rosebud hospital diagnose diseases from remote parts of the reservation, and then schedule these individuals for treatment. Because these individuals understood the culture, it was more likely these patients would arrive at the hospital for their scheduled appointments.

The Indian Mobile Health Clinic was a successful means to deliver health care across the reservation. The large trailer was equipped as a total outpatient clinic, complete with its own pharmacy. Doctor Sunandan Singh was the primary doctor on the Indian Mobile Health Clinic, and saw an average of thirty-five patients each day. During 1976, the Indian Mobile Health Clinic treated 3,500 patients. Doctor Singh used the mobile clinic as a way to increase health education as well, discussing good nutrition and emphasizing the importance of taking the medications he prescribed. If a patient needed hospitalization, Doctor Singh could also admit the patient immediately from the mobile clinic.

So what were the results of the first few years of the Indian Health Management project? Surprisingly, the number of recorded cases of individuals with disease actually went up, mainly because many more cases were diagnosed than had been previously reported. Immunizations

126

continued to rise during the project's existence; by March 1977, an impressive eighty-two percent of the reservation's children had been given shots against childhood diseases. The project showed real promise; it was even featured on a CBS news program about corporate social responsibility.

Unfortunately, circumstances on the reservation changed, and these circumstances greatly hampered the project. A tribal election was held and a new council was elected. To demonstrate their political power over government affairs, the new leaders fired nearly everyone in the health care service, replacing most of the staff with their political supporters and members of the reservation. As a result, much of the health-care effort was decentralized. Deciding they wanted to administrate the health care system themselves, the council essentially rejected several major components of the initiative. Control Data was essentially pushed out.

Another promising Native American business concept experienced difficulties as well. The Canadian government approached Control Data to come up with a business venture to improve the economy of an Inuit reservation in Churchill, Manitoba. Control Data proposed a data entry venture. The company had one of the largest payroll processing services in North America. To help facilitate its payroll processing service, Control Data would fly timecards from Minneapolis to Churchill. Workers on the reservation would then input these timecards through computer terminals. The mainframe computer would calculate the paychecks, and the resulting data would be sent back to Minneapolis over a phone line. The paychecks would then be printed in Minneapolis and distributed to customers through the payroll processing center. It was a creative concept that developed an application for an early computer network. Unfortunately, the tribe's leadership did not support it, and the venture never made it past the concept and planning stages. It appeared as if Control Data's ventures in Native American enterprises would all fail.

However, some aspects of Indian Health Management continued at Rosebud for many years, specifically the use of the mobile health care clinic. What remained of the original project was eventually taken over by the University of South Dakota Medical School. They administrated the program, and IMHI was able to secure federal funding for two fixed clinics within the Rosebud reservation towns of St. Francis and Antelope. Then during 1981-1983, relations between IHMI and the tribal leaders improved substantially, and this political change resulted in IHMI hiring a podiatrist, a nutritionist, a proctologist and a nurse-midwife. A women and infant health care program, which had worked so well initially but was abandoned during the previous council shake-up, was now restored as part of the program.

A study conducted and co-written by Robert (Sunny) Waln for Control Data Business Advisors on the tenth anniversary of Indian Health Management's founding summarized the progress of the organization: "IHMI has come a long way in ten years, from the point of one physician's assistant rendering care in a mobile clinic to a multi-service health organization playing an increasingly important role in the health of the Rosebud Sioux." Although IHMI did not turn into the model, cutting edge business Control Data had hoped, health care on the Rosebud Indian Reservation was given a significant boost by CDC's initial investment and ideas. In the same study conducted on the tenth anniversary, Sunny Waln compiled a list of observations about what a corporation should do when taking on such a project:

1. Firmly set your purpose, but maintain flexibility in approach.
2. As clearly as possible, identify the local problems and barriers to progress, then examine for interrelationships and promising points of attack.
3. Watch for situations where offering your organization's help to others will actually maximize the value of your organization's resources to the community.
4. Build a stable base within the community. In IHMI's case, this has been accomplished by stable medical services within the communities, and staffing from the local area.

The project also has an additional footnote. Control Data's presence inspired a young entrepreneur, Howard Valandra, to start a small business on the Rosebud Reservation. He founded a company which developed courseware for various classes in education institutions on reservations. This business, FIRST Computer Concepts, Inc., stayed in operation until 1986.

Prison Education

WHAT ARE PRISONS FOR? Should these correctional institutions deal out extremely tough punishment, with the intention that upon release, the prisoners live in fear of returning to them? Should these institutions be centers for inmate rehabilitation and education? Upon release from such a kinder, gentler place, would these inmates integrate successfully back into society? Is a combination of both ideas possible? These questions and more were raised (and continue to be raised), during the 1960s-1980s. Some alarming statistics were sparking this debate. Prison populations in the United States were rising at an exponential rate, growing to nearly 500,000 by the middle of the 1980s (by 2008, the U.S. prison population was 2.3 million). Because of tougher state and federal sentencing placed against a number of offenses, specifically illegal drug use, more and more Americans were spending significant hard time in prison. Laws were also changed that limited judicial and parole discretion, which in turn caused longer sentencing periods and conservative releasing decisions.

The net result of these changes was America's prisons were becoming rapidly overcrowded. Along with the increases in prison population came increases in costs at the local, state, and federal levels. New and expanded corrections facilities needed to be built, and quickly, to keep up with the expanding prison population. Related to the prison population was a larger issue, discussed both then and now. American prisons suffered from a very high recidivism rate, which is the percentage of released offenders who immediately return to crime and are eventually reincarcerated. What could be done to reduce recidivism so ex-offenders could enjoy productive, lawful lives outside the prison walls—and never go inside them again?

Control Data's involvement with corrections began in the early 1960s when the company showed a willingness to hire ex-felons to work in CDC plants. Members of the HR function worked with Richard Mulcrone, then the parole officer in Scott and Carver counties (Minnesota), and eventually chairman of the Minnesota State Parole Board, to integrate convicted but not incarcerated juvenile delinquents with the workforce, hiring these employees to work on various plant assembly crews. These programs worked well, as a percentage of these inmates were able to transition successfully into the work force and did not return to crime. Then as Control Data opened the poverty-area plants, HR personnel gained even more experience by hiring former inmates and maintaining the long-term employment of these at-risk individuals. Minnesota state officials took notice of both CDC's achievements with former inmates and the company's dedication to addressing social ills. These officials decided they should leverage Control Data's knowledge and experience to directly improve conditions within Minnesota corrections facilities.

In 1972, Governor Wendell Anderson created the Minnesota State Ombudsman Commission to develop an ombudsman function within the state prison system. This function would provide inmates with a direct way to voice issues and grievances, resolving conflicts with prison officers before situations erupted into fights, riots, and other dangerous, potentially fatal behaviors. He appointed Norbert Berg to be a member of the selection committee. This committee's purpose was to select an ombudsman for the Stillwater Correctional Facility, one of the largest prisons of male inmates in Minnesota. Within a few months, the committee was able to establish the starting makeup of this new pilot mediation program.

While the ombudsman program was taking shape at the prison, it was having difficulty setting up an efficient organizational structure. Governor Anderson asked Berg if an executive from Control Data could be loaned out to the Minnesota Department of Corrections to help get the ombudsman pilot program running within the Stillwater prison. Berg liked this idea, as it was a good fit with Control Data's efforts to explore new areas of social responsibility. Berg asked Richard Conner, an HR research manager who worked with the poverty-area plants, if he would be willing to help administrate this new corrections program. Conner was the HR manager who had led several studies investigating the employee experiences at the Northside plant, and these studies had helped the company discover the primary reasons why employees would leave their positions. Because of this experience, Conner was an ideal candidate for the position, and he agreed to take on the task. Control Data gave Richard Conner a six-month paid leave of absence to assist the new ombudsman, T. Williams, in launching the program for the Minnesota Department of Corrections.

Together, Williams and Conner worked directly with prison inmates and staff, easing them through their personal problems and any other problems they endured because of their incarceration. As he worked the ombudsman staff, Conner became heavily involved in researching all aspects of prison life. He experienced firsthand the dangers of prison life. Conner frequently received threats from the more hardcore prisoners whom he tried to help. During one visit to the Stillwater prison in Minnesota, Conner witnessed a riot. He was so close to the disturbance, he ended up inhaling a lot of tear gas. This turned out to be the first of three times Conner would be gassed during prison riots.

One of the major incidents Conner and Williams helped resolve involved the loss of inmate property. Normally prison guards handled inmate bad behavior fairly, but during one specific incident, the guards had gotten so upset they threw out most of the inmates' few possessions—particularly their televisions. The warden was not pleased and the prisoners were furious, creating a dangerous situation. The warden decided the prison should refund money to the inmates for what they lost. Conner got the job of interviewing each prisoner to find out what had been lost and how much these possessions were worth. The line of prisoners in front of Conner was huge and the task was fast becoming overwhelming. Suddenly Conner felt a tap on his shoulder, and he turned around to face one of the largest, meanest prisoners in the entire Stillwater facility. Previously this inmate, a convicted murderer, had threatened Conner with bodily harm. This time however, the inmate asked, "Can I help you?" While Conner was a little taken aback, he truly needed the help and agreed to let the inmate sit next to him. Apparently the inmate had felt bad about his previous threats and wanted to get back in good graces with the ombudsman staff. He proved to be a great assistant and together they were able to refund the inmates for their lost possessions. Through this and many one-on-one meetings with inmates, Conner learned firsthand the primary issues which faced the prison population. This knowledge would soon serve as a springboard for future Control Data prison program initiatives.

Working with the ombudsman staff, Conner helped set up the procedures which the program would follow to handle inmate problems. He also built an administrative function to ensure an efficient management structure was in place for dealing with the incoming caseload. He helped write legislation for the new government office, pushing for the corrections ombudsman program to become a permanent Minnesota state organization. Far from being an unnecessary government organization, the ombudsman function proved that when inmates were given some support and attention to their problems and concerns, some bigger, violent situations could be averted, preventing injuries and saving money. This had benefits for the prison as well, because by lessening the impact of these problems, fewer guards and administrative staff were required to run the prison. Safety was also increased for both guards and inmates. Richard Conner spent many hours shepherding the ombudsman bill through committee meetings, House of Representative hearings, and Senate hearings. His efforts were rewarded. Due to the success of the organization, the correction ombudsman office was permanently established by the Minnesota legislature as a state agency in January of 1973.

From this point on, Control Data had a direct relationship with the Minnesota Department of Corrections, and the HR function used this relationship to launch several prison initiatives. It officially created a new company, Prison Industries, in 1975, to administrate these various initiatives. Through his studies and work with the ombudsman program, Richard Conner concluded the reason many inmates broke the law initially was because they had extremely poor education, and as a result had low income and turned to crime to get ahead financially. Several inmates also had learning disabilities (in some studies, as many as two-thirds had such disabilities), which had prevented them from receiving an adequate education. This led to interpersonal and economic hardships, which in turn led them to crime and eventually prison. The results of these studies caused the Department of Health, Education, and Welfare (HEW) to give the HR function a grant to develop PLATO courseware that would treat the learning disabled. Control Data also collaborated with the University of Illinois to develop a computer-based education system designed specifically for prisoners. To give inmates a way to access this education, Control Data sold PLATO terminals to both the Stillwater and Red Wing correctional facilities, and prison inmates began logging onto these terminals to learn basic skills in math, reading, and other key subjects.

The advantages of using PLATO in a corrections facility soon became obvious. An internal Control Data memo described why PLATO was a strong fit for inmate education:

1. It is always available;
2. It is infinitely patient;
3. It is always positive and rewarding;
4. It is unique and entertaining;
5. It is one-on-one; and
6. It is instant feedback and positive reinforcement.

Control Data had discovered a unique market for its PLATO technology, and the company worked on selling computer-based education and training programs to correctional facilities throughout the United States. Gene Baker, former vice president of Human Resource Management Services, commented on this unexpected group of customers, "It's a marketplace we wouldn't normally have thought of for computer equipment. Yet there are several thousands of institutions detaining people in the U.S. At least 600 of these are places where education is part of the detention process." As a proof of concept, a study was done comparing inmates who had PLATO instruction against those who had a more traditional classroom experience, and the results proved that inmates made significant gains in reading and math in the former. This study was carried out in Minnesota, Texas, and Illinois prisons, and the results quickly spurred sales. By 1978, PLATO was installed and running in twenty-four prisons. By the early 1980s, PLATO was installed and running in over sixty correctional facilities in twenty-three states.

Through this platform, a multitude of remedial and high school level courses were offered to inmates, including mathematics, science, language, and vocational subjects. More social subjects were also introduced, including courses on life-coping skills such as balancing a check book and bargain shopping. Education was not limited to prison inmates either, as courses were made available to prison staff for developing administrative skills. This collection of primary courses eventually became the base for the FAIRBREAK educational system, a business designed for teaching at risk youth education and life skills before they got into trouble or for inmates while they served out their sentences. Later, a series of farming operation courses were developed and marketed to prisons. This course series, called the ADVANTAGE program, taught both inmates and prison managers various farm management and farm production techniques. This in-depth series covered many subjects—including farm business fundamentals; livestock enterprises such as dairy, sheep, and hogs, as well as crop-related knowledge on planting, fertilizing, and harvesting. Technology courses were released to inmates as well, modeled after the curriculum at the Control Data Institutes. This course curriculum taught basic computer operation and programming skills. Courses were also made available in office technologies like word processing and spreadsheets. Each year CDC offered more courses, all delivered to inmates through PLATO terminals.

This courseware was created and taught in the hope of reducing recidivism. By giving the inmates knowledge and skills they needed to find reasonable employment after their release, their time in prison would prove a rewarding one which could help them integrate back into society. This would result in reducing crime and lessening the demands placed on overcrowded correctional facilities. In effect, Control Data had developed the ability to install a complete school within a prison, creating private schools for prisoners. The company had found another way to apply its technology against a social need to build a new business and produce a positive outcome.

A 1982 article entitled "Spark of Hope in Prison Gloom" written for the *Daily Tribune*, a California newspaper, described how the PLATO terminals worked in the California Men's Colony prison at San Luis Obispo. Control Data had sold a PLATO basic skills learning program to this correctional facility; this program taught inmates third to eighth grade level education to minimum security inmates. The contrast between outcomes for the PLATO classes and the conventional classes was striking. In the traditional classroom, an inmate typically took nine months to advance one grade level in reading, writing, and arithmetic. When an inmate enrolled in the PLATO program, however, that time was reduced to just thirteen to eighteen hours per subject, and thirty-nine to fifty-four hours overall to advance one entire grade level. Keith Hayball, the assistant chief of education at the California Department of Corrections, described the unique advantage of PLATO, saying, "We're reaching the men we wanted to reach—the hardest ones, the ones least interested in education of any kind. Even the older cons are interested. They tried to fool their way around with classroom teachers, but they can't manipulate the PLATO program, they can't play games, so they apply themselves." The course curriculum was very popular among the prisoners themselves; at the time of the article, there was a six-week wait for inmates to begin receiving these classes.

While teaching rudimentary skills and basic knowledge was one way to reduce recidivism, giving inmates the equivalent of college degrees and job experience was yet another way. In 1975, Control Data sponsored a new business venture in Minnesota at the Stillwater

An inmate at the Stillwater Correctional Facility takes a course through a PLATO terminal. (Photo courtesy of the Charles Babbage Institute.)

and Lino Lakes prisons. INSIGHT, Inc. was an inmate-organized and inmate-led instructional program geared toward delivering college-level education. After inmates finished their normal daily work within the prison, they could participate in a series of college-level courses. If they finished the curriculum, they would receive college degrees from the University of Minnesota. The prison students were taught through both traditional classroom instruction provided by the University of Minnesota's education extension program and the computer-based training available from Control Data through PLATO terminals. The PLATO courseware proved ideal for the inmates, as they could take the courses at their own pace. And because the courses were private, the inmates were free from the embarrassment and ridicule they often experienced in the classroom setting. The available courses were primarily in adult basic education, GED equivalency, and secondary and post-secondary instruction. Additionally, the INSIGHT program delivered Control Data Institute computer programming education and training. To round out the offerings of the program, INSIGHT also later helped released inmates find employment through a job placement service. The INSIGHT, Inc. program essentially bundled together all the skills inmates needed to gain employment outside the prison, and then followed through by helping these inmates find employment upon their release.

The annual budget for this program was set at $150,000, but the novel approach was planned to eventually make the program self-sustaining through contracts which generated offsetting revenue. The students who received INSIGHT training could be contracted by Control Data or other firms to work on programming projects like courseware or other software deliverables.

These contracts helped pay for their INSIGHT training, and if enough of these contracts could be created and finished, they would offset the costs of the program. Another way the prison students could help pay for their training was by becoming programming trainers themselves—in this case for HOMEWORK students. HOMEWORK was created to rehabilitate partially able, former Control Data employees return to full-time employment. (HOMEWORK will be described in more detail within chapter four.) Now two social venture projects were assisting each other; for a time, prisonbound INSIGHT convicts were remotely teaching homebound HOMEWORK students how to use their PLATO terminals. The chairman of INSIGHT at the time quipped in an internal memo, "HOMEWORK instruction to the homebound is working extremely well and brings in steady revenue of $1,833 a month. We look forward to adding a second instructor position." Computer Based Education was another source of programming, and this brought in revenue of $1,000 to $2,000 each month. Because the program was largely self-supporting, prisoners received their education at no cost from other sources, including state government. The prison students would work for hire. Upon their release from corrections, they would have both the education and the work experience they needed to find a job.

Then in 1983, another source of revenue was developed for INSIGHT—telemarketing. A group of carefully selected prison inmates were trained on how to market products over the telephone, a task they could do within the prison walls. Telemarketing was a growing service in the 1980s, so the INSIGHT staff aggressively pursued telemarketing contracts. One of the first customers for this service was LEI, a book publisher. The INSIGHT inmates sold these LEI books to specialized markets around the country. The Minneapolis United Way also hired the inmates to carry out its fundraising campaign in the Minneapolis/St. Paul area. It gave INSIGHT its coldest corporate list, a list made up of people who had not contributed in three years or more. The inmates contacted more than 3,000 people on the list and raised nearly $6,000 in donations. The director of the United Way said it was the greatest fundraising drive from a cold list she had seen in the previous twenty years.

INSIGHT took on many telemarketing projects. At one point it even ran a physician headhunter service for a national health organization; this project was very profitable for INSIGHT. The telemarketing service was budget effective for many companies and non-profit organizations, as it cost much less to call potential customers than contact them through more traditional marketing methods like print media. Through the telemarketing contracts, prison students were able to offset more of the expenses of their INSIGHT courses. Three years after the telemarketing business was launched, INSIGHT was receiving $30,000 a year in additional revenue. By 1986, INSIGHT, Inc. was largely a self-supporting enterprise. It was also a very normal business environment. The inmates all sat in cubicles and used a state of the art phone system.

These inmates were housed in a special cell block run by inmate John Morgan. If these inmates had any discipline issues or other violations, they were kicked out of the cell block. In a report from John Morgan in 1983, he listed the following statistics for the program:

"We continue to operate at full complement—forty-four students and staff. Eight students will receive their bachelor's degrees this year, bringing to twenty-five the number of students who have earned their degrees in our eight-year history . . ." The following statistic though, was the most gratifying: "Of the 150-plus men who have participated in INSIGHT over the years, less than ten percent have returned to prison." The program also received attention from national political figures, especially Supreme Court Chief Justice Warren Burger. Perhaps the greatest moment for INSIGHT was when Chief Justice Burger came to the prison for the graduation ceremony to hand out diplomas to the INSIGHT graduates. The self-confidence, training, and work experience the inmates received was exactly what they needed, and the majority of inmates who made it through the program were leaving their criminal lives behind them.

Wheels Goes Flat

MOST OF CONTROL DATA'S social ventures either achieved successful outcomes or at least achieved modest results. In particular, many prison initiatives, like the PLATO courses, were popular and enjoyed demonstrative progress towards lessening a social ill. One prison initiative that did not turn out well, however, was Wheels, also dubbed internally as "Cars for Cons." The problem Wheels attempted to address was a simple but important need. One of the thornier problems inmates faced upon their release from prison was lack of transportation. While the education and work experience the inmates gained gave them better advantages in finding mean-ingful employment after they finished their sentences, most inmates were limited to taking jobs within walking distance from a metro bus stop. This greatly reduced parolee options for em-ployment, and so this situation was a contributing factor for their recidivism. If the released in-mates owned cars, Control Data reasoned, they could apply for jobs wherever they were available and have the means to get to and from this job.

Like every initiative, this HR business venture was an interesting concept, and it ad-dressed a dual need for the company as well. The Commercial Credit Corporation owned a car leasing business, McCullough Leasing. McCullough Leasing own a number of used cars, 30,000 of them, which it had purchased as a car fleet to lease to other companies. This business needed to retire around 5,000 vehicles a year as part of its three-year rotation schedule, and these used vehicles were sold to automotive dealers at car auctions. Rather than sell them all back to dealers, Commercial Credit could sell some of these cars to ex-felons. Commercial Credit would give the ex-convicts low-interest loans, and these individuals would then be able to purchase a used car. After leaving the prison, these inmates could drive out the gate with their used automobile. It seemed like a win-win concept. Commercial Credit would reduce its used car inventory and former inmates would have the transportation they needed to find better paying jobs.

What happened next was bitterly disappointing for all involved in the program. The first problem was that the Wheels program turned out to be very expensive for McCullough Leasing.

The inmates did not have to make payments on these cars for the first six months after receiving them, and McCullough had to absorb a loss on these cars during this grace period. While this was a financial hurdle that could potentially be resolved, a bigger issue emerged. The HR function hired an ex-felon to run the leasing program, giving a former inmate a unique opportunity to better himself by administrating the program. Instead, the ex-felon became a recidivist on the job. The easy access to the loan money proved too tempting, and the ex-felon began skimming small amounts of money from the leasing fund, ultimately embezzling about $25,000 before he was discovered. It was a stupid act, and it jeopardized the venture. An internal CDC memo euphemistically described the situation, "An ex-felon, who was hired to manage the program . . . misused his authority and misdirected the funds." The Wheels program and its problems were featured in several articles in newspapers. Complicating the situation were unproven rumors that some of the purchased cars had been used as getaway vehicles in robberies. Control Data had apparently made a blunder in one of its "out there" social programs, and the situation became the subject of much public derision.

Despite losing only $25,000 from the embezzlement, the bad press was brutal, and the program ended in 1980. Although some members of the HR function had hoped to revive the program under a new strategic plan, Wheels never got back on the road. CDC creditability was harmed by the incident, and many HR managers were loathe to try the program again. Gene Baker, who was involved with Wheels, summed up its painful outcome: "It didn't turn out to be the right idea." However, defenders of the initiative still argue it was a good business plan, as Wheels provided a way to give an at-risk population a tool to help them find a good job, while at the same time reducing excess car inventory and generating revenue for Commercial Credit from the loans. From this viewpoint, it was the implementation of the idea that was wrong, not the business plan itself. Regardless, Wheels became one of the few failures of Control Data's social business initiatives.

Factories with Fences

CHIEF JUSTICE WARREN BURGER wanted to dramatically change things in America's prisons. As the chief justice stated, the American approach to corrections was prisons that were primarily expensive warehouses—with revolving doors—for criminals. The warehouses "stored" the criminals for a time. Then, often within just a few weeks of their release, these individuals broke the law again and returned to the warehouse—and the vicious cycle of recidivism would continue. "To put a man behind bars to protect society without trying to change him," Chief Justice Burger stated, "is to win a battle but lose the war." Chief Justice Burger's solution was that job opportunities needed to be created within the prison, giving ex-convicts work experience they could leverage upon their release. In a speech the chief justice gave to the Nebraska Bar Association in 1981, he said, "It is predictable that a person confined in a penal institution. . . . who is then released without being able to read, write, spell or do simple arithmetic, and not trained with any marketable skill, will be vulnerable to returning to a life of crime. . . . What job opportunities are there for unskilled illiterates with criminal records?" The United States was about to start a multi-billion-dollar prison construction program to handle the surging prison population, and Burger reasoned American taxpayers deserved better results from this large investment.

For many years throughout his long career, Warren Burger had spoken frequently and consistently about this issue. A native of St. Paul, Minnesota and appointed as chief justice by President Richard Nixon in 1969, Warren Burger had thoroughly researched the corrections system and understood its problems. On multiple occasions he had traveled to Europe to study new approaches to corrections, particularly within experimental facilities in Norway, Sweden, and Demark. In some of these facilities, inmates lived almost normal lives and held manufacturing or service jobs. Instead of being dependents that cost their governments dearly and gave back nothing in return, these prisoners would actually be productive members of society, creating goods and services, which, when sold, helped defray much of the cost of their prison terms. Burger had found a solution, asking, ". . . are we going to build more 'warehouses' or should we change our thinking and build factories with fences around them, where we will first train inmates and then have them engage in useful production." In 1984, Americans spent $17 million each day to house inmates. Not only would prison jobs help reduce the costs of America's prisons, the potential employment which could happen for prisoners upon release would reduce crime. The use of the term "corrections" would actually become true, as criminals would use their prison time to correct their behavior and become productive, employed free citizens.

Throughout history, humanitarians and religious leaders have often stated that a nation's degree of civilization can be measured by how it treats its prisoners. The story of America's prison system is a story of brutality, compassion, and reform. Throughout the eighteenth and nineteenth centuries, prisons were staid fortresses where the reformation of inmates was solely based on solitary contemplation within cell walls and back-breaking, repetitive labor. Prisoners would work for private employers through contract labor. Through these contracts, the private employers paid the state, not the prisoner, so this basically was a legal system of slave labor. And as a result of these experiences, inmates left these prisons more hardened and resolved to a life of crime than before. Then early in the twentieth century, prison reform groups and the growing labor movement urged Congress to make contract prison labor illegal. Congress complied and the practice eventually disappeared.

Meanwhile, new approaches were applied to the prison population. Psychology and psychiatry were used in the hope of rehabilitating repeat offenders. While this approach produced better results, the level of recidivism remained high. Meanwhile, worries continued that jobs would be placed in prisons at the expense and economic well-being of law-abiding citizens. During the Great Depression, several states passed laws restricting the sale and manufacture of prison-made goods in an effort to protect the fragile jobs available during this difficult economic period. Congress also responded to the lobbying of labor groups and small businesses by passing legislation which regulated the interstate commerce of inmate-manufactured products. Under the Hawes-Cooper Act (1935), and then the Ashurst-Sumner Act (1940), prison-made goods could no longer be transported across state lines for private use. Manufacturing facilities were still allowed to be built within prison, but the products of inmate labor—for example, license plates—were almost exclusively sold to state agencies.

Chief Justice Burger particularly felt the law prohibiting the transportation of goods across state lines was counter-productive. He made these proposals for prison reform in 1984:

- Convert prisons into intensive educational and training facilities as well as "factories."
- Repeal statutes that limit prison-industry production or markets for prison-made goods.
- Repeal laws discriminating against the interstate sales or transportation of prison-made goods.
- Work with business and labor leaders toward cooperation to allow for more inmate job opportunities.

To this effort, he worked hard at convincing state and national lawmakers to make changes to the current prison laws that would allow more opportunities for private companies to employ inmates while they were in prison. Control Data was uniquely positioned to be an ideal match for the chief justice's proposals. The company's history of hiring ex-convicts, their experiences with former convicts at the poverty-area plants, and the prison education program made the company a prime example of what private industry could do within the corrections system.

The concerns of Warren Burger, prison officials, and industry leaders prompted Congress to partially relax the laws which prohibited interstate trade. In 1979, Congress passed the Prison Industries Enhancement Act (sometimes called the Percy Amendment), which was an experimental program that allowed seven projects in five states—Arizona, Kansas, Minnesota, Nevada, and Utah—to sell prison-made projects on the open market. The act also allowed these correctional facilities to make contracts for prison labor with private corporations. If the experiment worked, Congress could allow more exceptions through the Prison Industries Enhancement Act upon request. Control Data was involved in the creation of this bill, as the company saw it could expand its manufacturing needs and continue its social responsibility efforts by establishing plants within prisons. CDC now had the legal means to create a "factory with a fence," and it began efforts to do so within the prison at Stillwater, Minnesota.

The Peripheral Products business needed to expand its manufacturing capacity. Thomas Kamp, the executive in charge of peripherals, met with Norb Berg, requesting that work begin on finding a location, setting up the new factory, and hiring employees. Berg agreed this plant needed to be set up, but because of the new legislation, this plant also had to be built inside the Stillwater correctional facility. Kamp and other managers at Peripheral Products were strongly against the idea (in one interview, Berg stated, "At first, they complained like hell . . ."). The primary concern was that the quality of the manufactured products would not meet company standards. These managers also voiced more immediate concerns about personal safety as well. Because of the interstate commerce exception, however, CDC leaders felt it was golden opportunity to set up this operation inside the Stillwater prison. In many ways, this effort was similar to creating the poverty-area plants. A distressed, at-risk community needed jobs, and Control Data needed the increased production capability.

Corporate leadership made the decision to build a prison industries plant, and the Peripheral Products operation entered into a contract with the Minnesota Department of Corrections. Through this contract, Stillwater inmates could be hired to work within a computer component assembly facility. This facility was provided by the Minnesota Department of Corrections, and was placed inside an existing space that had once built agricultural implements such as manure spreaders and hay wagons (these implements had been exclusively sold to farmers within Minnesota). The contract, signed in October 1981, placed a major factory inside the walls of the Stillwater corrections facility, a maximum security prison. The prison inmates would assemble two key products, disk drive frames and electronic harnesses, within the walls of the correctional facility.

Soon 160 inmates were trained and put to work building these products. The inmates were employees of the Minnesota Department of Corrections, and they earned an income at or above the minimum wage of the time, roughly between a dollar and fifty cents and four dollars per hour, with the average monthly wage at $366.21 per month. Inmates typically worked seven hours per day, and production occurred during a five-day work week. The new plant also received no special treatment. The Stillwater factory was considered by the Peripheral Products operation to be another subcontractor, required to bid for jobs and held to the same deadlines and quality standards as any other supplier. It was now up to the inmates to make the Stillwater prison plant work.

The inmate employees, empowered with something much better to do than sit around and stare at cell walls, relished the chance to work. Not only were they earning money, they were working on what were at the time cutting edge technology products. In less than a year, the products assembled at the plant started meeting the same quality standards required from other Peripheral Products manufacturing facilities. Then beginning in April of 1982, the Stillwater plant began exceeding the CDC quality control standards every month. In fact, the inmates consistently turned out products more efficiently and at a higher quality than at other Control Data facilities. This output was primarily due to the intense motivation of the inmates. If an inmate did not do his job correctly, he would lose his manufacturing position. This meant spending long days in the cell block with no income for cigarettes, coffee, and other small comforts. The prisoners turned out to be highly motivated workers.

The inmates at Stillwater were proving the concept could work. The results were surprising and gratifying to everyone involved with the facility. Tom Kamp was so pleased, he felt the company should give the inmate employees some token of recognition for their hard work. He worried though, that inmates would not think very highly of his gesture. Berg assured Kamp these tokens would be the first gift of appreciation many of the inmates had ever received in their lives. Tom Kamp personally went to the Stillwater prison and awarded each prisoner a Gold Cross pen and pencil set in appreciation for their hard work, productivity, and quality output. Most inmates had never received such an award, and the pen and pencil set was very positively received by them.

Placing a factory inside a prison did present its share of challenges. The need for prison discipline could occasionally disrupt the normal working routine of the Stillwater factory. On the evening of September 11, 1983, a riot broke out in Cell Hall B and this wing of the facility was placed in lockdown—no prisoners could leave their cells. Normally lockdowns only lasted a couple days, but this situation was different. A racial incident had broken out among some of the inmates in the wing, and Warden Robert Erickson decided it would be prudent to remove the key actors to prevent more violence from erupting if all the prisoners were released. Most of the inmates who worked in the CDC assembly line were housed in Cell Hall B, so work on the disk drive frames was essentially shut down. The warden hoped he could release the CDC workers by Monday, September 19, and resume production. Warden Erickson was keen on meeting the output needs required by Control Data. "I . . . assure you", he wrote in a letter explaining the situation, "that we will hold up our end of the log by doing our very best to minimize down time and to continue to hold to the highest standards of both quality and quantity production. If a need to work overtime to meet production demands arises, we can handle that as well." Eventually production resumed at the Stillwater plant, and the quality output previously described showed they did indeed return to full production, meeting quantity demands and the production schedule. By the fall of 1983, the Stillwater plant had manufactured 10,000 disk drive frames. The frames were used in the final assembly of 300-megabyte disk drives at the Arden Hills facility; each of these disk drives were sold at a price between $25,000 and $30,000. The inmates were earning their keep.

Encouraged by this success, Control Data formed a new entity within the company, the Correction Systems Division, to coordinate its efforts with both prison industry and education. CDC was the first Fortune 500 company to create such a business. The project was assigned as an initiative for the City Venture Corporation, as City Venture's services and knowledge for revitalizing urban centers was similar to the expertise needed to market education and industrial opportunities to the corrections system. City Venture then hired an experienced individual to run this new division, Richard Mulcrone, the same official who had worked with Control Data years before to help hire parolees for work within Control Data plants. Mulcrone had a long career in law enforcement, starting as a street officer, then a probation and parole officer, and then eventually the head of the Minnesota State Parole Board.

Joining Control Data in early 1982, Mulcrone spent the first six months developing and analyzing the market potential for CDC's prison ventures. He also submitted major proposals for projects within Indiana, Michigan, and Iowa. During his time there, Mulcrone identified the main hurdles Control Data faced as the company began expanding the venture beyond the Stillwater prison. The legal issues he identified were:

1. What new legislation is necessary to allow the private industrial prison to be created?
2. What incentives would have to exist for the state to give up the authority of operating a prison?
3. What incentives would have to exist for the private sector to undertake this kind of responsibility?
4. What legal ramifications are there for a corporation in operating a prison?
5. What enterprise zone incentives could be applied to the private sector-operated prison?"

Mulcrone reasoned the demographics within the prison system were similar to the demographics found in economically distressed inner-city communities. The people within these communities were young, poor, unskilled, undereducated, disproportionally illiterate, and African-American. Prison industries, in fact, would be an ideal project for City Venture to undertake. "City Venture's initial excursion into prison problems," Mulcrone explained, "should be based on the belief that prisons are merely neighborhoods with walls around them." Placing a plant within a prison was essentially the same project CDC had done previously when the company launched each poverty-area plant. Jobs were the primary thing needed within poverty-area neighborhoods, so it made sense that providing jobs to inmates would also give them dignity and a new sense of self. Many inmates were angry young men, and in prison they were forced to be idle. By giving these young men a purpose through a job, these individuals would be less likely to reach a state of emotional combustion that would result in costly riots and other disorderly behavior. The money which the inmates made could be placed against a variety of costs, including paying for some of their room, board, and security at the prison; contributing support for their families; giving them needed money to pay for their education; and even providing restitution for the victims of their crimes. The inmates would also be eligible for health and life insurance benefits (even retirement savings) through the company, relieving some of the cost burden being shouldered by the state. The potential advantages for society could be enormous.

Mulcrone also identified three types of private industries that would work well within a prison environment. The first was that inmates could create entire products, building from a raw material all the way to a finished output. There would be some limits as to what kinds of products could be fully manufactured in a prison environment based on security concerns and space constraints. It would be possible, however, to manufacture a large number of items within a prison setting without much difficulty. The second type of industry was assembly work. For this output, inmates would manufacture a component of a product, which would then be transported to another plant for the final assembly. The Stillwater operation was an example of such an industry, as the disk drive frames were transported to the Arden Hills plant for final assembly. The third industry he identified was service work. Inmates could perform a service of some kind, such as deburring metal, renovating telephones, refurbishing school buses, or other services. Stillwater and Lino Lakes both had examples of service industries, as the inmates worked in the telemarketing service administered by the INSIGHT program.

Hiring inmates to work in these industries could be handled through a variety of business plans. The private company could set up a contract agreement with the commissioner of corrections for the work, or the inmates could be hired directly. A non-profit corporation could also be set up to handle employment functions. Formulating a prison industry would then be a very flexible process, as the potential opportunity could be tailored to the restrictions and needs of the facility and the legal requirements of each state prison system.

Mulcrone further reasoned all activities and amenities inside a prison should be nearly identical to the real world—prisons needed good housing, nutritional food, good medical care, and clean conditions. The current state of prisons, with their isolated cells and idle prisoners, was a weird environment that ran against America's culture of hard work and industry. It was little wonder that so many ex-offenders returned to crime, because they were not being taught a better way to live. If additional counseling services were provided for financial planning, nutrition, and mental health, inmates would be equipped with more ways to survive and thrive in the outside world. As Mulcrone argued in a 1982 speech to prison officials, "To change those in your charge, you must attack this abnormalcy of ignorance, of idleness, of self-depreciation, and of blocked access to opportunity." By making a prison a more normal environment, complete with access to a job and assistance with life skills management, a prisoner would be more prepared for life outside prison walls. All these initiatives would be done out of a sense of enlightened self-interest, as releasing prisoners who were better people than when they went in would be of greater value to society.

These prison initiatives—education, jobs, and improved environment—together amounted to a novel concept. Control Data reasoned these initiatives would work best if they were run by private corporations. The state would still provide much-needed security, but most of the services for the inmates inside the prison would be provided through contracts with private industry. As Mulcrone stated during a speech to the National Governor's Conference, "The states' monopoly on running prisons is based primarily on its superior knowledge of the policing function. But a partnership could be struck with the private sector to build and operate the interior prison if proper incentives were in place." The state would guard the walls, and corporations would guide the halls. Now that many of the company's education and manufacturing projects were either successfully profitable or self-sustaining enterprises, Control Data felt it had the proof it needed that such a pub-lic-private corrections association would work. The company soon set about trying to get the U.S.Con-gress to allow more interstate trade exemptions through the Prison Industries Enhancement Act.

To spur this effort, Control Data began an active relationship with Chief Justice Warren Burger. Warren Burger met with William Norris, Norbert Berg, and other CDC members of the board of directors to discuss prison reform. Control Data was enacting many of the ideas proposed by the chief justice, and so there was a strong tie between his platform and the Control Data prison initiatives. Control Data identified two legal areas which could be strengthened in order to stimulate more private industry in the corrections system. Of first importance, previously stated, was to grant more exemptions beyond the original seven allowed through the Prison In-dustries Enhancement Act. The second was to encourage private sector investment through tax credits. Control Data's idea was a company might receive fifty percent of a former inmate's salary back as a tax credit if the parolee was not involved in a crime within the first six months of release, seventy-five percent back if the parolee was crime free during the second six months, and a one-hundred percent rebate if the inmate was not reincarcerated for two years. The thought behind this rebate program was most ex-convicts commit crimes during the first 180 days of release, but then the chance of criminal activity diminishes quickly. The companies would thus be rewarded for their effort in rehabilitating criminals.

The chief justice liked Control Data's approach, and he used CDC's prison initiatives as an example of his prison ideas put into action (as described previously, he showed his support by passing out diplomas to INSIGHT graduates). Chief Justice Burger and William Norris ap-peared together in a forum at Racine, Wisconsin, in January of 1984, and then later in another forum at George Washington University in June of 1984. The theme of these forums was "Fac-tories with Fences," and both leaders used the event to advance their ideas to legislators, penol-ogists, and prison officials. That same summer, Norbert Berg testified before the House of Representatives on Control Data's positive experiences working with prison inmates. Berg framed the issue in this way: "Our choice is between a costly, multiple billion-dollar system whose end product has a fifty percent or higher failure rate and a new concept of how to deliver correctional services in a way which will truly prepare inmates for life on the outside, one which will embrace the most basic of America's ethics of work, education, and training." Control Data sought to either grant more interstate exceptions for goods and services, or even completely remove the restrictions imposed by the Ashurst-Sumner Act.

Meanwhile, Control Data's prison industries business continued to expand. The state of Michigan contracted with CDC to develop an inmate training center in one of its correctional facilities. This project came about partially through a grant from the Edna McConnell Clark Foundation, an organization devoted to improving the people suffering from poverty. This three-year project would set up a self-sustaining educational facility within the prison modeled after INSIGHT, as inmates would also work to help pay for their training. Control Data also won a contract at the Leavenworth prison in Kansas to set up an institute that trained inmates in digital electronics. Interest in prison industries and services was clearly growing, as Control Data was now one of thirteen companies competing over this contract. Stillwater wasn't the only exemption project in operation. Zephyr Products in Kansas was another of the seven pilot programs granted through the Prison Industries Enhancement Act. This company employed inmates in a sheet metal factory. Each employee earned roughly $1,700 a month to support their dependent families. In 1982, of the forty-two inmates who had worked at Zephyr who had since been paroled, only nine returned to prison. Best Western International, the hotel chain, employed thirty female prisoners as room reservation operators. This service was run from inside a women's prison in Phoenix. Yet another prison-based factory was run in Nevada, where inmates built fiberglass satellite dish antennas. By 1984, about 300 inmates were working in prison industries nationwide. Feedback from prison officials and the reduced recidivism results were encouraging results for this initiative.

But controversy loomed. The argument which had earlier caused the Hawes-Cooper and the Ashurst-Sumner Acts to be passed was essentially revived. Labor unions were concerned about the Stillwater plant and the other exemption sites, because the wage being paid to the inmates was less than the going rate for similar work outside the prison. Some states also had different categories of workers—employees and inmates. As inmates were a different category, by law they were not entitled to the same benefits as employees. However, this was not a problem under the Prison Industries Enhancement Act, as this law required that inmates receive the same benefits as the general workforce. Some clarification was needed, though, as obviously a prison workforce was less of a burden than a workforce made up of organized labor. And there existed the perplexing issue of union members who went to prison. Should these union members have the same benefits, including income, which they had before they went to prison? Did prison time revoke their union membership? Clearly some legal hurdles needed to be resolved before prison industries could continue to expand.

Unions also argued if prison industries became more widespread, it would reduce the jobs for organized labor, so this effort was really yet another veiled effort at union busting. They did have some reason to be worried. Fred Braun, the entrepreneur who founded Zephyr Manufacturing in Kansas, admitted, "I had to buy a company that was non-union. No union would realistically permit union people to be replaced by inmates." There was also the issue of exploitation. John Zalusky, an economist for the AFL-CIO, worried that, besides the issue of lower wages, inmates had no way to complain if the working conditions were unacceptable. "We tread a pretty thin line," he stated, "when we have this plan but protest slave labor in the Soviet Union." An additional concern was liability. Who was liable if an inmate was injured while working in the prison factory—the state or the corporation? Organized labor saw the threat of nearly 500,000 inmates (the prison population in the 1980s) being put to work as leading all workers down a path of lower wages and less jobs, and several unions lobbied against the efforts to expand the prison exemptions.

Chief Justice Burger was convinced these concerns could be answered. Labor unions also recognized the need for prisoners to do meaningful work. "AFL-CIO has very enlightened leadership," Burger remarked. " I've discussed with some of their leaders from time to time, and I think they have the natural concern right now that in a period of high unemployment they don't want to aggravate that . . . by having to compete with prison-made goods. But there are ways of dealing with that." He reasoned, as Control Data's leaders did, that even putting a half-million prisoners in the United States to work was in reality a small percentage of the nation's gross national product, and the impact on union laborers would be minimal. Privately, a union official even told a CDC executive that Control Data's prison industries were a good idea, but politically he had to oppose it. As for the concern of exploitation, Control Data and other companies argued that laws and business practices provided enough oversight to prevent abuse. But the concerns of labor unions would not go away. Despite some willingness by unions to originally support the prison initiatives, organized labor came out more and more against efforts to expand the number of interstate exemptions allowed under the Prison Industries Enhancement Act.

The unions had a surprising ally—small business. Prison-made goods, because of the lower wages, could be built cheaper than identical goods manufactured outside the prison. In some cases, small companies were being underbid by prison manufacturers, and the prospect of this sector growing even larger seemed a dangerous proposition to small business owners. For example, Anondson and Arntson was a small traffic sign manufacturer who sold signs to the state and local governments in Iowa. Inmates working through Iowa Prison Industries also made traffic signs, and during 1983, Iowa Prison Industries underbid the manufacturing company four times on contracts with local governments. These contracts were relatively small, but as co-owner Arntson stated, "What we have lost already is not going to break us. It's the fear of what they (Iowa Prison Industries) can do. They can break us." In 1978, total annual sales by U.S. prison industries was $180 million, but by 1984 this figure had grown to $300 million. Troubled by their potential loss of income and even the loss of their entire business, small business organizations joined labor unions in lobbying to prohibit the expansion of the prison industry exemptions.

An interesting side issue was whether these prison reforms were a conservative or a liberal approach to the problem. Warren Burger had been nominated to the Supreme Court by Richard Nixon because the president admired Burger's conservative credentials and his strict interpretation of the U.S. Constitution. When the chief justice spoke about changing America's prisons, however, some pundits complained he did not sound very much like a conservative. The chief justice responded to this criticism through a CNN interview, saying, "I don't know whether my views about prisons are conservative or liberal. To take those terms, I'd say they're conservative, not liberal, if I understand what those terms mean. I want to conserve values. I would like to see fewer crimes being committed. And one way to do it is . . . have these institutions run on the basis that we'll turn out at least a reduced number of repeaters." While the approach was advantageous for private industry, it was also a way to help a disadvantaged population. The issue was not a clear-cut conservative or liberal issue that could be divided along these polar opposite ideologies. The controversy these proposals generated was based more on economic concerns, as the unusual pairing of organized labor and small business organizations demonstrates.

The debate continued throughout the 1980s, and ultimately a compromise was reached. The prison industries had too many benefits to be ignored, so some form of this program needed to continue. The Stillwater plant, for example, demonstrated an increasing number of positive results. After seven Stillwater inmates were released from prison in 1983, Control Data hired them. Most of these former inmates worked in the Normandale South facility assembling disk drives. These parolees had the required work experience and several were able to find and sustain employment with the company. However, the concerns of labor and small business were also heavily considered by national lawmakers, and steps were taken to ensure prison industries remained as a small, controlled series of exemptions. Under the Crime Control Act of 1990, the Prison Industries Enhancement Act was continued indefinitely, and up to fifty exemptions (now called jurisdictions) are available to private corporations at any given time. As of this writing, thirty-seven state and four county-based certified correctional industry programs operate in the United States.

Eventually the Stillwater facility became obsolete and Control Data ceased its operations there. Circumstances were against Control Data's complete plan to manage an entire facility as well, as the company's problems in the mid 1980s ended the future expansion of its prison industries. The pioneering Stillwater plant, though, proved that employing inmates was good for both the inmates and the correctional facilities. Prison industries continue today, reducing recidivism, in large part because of Control Data's initiatives in this area.

Charitable Programs

While nearly all Control Data's social efforts, particularly service ventures, were ultimately intended to become profitable business ventures, some efforts were totally altruistic. These programs still reflect CDC's approach towards innovation, but they also show the company did contribute resources to charitable causes Control Data leaders and its social responsibility committee felt were important. These programs round out the community outreach principles Control Data followed; the company worked hard at improving the lives of as many disadvantaged individuals it could identify as needing help. The Committee on Social Responsibility was also responsible for assigning donations to these charitable groups.

Control Data was not the only organization focused on creating business solutions to address social needs. Some non-profit organizations held similar objectives. Because of this, CDC gave charitable contributions to organizations whose mission was to create business solutions, including the Minnesota Cooperation Office for Small Business and Job Creation, Inc.,

Minnesota Wellspring, and the Minnesota Seed Capital Fund. The charter for the Minnesota Cooperation Office for Small Business and Job Creation, Inc. states its purpose is to increase the number and quality of jobs and job creation potential within the private sector of Minnesota. Part of their services help entrepreneurs start new businesses. This mission was a perfect match for CDC's approach to entrepreneurship, so Control Data gave money directly to this organization. Control Data also sponsored research at various not-for-profit organizations for projects such as retooling computers for use by the handicapped. Courage Center is an organization which helps enable disabled people lead productive lives. Control Data donated a PLATO terminal to Courage Center, and several disabled individuals used this PLATO terminal to gain more skills through this courseware. The charitable giving was strategized to support organizations doing innovative projects, organizations who were (and in many cases still are) embracing social responsibility through groundbreaking methods.

The plight of runaway youth across the country also became a concern within the HR function. Runaway teenagers, especially girls, frequently turned to prostitution to survive on the streets in cities across America. Norbert Berg's nephew, who drove a taxicab in Minneapolis, mentioned to Berg that he and other taxicab drivers saw runaway teens regularly as they drove around the city, sometimes giving these teenagers rides wherever they needed to go. This information launched a simple, yet effective idea. Because taxicab drivers had frequent contact with troubled teenagers, they could be leveraged to help get these teenagers off the streets and hopefully out of trouble. It was a practical solution which was also easy to implement, so the HR function helped set this concept in motion.

To do this, Control Data collaborated with a series of safe houses in cities across the United States. These safe houses would bring support and services for the runaway teenagers, no questions asked. Control Data provided a fund these safe houses would use to pay for taxicab fare. With this fund in place, taxicab drivers were encouraged to look out for runaway teens. When a taxicab driver saw someone who looked like a runaway teen, the driver could offer the individual a free ride to a safe house. If the teenager agreed to go, the taxicab drivers could then drop off the runaway at the facility, where an administrator would reimburse the driver for the fare. This type of program was called different names in different cities; in Minnesota, this organization was called "The Bridge for Runaway Youth" and in Los Angeles, "Children of the Night." Plus, the program could operate on a small budget. The annual cost at "The Bridge for Runaway Youth," for example, was only six to seven thousand a year. The lives saved were well worth the expense, as these safe houses were able to take a number of runaway youth off the streets and away from harm.

In 1984, Control Data launched the Twelve Baskets food rescue program, a charity initiative designed to distribute previously prepared food to homeless shelters and other places in need. When the program was announced, Control Data said its purpose was "to move good quality, previously prepared, perishable food from Twin City restaurants and caterers to congregate eating centers for the disadvantaged." Instead of throwing away discarded food at the end of the day, standard practice for restaurants and caterers, this food could be picked up and delivered to homeless shelters and soup kitchens. Food normally wasted would instead go directly to the people who needed it most.

This Minnesota charity began because of a head cold. Berg was home recuperating from a nasty cold, and was watching television to pass the time. He saw a story on ABC news highlighting City Harvest, a program in New York that "rescued" prepared food from area restaurants. He was intrigued by the concept, so he sent Jane Belau, Control Data's vice president of public affairs, to visit City Harvest. The organization was thrilled to help set up a similar program in Minnesota. With City Harvest providing guidance, Belau returned to Minnesota and met with Control Data's Committee on Social Responsibility. Members of the committee were equally enthusiastic about the idea, so the committee provided the funds and administrative staff needed to start the project.

The key obstacle was ensuring the previously prepared food was safe and fit to eat. Health regulation rules would need to be strictly observed to make sure the program would gather and disperse untainted food. An advisory committee was formed with doctors, administrative health professionals, political representatives, and corporate representatives as its members. This group led efforts to learn how to handle food safely and how to train the food handlers to make sure they delivered good quality food. A set of quality standards were developed. One of the key rules was the previously prepared food could not have been placed before the public in any way; only prepared food which was not served could be donated. The donations could also only be collected by food rescue specialists. These certified food handlers would be trained following the standards required by the Department of Environmental Health and the Department of Agriculture. Refrigerated trucks were required for the food pick-up. This perishable food would then be delivered the same day to member agencies, including after-school programs, soup kitchens, and shelters.

The last hurdle to overcome was liability for the donor businesses. Control Data encouraged legislation to make it legally feasible for businesses to donate perishable food. As a result of this lobbying effort, the Bill Emerson Good Samaritan Donations Act was passed "to encourage businesses to donate food and grocery products to non-profit organizations for distribution to needy individuals." The law protects these businesses from civil and criminal liability. If the business can prove they donated food products in good faith that later caused harm to a recipient, the business would be absolved of liability. To complete the legal incentives, businesses would also get a tax deduction for the donated food, turning what would normally have been a business liability into extra income. With the legal questions resolved and health regulations in place, the food rescue program could begin.

The name of the CDC program, Twelve Baskets, was selected to reflect the biblical story of Jesus's miracle with the loaves and fishes. Despite just having five loaves and two fish, Jesus was able to feed five thousand people and had twelve baskets of food left over by the end of the meal. Likewise, Twelve Baskets would gather leftovers from similar feasts all over the Twin Cities. Working with the St. Paul Food Bank, the project began on December 3, 1984. By the next day, Twelve Baskets had already distributed about 400 pounds of food, mostly hamburger buns and yogurt. Several contributing restaurants were supportive of the project. Don James, owner of a Fuddruckers restaurant in Edina, Minnesota, stated, "Twelve Baskets is the reply to a voice in the wilderness. We make our bread fresh daily. Any leftover we give away." Twelve Baskets had found a way to both reduce waste and help improve nutrition for at-risk people. By April 1985, *Corporate Report* magazine stated that Twelve Baskets could collect—and distribute—up to 40,000 pounds of recoverable food per month. This program was entirely run by volunteers.

Large quantities of food were made available at the Twelve Baskets warehouse, and charities could pick up the available food each night. However, this plan didn't work for all charities, as some organizations wanted the food to be delivered, while still others would only pick up the food once a week. Ultimately this program worked very well for most charity groups, as it relieved some food costs at these shelters. It was not long before a group of charities began actively using Twelve Baskets. During the first year of the program in the Minneapolis/St. Paul area, 736 tons of discarded food were saved from the waste bin and given to homeless shelters. Soon more Twelve Basket chapters were created in locations across the country like Chicago, Tucson, and Atlanta.

Today, the Twelve Baskets program continues to be a successful, vital charity program, as the organization rescues an average of 183,300 pounds of food per month, totaling more than two million pounds of high quality food annually. Control Data found a home organization to run the program, and the food rescue program is now administrated by Second Harvest Heartland. Some of the current donors to the project include Embassy Suites, Honey Baked Ham, St. Paul Public Schools, Lund's, and Target Corporation. The simple idea of rescuing wasted food has helped thousands of people gain the nutrients they need to help get their lives on track.

From minorities in need of work to Native Americans in need of health care to the homeless in need of food, Control Data worked hard at identifying ways it could help disadvantaged populations achieve some level of economic stability and prosperity. Most of these ventures worked quite well, some worked partially well, and others worked not very well at all, but Control Data constantly explored innovations to help solve social problems. Along the way, members of the HR function gained vital experience working with disadvantaged individuals, who in turn gave them the knowledge and the confidence needed to tackle areas of social need within the company itself. Soon the HR function began to look at innovations that would improve the individual health and wealth of each employee.

Chapter Four

Employees First

"I just couldn't believe that a company this large would care about one individual."
—Michelle, Employee Advisory Resource client

CONTROL DATA CONSIDERED EMPLOYEES to be the core energy behind the company's success. Employee job satisfaction was a high priority for the HR function, as a dedicated, motivated workforce would create a vibrant and innovative company. Control Data was competing in the high stakes mainframe computer industry, so it was critical for the company to attract, retain, and motivate employees who were at the top of their profession within all departments and disciplines. Control Data management wanted the employees to do much more than just show up for work every day; they needed the employees to approach their jobs as product innovators and business entrepreneurs. Company employee mottos used throughout the years reflected this philosophy—"There's got to be a better way!" and "I can be a part of the solution." If employees embraced their job positions in a spirit of exploration and self-discovery, they would carve out their own niche in the organization and help ensure their long-term employment.

The HR function was tasked with finding the best, most qualified individuals in the job market, and then hopefully retaining these individuals for many years of employment. The first part of this HR mandate was to present a prospective employee with an interesting job position that had a competitive salary and good benefits. Once an employee joined Control Data, this individual needed both the tools and support to succeed at his or her job. The HR function was constantly considering ideas and implementing new programs designed to improve employee experience. Control Data innovation was evident in all these efforts. The HR function developed groundbreaking initiatives like the Employee Advisory Resource and Peer Review to help CDC employees resolve their problems both at work and at home. The company also launched Stay-Well, a comprehensive wellness program that encouraged employees to pursue better health habits. The company even supported temporarily and permanently disabled employees by giving them training in computer skills through the HOMEWORK program.

Central to these initiatives was the philosophy that Control Data hired the entire person, not just the employee who showed up for part of each day at an office cubicle or assembly line. The goals of these initiatives were to improve the internal workforce culture and to make CDC an attractive destination for job-seeking individuals. Many HR employee initiatives met these goals. Control Data was regularly cited as one of the 100 best places in the United States to work. Because of this positive publicity, the company was able to hire individuals who were "the cream of the crop," as Bill Norris frequently and proudly stated. These initiatives improved employees' lives in many tangible ways, and some even grew into independent businesses and standard corporate policies that exist in American corporate culture to this day.

Pro-Employee

IN ORDER FOR CONTROL DATA to roll out the first 1604 mainframe computers, the company had to hire assembly line workers to build the machines within their new manufacturing facility. The moment the hiring process for these individuals began, CDC was no longer a start-up venture of business managers and engineers; it became a manufacturing organization that needed a growing, skilled labor force. Items such as production line levels of compensation, regular hours and overtime hours, and manager/worker codes of conduct became a permanent, integral part of Control Data culture. In the past, Bill Norris and the other company founders had both good and bad experiences with employee relations. Now leading a new company, they had a fresh start. Company leaders wanted to ensure Control Data had the best possible relationship it could with the people who came to work for the organization.

Responsibility for developing a positive employee relations policy was placed on the HR function (called the personnel department during this time). As a founding principle, this group worked hard to establish an atmosphere of caring, fairness, and justice. From the first to the last days of Control Data Corporation, the HR function followed this basic principle. If the needs of both employees and management were proactively addressed, the company would achieve equilibrium. A satisfied workforce would be both efficient and productive, reducing costly expenditures on training new employees and battling employment-related lawsuits.

Control Data's policy toward employee relations was stated as being pro-employee, providing benefits and compensation competitive with what workers could receive elsewhere. The company followed these main principles in its employee relations strategy:

- Obey labor laws
- Avoid unfair labor practices
- Maintain consistency in employee relations
- Treat employees well so they would feel unions were not necessary

The last principle was of major importance—Control Data did not want to negotiate with employees through third-party union intermediaries. The company could not directly prevent workers from organizing, of course, as this was an unfair and illegal labor practice. Similarly, from a business ethics standpoint, aggressively fighting union organizing would go against the culture of fairness and justice the corporation wanted to cultivate with its workforce. Instead, HR managers actively researched the benefits their employees would receive through union representation, copying these benefits as much as possible and exceeding them where it was feasible to do so. Ruth Rich, a former executive of human resources, describes this approach, saying, "It wasn't about beating up the unions; it was about providing employees the things they needed. You don't fight your employees." Through this approach, the HR function tried as much as possible to get ahead of employment trends. Employees could have identical or better compensation than what they could get through a union contract, but without the additional cost of dues. Because they were free from paying dues, employees actually made more money than what they could gain through supporting and maintaining a labor union at their facility. By creating a strong compensation and benefits package, Control Data greatly reduced the need for its employees to seek union representation, providing benefit levels and job security provisions labor unions were aggressively negotiating for at other corporations.

Control Data employees never became or remained unionized in CDC facilities throughout the United States. If a union existed within an acquired company, it was eventually decertified through an official request by the employees. This decertification process was always initiated by the employees within the acquired organization. When CDC acquired a company, a union bargaining unit was occasionally in place. As part of the acquisition process, Control Data would work with the union leadership to deal with the new employees as directly as permitted by union rules. Initial contacts were thus made through the union leaders. At such a point when employees in the acquired organization expressed interest in decertifying their union, the HR function was permitted by law to advise them of the legal steps required under federal and state fair labor laws. One of these legal steps was a presentation through which Control Data was permitted to outline how the company treated non-union employees. The main CDC negotiator involved in these union meetings was Ed Vargon, Control Data's vice president of labor relations. Audiences were typically appreciative of these presentations. (One group of union employees were so impressed with Ed Vargon's abilities, they actually selected him later to be their impartial arbitrator to settle a grievance against Control Data.) During domestic acquisitions, the employees eventually voted voluntarily to decertify their unions and handle issues directly with Control Data management.

The decertification process itself was handled professionally and respectfully by the HR staff, ensuring the process was transparent and followed labor laws. Altogether, thirteen unions were decertified from Control Data's domestic acquisitions. After the unions were decertified, employees looked to the office of labor relations for support and representation for work-related issues. Later employees leveraged services like Employee Advisory Resource (EAR), Peer Review, and the ombudsman programs to resolve job disputes they could not resolve directly with their supervisor. In 1982, Frank Dawe, former senior vice president of administration, was interviewed in *The Weekend Australian* about the company's direct relationship to its employees, where he said, "Control Data's philosophy is not one of being against unions, but more one of feeling that we can deal better with our employees if we don't have to go through a third party. That third party inhibits our ability to communicate directly with our people." This philosophy worked very well in CDC facilities within the United States.

As for unions at international facilities, the laws were more complicated. Depending on the situation, union decertification was sometimes not possible or, in some cases, not even desirable. Control Data had to tread carefully to navigate through government politics and regional concerns. The most dramatic employee relations dispute occurred in South Korea in 1982. CDC had a manufacturing facility in Seoul, and most of the workers in this plant were young women, aged sixteen to twenty-six, who strung wires on magnetic memory cores. This assembly task was delicate work, and typically these wires were about the width of a hair and could only be mounted on the cores using a large, mounted magnifying glass. However, many of these workers were highly skilled and could string these wires without any optical assistance. Plus, the jobs were some of the highest-paying in South Korea. Unfortunately, with the development of integrated circuit memory technology, demand was fading for magnetic memory cores. Control Data decided the plant would eventually have to close.

A U.S.-based religious group, the Worldwide Council of Churches, found out about the closure plan and notified the leaders of a local union. The Worldwide Council of Churches was focused on improving the working conditions of laborers in Seoul, and Control Data's plans alarmed this group. These local union leaders, in turn, told some employees about the upcoming closure and offered to help them. In response, six employees tried to organize the plant in the hopes of leveraging the union to keep the facility open. Regrettably, they tried to organize the plant workers during company time, and in response, these six employees were laid off by their managers. Meanwhile, the South Korean government was not pleased these women laborers were trying to organize, and the government planned to punish the workers and the local union involved in the situation. This government action alarmed the Worldwide Council of Churches. The group publically accused Control Data of giving the South Korean government an excuse to violate the human rights of the female workers. It was a mess.

In response, Control Data sent Roger Wheeler, at this point in his career the vice president of human relations development, and Ed Vargon, as mentioned previously, vice president of labor relations, to meet with both the plant managers and the union leaders. As Wheeler and Vargon explained to the group, Control Data would be forced to close the facility because of declining demand, but would help the employees through a severance package that would provide income while they searched for new employment. After a few days of meetings, Wheeler and Vargon were getting ready to leave the plant and fly back to Minnesota. Suddenly eighty assembly line workers packed into the small conference room, demanding Wheeler and Vargon not leave until they restored the jobs of the six laid-off workers. These eighty workers, mostly women, now totally blocked the door.

Stunned, Wheeler and Vargon politely returned to their seats. Their captors gave them coffee and juice, but as the hours ticked by, this turned out to be more of a curse than a blessing. "I had to decide whether I could go to the bathroom in my pants with dignity," Wheeler later recalled in a *Forbes* magazine article about the incident. Sensing their growing pain, a South Korean plant manager led the two men to the bathroom, where they formulated a plan in the privacy of the urinals. None of the detaining workers spoke English. When they returned to the conference room, Wheeler called Bloomington headquarters using the pretext of discussing re-hiring the six former employees. Instead he called Norb Berg, explaining the hostage situation. Berg immediately called Dave Durenberger, national senator from Minnesota, who contacted the State Department. Early in the morning, the Korean police arrived and freed the two men. The next day, Wheeler and Vargon were on a flight back home to Minnesota.

The headaches, though, continued for Control Data. The South Korean government was directly hostile to unions, doing what it could to limit their power and influence. Control Data had actually shielded the union from the government's tough policies to help encourage better employee rights within this country. In this case, leaders from this same union had helped the HR managers learn more about the culture and circumstances of Control Data's South Korean employees. But because of this incident, the South Korean government capitalized on the situation to launch an anti-labor media campaign. This campaign also warned about the corruptive influence of religious activists. The HR function decided to address the situation directly by first contacting the Worldwide Council of Churches. The HR managers explained that when compared with other severance packages provided by competitors in South Korea, Control Data's compensations and severance package was significantly better than worldwide minimum standards. The church activists and the union leaders eventually agreed Control Data was doing the best the company could for these employees. Now with tempers cooled down, Control Data was able to close the plant without more incidents. Control Data's business ethic of doing well by its employees saved the company from further complications.

Regardless of the domestic or international location, the work environment Control Data established within its facilities was positive and supportive. As was demonstrated during the South Korean incident, Control Data tried to be responsive to the communities that surrounded CDC facilities—even when forced to reduce or even close a facility. Past employees speak warmly about the Control Data culture. Jennifer Enberg worked as a payroll clerk at the Normandale plant in Bloomington, Minnesota (a Peripheral Products operation which manufactured disk drives), in the early 1970s, passing out paychecks to the assembly workers. She describes, "I liked working for Control Data. They were a nice company, very considerate. I really liked my bosses during my time at the plant." The HR function stayed connected with the employees by regularly researching turnover trends at specific plants in order to evaluate the reasons employees left and to potentially improve compensation and other things in response. These personnel research reports were conducted at plants throughout the organization. Leveraging

Control Data technology, the HR function then developed one of the first automated systems for tracking compensation issues, constantly evaluating whether people in various positions were receiving competitive salaries, wages, and benefits. The members of the HR function also provided open communication channels between employees and the HR staff. The most important skill the HR staff members needed was the ability to listen. So the human resources staff used research, data measuring, and personal communication to stay ahead of the potential demands of employees, creating a proactive, rather than reactive, approach to employee relationships.

The other side of the employee relations see-saw was, of course, management. Line managers wanted rights to ensure work was getting done efficiently and profitably. To that end, the HR function also defined the following management rights. Managers had the right to:

- Define products
- Set schedules
- Control costs
- Make a profit
- Deal directly with employees rather than through unions

These management principles ensured every effort would be made to improve the economic health of Control Data. Management was in control of the strategic direction of line responsibilities, balancing the needs of employees with the needs of management. Managers had their own set of rights so they could do what they needed to accomplish within the organization. With this balanced approach, the company hoped to maintain a responsive, productive, and communicative relationship between management and employees.

Control Data publicly stated it was "pro-employee, not anti-union." Control Data was always vigilant about national and international compensation trends. Unions would occasionally try to organize one of the CDC plants, but Control Data responded by pointing out the competitive wages, benefits, and job security packages the company offered. As Ruth Rich explains, "Unions are created when management does not address employee needs." The HR function responded to these demands to counter the union proposal. So while it is true that Control Data successfully encouraged employees to voluntarily decide to not organize within their plants, the company was also directly influenced by union activities at other corporations. Though frustrated with Control Data, union leaders grudgingly admired the progressive, employee-first philosophy. A top union executive once privately told a CDC executive that if every corporation did as well for their employees as Control Data, there would no longer be a need for labor unions. By being a proactive company that continually worked at addressing employee needs, CDC could enjoy a direct relationship with its work force and likewise stay in control of its business strategies.

Recruiting College Knowledge

CONTROL DATA'S RAPID GROWTH during the 1960s-1970s meant the company had a great need for college graduates to fill a variety of positions. Control Data was creating positions for engineers, programmers, salespeople, business managers, and other young professionals at an accelerated pace. The company needed college-educated individuals to fill all aspects of the company's business, from designing and testing products, to manufacturing and distributing products, to then marketing these products and services to customers. The more qualified individuals Control Data could add to their workforce, the more profitable the company could become. However, Control Data was not alone in the hunt for these individuals. Other technology companies, like rival IBM, were actively recruiting college graduates for similar positions as well. It was a competitive era, and many college graduates had several job offers to consider after they received their diplomas.

To win over college recruits, the HR function launched its college relations program in 1959. This program was run by Eugene Baker, a young HR manager Berg had known at the Standard Oil Company, where they had worked together in a similar college recruiting program. This launched Baker's long career with Control Data (Baker later became the vice president of Human Resource Management Services in the 1970s). The company sent recruiters to a number of campuses and job fairs, presenting Control Data Corporation to soon-to-be and recent graduates. Control Data was a new, exciting company, and recruiters were able to convince many graduates to join the organization. Throughout the 1960s, the company was typically welcoming 400 to 450 new graduates a year as a result of the college recruitment program. Control Data had a competitive salary and benefits package, and since the company was growing so quickly, it was quite possible that young employees could advance rapidly to higher paying positions. Plus the compensation followed a "dual ladder for management/technical staff" policy—individuals who pursued a technical career would receive the same salary levels and benefits as individuals on the management track. This policy made the company especially attractive for engineers and programmers. As time went on, Control Data only grew more popular during the socially conscious 1970s, as the company's poverty-area plants and other social business ventures earned the respect of young people who shared these same concerns.

Recruiting college students to work for the organization was one challenge, and keeping these individuals within the company for extended periods of employment was yet another. A typical pattern for college recruits was they would work for a reputable company for two to three years to gain enough job experience to move on to a different company and a bigger salary. Luckily, Control Data's entrepreneurial culture and rapidly expanding business was challenging and stimulating, causing many college-educated individuals to share a large piece of their careers with Control Data. A personnel research report conducted in 1970 statistically demonstrated college-educated graduates had a lower level termination rate than employees without college degrees. The report came to this conclusion about retaining employees: "Control Data does not have as large a problem as other companies because it is a new company with many opportunities for advancement." This level of retention continued, as another employment study conducted in the 1980s discovered that seventy-five percent of the new graduates hired in 1960 were still working for Control Data Corporation in 1980. The HR function encouraged each new hire to become better than anyone else in a specific area of knowledge, skill, or ability, and "you'll never have to worry about job security." For many college graduates who joined the company, this promise turned out to be true for a large part of their careers.

Nonstop Education

INTERNAL EMPLOYEE TRAINING was also a key initiative strongly advocated and enforced by Control Data.

The better trained CDC employees were, the more knowledge and expertise they could provide through their roles. To support this effort, learning centers were built at facilities throughout the organization for the primary purpose of internal technology, process, and policy training. As new advances were made in the industry, all employees were required to spend a certain number of hours each month in these training programs. In this way, everyone was learning and growing in order to keep the company competitive. James O'Connell, a Control Data executive who worked in CDC's Washington government relations office, states this "sent a signal to the employee, questioning whether you were growing as a person in your role in the company." Though the time required for this training cut down productivity in their areas, Control Data felt it was in the best interests of the company to maintain an educated workforce with exceptional skills.

These training sessions were originally conducted with live instructors, but when PLATO terminals became available, the sessions were increasingly conducted through this early computer-based educational system. The flexibility of the PLATO terminals gave each employee access to individualized training on a schedule that worked best for them. Managers learned about new management techniques, engineers learned about new technologies, programmers honed their programming skills, and so on. Affirmative action and minority group awareness programs were included as part of the curriculum as well. By 1980, all Control Data managers averaged nearly forty-six hours of formal training and all new managers were required to attend a fifty-hour training program within the first three months of their employment. This learning center system was also used as a proof-of-concept initiative, as by leveraging PLATO, Control Data could demonstrate their educational technology in action to potential customers. While employees gained an education through the PLATO terminals, Control Data education service managers had a way to evaluate the effectiveness of their course materials. The next chapter details these computer-based education initiatives.

A Listening EAR

Appropriately enough, it started with a phone call.

When Norb Berg picked up the receiver, the person on the other end was frantic and distraught. Berg recognized who she was, a wife of a CDC executive. She was worried her husband's problems with drinking would ruin his career, his family, and ultimately their marriage. Could Control Data do something to help him overcome his alcoholism? Berg said they would surely try, and the phone conversation ended. He instructed his staff to arrange some private chemical dependency counseling for this individual. This incident got Berg thinking, however—how many other Control Data employees were being ruined by alcoholism? This disease could affect anyone. The cost to the employee and the employee's family was of course devastating, but the cost to Control Data was equally detrimental, because of both the loss of productivity and the likely loss of the employee. Statistics proved this was typically the case. Alcoholic individuals used group insurance benefits at a rate of three to four times more than what an average, non-addicted employee required. If alcohol dependent employees could break free from their addiction, it would benefit the employee, the employee's family, and ultimately CDC's bottom line in many tangible and intangible ways.

Control Data already had some alcohol-related initiatives in place. One was a free taxi service program. If employees were having a good time out on the town and became too intoxicated to drive, the HR function encouraged these individuals to instead call for a taxi service and get a ride home. These employees could then anonymously submit their receipts, and Control Data would reimburse them for the cab fare. The employee was never identified and no questions were asked. Bob Jones, an HR consultant who would become the prominent company expert on alcoholism, described this decision, saying, "We had some philosophical problems with the idea of paying taxi fares for drinkers. We don't want to encourage the abuse of alcohol. Our message still is if you drive, don't drink. But we recognize the reality that people may sometimes be in a condition not to drive." Another initiative was a no-alcohol reimbursement policy for all business functions. This policy was implemented in response to a tragedy. A Control Data auditor was on a business trip in Oklahoma City, had gotten drunk, and was killed later in a car accident. These policies were attempts by the HR function to reduce drunken driving fatalities, but neither initiative directly addressed alcoholism as a disease.

The HR function did have a "three strikes" policy toward alcohol dependency and treatment. If an alcoholic employee went into treatment, Control Data would hold the person's job while the person received care. Recognizing it might be necessary for an addicted individual to receive multiple treatments to break free from dependency, the company would hold the employee's job three times. If the employee could not stay sober after the third treatment, however, Control Data would terminate the individual. These interventions for treatment were always held as a last chance meeting to save the addicted employee's job. If the afflicted individual resumed the addiction after the second round of treatment, the HR function would go so far as to set up interventions between addicted employees and their families. In one case, the HR function held an intervention for a senior-level manager. This manager told the HR representative who initiated the intervention that he would someday kill the HR representative. Once this manager had completed his treatments, though, he apologized to this HR representative and thanked him for setting up the intervention. This "three strikes" policy defined the company's benevolence and its limits, but other than cases of extreme intervention, it did not directly give the employee tools for combating alcoholism.

The distraught wife's phone call crystallized the issue for Berg. Control Data needed an alcoholism program. Berg tasked the HR function to create such a treatment program and make it available to all employees. In order to launch a successful program that would make an impact, they needed someone with expertise in chemical addiction who understood how to build such a program. Bob Jones was an HR manager within the marketing organization, but he also had an interest in alcoholism. Bob Jones was reassigned to lead this initiative, and he created a complete alcoholics phone helpline system. On November 1, 1972, the HR function announced an "alcohol program," a service where employees could call in and receive the support they needed to combat their addiction to alcohol. Control Data would act as the intermediary, connecting employees with counseling services and alcohol treatment facilities. If all went well, the troubled employee would overcome the addiction and the company would realize reduced health care costs and improved productivity, as the afflicted employee would return to the job. This phone service was included as a supplemental offering as part of a new employee counseling service administered by the employee social problems coordinator. Employees could call into this service for a variety of issues, with alcoholic dependency being one of its primary purposes. The initiative seemed a win-win, value-added human resource service idea—another Control Data innovation expected to yield successful results.

Unfortunately, results proved otherwise. During the alcohol program's first year of operation, Control Data received only thirteen contacts from employees with alcohol addictions. And the total call volume for the overall services phone line was a dismal average of twenty calls a month. Likewise, few callers directly contacted the counselors hired by CDC to be front-line resource for these employees. Something was clearly wrong with the concept. After some research, the main reason for these poor results became apparent. Employees were uncomfortable about contacting Control Data directly about their addiction to alcohol. Bob Jones later stated, "Very little business was achieved partially because of the reluctance of the employees to expose their problems to people who also kept their personnel files." These individuals did not want to admit alcoholism to their employer, as they feared they would lose their jobs. In fact, they had little motivation to use the service at all—except as a last resort. The other problem was the narrow focus of the program. Alcoholism was only one of many drugs that could be abused, and troubled employees faced other difficulties, such as marital conflict, financial issues, and mental health complications. Control Data's experiences of working with employees at the poverty-area plants also demonstrated that, despite the willingness and ability of the employee, problems outside the job could have a negative economic impact on productivity and efficiency.

Problems on the job were equally worrisome. Although Control Data had a grievance procedure, it was basically ineffective at resolving actual grievances. Management controlled this system, and if the managers decided they wanted to bury an issue from their upper line managers to keep it from escalating and reflecting on their leadership, the lower-level managers could easily do so. Lower-level managers frequently did this to grievance incidents, as they had little motivation to support employees. In some facilities, their actions were effectively nullifying the grievance system.

Another troubling statistic was the number of recent suicides within the Control Data community. During the years 1969-1973, twenty people, either employees or their family members, had committed suicide. Although the common attitude was that employees left their problems at home before they came to work, in reality this assumption was a fallacy. A company hired the entire person, and it was foolhardy to assume problems at home would not also eventually cause problems on the job. As Ruth Rich, a former Control Data HR executive, states, "You can't assume that their lives won't impact their work; you have to look at the whole person." Perhaps a comprehensive service could be developed to assist employees with a range of issues. This in turn could result in even greater savings for CDC in health care costs, reduced employee turnover, and ultimately increased bottom-line productivity. The alcohol program was not implemented correctly, nor did it go far enough. A concept was out there that would work better, but what was it?

Another company was experimenting with a similar employee assistance concept. The Kennecott Copper Mining Company in Salt Lake City, Utah, was achieving good results with their Insight program. Jim Morris, an HR executive, accompanied Bob Jones on a trip to visit Kennecott Copper Mining and learn more about this company's employee program. Otto Jones was the Kennecott social worker who ran Insight, and Bob Jones and Jim Morris met with him and other members of the HR staff. One of the main principles of this program was all employee contacts made through the service would be kept confidential, away from their employment records. As the Kennecott HR managers described, ". . . many employees saw the counseling program as a preferable alternative to filing grievances with their unions." This philosophy fit well in Control Data's pro-employee strategy of addressing employee needs before unions interceded. Several principles of the Insight counseling program also complemented the principles provided through an ombudsman-type service, particularly in its approach to providing a means for workers to anonymously call the service for work-related grievances, improving work conditions and relationships between managers and workers. What further intrigued Jones and Morris was the Kennecott program had saved more than $500,000 from reduced health care costs, absenteeism, and employee turnover—an impressive return on an initial $90,000 investment. If Control Data could create a similar program, the overall cost savings alone would make the program well worth the effort.

The comprehensive employee assistance program was beginning to take shape. A key Control Data individual, highly instrumental during these early design stages, was Norma Anderson. She was the counselor in charge of the counseling service at the Northside plant. As described in the previous chapter, the purpose of this counseling service was to help transition Northside workers from their previously unemployed lifestyles into workforce culture. Besides having a deep understanding about the problems facing troubled employees, she also had direct knowledge about assistance agencies available both locally in the Twin Cities and nationally through government and private agencies. Pieces of the new program were fitting together into a complete, exciting new concept for an employee support service.

Confidentiality evolved as the key concept. The success of Kennecott Copper Mining's program was the employee could contact the service anonymously if desired, ensuring this employee did not have to fear an immediate supervisor would find out about an issue and use it as grounds for termination. Control Data would follow this same principle, making sure there was never a breach of confidentiality; the people involved at both ends of the conversation would be anonymous to each other if desired by the employee. The phone counselor would then link the individual to targeted resources so the individual could cope with the issue. The list of issues the service would tackle was enormous, but if the service had the right mix of staff, most employee issues could be addressed.

As the HR manager with the most experience and knowledge about alcohol addiction, Bob Jones became a key architect for the new service. He taught the rest of the design team that chemical dependency was often the warning sign for deeper, more personal problems. Resolving the chemical dependency would only help partway; additional services would likely be needed to completely rehabilitate a troubled employee. With that concept in mind, the design team described the program proposal in this way, "Control Data will provide a service to U.S. employees which will allow them to discuss personal problems and obtain assistance in solving these problems. This assistance may be in the form of help in processing a grievance through the grievance procedure, in personal counseling to deal with the roots of a personal problem, or referral to community resources which specialize in solving the particular problems an employee or a member of his/her family might have."

The last ingredient in the mix was, not surprisingly, Control Data technology. The mainframe computer system could be set up with a separate database that recorded employee calls, away from the corporate database that held sensitive human resource employee records. This call data would be kept under lock and key, separate from employee records. The name for the new service was also very important. The social venture was appropriately christened the Employee Advisory Resource, or EAR, a service which provided employees with a listening "ear" that would hear their problems and offer constructive solutions to them.

Within the human resources function, some HR staff members expressed concerns about the impact this program might have on staff positions. The service would take away some

HR responsibilities by reorganizing how counseling and employee advocacy functions were typically handled by human resources. Would this cause the loss of some HR employees? What would be Control Data's legal obligations? Plus, as Berg recalls, "Some colleagues told me that EAR was an outright admission that our employee relations system was inadequate. I agreed. We're not perfect. We have holes in our system and people get hurt or don't get the help they need." All of these concerns were considered, but the possible benefits overshadowed the possible risks. The costs in dealing with employee issues could not be ignored. In 1973, Control Data had a workforce of around 26,000 employees, and a percentage of these individuals would incur significant health costs and a subset of this group would eventually no longer work for the company. This would cause a loss of intellectual capital and skills that would take time, effort, and expense to resolve. The potential EAR had in both reducing company costs and doing good for employees outweighed the negatives of not taking on such an initiative. The employee assistance service would be launched, as so many Control Data initiatives were, in the spirit of enlightened self-interest. Control Data could potentially, by doing good for its workers, do good for the corporation as well. The Employee Advisory Resource took shape. It was the first comprehensive employee assistance program developed in the United States that dealt with both personal and work-related problems.

The primary individuals in charge for managing EAR were selected. Jim Morris and Bob Jones, the HR team members who had visited Kennecott Copper Mining, both assumed leadership positions. Morris became EAR's first general manager, while Bob Jones became the service's first chemical dependency counselor. Norma Anderson continued in her role as the leader of the Northside employee counseling program, but she was also available to provide referral connections to outside resources as needed. Another early leader of EAR was John Moe, a work problems ombudsman who had a background in HR relations. All these individuals ultimately reported to Richard Conner, now back from his six-month sabbatical at the Stillwater prison. Conner would oversee the developing project. The EAR management structure was in place.

The last ingredient the employee service needed was an experienced staff of phone counselors who would answer the front line calls. Norma Anderson and Bob Jones hired six phone counselors from Youth Emergency Services (YES) and the Crisis Intervention Center (CIC). These community services were integral in giving Control Data much-needed advice during EAR's development, and Control Data continued the relationship by leveraging their expertise as an employment resource. These six individuals were clearly not cut in the corporate mold. With their long hair, blue jeans, t-shirts, and other non-corporate attire, the phone counselors really stood out as they walked through a multi-national corporate headquarters filled with individuals wearing conservative business suits and closely cropped hair. As Jim Morris recalls, "They were skeptical about being corporate people. But these counselors taught us the ropes of phone counseling, and we taught them the ropes of corporate life." (Eventually this group would all decide to become regular Control Data employees.) Bob Jones, the counselor specializing in chemical dependency, would manage the six part-time phone counselors and the telephone center. Employee Advisory Resource now had a complete staff.

Employee Advisory Resource was promoted internally through *Contact*, the CDC employee publication newsletter. EAR posters were also permanently installed on all CDC facility bulletin boards. To ensure the entire domestic CDC community knew about the service, each Control Data employee directly received, through their home mail, a brochure about the program. This brochure described the services Employee Advisory Resource would make available. The information it contained emphasized it was a confidential support service; no records would be placed with the employee's personnel records. EAR was a new addition to each employee's total compensation plan, provided free of charge to all CDC employees as a thank you for their hard work in helping build the company. To complete each brochure, a pocket on the inside cover contained a small, red phonograph record. This record featured Dave Moore, a popular Twin Cities area television newscaster, interviewing Norb Berg about the service. Control Data used this interview to formally announce EAR, welcome employees to the service, and describe the support package it would soon provide. The finishing promotional touch arrived soon after the brochure. Each employee received a follow-up letter and a wallet-sized card that displayed EAR's phone number. EAR was now formally announced and each employee had the direct contact information they needed to use the service. The concept behind Employee Advisory Resource would soon be put to the test.

On April 8, 1974, the phone lines switched on and Employee Advisory Resource began. Would CDC employees use the service? The answer was a solid yes. Almost immediately, the phones began to ring from employees across the United States. By the end of that first month, EAR already had either phone or direct contact with 219 clients. Eight months later, over 1,500 people had requested some level of assistance from the Employee Advisory Resource. And, in stark contrast to the alcohol program that had helped only thirteen problem drinkers, 107 problem drinkers received treatment for their alcoholism during a single year of this new program. The internal system for handling the case load worked brilliantly. The telephone counselors ran the front line, resolving as many issues as they could through one-on-one interaction. If they were unable to resolve the issue, the caller was referred to one of the full-time, in-house staff counselors. Then if the counselor was unable to resolve the situation, the caller was referred to a state, community, or church organization that specialized in handling the specific issue. When Control Data discovered community resources were lacking in a particular area, the company would eventually hire an in-house specialist to address these issues. Additionally, Control Data developed a panel of outside consultants in medical, psychological, and legal areas that advised EAR; these consultants would also potentially receive client referrals directly from the service.

To make sure Employee Advisory Resource functioned independently within the overall organization, EAR became the first service administrated by Human Resource Management Services. This internal organization only reported to the human resources function, keeping EAR free from directly reporting to senior managers within the line organization. This meant

EAR counselors could act as independent agents throughout Control Data, assisting employees as needed to resolve personal and job-related problems without reporting these issues to line managers and senior executives. This structure gave EAR internal autonomy within Control Data's reporting hierarchy, allowing the service to have a set of records separate from employee job performance reviews. Through this organizational structure, Human Resource Management Services could keep EAR's records confidential. Employees would then be more likely to contact Employee Advisory Resource and openly discuss their issues. This independent structure turned into a win-win for both managers and employees, as many problems could be resolved through EAR before they became disruptive in the work environment.

At first the Employee Advisory Resource was only available twelve hours a day between 7:00 A.M. and 7:00 P.M. Not surprisingly, many issues the EAR team received were job-related issues such as worker difficulties with supervisors, and in turn, supervisor difficulties with workers. The number of work-related issues rapidly became overwhelming, and EAR hired additional phone counselors and expanded into a complete twenty-four-hour call-in hotline. The twenty-four-hour service was run through the communications technology available at the time. After-hours phone calls made to the EAR telephone room were automatically re-routed to an on-call service that would ring on a counselor's home telephone. Because pager technology was not yet developed, the on-call counselor was required to stay at home to receive any calls that might come into EAR. The EAR phone counselors would alternate weeks being on-call at home, tackling EAR calls in the evenings and throughout the night as needed. Appropriately enough, Bob Jones was actually the counselor on call for EAR's first time after-hours client. Deep in sleep, he received this phone call at one thirty in the morning. The message informed him to call an HR vice president at home immediately, which Bob did. The HR vice president had recently been awakened by a frantic call from a general manager who had just sobered up and found himself in jail. This general manager wanted help with his alcohol problem. EAR got him the help he needed.

During these first few years, Employee Advisory Resource emphasized short-term counseling either over the phone or through private interviews. Typically employees dealing with work-related issues, chemical dependency, and other issues were referred to existing community agencies better equipped to handle such issues. As Jim Morris described in a Minneapolis *Tribune* article about the service, "Our job is to make a gross evaluation, and often what starts out something like a marital or job related problem might turn out to have deeper roots in, say alcoholism—and then to find the help that is needed." The service also stayed true to its pledge of confidentiality. Employee names were not used in direct reporting; these calls were kept in confidential files never released outside of EAR. This confidential data also became important for research the EAR staff conducted, as it was used to measure the effectiveness of the counseling the troubled employees received. These studies were essentially a temperature test during these first years, demonstrating EAR was saving Control Data substantial amounts of money while simultaneously earning the employees' respect.

Demand for EAR's services continued to grow, so the EAR staff expanded during its second year, 1975, by adding financial and legal services. A financial counselor from Commercial Credit joined the staff, giving EAR another area of badly needed assistance. This individual helped Control Data employees resolve payroll and budget problems, answer credit questions, maintain emergency travel funds, and handle Commercial Credit loan requests. If an employee had to make an unforeseen trip because of an ill relative, funeral, or other family emergency, the financial counselor was authorized to make funds available through a travel account. During the rest of the 1970s, EAR gave out forty-six emergency travel advances, and arranged for re-payment through voluntary wage deductions.

Other pay advances were handled through EAR as needed. The financial counselor arranged voluntary wage deductions, through which payroll would deduct specific amounts each payday from employee checks to help the employee repay these debts. During the years 1976-1979, over 3,800 financial counseling cases were handled through EAR. The legal services EAR added in 1975 were also highly beneficial. Similar to what they were doing for the Northside plant, the Twin Cities-based Oppenheimer law firm supported Employee Advisory Resource with any legal services requested by the EAR clients. Attorneys from this law firm were available at the Employee Advisory Resource office two afternoons each week to do pro bono legal coun-seling. During this time period, they were available to answer basic legal questions, refer clients to other resources, and help resolve legal questions the EAR staff encountered during their day-to-day contact with employees.

By the third year, a second Employee Advisory Resource office began operations. The Commercial Credit Corporation opened its own EAR office, located at this company's Baltimore headquarters. Two counselors were available to listen and assist Commercial Credit employees, and the service soon averaged between sixty and seventy calls per month. To handle this demand, a third counselor was added to the Commercial Credit EAR staff in 1978.

Meanwhile, a clinical psychologist joined the EAR staff at Control Data headquarters in Bloomington, making the service better able to handle mental health care issues and provide additional support for the chemical dependency caseload. As the EAR team gained experience, the service began expanding its offerings through other means. Based on the knowledge gath-ered by EAR while handling issues of chemical dependency, a four-hour training seminar on alcoholism for CDC managers was developed. This seminar was conducted hundreds of times over a three-year period across the company, and it was soon turned into a PLATO courseware offering. A companion PLATO course was also created to assist people involved in a relation-ship with a chemically dependent person. Two videotapes were created from these courses, additional tools that could be used with the PLATO courseware or leveraged independently as an additional teaching tool for seminars. And while these PLATO courses were originally developed for Control Data employees, they soon were sold externally to public and private rehabilitation centers.

A significant number of those calling EAR also came from disabled employees on temporary or permanent medical leave, so in 1976, a rehabilitation counselor was added to the EAR staff. The objectives for this person were defined as the following:

1. Expedite a disabled employee's return to work by providing the necessary and appropriate rehabilitation services.
2. Ensure that a disabled person returning to work does not perform a job detrimental to his or her health.
3. Provide assistance to HR departments in modifying work assignments so work related accidents could be minimized.

One of the key roles for the rehabilitation counselor was to encourage employees on medical leave to continue their association with Control Data in the hope they could return to active, full-time employment. Principles were established to help make temporary and permanent disability less dehumanizing for the individual. EAR also began to research ways in which occupationally injured employees could return to work at the earliest possible date, and what additional services injured employees needed to minimize the effect of their disability and period of recuperation. By the end of the first year of the EAR rehabilitation service, 121 clients were given such assistance. A study was done on sixteen of these clients, and the results estimated Control Data saved approximately $300,000 through efficient use of resources and more rapid recovery times for the rehabilitated employees. The next year in 1977, the total caseload increased to 181 clients, with an overall cost benefit of $264,000. EAR had added another crucial area of responsibility and expertise to its offerings.

By the end of its first decade, Employee Advisory Resource was averaging over 500 calls per month. A trained staff of twenty-six full- and part-time counselors was now available to handle contacts from the domestic workforce. CDC expanded the service to support international employees, opening EAR offices in the United Kingdom, France, and Holland in 1980, and then in South Africa in 1981. An office was also opened later in Mexico. Unfortunately the word "EAR" was Spanish vernacular for "snitch," so the name of the service was changed in this locale to clarify the purpose of the employee assistance program. One by one, EAR offices opened in many international offices. EAR was now effectively available to nearly every Control Data employee throughout the entire international organization.

Employee Advisory Resource was making a deep impact improving the lives of Control Data employees. In 1975, a Minneapolis *Tribune* article described the program, highlighting the experience of Michelle. She was a twenty-year-old Control Data employee who had taken an overdose of barbiturates and alcohol, but had fortunately called a friend before the overdose could end her life. This was not Michelle's first encounter with EAR. "They'd gotten me into treatment before and all I'd done was lie to them. I wasn't really buying it—just going along to get everybody off my back and save my job," she said. Bob Jones showed up at the hospital any-way, helping her work through her treatment plan and break the cycle of chemical abuse. As Michelle remarked, "I just couldn't believe that a company this large would care about one in-dividual." The article concluded her story by stating she was back to work at Control Data again with no mention of her problems added to her personnel record. She was, in fact, aspiring to advance to a job position with more responsibility.

Often the EAR call center was alive with a variety of phone conversations. During one evening, a counselor was involved in an intense conversation, trying to prevent an employee from committing suicide, while at the same time another counselor was helping an employee locate a Santa Claus suit for a company Christmas party. EAR was not limited to helping just employees, as the service was often instrumental in assisting employees with family issues. In Kansas, an employee had a young daughter with hearing issues. The EAR staff was able to locate a doctor who specialized in addressing this specific hearing aliment, and the girl received the health care she needed. EAR was also instrumental in discovering positive or negative employee reactions to corporate-wide decisions which normally company management would not hear. Due to a downturn in the economy in 1974, Control Data decided to implement a ten percent pay cut across the entire organization. The executives asked various line managers what the em-ployee reaction was to this significant reduction, and the line managers responded that overall their employees were highly supportive of the move. However, the story that came from the EAR telephone room was significantly different. Many employees called and complained about what the ten percent pay cut would do to their livelihoods, a fact they were not willing to discuss openly with their managers. Through their anonymous ties to the CDC workforce, EAR was able to provide real, more accurate feedback to senior management about what the pay reduction actually meant to CDC employee relations.

While all these real-life results of jobs retained and lives saved were worth the cost of the service, Employee Advisory Resource was also improving the organization's bottom line. During the 1970s, it cost Control Data approximately $2,500 to hire and train a new employee. In contrast, EAR averaged costs of $1,500-$2,000 per recovery case, saving the company nearly $1,000 per each employee who was able to return to their position. Before EAR, the suicide rate among employees was five per year. During the first three years of EAR, there was not a single case of suicide, and despite the growing workforce throughout the 1970s and early 1980s, suicides were greatly reduced during the rest of Control Data's existence.

An evaluation of EAR was conducted in 1987, exploring employee usage of the service and the impact to costs incurred by the service. At this point, EAR had been in operation for thirteen years, and the service had amassed a significant quantity of data. The evaluation focused on data gathered between the years 1980-1985; altogether 635,000 electronic records from human resources, EAR, and health claim files were evaluated and compared to each other to arrive at the study results. And following EAR policy, employee ID numbers were encrypted on each record through an external vendor to preserve the anonymity of EAR clients. The study concluded, "EAR is associated with substantial medical cost savings in the area of chemical dependency, estimated at $10,200 per EAR intervention over the expected term of employment." Overall, the combined reductions in chemical dependency interventions per year was $635,000, the annual savings from reduced medical claims was $282,000, and the value of EAR interventions in reducing absenteeism was evaluated at $158,000 each fiscal year. With over a million dollars in savings gained after EAR costs, the study concluded Control Data was saving twenty-nine dollars per year for each employee (based on the total employee population at the time, averaging around 50,000). This cost savings was not a "soft" data statistic; these savings were based on actual hard data. Thanks to EAR, Control Data was saving millions in employee costs, while at the same time maintaining a healthier, more stable work force.

In 1977, Control Data was selected by the Mental Health Association and the President's Committee on Employment of the Handicapped (PCEH) to receive the Mental Health Employer of the Year award in recognition for the benefits achieved through EAR. Employee Advisory Resource had grown into a well-regarded, multi-faceted employee mental health program that succeeded in its goals. That naturally led Control Data managers to ask the next question: would external companies be willing to pay for such a service? Control Data began marketing EAR to other corporations, emphasizing the cost savings and employee satisfaction that could be gained through implementing the service. The marketing effort paid off. The Bondhus Tool Company, a manufacturer located in Montevideo, Minnesota, bought a contract from Control Data for EAR services. This purchase marked the start of a new nationwide services industry. Many companies began purchasing EAR contracts, and by the mid-1980s, the service was supporting 250,000 employees from 155 different organizations. Employee Advisory Resource became a profit center for CDC, providing $3 million each year in annual revenue. Other companies now saw the business opportunity EAR represented, and competitors began developing and marketing their own employee advisory programs.

To advance the work of this growing business sector, the company's expertise was sought after by human resource advocacy organizations. John Moe, now the second general manager of EAR, joined Norbert Berg to co-author a chapter in the 1978 *PAIR Policy and Program Management* publication. Within this chapter, they describe the reasons for developing an employee assistance service, writing, ". . . on the one hand there are the costs of implementing and maintaining the program, but against these on the other hand, are the costs of not implementing an assistance program." They describe the EAR's approach, explaining, "The troubled employee is best defined as an individual who has unresolved personal or work-related problems . . . The context is the ever-changing environment in which the work functions . . . Vulnerability can be defined as the person's inability to cope with the environment and still keep functioning. It is when these three factors overlap the troubled employee appears." Because of the detrimental effects a troubled employee has on an organization, the article further describes how a company should implement the program, by explaining its purpose in detail to company managers in order to ensure high-level support. Internal politics and reporting structures should not interfere with the most efficient means to implement the employee assistance service. If the company employed workers who were union members, ". . . management and union leadership must decide how to handle job-related problems identified as a result of the program."

The concepts of the modern employee advisory providors (or EAP) were now becoming a thoroughly entrenched, accepted part of American corporate culture. As Berg and Moe's chapter on Employee Advisory Resource concluded, "The value of the employee assistance concept is demonstrated by the fairly rapid growth of employee assistance programs in a relatively short period of time." A new industry emerged within the United States, as competing employee services were spreading rapidly as an ethical, cost-effective way of conducting business and maintaining productive employee relations. It all began with EAR.

Peer Pressure

FROM THE DAY THE FIRST manufacturing center opened and workers started assembly on their first mainframe computer, the HR function focused on developing a just and equitable workplace. To encourage a just environment, the company set up a grievance system so employees at all positions in the company—mangers, assemblers, clerical staff, and so on—would have an avenue to resolve work place conflicts. Its purpose was to provide a systematic approach to resolving issues internally so employees would not resort to an outside intermediary, such as a lawyer or union representative, to negotiate with the company. This system was designed with a simple, up-the-chain structure through which, if needed, employees could escalate issues. The grievance system worked as follows:

1. The employee would first speak with the immediate manager to resolve the issue.
2. If the employee was not satisfied with the immediate manager's decision, the HR representative at that facility would help the person move the issue up the management chain—to higher and higher managers until the employee was either satisfied or received a final decision from upper-level management.

This system remained the primary method of handling grievance issues during the first fifteen years of Control Data's history. This system worked very well as long as managers were genuinely interested in actively and honestly supporting it. As discussed previously, however, by the early 1970s serious problems with the grievance system emerged. Because the first level of the system was administered directly by managers, they could, if they wished, prevent grievances from advancing to the HR function for further resolution. This situation grew increasingly untenable. For employees who found themselves in difficult situations on the job, the Control

Data principle of justice and fairness became a hollow promise, and they were not pleased. Eventually some employees completely bypassed the grievance system and wrote letters of complaint directly to Bill Norris. After Norris reviewed these letters, and he would be disturbed by many of them, these letters would cascade down through the management chain and eventually end up on the HR manager's desk. Only then could the HR manager act to resolve the situation through the grievance process. Members of the HR function did not want to include Bill Norris in resolving these issues, so the system needed to change.

While combating chemical dependency was the original impulse for Employee Advisory Resource, this increasingly unsatisfactory grievance system was another motivating factor. When EAR was launched, a work-related problems counselor, John Moe, was included as a full-time member of the counseling staff. Almost half of the first calls to EAR were for work-related problems, and this statistic remained consistent throughout the years Employee Advisory Resource was implemented by CDC. Employees now had a direct means to place a grievance to the HR function and receive the counseling they needed. Managers were no longer filtering issues, and the additional structure to the grievance system worked much, much better. (Perhaps best of all for HR managers, Bill Norris stopped receiving letters of complaint.) To handle work-related problems, the EAR counselors followed a four-step system to make sure all work-related issues were handled consistently and fairly. The four steps were as follows:

1. Define the problem and repeat it back to the client for clarification and confirmation.
2. Establish what has been done so far—has the problem been discussed with the client's supervisor or HR department?
3. Describe the grievance system to the client, so the client understands the work problems policy and procedure.
4. Discuss with the client how to use the grievance system and facilitate an active plan for the aggrieved client to follow.

As much as possible, the EAR counselors encouraged the employees to leverage the grievance system first, and this approach helped restore the grievance system to better effectiveness.

If the grievance system failed to address the issue, EAR developed an additional function to help resolve work-related difficulties. One of the full-time EAR counselors would also function as an arbitrator, or ombudsman, between the conflicting parties. Directly influenced by the ombudsman concept facilitated by Richard Conner at the Stillwater Correctional Facility, the ombudsman for EAR reviewed the complaint and then guided the parties involved to resolve the conflict as equitably as possible. Together, with this arbitrator evaluating the issue, an amicable settlement could typically be reached. The ombudsman would focus on fighting for a middle ground fair to both the company and affected employees.

The ombudsman was a much-needed component the previous grievance system had lacked, as this person was a disinterested referee whose only motivation was to find common ground. The ombudsman advocated the standards of resolution between the parties, and was not positioned to favor one side over the other. Most workplace conflicts could now be diffused before they erupted to the point of a discrimination or wrongful termination lawsuit. While the ombudsman function was designed to help the employee, it also was another example of the HR function innovating in the spirit of "enlightened self-interest" for the company's bottom line. The cost of an ombudsman program was far less than the cost of a lengthy, expensive court battle. Typically the results the employee gained by the ombudsman were better than the results of a court decision, so this arbitration program was in the best interests for the employee as well. If the issue was resolved satisfactorily, the employee would most likely continue working for Control Data, preventing the loss of talent and skills. The amount of money the ombudsman saved the company throughout the 1970s and 1980s is impossible to estimate, but clearly substantial losses were avoided every year.

However, as the 1970s moved along, even the ombudsman confronted situations too thorny to resolve. In some cases, the employee had exhausted all available channels through the grievance system and also was not satisfied with the recommendations of the ombudsman, and so the individual continued to press the grievance. To keep ahead of these situations, the HR function began exploring more innovations to add to the grievance system. The main aspect of the process which was troubling for employees was that, at every level, they were still working with Control Data managers—whether through their department line managers or the HR managers. The viewpoints of these individuals, despite trying to be fair, would still have a tendency to be more loyal to other managers involved in the dispute. The EAR ombudsman was a more balanced arbitrator, but this individual advocated for the system, and the system was set up to ultimately help the company. A more objective method was needed that would satisfy the employee's desire to see the issue resolved justly and competently.

The Employee Advisory Resource staff set up a task force to create a final internal level of arbitration. Leading this task force was Fred Olson, the director of work problems counseling and international programs for EAR. Throughout the last half of 1982 to the early months of 1983, this task force explored a number of ideas and proposals. The main idea that emerged was some type of panel review would be the best model for a final, binding level of arbitration. To avoid management from having too much influence over this panel process, the task force decided this arbitration panel should primarily consist of peer individuals who would potentially have a better grasp of the situation facing the employee. In order to set up such a panel to be fair to both the employee and the company, the human resources staff would select two peer level employees, individuals who worked within the same job family at a grade level or slightly higher equivalent as the aggrieved employee. They did this by choosing two employees through a random nationwide search from a computer-generated list.

To round out the panel and ensure a final decision, a third individual would also be randomly selected through a computer-generated list. This individual would be a disinterested executive whose role was to provide a corporate perspective on the situation. The majority vote of the three individuals would prevail. Because of this, the power to decide for or against the grievances was placed totally in the hands of the peer employees, as they made up the majority voting block on the panel. This new level of arbitration was called Peer Review, and the three-member group made up a peer panel. Now if a grievance situation required it, a peer panel could be assembled and charged with reaching a final resolution for the grievance. The Peer Review process was formally announced throughout the United States workforce in February of 1983.

The grievance system now had additional steps that led up to final arbitration to the peer panel. The steps for the revised grievance process were:

1. Discuss your issue with your immediate manager.
2. If not happy with the manager's solution, contact your HR manager to help work out a different resolution.
3. If this decision fails to resolve the issue, instruct your HR manager to escalate the grievance to the person identified as "the focus of power" in your specific job line situation.
4. The HR manager writes up your grievance as a report, verifying the report accurately communicates the issue.
5. The local upper-level management reviews your grievance report and suggests a resolution.
6. If you are still not satisfied with the resolution, you may ask for a peer review.
7. The responsibility for the grievance process now shifts to Employee Advisory Resource. The EAR ombudsman helps the aggrieved employee complete the written presentation, assembles the members of the peer review panel, and guides it through deliberations as a non-voting chairperson.
8. The peer panel votes on a resolution.
9. Hold a meeting with the corporate vice president of HR. If the Peer Review resolved the case, the corporate vice president approves the resolution. This resolution is final and binding.
10. If in the very rare outcome that the peer review panel could not agree on a result, the corporate vice president then makes a final decision (this step was mostly unused in the process).

The system was in place and soon would be put into action. Would the peer review process satisfy employee grievances? In an article Fred Olson wrote for the *Harvard Business Review* entitled "How Peer Review Works," he describes the first case resolved by a peer panel.

This case occurred in May 1983, and it was a conflict over how a plant manager applied a performance improvement program against a lower-level department manager. Division executives had reviewed the performance of this department manager and decided the work of his department was satisfactory. The plant manager, however, blamed him for cost overruns and several other problems and placed him on a two-month performance improvement plan. When the two-month performance plan ended, the plant manager extended the performance period without explaining what was unsatisfactory about the department manager's performance. The department manager became convinced the plant manager was trying to get rid of him, so he in turn refused to sign the plan or even respond to it. The plant manager stated this was more evidence of uncooperative behavior, and he immediately fired the department manager.

At this point, human resources became involved and the grievance program was put into action. Because the plant manager was both his boss and "the focus of power" within this division of the company, the situation went quickly through the first few steps of the grievance process. The HR manager arranged for a grievance meeting at the plant between the aggrieved manager and the plant manager, but no common ground was found and the job termination continued. The situation was then moved up to the executive in charge of the plant, and this executive upheld the decision of the plant manager. The department manager now had exhausted the options within the plant leadership hierarchy, so he turned to Employee Advisory Resource, requesting a peer review. The EAR ombudsman first tried to mediate between the parties, but these meetings failed to change the situation. The plant manager strongly felt the department manager could not handle his job. The last remaining recourse the department manager had was a peer review. As Fred Olsen relates, "We then assembled the materials and called together a board. The board found for the aggrieved manager. Accordingly, he was reinstated and given additional training, since he acknowledged that there were areas where his performance could be improved." The process worked, ruling in favor, at least in this situation, for the aggrieved employee.

Because this first case of peer review restored the department manager to his job, Control Data employees and managers suddenly took notice that peer review was a recourse with serious consequences. When the next peer review case also went in favor of the complainant, some executives became concerned peer review would prevent management from effectively managing their line organizations. "Fortunately, the careful deliberations of the first two boards indicated that whatever the outcome," Olson writes, "panel members were serious about getting at the facts and making the right decision." Monitored by the ombudsman, the debate within the panels was always very calm and thoughtful. A losing panel member often felt a need to explain his or her decision, and HR requested these positions as part of the feedback of the entire process. However, many executives were wary about peer review until the third case, one which went against the complainant in favor of management's position. The peer review process was now viewed, at least by the majority of CDC executives and managers, as an important last step in resolving on-the-job conflict.

As the second year of Peer Review ended in 1984, eleven cases had been escalated to the peer review stage. The statistics of these cases demonstrated the concept was a credible means of resolving conflict. Of these eleven cases, four were decided in favor of the aggrieved employee. In these four, two were unanimous decisions; in the other two cases, the peer employees outvoted the executive in favor of the grievant. Of the seven cases ruled in favor of management, six of these cases were unanimous decisions. During the seventh case, one of the peer employees sided with the executive in supporting the original management decision. Not surprisingly, nine of the eleven cases involved a grievance over job termination.

Peer Review became a permanent part of the Control Data grievance process. Peer review cases continued to appear periodically, resolving the most difficult work-based problems. The decisions of each peer review were implemented quickly and were also publicized in the management newsletter, but the individuals involved in the grievance case were not identified. Peer Review had other positive side effects, as plant and department managers began to aggressively and fairly resolve problems before they escalated to the peer review level (coincidently, in one HR survey, middle managers asserted that Peer Review was not needed.) Assembly workers and other non-management employees felt they now had a solid way to fight against arbitrary management decisions. Corporate leaders were also very pleased with the peer review process, as they believed it prevented litigation. The grievance process created during the early days of Control Data had now fully evolved and matured to satisfy its initial promise.

Better Health, Better Life

CONTROL DATA CONTINUALLY EXPLORED ways the company could help employees improve themselves. One of the company's primary concerns was safety. During the first years seat belts were introduced in cars, few people regularly wore them. Even though several public service campaigns were launched to encourage seat belt use, most drivers felt they were a nuisance. Human resource managers wanted to encourage CDC employees to wear seat belts everyday when they came to and from work. A variety of methods were used to calculate how many drivers were wearing seat belts. The results of this analysis were disappointing—only sixteen percent of employees buckled up. The company used this percentage when it launched a public relations campaign, directed at all employees, advocating the use of seat belts.

As the 1970s continued, an issue gaining more and more national attention was the overall state of employee health. People increasingly worked sedentary jobs behind desks and were not getting much-needed exercise. Meanwhile, fast food restaurants became more common, springing up near office parks and providing cheap, high-caloric meals to these sedentary employees. And more often than not, these employees were trying to beat stressful deadlines—many relieving this stress by taking frequent smoke breaks with their favorite brand of cigarettes.

This state of affairs was bad for both employees and corporations. The employee's lifestyles often led to serious health-related problems, hurting productivity and sometimes ending careers prematurely through chronic illness or death. Health care expenditures for corporations were also rising due to the rapid advance of medical technologies. These new technologies offered cutting edge, effective treatments for patients, but these treatments also came at a higher cost—causing insurance premiums to take bigger cuts out of company budgets. To counter this negative trend, some companies added exercise and fitness centers to their facilities. While this was a positive direction, Control Data recognized exercise was only part of the total equation needed to improve employee health. Bad lifestyle choices like smoking, overeating, dangerous driving, and inadequate sleep habits were all items that adversely affected a person's well-being.

Following the principle that Control Data hired the whole person, the company acquired the Life Extension Institute to develop a much more holistic approach to employee fitness. Irving Fisher began the Life Extension Institute in 1913 to promote the overall concept of "wellness" and created several programs to improve the overall health of people. This organization focused on developing a comprehensive approach to better health. The Life Extension Institute had developed a core system of preventative health plans focused on a specific area of behavior modification and lifestyle change. As an example, the Life Extension Institute developed a body mass index that measured a person's proper weight based on size and age.

Building upon the plans created by the Life Extension Institute, the company created an entire package of health-related programs. This package was named StayWell, and it became a new internal employee service. The StayWell family of offerings included wellness programs for improving diet, reducing stress, stopping smoking, increasing exercise, and developing better physical fitness. The stated goals of the service were to:

1. Increase productivity.
2. Reduce lost time due to illness or accident.
3. Reduce the cost of medical insurance.
4. Reduce absenteeism.

StayWell began operations in 1979 as a pilot project within Control Data's New York and San Diego facilities, which together had a population of 1,200 employees. Members of the HR staff helped facilitate the program. Individuals and their spouses could voluntarily participate, selecting the wellness plans they felt best applied to their circumstances. For example, if an employee wanted to break a smoking habit, the employee enrolled in the smoking cessation wellness plan, following its direction to lose the cigarette addiction. Another employee would enroll in the diet plan, and yet another employee enrolled in a fitness plan. Employees could, of course, take on multiple plans if they wished. The program was structured around four concepts designed to help the individual achieve better health—awareness, assessment, behavior change,

Control Data employees participating in physcial exercise through the StayWell program. (Photos courtesy of the Charles Babbage Institute.)

and maintenance. Each health condition was evaluated through these components and provided the employee with a process to follow for improving their health.

After the first year of testing, the wellness plans were sufficiently developed to handle a wider audience. StayWell was expanded, becoming a voluntary benefit offering available in forty-eight additional Control Data offices and plants. By 1983, StayWell was available to all Control Data employees and their spouses throughout the United States, and by 1985, StayWell was implemented at most Control Data facilities. As Robert Price describes in his article "Sowing the Seeds of Innovation," "We developed a comprehensive education program to help employees understand that a healthier lifestyle could lead to both a more enjoyable life and a reduction in medical expenses for themselves and the company." The motivations for both Control Data and the employee population were totally synchronized, as everyone was poised to benefit from improved health and personal well-being.

The wellness programs were administered by a staff of counselors and a number of assisting practitioners, such as fitness instructors, who were present to help employees pursue their selected wellness plans. Control Data technology was also incorporated in StayWell, as the service provided seventeen PLATO individualized courses. Five of these courses explored lifestyle choices, while the other twelve focused on wellness education. Employees could launch these individualized courses from an available PLATO terminal, following the wellness plan as outlined by the courseware. Booklets were included as part of each wellness plan to keep the employee on track for success. Central to the wellness plan was the "StayWell catalyst." As the introduction to a fitness wellness plan describes, ". . . a catalyst is that important extra ingredient needed in a process to make it work. This series of StayWell booklets will be your catalyst for action. Each short book supplies the important how-to information you will need to initiate your own program for health."

StayWell also internally released a regular newsletter, the *Wellness News*. Each newsletter gave employees health tips and articles about pursuing more fit lifestyles. Later the *Wellness*

News was transformed into the *Well Times*, an expanded publication sent to employee's homes. This publication explored a variety of health-related subjects like pain management, mental health, and aging. It also examined specific illnesses such as Lyme disease. In order to keep the national staff of StayWell counselors and practitioners up to date on current wellness issues and practices, the service published the *Staywise* newsletter. Through these lines of communication, the wellness service became a popular benefit, frequently used by CDC employees.

The StayWell service also had a research component, and surveys were conducted to evaluate the overall health of Control Data employees. These large surveys were gathered in 1983 and 1986. Employees were asked what, if any, risk factors they felt threatened their health the most. Lack of exercise, stress and anxiety, bad nutrition, obesity, bad sleeping habits, and other risks were included as part of the surveys. The results were consistent, as about sixty-nine percent of Control Data employees selected at least three of the risk factors listed in the survey. Meanwhile, many individuals reported positive results from the wellness plans they pursued. Jim Morris, the first general manager for Employee Advisory Resource, enrolled in the smoke cessation wellness plan and succeeded in ending his smoking habit. Another Control Data employee, James J. Bowe, described in an article about StayWell that he quit smoking, lost forty-five pounds, began doing distance running, and lowered his blood pressure by forty points. He concluded that StayWell "added eight to ten years to my life." These examples are just a couple of the success stories attributed to the wellness plans available through this service.

StayWell-influenced behavior modifications began to crop up within several areas of the corporation, each of these modifications designed to improve employee health. Restrooms in many Control Data facilities across the United States were each fitted with a scale which employees could use daily to measure their weight. Another behavior modification StayWell advocated was seat belt use. During this time period, few states had mandatory seat belt laws, but much accident research indicated lives were frequently saved through the regular use of seat belts. StayWell emphasized their use as part of an overall lifestyle modification plan.

Like EAR, StayWell was created for the ethical purpose of improving the lives of employees. Its aim was to develop methods to encourage positive, healthy behavior. Because it was a voluntary service, those employees and their spouses who enrolled in the benefit plan used the program because they wanted to better their health and ultimately extend their lives. As more and more employees enrolled in the various wellness plans, Control Data also benefited, as StayWell cut overall insurance costs for the company. The business venture had achieved its primary goals—reducing health care costs and improving employee lives.

More benefits were to come. Just like EAR before, Control Data began marketing Stay-Well services to outside companies. Using statistics from Control Data, the marketing team demonstrated a company could save up to twenty percent on their health benefit costs. Outside companies were soon buying StayWell services. One of StayWell's first major customers was Chrysler Corporation, who in cooperation with the United Auto Workers, began offering StayWell to both union members and Chrysler employees. StayWell became a profitable business, turning what had been an added cost employee benefit into a new stream of self-sustaining income.

Some Flexibility

Employees in today's corporate workplace frequently use a flexible work schedule. While the hours required for the employee remain at the level of a full-time job, the times when employees arrive and leave the office fluctuate based on their personal and family schedules. Employees with children, for example, have time pressures on either end of the work day, and they frequently leverage this policy. If an employee needs to stay at home in the morning to get children on a school bus, that employee can do so and come into work at a later time. Likewise if an employee needs to leave work early to get children to and from after school activities, the employee can take this time as well. As long as the employee can keep up with the workload and maintains a consistent presence at the company by working core hours, management does not frown on the adjusted schedule. This flexible time policy is proven, in fact, to both improve productivity and reduce stress. Control Data is credited as being the first company in the United States to start what is now a common employment practice.

The flexible time concept originated in Germany. Flexible time (in Germany, it was called gliding hours) was a simple, elegant idea. Employees at some German companies were able to tailor their work day to meet their own scheduling needs, whatever they may be. Norb Berg learned about this policy while he was on a trip to Germany, and upon his return began advocating Control Data employees in the United States also work using a flexible time schedule. The HR function made plans to implement flexible time. Some line managers were skeptical about the policy, concerned employee productivity would suffer. Backed by evidence in Germany that employees actually became more productive, the HR function continued to advocate for the policy change. Control Data eventually implemented flexible time across the company's United States locations in 1972. Employees began coming to work on a flexible schedule, and this change did not adversely affect employee output. Soon other companies began adopting flexible time as well, and it became a corporate trend during the 1970s. *Business Week* magazine, in an article about the trend in flexible hours, cited Control Data as the first major corporation to implement this policy.

To make the case that flexible time was a beneficial policy, the HR function surveyed Control Data's domestic employees in 1979 to see how employees were using flexible time. The team discovered it was indeed popular, as around sixty-five percent of the U.S. employees used flexible hours in some way during their work week. One of the most notable statistics was the amount of stress experienced by the employees, as seventy-three percent of employees felt the pressure of getting to work on time was reduced and sixty percent also felt their need to leave work right after quitting time was reduced. The survey found managers were also happy with the flexible time policy, as when measured against previous years when flexible time was not available, employee tardiness was reduced forty-six percent and employee use of sick leave was reduced by sixteen percent. Because of this, managers stated that employee productivity greatly increased as well. The policy even had a positive impact on the environment, as employees reduced their total driving time each week by fifty-seven percent, lowering gas consumption and carbon monoxide emissions significantly. As the results of this internal survey proved, flexible time was a win-win not only for Control Data, but also for many corporations throughout the United States.

Personal Days Off

THE HR FUNCTION ALSO LAUNCHED a major change which was initially received much less favorably by Control Data employees. The company originally granted leave time using the traditional model—employees had both sick days and vacation days. Employees accrued these days off in two separate accounting buckets. When employees were sick, they took days from their accumulated sick time. When employees went on vacation, they took days from their accumulated vacation time. Two separate purposes, two separate times. The accounting department calculated these times separately as well. However, from the company perspective, both sets of time off meant exactly the same thing. The employee was away from the office or plant during these periods and not contributing to the productivity of the company. From the employee's perspective, complications could occur when the employee had used up vacation leave, but had not been sick, leaving the sick leave days unused. Likewise if the employee had battled an illness and had used up the accumulated sick leave, they couldn't touch the vacation leave to get additional days to recover. There were also cases where some employees were using up all their sick days each year to essentially get some extra days off, while other employees took no sick leave at all. The wrong people were getting rewarded, as honest employees were getting less time off than those who chose to be dishonest.

Financially, the members of the HR function became increasingly alarmed at the growing liability to the company for sick leave and vacation time. Vacation and sick time were required by law, but how this time was administered was up to Control Data's discretion. However, there was some concern the federal government would change labor laws to make sick leave an entitlement. If that happened, Control Data would have been in a difficult financial position. When employees did not take vacation and/or sick time, they carried over this amount into the next year. If the employee kept this accrued time year after year, they could use it to retire early by as much as six or more months. This translated into a growing pile of debt that would result in real losses for the company when these employees retired. While on the books these employees were still employed and receiving full pay, they were no longer contributing to the organization. This ballooning vacation/sick time was essentially an unfunded liability which grew alarmingly more significant on the company's ledger year after year. This joint liability of vacation and sick time was in the tens of millions of dollars.

To improve the situation, the HR function developed a new, more flexible concept for administrating leave time—personal days off, or PDO. Employees would accrue leave time as they had always done in the past, but instead of categorizing the types of time the employee was using, all paid time off was placed inside one bucket. The employee could use this time for whatever was needed—health needs, personal days, family vacations—and the company would only track one bucket of accumulated time. This concept simplified how the hours were tracked and it gave the employee the freedom to decide how to best use the accumulated personal days off. The policy also encouraged employees to use their sick leave time more responsibility, as now both sick leave and vacation leave came from the same pool of time. Starting employees received fifteen days total, which amounted to an equivalent of a two-week vacation and five days of sick leave. As employees continued to work for the company they would receive more personal time to use. Employees were also required to use up this time by the end of the year or they would lose it. The company would obviously benefit the most from this particular change, as it would remove the accumulating liability. The trade-off for the employees was they gained more freedom in how they chose to use their PDO time.

The switch from sick leave/vacation leave to PDO was highly controversial. Many employees had accumulated a large backload of sick days and vacation days over the years which they had not yet taken, and they were worried their accumulated time would be lost. To ease employees onto the new system, a grace period was put in place where employees could use up their accumulated days before the personal days off policy was put into effect. However, some employees were forced to give up some time through this change, and they were not happy about the loss of their earned vacation time. This also required a cultural transition, as many employees viewed sick leave as an individual right. By placing this time all in the same category, there was effectively no more sick leave time.

The personal days off policy also had its advantages for employees. Time off was no longer constrained by the purpose for which it was being used, so employees actually gained more freedom through PDO. The time was completely theirs to do what they wanted with it. The policy encouraged a new level of honesty, as employees no longer needed to pretend to be sick in order to gain some additional time off. And with all the leave time going into the same total amount, employees found themselves with time to take longer vacations. Gradually most employees began to support the new system. Like flexible hours, the personal days off policy proved to be a better way to manage leave time for both management and employees. Today this leave time policy is more commonly called paid time off, or PTO, and it is used by over half of corporations in the United States today.

Through both flexible hours and PDO, the company gave employees more control over their private lives, providing them with the ability to balance their personal needs with the needs of their jobs. These policies were another means though which the HR function could help employees and simultaneously help the organization.

Into the Great Outdoors

Even though he was one of the leading technological evangelists of the new computer age, Bill Norris was still a farm boy from Nebraska. He had baled hay in the blistering sun, been kicked in the shins by uncooperative calves, and experienced thousands of other similar experiences that life on a farm brings. Now it was 1972, and he was inside the new Control Data world headquarters building. As he worked in his office inside that tall, air-conditioned gold-and-green skyscraper, there would have been moments when he wondered how he came to be there. He had a lot to see out his window. The Bloomington headquarters was built on an empty expanse of land about ten miles south of downtown Minneapolis, and nothing was around to obstruct the view. Cranes were now working steadily on the downtown skyline as its tallest skyscraper, the thirty-story concrete Foshay Tower, would soon be eclipsed by the fifty-seven-story steel-and-glass IDS Tower. Control Data's largest neighbor to the west was Metropolitan Stadium, home to the Minnesota Twins baseball franchise. In anticipation of future growth at its campus headquarters, Control Data had purchased many acres of former cropland. The company was not yet using all of this real estate, and sitting right next to Control Data's main tower was six acres of idle land. Bill Norris, the former farmer, would not have liked looking out his window and seeing all of that good soil lying fallow.

During the same trip Berg took to Germany when he learned about flexible time, he also saw villagers tending gardens in common plots located outside their towns. Berg, a former rural youth as well, thought the land around Control Data's world headquarters could be ideally used for a similar purpose. The company could turn the idle land into a place for employees to plant gardens.

After the snow thawed in the spring of 1974, the gardens began. Control Data had the six acres of available land tilled, and then staked it all out into ten-by-fifteen-foot plots. Water was made available at convenient locations. Each plot was offered as a free garden to any employee at corporate headquarters who wanted one. Over 900 employees jumped at the chance to have their own garden space, and soon many were outside in the dirt both before and after work, planting neat rows of vegetables and flowers. The HR function also provided assistance to help novice gardeners get started in their new hobby. They contacted the Agricultural Extension Service, a farming advice service provided through the University of Minnesota, to help employees learn how to successfully grow produce and flowers.

As the spring and summer of 1974 moved along, the six fallow acres were transformed into a series of small, blooming gardens. Each garden was unique, as employees chose a variety of colorful flowers, tomatoes, cucumbers, green beans, and any other plants to grow. It was a great way for the employees to get out of the office, put on some gloves, and dig into the dark loam. But since this was a corporate-sponsored program, there also had to be some friendly competition thrown into the mix. During the month of August, members of the Minnesota Agricultural Extension

Recipients of the Golden Hoe award. Notice Control Data Headquarters in the background. (Photo courtesy of the Charles Babbage Institute.)

Service would return to Control Data's campus and inspect the gardens. Each of the 900 gardens was judged on the neatness of the plants (no weeds, good leaf structure) and the overall quality of the flowers and produce. The winner of the competition would receive the "Golden Hoe" Award— a major accomplishment, considering over 900 gardens were involved in the contest. This became an annual tradition at corporate headquarters; employees could raise fresh vegetables and flowers every summer and bring them home for their families to enjoy. Plus when Bill Norris looked out his window, he saw Control Data's land being put to efficient use.

Norb Berg's love of the outdoors did not stop there. Another dream project he initiated was to develop a recreational facility for exclusive use by all Control Data employees. This park would be provided free of charge, so employees who worked together could now play together as well. The HR function developed a plan wherein the profits from the company's vending machines would be used as a fund to finance employee recreation programs. Starting in 1960, the company increased the cost of soda, coffee, and candy by five to ten percent, and this additional money was deposited into this designated fund. Over the next decade, the fund grew into a substantial amount of money. A portion of this fund was set aside for a capital expenditure—the purchase of a recreational facility. Ron Hurst, the employee recreation manager, was charged with the responsibility of purchasing a property, and he bought 560 acres of land bordering the St. Croix River in October 1970.

During the next few years, the land was developed into a fully realized recreational park. A picnic shelter was built near new softball diamonds and tennis courts. A marina was also developed, complete with boat launches. A cottage that was already on the property was remodeled to hold company events. The majority of the site, however, was left alone to be open for hiking and camping. Bathroom facilities, firewood storage buildings, and fire rings were also built. A full-time park director was hired to maintain the grounds. All of this was financed with the profits from the vending machines.

It took nearly five years to get all the legal permits required, but finally the recreational park was ready to open. During a spring day in May 1973, Norb Berg cut the ribbon at the picnic shelter, and Control Data's new park and recreational facility was initiated. Any Control Data employee could use the park, and it turned into a major perk for Midwest-based CDC employees (and those more distant employees in the Twin Cities on business). Employees gathered at the facility to play softball, baseball, tennis, and other athletic pursuits. Control Data employees frequently brought their children out to the shelter for picnics. The cottage was large enough to use as a conference center, so some business meetings and company celebrations were held at the St. Croix recreational facility as well. As Susan Willette, a former StayWell employee relates, "A truck would deliver wood and water. It was a top-notch campground." Many former CDC employees and their children have fond memories of the times they had at that recreational facility, toasting marshmallows by the campfire, looking up at the stars.

These outdoor assets—the employee gardens and the recreational facility—were additional aspects of Control Data that made the company unique. They provided CDC employees with an outlet to unwind, inhale fresh air, and absorb some sunlight (or moonlight). These individuals could meet each other in an environment outside of the office or plant, developing friendships that would last a lifetime.

The employee gardens came to an end when Control Data became Ceridian and moved out of the Bloomington headquarters. Grass and flowers replaced the garden plots. The recreational facility was also sold during the transformative years during the late 1980s, becoming part of the local county park system. The recreational facility still exists, and as part of the selling agreement, former Control Data and Ceridan employees have special rights to use the park. These past employees can make reservations and have priority access to the facility. The proceeds from the land sales and the profits from the vending machine funds that financed so much of Control Data's recreation activities exist today as a special fund, and this money is used to finance events for Control Data and Ceridian retirees. The spirit of this special outdoor place lives on in the former employees that still enjoy it.

Enable the Disabled

Perhaps the most intriguing employee assistance venture Control Data developed was HOME-WORK. This internal training program was created to help CDC employees who, for various reasons, were either temporarily or permanently not able to return to the workplace. The individuals eligible to participate were Control Data employees who had suffered a loss of mobility due to accidents, required reduced stress because of heart ailments, were afflicted by chronic diseases, or had any other condition that prevented them from returning to their original job. Even though many of these individuals either were no longer physically active or were placed on company disability, they were still mentally alert. Unfortunately, their physical conditions also prevented them from attending alternative or vocational training. Because of their debilitated situations, they were considered unemployable and were now receiving some form of government welfare assistance.

The HOMEWORK concept was that these individuals could leverage technology to learn about technology. They would receive training in computer programming skills, something they could do successfully from home, and return to active employment with Control Data. Along with the obvious benefits of real income, these individuals would gain the added satisfaction and self-respect of working either full or part-time once again. They would also no longer require as much government welfare and insurance assistance. Testing of this concept began in 1978, and the program was announced and fully implemented in 1980.

Three important factors led to the HOMEWORK program. The Employee Advisory Resource (EAR) service was involved with all of these individuals. While the EAR service was able to coordinate financial benefits to these disabled employees, staff members felt they were not giving these employees enough emotional support to maintain a good quality of life. The PLATO technology had also sufficiently advanced so interactive education courseware could be launched and administered through multiple remote locations over telephone lines. Another main factor was the cost of providing disability benefits programs grew higher every year, and the HOMEWORK program could potentially help reduce these overhead costs.

HOMEWORK was a mix of education, job placement services, consulting services, and a computer-based instruction system. The program leveraged the PLATO technology in a unique way. A PLATO terminal was installed at the participant's home, rehabilitation center, or extended health care facility. This terminal was connected through phone lines to a central PLATO mainframe computer. The individual would then receive programming instruction through the courseware piped in over the phone lines through the terminal. Each participant was also provided with personal consulting and training as needed. The results of the training were then evaluated by the central PLATO mainframe computer. These results were reviewed by instructors who were then available to help the student master the programming skills. The advantage of using courseware was huge, as these partially able individuals could study the programming courses at a pace best suited for them. Control Data had, in effect, created one of the very first online universities.

The ultimate goal of the HOMEWORK concept was to rehire the individual to work from home through a mainframe terminal. Long before working from home through a computer became more common, Control Data leaders understood technology could be implemented as remote work centers and because of that, employees could be equally productive—perhaps even more productive than in a traditional office. After the participant successfully completed the

A HOMEWORK student learns programming through a PLATO terminal installed in her home. (Photo courtesy of the Charles Babbage Institute.)

training, the PLATO terminal would be removed and the employment application process began. If work was available, the individual would be rehired by Control Data as a programmer, and a standard mainframe terminal would be permanently installed in the individual's home. This person then would be assigned programming projects and resume active employment. The company gained a new programmer whose productivity would eventually pay for the initial investment of installing and using the PLATO terminal.

The educational component began after technicians installed the PLATO training terminal at the individual's home. Once this terminal was running, an instructor would arrive on-site to first teach the student how to log on, launch the courseware, and other basic technical skills. The formal role between the instructor and the student would then be complete, but the instructor could still be contacted as needed, even returning for follow-up visits. Because the participant would be self-taught and work at his/her own pace, the instructor and the student would agree upon a series of goals and a schedule of completion. The standard length of time for the training was eight months, but due to the participant's health and other factors, it usually took most participants longer than eight months to complete the curriculum. The courseware taught the participants the PASCAL programming language.

An impressive variety of consulting services were also made available both during and after the programming training ended to help facilitate progress. At any point, the HOME-WORK student could request educational consulting for help with the curriculum. Consultants were also available to provide assistance for any technical problems which occurred with the courseware or the PLATO terminal. Both of these services made practical sense, but the HOME-WORK program also provided psychological consulting services to help students deal with problems of depression and other mental health issues that might occur as a result of their disability or other personal issues. When the student completed his or her training, a job placement consultant would help the HOMEWORK graduate prepare a résumé and locate job opportunities within Control Data. These consulting services helped complete the training for each student.

Twelve students enrolled in the test program in 1978, called HOMEWORK I. All twelve students were on long-term disability. Besides participating in the course load, these students critiqued the materials, which led to later refinements in the delivery and execution of the program. The HOMEWORK II program was conducted in 1979 with another group of long term disability individuals. During both testing years, issues with the courseware were identified, and refinements were repeatedly made to improve the impact of the courseware. The printed materials, for example, proved to be hard for some of the students to use, so new strategies were developed for organizing and laying out these materials to make them more user-friendly. The participants admitted that personal problems, like health conditions and financial worries, were also factors that interfered with learning. Based on these concerns, the HR function decided consulting services should be included as part of the overall package. When the two test years were complete, the HOMEWORK training service was considered ready for deployment, and CDC employees began to be admitted on an individual basis in the fall of 1980. Some external HOMEWORK students were also admitted in a parallel program to test market the service for potential sales outside of Control Data. Once again, the HR function was experimenting to see if HOMEWORK could be turned into a standalone business.

Many of the struggles identified during the two test years were now handled with more positive results, and partially able individuals began developing the programming skills they needed to be rehired. However, the HOMEWORK training program created an interesting and very human side effect. To give students a way to simulate interaction and mirror a real class environment, the PLATO network utilized early forms of email and instant messaging. It was not long before the email sent between the participants became more personal. The HOMEWORK participants grew into an online support group, one of the first of its kind, encouraging each other to continue working through the difficult material. Friendships sprang up over the PLATO network, and soon participants were logging on just to meet (or "chat") with each other. Some sources cite this feature of the system as one of the first Internet chat rooms. The group became a special family, celebrating birthdays and even weddings together online. HOMEWORK administrators were basically pleased with this result, although this situation made it difficult to remove the PLATO terminals when the instruction was complete. It even caused some students to delay work on their courses, because completing their courseware meant the PLATO training terminal would be taken away—and they did not want to sever their connection with this online community.

The HOMEWORK managers were very surprised students preferred communicating through email instead of by letter or by phone. During an online evaluation of the program, one participant theorized why this was the case, "It may be that computer technology fills a communication gap that letter writing and phone conversation do not provide. Letters may take too long a turn-around time, and phones may be too intimate a medium to use, at least at first. The terminals may provide for freer expression, allowing people to write out their feelings with the opportunity for an immediate response." Considering how much public and personal communication was handled through email on a massive scale just fifteen years later, this early online community within the HOMEWORK program was a foreshadowing of the communication future soon to come.

Unfortunately, one negative result was that some participants, after they successfully finished their training, found themselves in a perilous financial situation. Going back to work, especially in a part-time capacity, frequently meant their social security disability insurance payments and regular insurance payments would end. In some cases, insurance companies would immediately try to terminate the benefits after the participants completed the PASCAL training. Another worry was that, even if the participant was able to work full-time, there was always the possibility that this individual would suffer a relapse, and not having their disability payments available would put them at a great deal of financial risk. As one participant exclaimed, "the stress caused me to have another heart attack."

Clearly more flexibility was needed, and Control Data advocated for changing Social Security legislation so individuals on long term disability could return to work on a limited basis. Gary Lohn, the HR manager who had assisted employees at the Northside facility, testified before Congress on this issue. In the meantime, any HOMEWORK participants who could not work for pay were allowed to work as volunteers, but then received some compensation from Control Data. However, the issue with the social security disability and insurance payments did not resolve quickly, and this situation dogged the HOMEWORK program throughout its existence. This financial burden, the loss of the PLATO terminal, and insecurity about re-entering the job market made the transition out of the HOMEWORK program very, very difficult, and in some cases, nearly impossible.

The program did have limited success. A review of HOMEWORK results was conducted in 1985 to evaluate its effectiveness since the program was launched in 1978. Up to this point, seventy-six Control Data employees had participated in HOMEWORK (and 117 in total, including the outside students). Of the Control Data employees, twenty of these individuals were working, but only eight individuals were in jobs that leveraged their HOMEWORK training. Another eleven had worked for a period of time but now were unable to work again. Of the twelve original HOMEWORK I students from the 1978 test program, five were successfully re-employed and four remained active on their home terminals but could not work because of social security and insurance issues. The last three of the original twelve could not rejoin the workforce due to their health problems.

The main issue with the program, the study concluded, was job placement after the training was not very effective. The study recommended, "Better communication is required to emphasize that job placement is a corporate-wide responsibility. It does not rest solely with the HOMEWORK or Disability Management staff." While the resulting job growth was disappointing, some real outcomes from HOMEWORK could not be measured. The nature of the program had provided some therapy, stimulated mental ability, and created a support group. In the words of one participant, ". . . if it hadn't been for HOMEWORK, I wouldn't have made it . . . They've saved my life. HOMEWORK has really given me a new start on life." Unfortunately, as the industry changed in the middle of the 1980s, the amount of subcontract work available to this group diminished, and by 1988, the HOMEWORK initiative was significantly reduced in size. The concept behind the program was sound, and the knowledge learned through this program helped the HR function gain new insight into how the company could help this underutilized segment of the population. The HOMEWORK program represents a model for empowering the disabled by creating opportunities for self-sufficiency through training and regular employment.

Serve the Community

When Richard Conner came back from his six-month paid sabbatical at the Stillwater Correctional Facility, he had gained additional insight and skills into how to resolve conflict. This sabbatical turned out to be well worth Control Data's investment, as the HR function leveraged Conner's newfound knowledge to develop the ombudsman function within Employee Advisory Resource. The ombudsman function was a real benefit for Control Data, as it now had a solid process for internally resolving work-related problems through employee counseling and advocacy. And as previously described, the ombudsman function became part of the peer review process that resolved many serious employee grievances. Likewise, Richard Conner's managerial expertise was invaluable for establishing the prison ombudsman, setting the stage for Control Data's manufacturing facility within the Stillwater Correctional Facility and the company's other prison industries initiatives. Given the success of Conner's sabbatical experience, the HR function established a special program to encourage employees at any level of the corporation to take time off with full pay and benefits to develop community, national, or international projects. Administered by Employee Advisory Resource, employees could submit proposals to EAR, where the staff reviewed the merits of the proposal. If the proposal was accepted, the employee would begin the paid sabbatical term, temporarily leaving the company to work on the project.

Hilda Pridgeon submitted one of these social service leave proposals. Hilda was working as a Control Data secretary, but she had only been on staff for a short time. She was married to Al Pridgeon, a World War II veteran who had served as a B-24 gunner and aerial engineer, flying in fifty-two missions. After the war, Hilda and Al married and had three children. He worked as a branch manager for a drapery hardware company, and because of his position with the company, they moved to several cities across the United States. Hilda worked as a secretary wherever they went to bring in extra money. Eventually Al's job brought them to Minneapolis for the second time in the late 1970s. They settled down into their usual pattern, but their lives suddenly changed. Hilda became worried about Al's behavior. Though only in his late forties, he was forgetting things and getting confused. Fearing that she might need some level of financial security, Hilda applied for and received a secretarial position at Control Data. Her fears were justified. Shortly after joining CDC, Al abruptly, irrationally, decided to quit his job of twenty-five years at the drapery company. Al had always been a fun-loving guy, enjoying life, his kids, and work, so something was definitely wrong. Hilda took Al to the doctor, and after several tests, Al was diagnosed with early-onset Alzheimer's disease.

Hilda was stuck in a very difficult position. Because Al had voluntarily left his job, he was not given retirement and disability benefits by his former company. Al needed care. Hilda also needed to raise their three children. The financial stress caused by Al's unemployment, the parental needs of her children, and the emotional distress of watching Al slowly decline were all taking their toll. Desperate, needing some way to keep all these balls in the air, Hilda decided to call EAR. The counselors immediately brought her case to Oppenheimer, Control Data's law firm. Paul Hannah was assigned as a lawyer on her case, and he first took on the drapery hardware company to restore Al's disability and retirement benefits. He won the case for Al, since he had clearly left the company because of his illness. Paul Hannah also helped Hilda leverage other financial avenues like Social Security and mortgage disability insurance. Their financial issues were resolved. Hilda was now free to improve her career, and she began working in the shareholder relations function. During this time and encouraged by her manager, she earned her college degree.

Taking care of Al at home, though, was still quite a challenge. Hilda connected with other women dealing with the same circumstances, and together they decided to organize a support meeting for families who were caring for a relative with Alzheimer's disease. To prepare for the meeting, they gathered materials from the National Institute of Aging. They then reserved a conference room at Control Data's headquarters and ran an advertisement in the Minneapolis *Star Tribune* about the upcoming support meeting. The response was incredible. The conference room did not have enough chairs for everyone, so some spent the entire meeting standing up. Hilda decided these families needed a national support organization to help them deal with this devastating disease. Hilda devoted many of her nights and weekends to organizing the support group. She had the business skills needed to get the support group running, but unfortunately not the time. When Control Data announced its social leave program, Hilda wrote a proposal for a year-long paid sabbatical. Her proposal was approved.

Her paid sabbatical year started on August 1, 1979. Hilda turned a room in her home into an office, but she needed some office equipment. As Robert Price relates in his book *The Eye for Innovation*, "A Control Data truck arrived with a typewriter, desk, filing cabinet, and office supplies. She had permission to use the company's photocopy machines at any time, and she could use the company designers for her newsletter." By August 28, Hilda had registered the first nonprofit (50IC3) organization for Alzheimer's disease in the United States. Thanks to her continuing connection with the National Institute on Aging, letters from family caregivers struggling within the disease began to arrive at her office from all across the country. She and her co-founders made public service announcements on various television stations, gaining more local and national support for the organization. Control Data continued to help Hilda by creating a mailing list database.

On April 10, 1980, nine months into her sabbatical, the organization was registered as the Alzheimer's Disease and Related Disorders Association, Inc., or as it is more commonly called today, the Alzheimer's Association. Seven chapters were founded nationally in Boston, Columbus, Minneapolis, New York City, Pittsburg, San Francisco, and Seattle. Hilda Pridgeon joined the board of directors, and, when her sabbatical year ended, she returned to work at Control Data. However, she continued to guide the Alzheimer's Association by remaining on the board for seventeen years.

What had started as a support meeting in a Control Data conference room now became a national organization—both helping families cope with the illness in every state and lobbying for government and private funds to research the disease. As the organization describes on its website, "The Alzheimer's Association, today a multi-million-dollar organization, has been the catalyst and leader for a generation of advancements in Alzheimer research and care. Our organization's achievements and progress in the field have given thousands of people a better quality of life and brought hope for millions more." By providing Hilda with the basic support she needed in time and resources, Control Data helped an employee turn a terrible illness into a national call for action. If a cure for Alzheimer's disease is discovered someday, Hilda Pridgeon, former secretary, will be one of the reasons why it was found.

Money and Jobs

As CONTROL DATA STRUGGLED with the massive technological changes of the mid-1980s, the HR function developed some innovative approaches to protect and help employees as much as possible with wage pressures, career transitions, and job layoffs. It was a challenging period, but the HR function continued to examine ways the company's most important asset—the employees—could be supported and maintained throughout the difficulties. While the Control Data brand name ultimately disappeared and many jobs either transitioned into other organizations or were lost, the HR function never gave up on its role of advocating for CDC employees as much as possible.

One major pressure that became an increasing management headache was inflation. Inflation was on the rise during the late 1970s and early 1980s, and while Control Data enjoyed its largest years of growth during this period, inflation was a growing threat to the company's profitability. As the dollar dropped in value, corporate budgets and personal wallets had less buying power. One obvious method Control Data and other companies used to battle inflation was to raise product and service prices, salaries and wages, costs of benefits, and so on to keep up with the decreasing value of the dollar. Raising these costs, however, created more inflationary pressure, so this cycle had to be slowed to prevent inflation from unraveling the marketplace. Both the public and private sector took action during this period to keep inflation from going out of control.

As the value of the dollar dropped, CDC employees demanded higher wages to make ends meet. Control Data could only raise these costs so far, before their products and services rose to uncompetitive price points. In response to these wage demands, the HR function developed a financial management program to help employees make more effective use of their earnings. This educational service was called WiserWays. Announced in 1981, the annual report for this year stated, "WiserWays is a program covering many activities to help employees cope with persistent inflation by making better use of their incomes, stretching their paychecks." By teaching employees how to more effectively use their money, Control Data hoped to stave off wage demands.

The backbone of this educational service was a series of video and audio tapes that contained financial management and consumer education materials from a number of financial planning services. Financial courses were also made available through PLATO. For example, one of these courses explained how to bargain shop, while another course explored how to manage a family checkbook. Employees were encouraged to leverage these educational resources to better handle the income they received. By providing employees with increased financial skills, they could make more efficient use of their money and Control Data would have an easier time maintaining current wage levels—keeping more individuals employed in the process. WiserWays continued to be offered by the HR function throughout the 1980s in the hope that it would help keep costs down.

When the financial liquidity situation became extremely difficult in 1985, the HR function developed two important downsizing models which Control Data used to help mitigate the damage and hoped would return the organization to profitability. These two models were the rings of defense and the adverse impact statement. While the corporation had no choice but to constrict the employee population, Control Data needed to manage the layoff process responsibly through methods that would increase the chances the company could rebound when the economic situation improved. These models were also designed to help ensure the downsizing process would not incur additional costs through lawsuits. Using these downsizing models as a guide, company leaders were able to continue many areas of business as long as it was economically viable to do so.

The HR function developed the rings of defense model by examining job roles within the entire CDC employee population. The module examined the people doing the work, analyzing how many employees could be reduced but still maintain the productivity of the business at the highest level possible. The model placed employees in different rings of business functions, positioning those employees with skills and knowledge necessary for the business to survive within the core rings, and those employees with less vital skills and knowledge within the middle and outer rings. Permanent employees were thus placed within the inner rings and cushioned from job cuts as much as possible, while temporary employees and contract workers were placed in the more vulnerable outer rings.

Before the jobs of any of these individuals would be considered for layoffs, the rings of defense plan established further channels of contraction to explore first. One of these outer rings was to cut back spending throughout the company. CDC would take a detailed look at everything to find as much savings as possible. For example, in 1982, the company reduced the number of telephones in the Twin Cities offices by five percent, saving the company over $350,000 during the fiscal year. After this point, the rings of defense started the job layoffs by first evaluating the company's efficiency. Human resources would examine positions across the entire company and eliminate any role redundancies in order to improve overall efficiency. The next ring targeted contract positions—any outside contractors would be terminated by the organization. However, to ensure these contractors were not put out of business, Control Data also required that those cut could only have fifteen percent of their operations dependent on CDC projects. This policy was implemented in the hope that should business improve, these contractors would still be available for work again.

The next ring was eliminating overtime pay, because if the economic climate was poor, it was likely the company would not increase production costs to build more products not in demand. Employees could also be given the option to voluntarily take time off without pay, but still keep their benefits. These employees could then opt out of the workforce for a specific period of time, helping protect other employees who really needed the work. Control Data had been making this an option for several years. During the industry downturn in 1970, Ruth Rich, then a secretary (later an executive of human resources) decided to take some time off without pay. "I had wanted to go to Europe," she relates, "so I took ten days without pay and traveled."

If the savings gained through overtime and voluntary time off were exhausted, the company would next begin larger targeted layoffs, starting with temporary positions and then regressing up through the inner rings. Because these rings contained the company's core resources, individuals, these layoffs would be gradual. Hopefully the organization would return to profitability through the layoffs at one of the outer ring levels, but if needed even the core positions would be shed—at which point, the organization might no longer exist.

The rings of defense module was used to plan layoffs during the 1985 crisis and then again during the tough days of 1989. The model gained acceptance throughout the industry; it was described by Jocelyn F. Gutchess in her book *Employee Security in Action: Strategies That Work*, published in 1985, and the Honeywell Corporation used the rings of defense model as a plan for layoffs they needed to carry out as well. Today other companies have created similar rings of defense models specific to their organizational structure and lines of business. Through these models, companies can develop strategies for defending themselves during adverse economic times in order to emerge in flush times as a stronger, better company.

While the rings of defense defined an overall layoff strategy for Control Data, the company needed to define an ethical approach to employee layoffs that was fair and just. To define this approach, the company developed the adverse impact analysis model. Through this job termination plan, the HR function established guiding principles to assure layoffs did not adversely focus on a specific group of the employee population. As Frank Dawe, the former senior vice president of administration explains, "We would not target women, minorities, or people over the age of forty. We would make sure there was no adverse impact on protected classes." The HR function researched what would happen if different people from the company were laid off, and what that adverse impact their loss would have on the overall organization. The adverse impact analysis developed a series of performance categories through which employees would be rated. If layoffs were needed within one of the rings of defense, these performance ratings were used to evaluate which specific employees would be let go. These performance ratings were solely based on job output and other measurable factors—free from race, sex, and age discrimination. The company had worked hard to eliminate discrimination in hiring and promoting people, and now it applied these same ethics to job terminations. Through this plan, Control Data would know whose jobs to terminate should the need arise.

The adverse impact analysis was a major tool that helped the company downsize responsibly during the final years of the organization. Despite the upheaval, Control Data was able to contract in size without too many legal hurdles. There were exceptions, as the company did have to resolve a few wrongful discharge lawsuits. During one of these lawsuits, Control Data was accused of wrongfully targeting older people for job cuts. Control Data's legal team was able to draw on the rings of defense and adverse impact analysis models to build its case for defense against the wrongful discharge claim. When they presented their case to the prosecution team, the lawsuit was settled for a couple thousand dollars (to cover legal fees) before it made it to court. Settling before trial became the pattern for similar lawsuits, and the HR function was able to demonstrate Control Data had used performance, not discrimination, to carry out its job cuts.

Both the rings of defense and the adverse impact analysis were designed to protect Control Data as well as employees. By ensuring layoffs were handled in an ethical manner, company management was able to strategically navigate the business through difficult times and reduce potential liability. Control Data even turned the layoff situation into an entrepreneurial opportunity, as the HR function developed an outplacement consulting service to help former employees find jobs. This service eventually became a standalone job placement business (this business will be discussed in the next chapter). Control Data's culture of innovation continued to find new ways to respond to employee problems as the company transformed into Ceridian Corporation and its other spin-off child organizations.

The result of these policies and employee services was Control Data enjoyed a very low turnover rate compared to other corporations of a similar size. Robert Price explains the motivation behind these employee service ventures, "The policies and practices . . . all were rooted in a basic belief in the individual. This was based on a deeply held conviction that each individual has untapped potential for innovation, and each individual has a responsibility for personal growth and skill development." Because the workforce was so well supported through these services, Control Data employees had a high level of morale, bringing the best of their skills to bear against work challenges. Many employees would stay with the company for a major portion of their careers, reducing the job turnover rate. And by reducing turnover, the costs of recruiting, hiring, and training new employees was reduced as well. Whether it was during the boom times of the mainframe era of the 1960s, the diversification of electronics industry in the 1970s, or the transformative struggle to survive the business climate of the 1980s, employees benefited from human resource practices designed to fulfill their needs as reasonably as possible. They even had a great place to camp.

Chapter Five

HR Entrepreneurs

"We rejected the traditional do-gooder concept in favor of one that says we shall address society's unmet needs as profitable business opportunities."
—William C. Norris

NEARLY ALL THE SOCIAL BUSINESS VENTURES were experiments testing the possibilities of the free market. To Control Data's leadership team, a social need was viewed as unmet demand. Where there was unmet demand, there existed a potential business opportunity. During the company's peak years of business, Control Data invested in a number of social need areas, resulting in such ventures as the prison industries, Employee Advisory Resource, and HOME-WORK. If the venture demonstrated potential, the next phase of the venture's development began wherein it was marketed externally to turn it into a standalone, profitable business. Some of these efforts were extremely successful, some made modest gains, and others failed to make the transition. Regardless of the result, the company's entrepreneurial approach to both business and society made sure employees were constantly searching for new ideas to enrich and expand the company.

The HR function was influential through several ventures intended almost from the beginning to be standalone businesses. The first such business was the Control Data Institute, an international chain of vocational colleges that taught students the primary skills they needed to enter the computer industry. This business became the point of entry for thousands of young professionals who wanted to create and develop computer technology, whether within Control Data Corporation or destinations elsewhere. The company's experience with prison inmates gave the HR function the knowledge and expertise to develop FAIRBREAK, a business designed to teach basic knowledge and job retention skills to unemployed individuals. Then Control Data perhaps attempted the ultimate experiment by spinning off the corporate human resources staff into a separate business entity that would contract its services back to Control Data and outside clients. The corporate HR function became a major service area within Control Data Business Advisors, Incorporated—a venture designed to support the development of new companies.

All these ventures were in keeping with Bill Norris's strategy of gradually transforming the company from a solely hardware manufacturing company to a more services-centered organization, and so the HR function actively pursued these ventures in support of Norris's vision.

He strongly believed the products and services developed through Control Data's social responsibility activities would gradually evolve into one of the company's major sources of income. This chapter describes what happened when the HR function turned some of its social ventures, including itself, into standalone ventures. This chapter completes the journey many of these ideas took from their early concepts to their final incarnation as profit and loss business opportunities.

Teach the World

MOST EMPLOYEES WHO JOINED Control Data in the early 1960s knew very little about computer technology. This field of study was so new, few colleges and universities actually had degrees or even courses students could enroll in to master the discipline. So Control Data frequently hired many individuals with the assumption the company would need to teach these new hires the skills and knowledge required to do their jobs—whether it was to assemble, program, operate, or maintain mainframe computers. To accomplish this task, CDC developed an internal training curriculum designed to efficiently teach new employees the knowledge they needed to successfully work in their Control Data positions. This internal training program was well structured and thorough; employees were often ready to perform their jobs after just a few months of study.

The curriculum continued to expand, covering an increasing range of subjects Control Data employees needed to master within the rapidly evolving computer technology industry. Of course, there was a downside, as running this internal training program was an added expense to the company's bottom line. The training program was needed, so it became part of the company's expected cost of doing business. After a few years, the training curriculum evolved into a complete field of study. The administrators of the training program realized they could make this technical curriculum available as a complete vocational education program, marketing it externally and charging the students tuition to enroll. Instead of being an internal educational cost liability, the training program would be turned into a potential profit-making business venture.

The first Control Data Institute opened in Minneapolis in 1965. The purpose of the school was to provide entry-level training to individuals within the Twin Cities area who wanted to pursue a career within the young, quickly growing computer industry. A number of these first students were Vietnam War veterans who had served as military technicians in the army, so the Control Data Institute was a terrific way they could build on their technical skills. The programs varied in length from a few months to almost a year. The Control Data Institute was a complete school, set up as a separate business from the mother company. Interestingly, the students were not obligated to become Control Data employees and likewise, Control Data was not obligated to hire these students after they graduated. The company hoped to hire many graduates who successfully completed the technical coursework, but the students were free to seek employment at other companies. While this seemed a strange policy, this approach was in

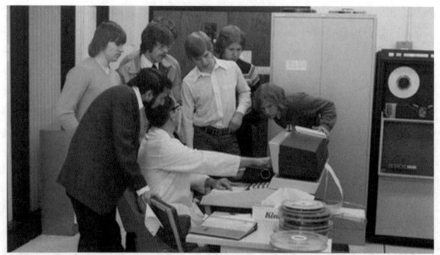

Students learning computer technology at a Control Data Institute. (Photo courtesy of the Charles Babbage Institute.)

line with the entrepreneurial strategy at CDC—the Control Data Institute would succeed or fail as a separate profit center.

Frequently, students who graduated from the Control Data institutes went on to earn higher degrees at universities. Many students also did decide to work for Control Data after completing the program. Instead of having the added expense of training the employees after they were hired, Control Data instead profited from the tuition fees and then hired individuals who were immediately prepared for their positions. For the students who found work at other companies and institutions, the company had at least received income from their tuition. After a short time, the Control Data Institute expanded the curriculum to include a multi-year program where the students would work part-time at Control Data to gain job experience. In this way, the educational curriculum gave the company much needed entry-level assistance at facilities near the Control Data Institute.

The first Control Data Institute in Minneapolis did very well, and it was not long before more locations were opened near corporate facilities across the United States. By 1967, five Control Data Institutes were in operation, including an international facility in Frankfurt, Germany. The company continued to expand these training centers until at their peak, fifty Control Data Institute facilities were in the United States, Australia, Canada, and Western Europe. Each year, the institutes enrolled an average of 8,000 students. They were heavily advertised on television, with commercials regularly airing throughout the 1970s through the 1980s. Many young people who grew up during this time period remember these commercials, as the Control Data Institutes helped make CDC a visible household name.

The international locations were not enough to address the worldwide demand for computer technology education. Since much of the hardware engineering and design was taking place in the United States, foreign companies who purchased Control Data hardware wanted their employees to gain more direct experience with the systems. To address this need, the institutes based in the United States frequently served as training facilities for international employees. These international students would enroll in the program at a Control Data Institute and stay within the United States for the duration of the training program. To accommodate these students, Control Data rented entire apartment buildings near Control Data Institute facilities. When these foreign students completed their training, they would then return to their home country, working for the employer who had sent them. Because of this, the Control Data institutes essentially taught the world how to use computer technology during the early days of the industry.

At the original Minneapolis location, the Control Data Institute eventually partnered with the University of Minnesota to start an Associate of Arts degree. This computer degree was very popular, and soon Control Data Institutes collaborated with other colleges and institutions to create similar degrees. Through these partnerships with the Control Data Institutes, colleges began fashioning their own academic programs. Degrees in computer programming became popular disciplines within many educational institutions. Because of these collaborations, the institutes were not only a major service for educating potential future employees, they also became one of the foundations for computer technology education throughout the United States and at some international educational institutions. As time went on, new programming languages and technologies expanded these disciplines into their present form. Degrees in computer programming and engineering are now standard offerings at colleges, universities, and technical colleges. It was Control Data's initial decision, as an industry leader, to be one of the main catalysts that helped elevate computer sciences into becoming a major academic discipline.

The Control Data Institutes continued as a vocational education business throughout the 1980s. They were eventually sold in the late 1980s as a spin-off organization during the company's transformation into Ceridian. Some of these education facilities still exist today under different names in Canada and elsewhere as vocational technology training centers.

The Business of HR

WHILE EMPLOYEE SERVICES like Employee Advisory Resource and StayWell were initially created to retain employees and reduce internal HR costs like health insurance, Control Data's emerging strategy was to sell these employee service ventures to other companies. Although this was not the initial long-term plan for these services, when the service clearly worked well internally, the company eventually decided to sell the service externally to offset some of its costs and potentially turn it into a self-supporting business. But that was a task these services themselves could not always take on. The Employee Advisory Resource staff had plenty to do by maintaining a 24/7 hotline and handling acute cases of work and non-work related problems. The HOMEWORK group was busy teaching and assisting partially able former employees return to work. So Human Resource Management Services was tasked to become a resource gathering organization, acquiring and organizing the resources needed to begin the marketing project for these services.

When an HR product or service seemed like it could be something the company could market, Human Resource Management Services could then leverage corporate resources that existed elsewhere within CDC to market and produce these services. By utilizing the knowledge and expertise of the CDC marketing function and leveraging any engineering and hardware resources required, Human Resource Management Services could bring the best possible effort towards each HR venture's successful introduction into the marketplace. Control Data was now embarking on an almost entirely new business concept. The company was one of the first organizations to launch the strategy of outsourcing internally developed services. This "early-to-market" idea was a cutting edge concept, as Control Data Corporation, a manufacturing organization that originally developed these internal services to help its bottom line, was now setting out to open new markets for employee support and development services.

The choice to market Employee Advisory Resource externally was not initially planned when this service was launched. EAR proved so surprisingly cost effective, it wasn't long before company leaders thought other organizations might want to purchase the service. The marketing campaign for Employee Advisory Resource began in earnest throughout the winter in 1974-1975. However, the daily cold calls made to the prospects were about as cold as the ice crystals hanging outside the windows of the Bloomington office. Most companies were not at all interested in purchasing EAR services. The marketing team emphasized the benefits the service provided for employees trying to cope with alcohol addictions. Most companies denied they had any employees with alcohol addictions. If they did discover an employee with this addiction, their typical response was to terminate employment instead of supporting the person's recovery. How could EAR possibility save their organizations any money? EAR was a difficult sell, and it looked like Human Resource Management Services effort on this project would be short-lived.

Then an amazing, hard fought event occurred—the HRMS marketing team finally sold EAR services to an outside customer. The Bondhus Tool Company of Monticello, Minnesota, signed a contract to receive EAR services on April 23, 1975. The Bondhus Tool Company also purchased other HR offerings, including management development training and personnel consulting, both services purchased to help improve the productivity of employees at its tool manufacturing business. Starting with this first significant sale, other companies began purchasing both EAR and other HR services. The Southland Corporation, owner of the 7-Eleven convenience stores, contracted with Human Resource Management Services to deliver Employee Advisory Resource. EAR eventually was contracted to provide counseling services for the National Basketball Association and the Major Indoor Soccer League. During 1976, Control Data received $173,000 in revenue from EAR contracts alone. During the next few years, EAR contracts grew into a stable source of income. By 1985, Employee Advisory Resource was supplying services to eighty-seven other companies, supporting an employee population of approximately 135,000 individuals.

The EAR organization was later expanded to include a consulting services business. Through this additional business line, Employee Advisory Resource would evaluate other companies' employee assistance programs through short-term consulting and employee policy review services. Several companies decided to purchase these services instead to improve their existing programs, rather than totally contract these services out to Employee Advisory Resource. Through the number of companies either contracted directly with EAR or assisted through EAR consulting services, revenue from Employee Advisory Resource grew to generate $2 to $3 million in annual revenue throughout the 1980s. It was also estimated during this time Employee Advisory Resource saved Control Data $10 million a year in health insurance costs, employee retention, and improved productivity. Employee Advisory Resource also became one of the major components within Ceridian's service offerings, and so EAR remains one of the premiere employee advisory assistance plans.

HOMEWORK was also sold externally through Human Resource Management Services. HOMEWORK had limited sales, as this service was primarily focused as an internal employee educational service and could only accept a small number of external students. This marketing effort was primarily created as a pilot project to test if HOMEWORK could be sold externally, so this service never was marketed past the prototype level.

Some human resources services did not fare as well in the market place. A personnel consulting service, created by HRMS to help companies achieve better results through their job recruiting, did not achieve its goals. It proved difficult for Human Resource Management Services to market this consulting service to HR professionals in other companies. However, the HR function expected some of these services and ideas to fail, so the personnel consulting service was just an entrepreneurial endeavor that could not find a market.

Human Resource Management Services was also in charge of administrating several social initiatives described in previous chapters. HRMS was in charge of administrating the Indian Health Management corporation. The strategic plan was to eventually market these services domestically to other Native American reservations across the United States and then internationally to third-world countries. Likewise, HRMS was responsible for administrating prison initiatives like INSIGHT, Wheels, and other prison services. Human Resources Management Services was largely responsible for making sure these initiatives were given the support and patience needed to develop into businesses.

Most Control Data initiatives involved applying computer technology in some way, so one of the major directions HRMS explored was developing groundbreaking computer applications for human resource purposes. A significant task HRMS felt could be improved by the computer was résumé evaluations. HR professionals had to constantly evaluate numerous résumés companies received to fill available positions. This process could be inefficient, potentially overlooking qualified candidates whose résumés were reviewed at an inopportune moment (for example, at the end of a long day). Computer technology could be leveraged to handle this sometimes challenging task. Working toward the goal of turning this efficiency idea into a profitable venture, Human Resource Management Services acquired Lexicon Software. This start-up software company had developed SKILTEC, a database query application designed for human resources. Through this application, users could enter their résumés and then these electronic résumés would be available for review by employers when they entered search criteria into the database. SKILTEC was a broad-based database that could be customized for various job recruiting purposes and focuses.

The first customized product created from SKILTEC was developed for college recruiting. This computer application, SKILSOURCE, was a job matching application. It was first installed and tested at Southern University, an African-American university located in Baton Rouge, Louisiana. Students entered their college résumés into SKILSOURCE. This data was then made available to potential employers. The employers could enter search parameters on the areas of study and skills they were looking for in college recruits. The résumés that matched the search criteria could next be printed and reviewed by employers. After reviewing this more effectively targeted group of résumés, the employers could arrange interviews with the students they felt were good matches for their positions. The new concept proved to be a good application for computer software, and soon SKILSOURCE was in use by many colleges. The job matching (and ultimately hiring) achieved more accurate results, as potential employers could rapidly locate a pool of qualified students at the university or college level.

The SKILTEC system had the potential for a much larger job recruitment market. The question was how to apply this technology in an effective way. At the same time SKILSOURCE was in development, Control Data was also actively pursuing applications that could leverage a new data-sharing technology. Packets of information could now be transmitted between multiple mainframe computers connected remotely through a network. The first such network, ARPANET (Advanced Research Projects Agency Network), was developed to connect multiple mainframe computers for research purposes. This network was intended to be a closed system to link university research departments and Defense Advanced Research Projects Agency facilities (DARPA, the research agency for the Department of Defense). Demand for this technology grew throughout the 1970s, spurring the development of an open architecture network environment. Through this environment, users could send and receive information packets across multiple networks. This new architecture became a protocol called the Transmission Control Protocol/Internet Protocol (TCP/IP). During the 1970s and especially during the 1980s, increasing numbers of mainframe computer networks became available for research, military, and commercial purposes. These early networks are the foundation of the modern Internet.

To leverage this new, interconnected communications protocol, Control Data developed CYBERNET, its version of a data-sharing application that could pass packets of information across such a network. This application was an exciting technology with virtually unlimited uses. The first application developed for CYBERNET was for the services organization. Control Data used CYBERNET as a means to run payroll processing for large organizations that needed to distribute amounts in multiple locations. Control Data also used the technology for other data-sending services, and it became an early "e-commerce" application that could move business information through a national computer communications network. However, as a result of the IBM lawsuit, the original application for CYBERNET was no longer needed. Control Data acquired the Service Bureau Corporation (SBC), and this organization already had a similar communications system in place that served more customers. The CYBERNET payroll processing service was moved to the data-sending system at the Service Bureau Corporation. CYBERNET was still used for some limited data sharing services, but now with the Service Bureau Corporation's acquisition, company leaders needed to find more ways this technology could be utilized.

Within the HRMS idea factory, an exciting concept emerged. What if the SKILSOURCE application was modified to accept Internet database calls through this CYBERNET data sharing system? Job applicants could enter their résumés through the SKILSOURCE data inputs as before. Now, however, this résumé data could be stored within a mainframe computer connected to the network. Potential employers would then be able to search this résumé database through any mainframe terminal connected to the CYBERNET data sharing system. By leveraging the query tools available within SKILSOURCE, they could filter out a group of potential employees who had skills matching their search criteria. Both the job applicants and the employers could conduct their job recruiting and job searches nationally, opening more possibilities to match the skill sets of the applicants with compatible jobs and, at the same time, connect employers with a much larger pool of qualified candidates. It was a terrific idea. Programming work began on linking these two applications, and the concept became a reality. This resulting application was called CYBERSEARCH, the cornerstone technology for Control Data's electronic employment bureau franchise.

CYBERSEARCH was one of the first computer applications created for the job recruiting sector, and Human Resource Management Services invested heavily in this network data-sharing software. Roger Arent, vice president of operations, led the development of this service. To make CYBERSEARCH truly a national job recruiting service, multiple employee bureau offices linked to the same network needed to be established throughout the United States. The first CYBERSEARCH employment office was opened in Chicago, but within a year, CYBERSEARCH offices unlocked their doors elsewhere in Houston, Dallas, Los Angeles, Philadelphia, Irvine, San José, and Minneapolis. This business concept quickly became a profitable business application. During 1977, the first year CYBERSEARCH was in operation, the service generated $300,000 in sales. The next year CYBERSEARCH earned $1.7 million. Revenues increased by another million dollars in 1979, resulting in earnings of $2.7 million. By joining these separate computer applications, Control Data innovation had created a highly successful HR business. The recruitment service was also used internally by members of the HR function. Control Data job recruiters heavily leveraged CYBERSEARCH to locate potential employees to fill a variety of positions. So while Human Resource Management Services had facilitated the launch of a new business, it also developed an important recruitment tool to help Control Data locate and recruit new employees as well.

Human Resource Management Services was also tasked with developing various educational courseware offerings available through Control Data's PLATO technology. In 1975, HRMS purchased the General Mills Creative Learning Center. This business had two educational centers located in Edina and Roseville, locations within the Minneapolis/St. Paul area. These creative learning centers became the testing center for many of Control Data's education initiatives. PLATO terminals were installed with the two centers. Both locations were then used to test the courseware created for high schools, colleges, FAIRBREAK courses, and manager training (such as the minority group dynamics course mentioned previously). Focus groups would attend the creative learning centers to test the effectiveness of PLATO courseware. Individuals ranging in age from junior high school to adult learners were often within these centers, helping the courseware creators evaluate the challenge level of each course. These facilities were also used to conduct internal company training when other educational facilities within the Minneapolis/St. Paul area were not available.

The PLATO courseware went through extensive testing to make sure each course was ready to market as an effective educational tool. Members of the target audience were frequently involved in testing new courseware. One such courseware program was created to help the learning disabled master basic reading and writing skills. In 1979, the Minnesota Learning Disabilities Consortium selected Control Data's PLATO system to be the test delivery mechanism for its special learning needs curriculum. The Minnesota Learning Disabilities Consortium felt the

College students using PLATO at the University of Iowa. (Photo courtesy of the Charles Babbage Institute.)

Children learning on PLATO courseware. (Photos courtesy of the Charles Babbage Institute.)

PLATO terminals gave students a unique and repetitive way to learn cognitive skills. Because the results of the students' efforts were recorded as computer data, the platform was ideal for both teaching learning disabled adolescent students basic skills and providing special education classroom teachers a platform to monitor the progress of these students.

To test the special needs curriculum, two junior high school resource rooms were set up with PLATO terminals. Each terminal came with a keyboard, a touch sensitive display screen, and an audio system. The courses consisted of a remedial reading and language arts curriculum that incorporated methodologies used successfully with learning disabled students. An article, "Project Overview Minnesota Department of Education" written about the special needs project described the curriculum in this way: "Instruction begins with drill and practice lessons that are designed to improve the student's encoding and decoding skills. The lessons focus on letter identification, phoneme/grapheme relationships, vowel/consonant patterns, spelling and syllabication." The students primarily interacted with the PLATO terminal through touch screen responses, working on the PLATO lessons for twenty minutes each day. Some keyboard interaction was also required to improve each student's visual motor skills. When the PLATO session was finished, the students then attended a learning disabilities resource room for part of the day to recap the instruction and work one-on-one with the special education teacher. Each lesson focused on a specific skill so the students could focus on improving one skill at a time.

Students were also continually assessed individually to determine whether the various basic skills presented through the software were mastered. When a student was not able to complete a skill, the program was modified to match the deficiencies discovered through the assessment by the computer program. As the Minnesota Department of Education article describes, "Every PLATO lesson is, in effect, constructed on the spot for each student, using on-going diagnostic information collected from daily performance." Repetition and structured drills were designed so students would retain the new skill. Before a learning disabled student could move on to the next area, the student was required to achieve at least eighty-five percent mastery over the skill set during three consecutive PLATO sessions. This standard was in place because students in this population typically have problems with short term memory loss.

Since data on each student was collected after each PLATO session, the special education teachers were freed from evaluating and could spend more time helping each student overcome the learning difficulties uncovered through the PLATO program. The goals were to give students the necessary skills to overcome reading deficiencies so they could comprehend academic subjects, and also reduce teacher preparation time by more accurately identifying problems with individual learning patterns, styles, and needs. This learning system also provided more accurate accountability by tracking each student's progress in developing the basic skills needed to overcome learning disabilities and achieve academic success. Through this experimental project and several others, Human Resources Management Services encouraged the exploration of the possibilities of computer-based education, principles still used by many educational and occupational computer-based training programs.

Additional learning centers were built as delivery facilities for PLATO computer-based education. A new facility was built in the Twin Cities area, the Arden Hills Learning Center. The rest of these centers were built in regional locations across North America, with new facilities opening in Sunnyvale, California; Rockville, Maryland; and Toronto, Ontario. These creative learning centers formed the backbone of the educational initiatives launched by the HR function during the mid-1970s. A wide range of individuals took part in the computer-based education offered through the PLATO terminals—from high school students struggling through algebra to CDC engineers mastering a new technology, from young adults preparing for their Graduate Educational Development (GED) certificate to CDC managers grumbling through their forty hours of required management training. Tapped for use in these multiple functions, these educational centers became central gathering places for a diverse range of humanity.

With the creative learning centers in operation throughout North America, HRMS was able to market packages of computer-based education courses. One of these groups of courses was a management training program targeted nationally to businesses in 1975. Through these courses, managers would explore financial management, leading through objectives, planning analysis, and decision making. Another group of courses was built off StayWell, focusing on behavior modification and healthy living. The courses available in this offering included weight control, relaxation, personal finance, and insurance buying strategies. Another interesting computer-based course was for police officers in California. This course taught police cadets how to safely use firearms, follow arrest laws, and search and seize property. Another course was designed for M.I.T. students learning about steam traps. As the course explained, "Upon completing the module, you should be able to determine whether a particular steam trap is malfunctioning and if so, how it is malfunctioning." Yet another PLATO offering, the handicapped awareness course, was created to ". . . give students an increased awareness of the individuality

A Control Data Learning Center, offering training courses through PLATO which could be tailored to fit customers' needs. (Photo courtesy of the Charles Babbage Institute.)

and abilities of disabled people." This equal opportunity training course was developed for HR specialists, supervisors, and co-workers of handicapped individuals to improve attitudes and assist partially able individuals achieve successful employment at Control Data. And much like the Control Data institutes, PLATO technology was leveraged through a number of strategic partnerships with high schools, businesses, colleges, and universities to teach computer literacy and skills.

In keeping with the fluid state of everything at CDC, the educational components of this business initiative were eventually moved off into a separate organization from Human Resource Management Services. Control Data Education was created to administrate the development of courseware used by all Control Data education initiatives. PLATO courseware development now fell under the responsibility of the Control Data Education organization, creating the internal training programs, courseware for business centers, and the basic educational curriculum.

Another major employee related service was marketed outside of Human Resource Management Services. StayWell, while an employee benefit, always remained a self contained service. Because StayWell was an acquisition of the Life Extension Institute, this service handled its activities largely outside of the human resource function. Starting in 1985, Staywell began marketing its services externally to outside customers. One of the first major organizations to purchase

StayWell services was the Chrysler Corporation. Working through a cooperative agreement with the United Auto Workers union, Chrysler began offering the StayWell program to union members and, as of this writing, continues to do so. With Chrysler as a major client, StayWell enjoyed significant market exposure. Several corporations embraced the cost savings possible through Stay-Well's health plans; sales of StayWell became quite significant throughout the late 1980s. Several companies purchased StayWell health management services to reduce their overall insurance costs, and StayWell grew into a profitable business unit.

Employees as Entrepreneurs

BILL NORRIS AND HIS CO-FOUNDERS launched Control Data Corporation because the Sperry Rand Corporation had starved their Univac division from resources this engineering group needed to develop groundbreaking technologies. Sperry Rand effectively prevented its employees from being entrepreneurial, self-sufficient employees who would design, develop, and market the innovations the company needed to stay competitive in the fledgling computer hardware industry. As a result, Bill Norris and other founding innovators left the company to launch their own entrepreneurial venture. They created the environment in which Seymour Cray, Jim Thornton, Bob Perkins, Lloyd Thorndyke, and many other innovators were able to engineer cutting edge technologies that put Control Data on a path to success and, at the same time, greatly advanced computer technology. Particularly because of Cray's success, everyone at the company wanted to become the next Seymour Cray, inspiring other creative entrepreneurs to develop equally groundbreaking peripheral devices and computer services. When the situation at Control Data no longer suited him, Seymour Cray left the company to start his own entrepreneurial venture, Cray Research. Bill Norris made the surprising move of investing in Cray's new company, and CDC received a good return on their investment. More than anything, Bill Norris always worked hard to keep the entrepreneurial spirit alive and well both within and without Control Data.

With that principle in mind, Control Data started the employee entrepreneurial advisory office (EEAO), a unique employee support service. This office was located in the Arden Hills manufacturing facility, and it was run by Bob Wesslund. Employees could approach EEAO on a confidential basis, pitching a business idea they would like to pursue as a venture outside of Control Data. Through this service, the employees could receive advice and ideas about how to set up their new business. Wesslund would first evaluate whether the idea made sense. If it had potential, he then passed the concept along to a group of business counselors. These business counselors were made up of senior technical, marketing, and financial executives. They would first evaluate the idea to see if it had any possibility of commercial viability. If the EEAO advisors felt the idea had promise, this group would give the employee access to services, knowledge, and other support. The employee could then begin the process of developing his or her business while still working for Control Data. These employees even had a workspace and access to office machines—all the main resources needed to make their entrepreneurial dreams come true. Control Data was, in effect, encouraging driven, talented employees to leave the company!

The rationale for the employee entrepreneurial advisory office followed the approach Control Data used when Seymour Cray left the company. As Bob Price explains, "Such people will leave anyway." By becoming the avenue an entrepreneurial employee could use to get started on their dream, Control Data was actually building a relationship with an individual the company may want to partner with in the future. While the loss of the Control Data employee would be unfortunate, the income from a continued customer or supplier relationship with the former employee had the potential of returning even more revenue than if the employee had remained with the company. Business reality was on Control Data's side as well, because statistically only one out of every ten would-be entrepreneurs actually left the company. By providing EEAO as an employee benefit, most individuals instead learned how difficult it was to create a new business. Consequently, many of these individuals stayed employed with Control Data, relieved they did not make the risky move to leave the company, pursue their venture, and then unfortunately fail. In the meantime, these employees would spend some time thinking about and even developing a new technology. So, ironically, the employee entrepreneurial advisory office was also a means to retain employees. Through this service, the HR function found another way to keep employees happy with the corporation—while at the same time potentially opening the door to gain a future innovation or a new business partner.

Not every employee with a creative business idea would actually want to leave the company. Some would rather develop an innovation Control Data could then pursue as a new product line or service. What was ultimately even more in the company's interest was developing a way where these employees could suggest and develop business proposals for executive review. With the support of Robert Price, a group of executives and managers within the business development group started the entrepreneurial advisory program. This program created a formal means by which employees could develop business plans and promote them at the executive level. The program had a clear premise: because "today's ideas are the basis for tomorrow's prosperity, it is proposed that Control Data institute a formal practice which identifies and effectively promotes sound business ventures suggested by Control Data's employees." The term used for these employees is "intrepreneur," an individual who wants to develop an innovation internally within a company.

While this program was set up to provide a formal channel for developing internal entrepreneurialism, it also had another benefit. All executives involved in analyzing the proposals would be equally challenged to properly assess the opportunities and risks that came with each proposal. The executives would review these proposals through an underlying methodology used as a basis for deciding whether to pursue a business proposal. The employee submission program would then help foster Control Data's future viability by having both management and employees think imaginatively about the potential business ventures the company could create internally.

Employees who submitted proposals through this program went through the following process:

1. The employee develops a business venture proposal using a format submission that meets the standard for executive review.
2. The business development group previews and screens the documents to verify the proposal is consistent.
3. If the business development group decides the business venture should be considered, the proposal is then given a complete review by a group of executives (the executive forum) to consider the business plan and the overall strategy for the business venture.
4. If the executive forum endorses the proposal, the business development group assumes responsibility for the salary, space requirement, and any other expenses the employee may have to support the business venture's development.
5. Members of the business development group would then help the employee create and present a more thorough business plan to the executive forum.
6. The executive forum would then meet to evaluate the complete proposal.

Depending on the decision of the forum, the employee would either be assigned to the business development group for further support, return to his or her original job, or be assigned to another organization to develop the business venture concept. The executive forum was a structured meeting during which each executive verbally expressed his or her opinions. After each executive had presented an opinion, the outcome for the business proposal was decided.

To recognize employees who came up with promising new business ventures, Robert Price sponsored a formal honorary organization—the Great Performers. Their symbol was the porpoise. If an employee developed a business venture, submitted it through the appropriate format, and had their venture suggestion pass through the first level of executive review, they would become "porpoises." These individuals were given a porpoise pin and accepted into the club. The porpoise was selected as the club's mascot because it is an intelligent creature "that moves with admirable swiftness and occasionally surfaces for exposure." Control Data had other recognition clubs for employee achievements, like the "Sharks" who were members of the sales team, swimming out in the open seas, capturing big sales, primarily away from IBM. If the salesperson had really achieved an impressive sales number, this person became a member of the much smaller, elite "Bull Sharks"—the highest level club honor one could receive in sales.

The most visible and popular internal employee entrepreneurial initiative was the Bright Ideas program. This program was launched in conjunction with the twenty-fifth anniversary of Control Data Corporation in 1982. The rationale for the Bright Ideas program was to both celebrate and recognize that over the previous twenty-five years, CDC employees had driven the innovation of the organization, creating products and services that increased the size of the company from just four individuals to 60,000 employees. Control Data leveraged the entire organization through this program, as it was open to full-time employees, part-time employees, and temporary employees.

Through the Bright Ideas program, employees or groups of employees could submit new ideas that would improve the work they did at Control Data in some unique way. All ideas could be submitted, from simple changes that made a task more efficient to major ideas for new businesses. If a group of employees submitted an idea, they needed to be employees within the same work group (all having the same manager). These ideas were submitted through an official entry form to corporate communications, the department that handled all internal communications. As part of the submission form, each idea needed the signature of the employee's immediate supervisor to make it official. The final requirement was the employees either had to implement the idea immediately or develop an action plan for implementing it in the following months. The deadline for the Bright Ideas program was December 31, 1982.

What would the employees receive if they submitted an idea? The first gift was highly symbolic, as each employee would receive a "Russian thistle" pin (only received for the first submission). This pin symbolized the idea Bill Norris had while he was a young farmer in the 1930s. When his cattle were on the edge of starvation, he had cut budding Russian thistles for hay and saved his herd. Now Control Data was looking for similar ideas to help the company solve all kinds of problems—large or small. The real incentive was much more concrete. All submitted ideas were put into a corporate-wide drawing, and the winners would receive up to a maximum of two extra weeks of vacation. If a group of employees submitted the idea, the number of days would be divided evenly between them, but each employee would receive a minimum of an extra day of paid vacation. Control Data's HR function was giving away a total of 1,300 weeks of vacation, the equivalent of twenty-five years of time, commemorating twenty-five years of Control Data business and innovation. All the vacation time would need to be taken during the 1983 fiscal year.

The company launched an extensive internal promotion campaign to make all employees aware of the Bright Ideas program. It was first introduced in a novel, technological way on October 14, 1982. Scott Meyer, an executive who worked with Bob Price, called every Control Data facility in the United States through a single conference call. The call reached approximately 40,000 employees at the same time. Bob Price then announced the program. This call was the largest corporate conference call ever made in the world at that time. It was also recorded and made available through a hotline, so employees could hear it again whenever they needed. Interested employees could additionally contact an information center to ask more specific questions. All Control Data learning centers were provided with videotapes describing the Bright Ideas program. *The Current* and *Contact*, the internal corporate newsletters, printed updates about the progress of the program through regular articles. "Control Data, more than any other company I know, has always relied on the ideas and entrepreneurship of its employees," Price stated in one of these articles. "If we could look back down the road Control Data has traveled, we'd see an unbroken string of ideas lighting the way—ideas generated by the individuals who are our company." The cartoon symbol for the program was a friendly light bulb wearing sunglasses. Control Data had done everything possible to spur employee interest in the program. Would it work?

The response to the Bright Ideas program was amazing. Starting right away in October, corporate communications received an average of 100 submissions a day. The range of ideas was as broad as the planners had hoped. Many were simple changes that saved money and often were "green" solutions to make better use of resources, such as the following: "My idea is to save some of the packaging materials we receive from vendors and use it again when we have to send materials out. By reusing packing materials, we could save money and would not need to order as often." Other ideas involved a technological innovation to make a task more efficient: "I have designed and implemented a new information retrieval system for our telephone support staff. Instead of distributing a multi-page listing of program revision level information, the same data is now instantly available to the telephone support person on his/her terminal. This saves both time and paper." Other ideas were more employment and social conscious based: "We have diffi-cult[ies] hiring qualified minorities for insurance technical and professional positions. Like other companies, we don't have a training program. We could conduct training for specific insurance disciplines—claims, underwriting, and marketing. Training would be for minorities still in college (or recently graduated), who have no specific job career plans." The ideas kept rolling in through-out the fall and early winter, each one solving a problem and making Control Data a more effi-cient, productive organization.

At the close of the business day on December 31, 1982, corporate communications had received 13,650 total Bright Ideas submissions. The company held the last drawings for the vacation time, and all twenty-five years of the allocated vacation pool was distributed among the employees. Most importantly, these ideas were being implemented across the organization, a savings that one article in *Contact*, early in 1983, estimated would save the company a million dollars a year. Corporate communications did indeed enter all the ideas within a database; man-agers across Control Data could search on them, implementing any ideas that applied to their processes and business needs as well.

Because the Bright Ideas program was so successful, Control Data decided to make it a recurring, permanent program. Corporate communications announced that submissions for the next Bright Ideas program would open again in 1984. Following the incentive template of the previous program, employees would compete for a total of twenty-six years of extra vacation time, commemorating the now-twenty-six years that Control Data had been in business. The 1984 program turned out to be even more popular than the original Bright Ideas program, as corporate communications received 20,409 submissions by the close of the second program. The employee magazine, *Contact*, also began running a Bright Ideas column in each issue. This regular column showcased the ideas of specific individuals, putting a face on each person by including a photograph of the employee with their innovation. Control Data had found a way to encourage new thinking, improve efficiency, and increase employee loyalty within the organization.

A Second Chance

THE ST. PAUL SUPERINTENDENT OF SCHOOLS gave Bill Norris a challenge. Could Control Data find a way to help high school dropouts get into jobs and lead productive lives? Norris took on this challenge, tasking the HR function to come up with a concept they could present to the St. Paul superintendent.

Meanwhile at the prison industries facility within the Stillwater Correctional Facility, HR staff members regularly came in contact with inmates, using this opportunity to learn more about the individuals who made up the prison population. One recurring aspect was the majority of the inmates were young men in their twenties who had little or no education. This situation was true in prisons across the United States. Most prisons contained young men and women, predominately minorities, who did not have sufficient education to secure good employment— and as a result had turned to crime. National unemployment statistics backed up this observation. In 1976, 14.7% of sixteen to twenty-four-year-olds were unemployed—twice the rate of Americans over twenty-four years old. For minorities in this age group, the statistics were even more troubling, with forty percent of sixteen to twenty-four-year-olds classified as unemployed. Half the individuals in these statistics were functionally illiterate, unable to read or comprehend material at a fifth-grade level.

However, within these discouraging statistics, members of the HR function saw a potential business opportunity. If these young people were given a second chance at a basic education in reading, math, and language arts, at least at a high school level equivalency, they would have a better chance to find a better paying job. But if this educational experience took these students the next step further by combining the offerings with job counseling, job seeking, and job retaining skills, the students would have an even better chance of staying employed and not resorting to crime. Control Data was uniquely positioned to make such a concept work. The company could merge its basic education PLATO courseware with the expertise the HR function had gained helping people adjust to full-time work at the poverty-area plants. Control Data Education could develop further basic skills courseware in reading, math, and other areas. Meanwhile, HR could use the materials and knowledge from Employee Advisory Resource to develop the job counseling component for the service.

While the concept had a lot of potential for addressing a social need, how would Control Data turn this concept into a profitable business? The individuals this service would assist, unemployed young people, would not have sufficient funds to pay for this training. The company needed a financial incentive to invest in this business concept. This incentive came from the federal government. In 1973, Congress had voted into law the Comprehensive Employment and Training Act, frequently called CETA. The purpose of this bill was to train long-term unemployed workers in basic skills, then employ these workers for a period of twelve to twenty-four months within public agencies or private non-profit organizations. These individuals would then have both a marketable skill and job experience they could use to move into an unsubsidized private or public sector job. The business concept being considered by the HR staff was a match with the intent of this bill. Other federal and state funding sources were available, like the Work Equity Fund, which would offset the costs of the training program.

An HR team was assembled to develop the concept and answer the challenge from the St. Paul Superintendent of Schools. Richard Conner, the executive who helped launch the ombudsman program at the Stillwater Correctional Facility, was put in charge of this project. He was tasked with leading the team that would bring all these concepts together under one complete package. As Conner recalls, "We came up with some good ideas and developed a flow chart and a business plan. We gave the presentation to the superintendent. Within a half-hour, I had a new job."

During the last half of 1977, Conner and his team researched and tested some methods that could be used within the educational service. The new educational service was originally given the working title "Second Chance" or "Another Chance," but eventually another name emerged that better described the concept—FAIRBREAK. Any individual who had been dealt a bad hand by society would now have a way to break away from their past difficulties through a fair, complete service that would teach them basic skills and prepare them for long-term employment. The FAIRBREAK program would first teach students the concepts and skills they needed to become more effective learners. Comprehensive retention strategies would be taught so these individuals would absorb the material more effectively than they had during their early years in school; they would be "learning how to learn." Then the students who needed remedial training would embark upon exploring the basics—reading, writing, arithmetic—in order to achieve their high school equivalency diplomas. The last section of the learning component was that these students would receive additional education beyond the high school level so they could truly transition into the labor market and better job opportunities.

Meanwhile, the students received additional support through job counseling. This counseling explored the students' long-term and short-term career needs, gave the students additional tools to maintain self-esteem, helped them make job and education decisions, and taught them how to find occupational information. An added component was inspired by Employee Advisory Resource, as the students could receive supportive services to help them through personal problems—whether immediate crisis situations or long-term problems. A brochure about FAIRBREAK succinctly summed up the purpose of the service: "Integral to the FairBreak program is the continuous availability of support services to resolve individual problems in the areas of health, personal problems, and life management. Professional staff monitors each individual's progress and prescribes computer-based activities in the areas of health assessment, chemical dependency, personal finances, etc., as well as individual and group counseling." When their FAIRBREAK experience was over, the students would hopefully have acquired the skills and tools needed to handle the long-term challenges awaiting them in the labor market.

Toward the end of 1977 and the beginning of 1978, the FAIRBREAK team ran a small test run of the educational program, evaluating the concept on a group of ten young unemployed students. The results from this early group were encouraging, demonstrating the FAIRBREAK mix of basic education and job skills training was an effective way to reach these students. The result of this first phase was Control Data received federal and state funding to continue developing the business concept.

To secure major funding, the FAIRBREAK team needed to demonstrate the effectiveness of the service through a more complete "proof-of-concept" test run with a larger student population. The HR team decided to build a FAIRBREAK facility near the Selby-Dale bindery plant in St. Paul, Minnesota. This area of the city was strategically ideal for the test facility, as the local population consisted largely of low income households. Because of the successful Selby-Dale poverty-area plant, Control Data was a respected corporate partner within this community. CDC had the support of local leaders, so creating a prototype facility in this location would ensure the company could get the support needed to recruit a cross-section of individuals from the target population. This test facility was called Operation Inner Dale, and it officially opened its doors in April 1, 1978. Members of the original ten students enrolled at this facility, mixing with a larger group of students from the surrounding community.

Each student was first evaluated by the FAIRBREAK staff to determine what level of education and service was needed. This evaluation was the intake/assessment process, and this process involved the following steps:

1. Identify the reasons why the student is unemployed. This information was gathered through a self-assessment that asked life situational questions like "Who is in charge of my life?," What do I want to do?," and "What barriers do I need to overcome?"

2. Develop a basic skills assessment to determine the degree to which remedial training is necessary for the student.

3. Develop an employment skills assessment to determine the present skill level of the student for temporary part-time employment.

4. Develop assessment materials to determine why the student is unemployed. Included in this process was an analysis of the person's work habits, interpersonal relations, physical health, financial health, and family situation.

Students using PLATO at a FAIRBREAK center. (Photos courtesy of the Charles Babbage Institute.)

5. Develop assessment materials to determine what degree and type of support services are required for the student.

6. Select a sequence of services necessary for the student to effectively participate in Inner Dale.

7. Implement the assessment components for each student.

Based on this assessment, the FAIRBREAK staff could then develop an individualized program, training the students to identify their work-related skills and assist them in establishing their career goals. This individualized approach tailored the curriculum to fit each student's specific needs, helping insure more successful results. The FAIRBREAK staff then helped each student secure a temporary part-time job that matched their skills. Some of these jobs were obtained through a work experience training program launched within the CDC subsidiary Magnetic Peripherals, Inc., where they worked on manufacturing the company's disk drives. Each individual would then work at this part-time job for the duration of their participation in the FAIRBREAK program, earning money to offset the cost of the service and gaining job experience they could build upon during the job hunt process to come.

The FAIRBREAK classes themselves were primarily taught through PLATO courseware, so the individuals could take these classes whenever it best fit their part-time job schedule. If a subject was not available through PLATO, the FAIRBREAK service held traditional classes as well. The academic subjects taught were basic math skills and reading courses. Students were also taught life-coping skills like bargain shopping and balancing a check book. The job skills taught through FAIRBREAK included how to fill out job application forms, how to write a résumé, and how to write a job application letter. When the student finished the program, the FAIRBREAK staff assisted these job-ready individuals search for permanent, career-oriented jobs. To open up their job hunt to a national level, the students entered their resumes into CYBERSEARCH. Once the employee found a permanent job, the FAIRBREAK counselors would follow up with the student during the first few months to make sure this individual was doing well and transitioning into permanent full-time employment.

The basic skills curriculum was carefully constructed, blending introductory videos, PLATO courseware, and textbook materials seamlessly to present a complete package of educational delivery. This curriculum was made up of specific "strands" of lessons, and each student would select the strand he or she wished to explore. The three learning strands consisted of reading, language, and math, and each strand itself contained several lessons for each student to complete. The basic skills curriculum gave each student three kinds of material:

1. PLATO lessons—These materials were direct lessons conducted on terminals that interacted with the PLATO mainframe computer. Each lesson was designed for the student to learn a specific basic skill.
2. Strand booklets—Each strand contained a series of practice exercises that related to the PLATO Lessons for the specific strand. Students used the booklets to work on the exercises available within the strand. These books also served as take-home textbooks.
3. Videotapes—Each curriculum contained overview videotapes that introduced a new strand.

An instructor was available to help each student log in to the PLATO terminal and set up their own learning account. The basic skills curriculum required each student to take an inventory of their current skills to evaluate which strands they should pursue. The PLATO system automatically created a record of the student's starting skill levels, and placed the student in the appropriate strands. The strands themselves were organized in a logical sequence, from simple to complex. As each student worked through the strand, the computer checked the student's progress and gave credit for the knowledge and skills mastered so far. When a student had trouble with a particular skill, the PLATO lesson would provide the student with additional instructions to help master it.

The computer-delivered materials available within each PLATO course were tutorial lessons, drill and practice lessons, remedial help sequences, and mixed practice lessons. When the student was not in front of the PLATO terminal, FAIRBREAK provided additional materials for the student to continue learning outside of the FAIRBREAK facility. These materials consisted of overviews, exercise manuals, and off-line mastery tests. Review periods were built into the computer program to evaluate each student's retention and review the skills learned so far in each course. As each individual mastered a specific skill, the student then had the option to choose which strand to pursue next. By the time a student successfully completed a strand, this person became much more skilled in reading, math, and comprehension—skills they could now utilize in the real world.

Once the student started a new, full-time position, the FAIRBREAK job counselors continued their relationship with the individual. The job counselors would meet with both the individual and the employer to make sure any job-related problems were resolved so the FAIR-BREAK student could remain employed. These sessions included making sure the individuals continued to follow their career plans and if further education was needed, these individuals were pursuing educational opportunities to follow their career plans. This final part of the process completed the FAIRBREAK service, ensuring the individuals made the successful adjustment into long-term, gainful employment within the workforce. Thus FAIRBREAK gave each individual a complete palette of skills training and job placement services—assisting each individual from start to finish.

Tom Varley, an HR executive who had run the internal management training program, became the general manager of FAIRBREAK. Varley had run the management program because of his master's degree in education, so his dual experience with both management and education made him a good fit for leading this new basic skills training service. He assisted Richard Conner to develop the program, so he completely understood the concepts behind the venture. As Tom Varley relates, FAIRBREAK was an ideal way to combine social objectives with business objectives. Control Data had a need to expand the company's manufacturing capabilities, and FAIRBREAK gave the company the opportunity to educate and train potential employees from the inner cities.

The marketing effort for the new venture began. During the first few months, it was difficult for CDC to sell the service to communities because, as was described in an inter-office memo at the time, "The advantages we 'bring to the table' are not perceived, appreciated, or believed by most. We are still viewed by many as just wanting to sell terminals, computers, and are looking for labor dollars to do so. The barrier of being a computer company and not really understood as being experienced in human resources delivery is formidable." This situation would rapidly change. Most of the first graduates from the FAIRBREAK program went on to permanent employment, and this significant outcome was noticed by federal government officials.

In the summer of 1978, Control Data received its first round of financial support through the CETA fund. Control Data then proposed the Department of Labor increase funding so the company could open five more FAIRBREAK centers to locations across the country. As part of the proposal, Control Data emphasized the expertise the company had gained with assisting the target population through its poverty-area plants. The Department of Labor accepted the proposal and worked out a counter-proposal of its own. The Department of Labor ran a similar program, Job Corps, in which young people were trained in basic skills for employment, but demand for these skills was low. Would Control Data offer Job Corps graduates advanced training in computer skills?

Because a large component of the FAIRBREAK program involved improving computer knowledge and skills, the Labor Department's proposal was a good fit for an advanced training and hiring program within FAIRBREAK. In response, Control Data proposed creating an off-shoot FAIRBREAK program called the Advanced Career Employment and Training program, or ACET. Job Corps students would receive advanced computer skills training in data entry, programming, and computer maintenance. These students would move from whatever school they were in and then relocated to Minneapolis for training at the Control Data Institute. If some students were not able to handle the advanced training, they could leave the program and pursue less technical coursework. Upon successful completion of the training, Control Data would guarantee these graduates would be hired by the corporation. The Labor Department liked the proposal and awarded Control Data a $3.3 million contract to train Job Corps youth for positions within the computer industry.

On March 1, 1979, William Norris and other Control Data executives attended a formal signing ceremony for the ACET program with the Department of Labor in Washington, D.C. The ceremony was held in the White House Roosevelt Room; Vice President Walter Mondale was in charge of the event. Vice President Mondale noted during the ceremony this was "an outstanding example of how government and business can work together to solve structural unemployment." The secretary of labor, Ray Marshall, signed the financial support grant for the Department of Labor. William Norris spoke at the event, stating, "One of the keys to solving our problems like health, crime, housing, food, employment, jobs, is through the immediate skills-related education which is easily available in a systematic nontraditional computer-based form." He then described the major functions of the FAIRBREAK program, explaining his vision of how solving the problems of unemployment within the United States had the potential of becoming a multi-billion dollar business. This Job Corps program was centered in Minneapolis, and the FAIRBREAK staff administered the skills program for many years.

Now infused with sustainable funding from the Department of Labor, the HR function rapidly created FAIRBREAK centers. By July 1980, the company had created thirty-two FAIRBREAK programs in multiple U.S. locations. Nearly all the individuals who enrolled in FAIRBREAK remained in the program from beginning to end, as the retention rate was eighty-seven percent. As Tom Varley recalls, students who completed sixteen hours of computer-based training were increasing their basic skills by about one grade level.

While the 1980s continued, forty locations were launched nationwide in cities like Phoenix, Seattle, Boston, Portland, New York, and Washington, D.C. The retention rate increased to ninety-two percent, and fully eighty percent of these graduates went on to receive full-time employment. As a brochure describing FAIRBREAK asserted, "In the last few years, research has also uncovered several methods for helping individuals with low self-esteem change their feelings about themselves and their environment. The computer has been found to be a useful device in this area because of its ability to consistently and continuously reinforce positive behavior." While it was originally intended for young men and women, older students also enrolled in the educational service. FAIRBREAK grew to serve individuals ages sixteen to sixty, and many of these individuals were the heads of their households.

The HR function also spun off a version of FAIRBREAK for internal purposes. Launched in 1980, this in house version of FAIRBREAK was called the skills enhancement program. This initiative was included as a service for employees in low skill positions who had not received a good education before joining Control Data. The goal of the internal skills enhancement program was to improve the productivity and job satisfaction for this target group of employees. The skills and knowledge taught through this program were virtually identical to the public FAIRBREAK system. Almost immediately, this internal version gained positive job retention results. In 1978, before the internal program, Control Data employees in this target low skills population had a thirty percent turnover rate. After 1980, the HR function reported the turnover rate for this segment of Control Data employees dropped significantly to just three percent. Employees who enrolled in the skill enhancement program now had the necessary skills to advance within the company,.

Control Data had another motivation for creating the FAIRBREAK centers. This program was an ideal way to promote the PLATO computer-based education technology. Prospective customers would attend a FAIRBREAK center to see PLATO's courseware, watching the students as they interacted with the computers. By showcasing PLATO in action, the FAIRBREAK centers helped increase sales of Control Data Education's basic skills courseware for customers as well. So besides becoming a revenue generating social venture, FAIRBREAK also helped promote PLATO and its accompanying courseware, making this program a proof-of-concept marketing tool for the PLATO computer-based education system.

Meanwhile, the statistics kept increasing in the right direction. During the early years of the 1980s, eighty-three percent of the FAIRBREAK students successfully completed their training, and the overall job placement percentage remained high at eighty percent. FAIRBREAK continued to refine its offerings, and several centers tailored their programs to match the business needs of the local economy. In Atlanta, for example, students received training in retail sales, clerical office work, and computer programming—all skills that readily transferred into actual jobs available within the Atlanta metropolitan area. By using a combination of state and federal funding, leveraging internal HR experience and know-how, and including PLATO technology in the mix, the HR function had created one of the most important social business ventures in its history.

Then the transformative years of the 1980s placed their significant stamp on FAIR-BREAK. When the CETA funding came up for reauthorization from the federal government, the Reagan administration refused to reinstate the program as part of its effort to reduce the size of government. Now without major government funding, FAIRBREAK was forced to come up with new sources of income. Sustainable income was difficult to find. As Tom Varley describes, the loss of the CETA funding was a significant hurdle that made the FAIRBREAK centers less financially viable. Additionally, FAIRBREAK faced resistance from both local governments and social organizations like the Urban League and the NAACP, as these institutions were providing similar educational services. In several cases, these institutions had a staff of basic skills educators and counselors already in place, so a FAIRBREAK center created a situation where two organizations were providing redundant, competing services.

Because of lack of funds and competition with local educational services, the FAIRBREAK centers were eventually all sold to local institutions. Then the city or social organization's staff gradually assumed the administration over the education center. This occurred with the FAIRBREAK center in Minneapolis. The FAIRBREAK center was sold to the city, but the center went through a two-year transition period where Control Data staff was gradually replaced by city staff. These city and local government centers typically retained the FAIRBREAK basic skills curriculum, but by 1984, FAIRBREAK was essentially over. The main piece that remained was the basic skills courseware. Control Data Education continued selling the courseware to schools, prisons, and corporations—finding a sustainable market for this software. The configuration of the courseware was modified to fit whatever target audience the marketing team was trying to reach, and so the computer-based education system became a major product series all on its own. The only component that did not continue was the job counseling, but the rest of the basic skills components were sold in various configurations throughout the end of the 1980s.

The basic skills computer-based education system became accepted as one of the best curriculums available. Today the basic skills curriculum developed by FAIRBREAK is still a major offering provided by Plato Learning Systems, Inc.

Opportunities in Employment

DURING THE 1980S, THE HR FUNCTION discovered a way to turn typical employment liabilities into positive, profitable outcomes. The function developed two successful ventures that grew out of temporary job recruiting and job layoffs. In both businesses, difficult employment situations were overcome by creating entrepreneurial solutions that additionally benefited Control Data.

Control Data always had a number of temporary secretarial positions open throughout the organization. To fill these positions, the HR function either recruited secretaries through temporary employment services, employment agencies, or through a direct job application process. These hiring methods cost Control Data a great deal of money and time. To reduce these inefficiencies, the HR staff created its own internal temporary agency and charge other line organizations for the use of this service. This business venture was called Control Data Temporary Help Agency, or Control Data Temps, for short. Departments could no longer hire temporary secretaries through outside recruitment services; instead, all these secretarial positions were handled by Control Data Temps.

Control Data Temps was better positioned than the outside temporary agencies to match secretaries who had skills line organizations needed, so the service was embraced by most managers. Soon Control Data Temps expanded to handle all temporary positions within CDC, wherever temporary workers were needed. The Control Data Temps organization created a database of job openings and résumés, using computer technology to match these résumés with job openings. Although not every manager liked being required to hire through this central recruitment service, it generally did reduce costs and improve hiring results. By shifting these needs to an internal service, the HR function was more involved and was able to exert a higher level of control over who was hired. But the evolution of this business did not stop there. Following the CDC entrepreneurial pattern, Control Data began offering the service to outside customers. The result of this transition paid off, as by the mid-1980s, Control Data Temps was receiving $15 million in average annual revenue. Through this employee service innovation, the HR function satisfied internal demand and built a profitable employment service.

The next employment service the HR function developed turned adversity into opportunity. When Control Data began the painful process of downsizing the employee base during the mid-1980s, the HR function discovered an unlikely business concept. The company created Transition Services, an internal group of offerings designed to help former Control Data employees find new jobs. These services were managed through two divisions—transition services development and transition services operations.

Transition services development focused on providing former CDC employees with resources and support to find their next employment positions. Employees now had access to career consultants who helped them prepare résumés and learn about unemployment benefits they were eligible to receive. Transition Services obtained lists of job openings from other companies, and the former employees had access to computer terminals linked to databases they could use to launch their job hunt. Printers were also installed within these centers. Former employees could use these printers to create hard copy letters and résumés for their job campaigns. These employees also received interviewing skills training to help them answer questions better during upcoming interviews with potential employers. To complete these transitions service offerings, support groups met regularly. These groups discussed the stress of the job search and shared hopes, frustrations, and fears of the process. These support groups provided a social cushion that helped participants feel they were not alone.

Transition services operations ran the facilities required to administrate these services. These facilities were called outplacement centers, and they housed the transition services. Care was taken to ensure former employees were made to feel comfortable returning to Control Data to receive these services. For example, one outplacement center was located within the main CDC headquarters building in Bloomington, and this outplacement center took up a large space directly on the first floor of the building. The former employees could enter the outplacement center without having to walk past working Control Data employees. This separated the activities of the center from the daily routine and prevented potentially awkward situations where former co-workers could cross paths in the hallways.

The outplacement centers were created as an ethical response to reducing the labor force. These individuals, through no fault of their own, had lost their jobs, and Control Data responded by helping them transition into new careers. But what began as an ethical response to adversity developed into an entrepreneurial venture. The outplacement centers became very successful at placing former employees into new positions. Capitalizing on this success, the HR function began selling these outplacement services to other companies going through layoffs. This outplacement consultation service eventually became a standalone business. Downsizing corporations leveraged Control Data's expertise to help employees transition into new jobs. So even in the midst of reducing the size of the company, the HR function found an entrepreneurial way to build an entirely new business. The outplacement centers played an important role during the final years of Control Data's transformation, easing employees back into the job market and into the next stage of their careers.

Not Business as Usual

THE ENTREPRENEURIAL VENTURE that caused the most structural reorganization of the HR function was Control Data Business Advisors, Incorporated (CDBAI). The business concept behind this organization was to assemble a complete support service for existing and start-up businesses. These companies could hire Control Data Business Advisors to gain assistance for everything from acquiring venture capital to organizing their human resources function to marketing their products and services. The purpose of CDBAI was to give these businesses the management tools and advice they needed to handle the pitfalls of launching a start-up venture or overcoming a major obstacle. Control Data Business Advisors would increase the chances these client companies would grow into successful organizations. As Bill Norris described in an article for the *Barcelona International Academy of Management* after his retirement, "The greatest entrepreneurial opportunities always lie in areas where existing goods and services fall most critically short of meeting needs." Through CDBAI, Control Data hoped they had found a niche service space where there was a great deal of pent-up demand. Many CDBAI services could be sold to a huge spectrum of companies, large and small. Through this diverse mix of offerings, CDBAI was uniquely positioned to become a profitable business venture.

The odds were (and are) against a start-up business surviving longer than just a few short years. It typically takes a new organization ten to twelve years before the return on investment is fully realized. And at the time CDBAI was set up, it was calculated nearly eighty percent of all start-up ventures failed within just the first five years of operations. Control Data Business Advisors' primarily mission was to drastically reduce this failure rate, setting forth a goal of reducing this rate to around twenty percent for its client companies. CDBAI, through its educational offerings and enterprise consultants, would be the backbone entrepreneurs could leverage for help in any areas where they were experiencing problems. This concept personified the business philosophy of Bill Norris—because entrepreneurs are the key to economic vitality, these individuals needed support by whatever means was available. New business ventures are the largest source of new jobs, with some studies indicating nearly eighty percent of all new jobs emerge from small businesses. Similarly, the career opportunities available in an emerging business are greater because a growing company has more room for advancement than a larger, mature business. As long as America continued to foster a cultural environment that gave entrepreneurs better chances to thrive and prosper, the economic future of the country would also thrive.

With the rationale for Control Data Business Advisors clearly defined, Control Data began to build the organization. The genesis of Control Data Business Advisors came about through a five-member team representing the services provided through CDBAI. This group, led by Peter Bailey, an executive with entrepreneurial skills formerly in charge of business products, was a group of specialists targeted from disciplines that would make up the products and services available. These individuals were Jim Bowe, a vice president of communications; Marv Swenson, a vice president of marketing and sales; Henry Hodde, an executive within strategic planning; and Bob Rutishauser, a corporate vice president of finance. Together, these executives developed the strategic plan for the new organization. Armed with this plan, the CDBAI team began tobuild the new business venture.

Just like the business ventures Control Data Business Advisors wanted to guide, the CDBAI organization needed its own flow of start-up venture capital. To secure this income, the company decided to split off a management function typically wrapped inside the overall cost of the parent organization—the corporate-level human resources function. The corporate HR function would become a separate line organization required to have a profit/loss statement like any other product or services group. However, HR offices within other line organizations would not be moved; only the corporate-level office would become part of CDBAI. The strategy was if Control Data moved its corporate human resources staff into a profit and loss environment, and this group sold its HR services to outside organizations, the cost of the function would be substantially reduced. Because Control Data no longer had an internal HR staff at the top corporate level, the parent company would have a competing roster of independent human resource contractors from which it could receive bids for various services. These competing contractors would respond to needs quicker and offer competitive pricing, reducing the overall expense of these services. The cost of the HR function would then be offset by the income CDBAI received from outside client companies. Perhaps best of all, many human resource products and services were already available to roll out and market.

The CDBAI strategy looked promising. The HR function's employee attitude surveys and job evaluation systems were already in demand by outside companies. By combining these offerings with other business advisory and marketing services, Control Data would have a separate, potentially profit-making organization almost immediately. Starting in 1982, this concept was put into action when a majority of the members of the corporate human resource staff moved out of the CDC Bloomington headquarters to a leased facility five miles down the freeway. This facility became the regional office for Control Data Business Advisors in the Midwest area. Overnight the corporate HR function was spun off into an independent business, as several HR managers took new roles as line managers. The split from Control Data was complete; Control Data Business Advisors would now sell all its human resource services back to the parent corporation through negotiated contracts with other CDC line organizations.

Including the regional office within Bloomington, Minnesota, Control Data Business Advisors set up four other business advisor center locations across the United States. Two international business advisor centers were also set up in the United Kingdom and Australia. George Troy was selected as president of the new organization. Control Data Business Advisors was ready to take on client companies through its three main business groups:

1. Business Services—This group focused on developing courses and consulting resources to help CDBAI client companies both start and manage their businesses. Gail Bergsven was placed in charge of this service organization. Starting her career as an administrator, Bergsven (later Gantz) was now a senior line manager.

2. Human Resource Services—This group was in charge of all human resource offerings, like benefits and compensation services. They also administrated the pool of business consultants available to customers. Roger Wheeler, the architect of so many HR initiatives, was the president of Human Resource Services.

3. Marketing and Planning Services—This group handled the marketing strategies and services Control Data had available for assisting new small businesses advertise and sell their products. Jim Morris, one of the early managers of Employee Advisory Resource, was selected to head Marketing and Planning Services.

The foundation for the business services was a courseware series—available both on PLATO and in live classrooms—that explored the principles of raising capital, planning company finances, creating marketing strategies, and other key aspects of business development. As for the advising services, Control Data Business Advisors set up a consulting talent pool of 2,000 technical, professional, managerial, and executive personnel from within Control Data, other participating corporations, and various academic institutions. Members of this talent pool could be called upon by CDBAI to help business clients. These experts were available to clients on an "as needed" basis. If CDBAI called on an organization to provide a consultant, this organization was required to release the individual. CDBAI thus could tailor the consultant options to fit a specific entrepreneur's business needs. Because these individuals were full-time and available on-call, Control Data Business Advisors could also keep the cost of these consultant fees low, making them more affordable to a wide range of client companies. Lastly, to help business ventures leverage the possibilities of technology, CDBAI contained technology service operations. This group consisted of computer industry advisors who helped clients decide which technologies would best suit their day-to-day business flow.

A new business cannot survive without an initial investment of venture capital. Another specialized service, Venture Capital Support Operations, was available to assist clients in securing much needed capital through various investment companies. Control Data Business Advisors developed educational courses and advisory services designed to help business ventures secure capital on their own. One of these resources was the *Guide to Soliciting Venture Capital*, a book that described how to develop business plans to attract potential investors. The guide identified the key hurdle in obtaining venture capital, stating, "Entrepreneurs just starting a business has additional disadvantages to overcome in establishing the credibility of the business with potential investors." The guide explained how a financially oriented business plan differed from venture capital financing:

1. The main purpose for the business plan is to gain capital as debt, equity, or a combination of the two sources.
2. The business plan succeeds when, after it describes all of the financial elements of the business, the plan attracts an equity investment or loan.

Client companies could purchase packages of these consulting and educational services, leveraging the business expertise and experience available through Control Data's consultants, many of whom had experienced several years of highs and lows as the parent corporation carved its path within the computer technology industry. Control Data began as a start-up venture as well, so the CDBAI advisors understood the unique challenges faced by young companies.

These client companies could also receive venture capital directly from Control Data. These venture funds were administrated through two internal organizations—Small Business Investments and the Community Venture Fund, Incorporated. When these clients received funds from Control Data, they were essentially considered cooperative ventures by CDBAI. These venture capital investments were typically small, less than fifty percent of the total capital of the new business, but these investments did entail that Control Data would now have a major stake in the strategic planning of the venture. To begin, Control Data would analyze the business plans for the potential affiliate, calculating the effect the investment could have on the CDC organization. If needed, Control Data Business Advisors would then give the business venture educational materials and expertise for developing a well-structured business plan. Once the plan was satisfactory, Control Data would then make the investment in the client company.

Because Control Data was now directly contributing capital to the venture, a member of CDBAI would function as a direct observer of the investment to make sure both the business and Control Data's interests were observed. The advising CDBAI executive had to walk a fine line in this role. As the CDBAI standards book, *A Guide for Managing Cooperative Ventures*, states, "Managing in this context means the process of hiring management responsibility for the investment. It does not mean having a management role in the affiliate." For this role, the CDBAI executive would closely monitor the performance of the cooperative business venture. This person would develop good rapport with the top management of the business venture and also provide regular reports to Control Data's management. The executive was charged with analyzing the available information by comparing actual revenues and profits against the strategic plans of the fledgling organization, reviewing the expenses to verify none of them were "out of line" and wasting capital, and lastly computing business indicators and plotting their trends. The CDBAI executive would guide the strategic direction for the venture as well as the strategic exit for Control Data. The goal was Control Data Business Advisors would eventually gain back a return on Control Data's initial investment and the new company would become a fully independent organization.

When the cooperative venture encountered problems, the business advisor was instructed to review the situation with the CEO of the organization and recommend a plan of action. The CDBAI book, *A Guide for Managing Cooperative Ventures*, contained this procedure for helping resolve issues:

1. Understand the problem. Get at the true problem behind what may be just a symptom.
2. Analyze the problem and its situation.
3. Develop a solution that falls within the resources and capabilities of the company.
4. Implement the solution. Address the problem in a timely fashion, and work to avoid its recurrence.

Ultimately it would be up to the company's CEO to decide what plan of action to take. The CDBAI executive could arrive at possible solutions, but Control Data could not dictate the final decision made by the company's CEO.

From venture capital assistance to executive consulting, the Business Services group had a complete range of management services. Client companies could use these services to gain an advantage in both managing and growing their business venture.

The human resources component of CDBAI offered six services. One of these offerings was the employee attitude survey, a survey that measured the job satisfaction level of employees. The job analysis provided client companies with a thorough review of each position within the company, defining the tasks performed by each individual to create an overview of the functions within the organization. A workforce alternatives service drew up a plan whereby the client company could consider some different hiring options to complete all tasks required by the business. CDBAI also leveraged Control Data's considerable background in affirmative action to help guide clients with their equal opportunity employment policies and procedures. Control Data Business Advisors also provided a personnel advisor program which helped client organizations establish their HR policies and procedures.

Likewise, a performance appraisal system was available, ". . . developed specifically to help open up the manager/employee communication process and assure that every employee is treated with fairness and consistency." Through this system, the client company would set up a solid process for employee review. This performance appraisal system was sold through four levels of service. Each subsequent level provided more HR services than the previous level.

The human resources group could help client companies design and manage a complete HR function. The HR group provided the tools a client company needed to develop its internal employee relationship culture. By leveraging the many groundbreaking HR services Control Data had developed to hire, retain, and motivate its own employee population, client companies would have better results hiring and retaining qualified, committed employees.

Through its third advisory group, marketing and planning services, Control Data Business Advisors emphasized if a business was going to succeed, it needed to create a series of high quality products and services sold at competitive prices that, in turn, satisfied a customer demand. The business venture needed to spend large sums on researching and developing its product line as well as spending equally large sums on a marketing campaign that supported this product line. The CDBAI marketing and planning consultants would review the market space through which the client company planned to sell its products and services. One key ingredient the market advisors looked for through this analysis was whether this market space was rapidly growing; this ensured that strong competition existed within the sector so all companies were creating innovations to survive and distinguish themselves. Once the parameters of the external market were understood, the marketing and planning advisors would then look inward at the client company. These advisors would evaluate whether the client organization had enough available production capacity to meet the market demand. The advisors also recommended the client corporation have as wide a range of products available as soon as possible, so the income on the business venture was not dependent on the volatile market space of only one or two products or services.

The business, human resources, and marketing services made up the three legs of the stool a struggling business needed to be successful. This complete patina of offerings reflected both Control Data's history as a small maverick organization and its ongoing philosophy to foster the growth of similar entrepreneurial organizations. Now with its products and services offerings in place, CDBAI began its marketing and sales effort.

During the first years of Control Data Business Advisors, the clients who purchased services were primarily larger organizations who contracted for various parts of the human resource offerings. However, because the goal of the new company was to support small start-up businesses, the staff investigated ways the capabilities of these larger HR services could be downsized to make them more affordable for smaller companies. Control Data Business Advisors eventually began receiving contracts for its services by large and small business ventures, and the new organization was able to build and improve upon its base of services.

To make the concept work, Control Data Business Advisors would have to overcome some internal hurdles of its own. The plan was to have a year-long transition period, during which CDBAI gradually wean itself from corporate funding to become an independent subsidiary. As described previously, members of the former internal HR function would make this transition by actively marketing the human resource services back to Control Data and external customers. Unfortunately, the decision to split off the corporate level HR function as a separate line organization was not vetted through all the HR staff, and some individuals were not happy in their new role. David Noer, the third president of CDBAI during the mid-1980s, explained, "They became a draftee army." These HR employees now had to become salespeople, and not everyone was eager or had the skills to take on these marketing tasks. Some of these individuals were afraid of meeting potential customers and others just outright feared rejection. Most importantly, several individuals felt if they did not receive a one-hundred-percent response in their sales, their paychecks would be reduced. This insecurity translated into higher levels of stress that made the transition difficult for several corporate-level HR professionals.

There was some internal political fallout within the corporation as well, because now HR managers had to provide quotes for the costs of their services to former Control Data colleagues. Many of these relationships, previously quite informal and friendly, now became much more formal and professional. Control Data executives and line managers treated the HR consultants like any business cost that needed to be kept in check, receiving bids from other outside HR services to force CDBAI to reduce the prices on their bids for HR services. This was a significant, distressing change in culture for the HR staff, as it had the consequence of doubly harming professional friendships and reducing the income for CDBAI. Now that the HR function was split away from the corporate organization, it was soon revealed just how much expense was required to run the corporate-level HR function. Generating the income to offset these expenses proved difficult, and it soon became clear it would take longer than a year to wean CDBAI from the financial books at corporate headquarters.

Control Data Business Advisors recognized these issues and made some adjustments to improve how the HR function worked within this new environment. Other companies were interested in Control Data's experiment in spinning off the HR function, and the company was honest about how difficult it was to make this transition. One of the main things CDBAI worked at maintaining was a stable work environment. Despite the stress of these changes, the spin-off corporate HR organization needed to continue to nurture creativity and support employees in their new roles. The spin-off organization had to instill a spirit in the new culture that would overcome fear of failure and reject the status quo of the original work environment. Individuals also needed to continue to maintain ownership over their creative ideas and have enough time to think through their ideas without distractions. Ultimately, the spin-off organization should become a more dynamic and exciting organization than the one which had existed. David Noer, the CDBAI president mentioned previously, delivered a speech at Utah State University in 1985, in which he illustrated the principles Control Data recommended when separating a corporate function into an independent business:

1. The business should be consistent with (but not identical to) the company's own goals.
2. The company should take an equity position in the new business, thus participating in both the risk and reward.
3. The individual should take a well-defined risk, for example, a salary reduction which would apply toward his or her own equity position for increased income later on.
4. The entrepreneur should also have a well-defined reward, based on the development of the business.
5. Since the business is to be independent, there should be rules facilitating the build-up of capital.

But even though CDBAI was able to overcome the shift in internal culture and structure, the organization faced an even larger hurdle in the marketplace. While many companies were interested in the educational services available, the concept of giving even partial control over a private company to a Control Data executive was not a comfortable proposition for most independent-minded entrepreneurs. Plus, through its human resource services, CDBAI could potentially have fairly intimate knowledge about the compensation and benefits specific individuals received in the client companies. Control Data would have a lot of influence over how a company conducted its business, and for many corporate executives, this was not attractive. The market stubbornly, slowly took its own dogged time to develop, and many critics within Control Data concluded there was not enough demand for CDBAI to justify continuing the organization.

Still, Control Data Business Advisors continued to gain creditability and the organization did assist many businesses, large and small, overcome obstacles. Just like any other start-up venture, CDBAI needed some time to grow and hone its services before it could completely return its initial promise. Control Data Business Advisors did achieve one of the primary goals of reducing corporate expenses. Unfortunately, time was against CDBAI. The problems within the larger organization in the second half of the 1980s caused support for the organization to eventually wane. Although Control Data Business Advisors survived the first troubles of 1985, its slow growth made it an easy target during the second round of problems in 1989.

David Noer described the sad, final outcome of CDBAI, saying, "Control Data implemented an innovative effort that would have succeeded despite many tactical errors if the parent organization had not been in such a period of decline." Eventually its budget was significantly cut and CDBAI ceased to be a major part of Control Data. Its various parts were spun off, sold, or re-absorbed back into Control Data. Finally only the business consulting services remained in Control Data Business Advisors, and the remaining organization was discontinued in 1990. However, many former employees still feel that had Control Data been in a better position to support the organization in the long term, CDBAI would have prospered into an independent, viable business. Control Data Business Advisors was either an interesting business concept that ultimately did not work, or an innovative concept ahead of its time. Regardless, Control Data Business Advisors was yet another example of the direction Norris had for the overall organization—create a service business that would improve the survival chances of new businesses. CDBAI was a noble experiment.

Advocating for Small Business

DURING THE EARLY 1980s, the HR function collaborated with other business functions within Control Data to extend the Employee Advisory Resource concept to small businesses. The motivation behind this program was, "Control Data is concerned about the survival of small business as one of society's major needs." The company was now implementing its employee relationship ethics to external businesses. To do this, the company set up a twenty-four-hour hotline specifically for small business owners who had an issue with Control Data they wanted the company to resolve. Small business owners could call this hotline and EAR operators would assist them, providing the small business owners with contact information and low-level assistance on various business matters.

However, if the initial EAR contact failed to resolve the situation, the EAR counselors would refer the matter to a new support organization, the small business advocate office. Launched in 1981, this organization acted as a liaison to help resolve problems related to purchasing, sales, accounts payable, government contracts, service contracts, or special funding programs. It did this by connecting the small business directly with the internal resources that could help resolve the problem. Legal services were also available through the small business advocate office. Administered by Control Data Business Advisors, these services gave small businesses that had a dispute with CDC another alternative for the legal support they needed without having to seek out more costly legal services elsewhere. The purpose of the small business advocate office was to enhance the company's relationship with small organizations: "Our business strategy encourages the promotion of small business in this country, so that the company actively seeks both vendor and customer relationships." The combination of the EAR hotline and the small business advocate office ensured the company would cultivate positive business relationships between small organizations and CDC. The small business would get its issue resolved in a responsible, rapid, and fair manner, serving both to resolve the issue and help make it more likely the small business would want to continue its relationship with Control Data.

One of the most common issues resolved by the small business advocate office was Control Data would occasionally have an overdue payment with a supplier. In a 1982 article written about the small business advocate office in the *Management Current*, Jim Morris, the head of the service at the time, stated about twenty-five percent of the cases involved late payments. As Morris described, this problem was very infrequent. However, because CDC's accounts payable department processed 40,000 invoices each month, odds were likely a payment would be missed or inadvertently delayed. This could be a significant problem for a small business, as these organizations might only have income from a few major sales to rely upon at any given time. Because of this situation, these companies leveraged the small business advocate office to receive their late payments. By contacting this service, small businesses had a direct line with Control Data management to resolve these issues.

If the normal connections and resources provided by the small business advocate office were not sufficient to handle the issue, the company utilized yet another concept from EAR—the ombudsman. If an outside vendor or customer had a conflict with a Control Data department, the small business advocate office would assign a CDC manager not connected with the department in question to evaluate the situation and arrive at a fair resolution between the outside party and the CDC department. Just like the ombudsman function utilized to resolve employee conflicts, the small business ombudsman would advocate for the system rather than either party. Through the impartial ombudsman role, the small business advocate office was able to resolve a number of difficult issues, reducing the likelihood that many of these issues would escalate into litigation.

Some of these small business ombudsman meetings could grow heated. Jim Morris, one of the architects of EAR and, at this point in his career, a member of Control Data Business Advisors, was often called upon to serve as the small business ombudsman. During one specific incident, he had to face and attempt to calm down a very irate contractor. This individual made it known that he had served in Vietnam and claimed he had killed over one hundred people during the war with his bare hands, and had no qualms about revisiting his combat experience again on various individuals within a certain CDC department. Fearing this meeting could turn dangerous, Jim asked that Jeff Roller, a large security guard and former police officer employed by the company, be visibly near during the deliberations with this irate vendor (whenever Jim Morris would say, "Better get Jeff," the secretary knew the ombudsman meeting would be a thorny one). Morris was eventually able to clearly state that he was advocating the process for resolution between this contractor and Control Data. As the small business ombudsman, Jim Morris was able to calm down the irate contractor, cut through the red tape, and arrive at a solution beneficial for both parties.

The HR function defined the target audience for the small business advocate office to include suppliers, customers, other small businesses, businessmen's organizations, large local corporations, large national corporations, and Control Data employees working in various divisions that served small businesses. In 1981, the performance of the small business advocate office was reviewed. During the first ten months of the year, twenty-six contacts were received by this office. About half of these calls were received through EAR and the rest either directly from the executive office or from other employees and executives. Sixty-one percent of these contacts had an issue they needed to resolve with the company. The remaining contacts were primarily requests for information about Control Data. Through this interesting service, the company demonstrated its commitment to encouraging the growth and prosperity of small businesses.

Providing the Place

IN THE BIG PICTURE, Control Data Business Advisors was a very large piece of the total pie which Control Data wanted to provide entrepreneurial business ventures. Control Data Business Advisors was intended to be a backbone management services organization that assisted small businesses with marketing, financial counseling, strategic planning, capital investment, and HR practices. However, this organization didn't provide the physical incubator which a new business venture needed to actually develop its products and/or services. To complete the offerings available to small and start-up businesses, Control Data established a connected chain of support centers that pulled together the services and facilities a small business needed inside one facility. Bill Norris had visited such incubators in his travels to Europe, and wanted to support a similar concept in America. Now it was the late 1970s, and the United States was in terrible economic shape as the country struggled against both double-digit inflation and double-digit unemployment. If Control Data created a chain of support centers to help emerging businesses, these new businesses might help jumpstart the struggling economy.

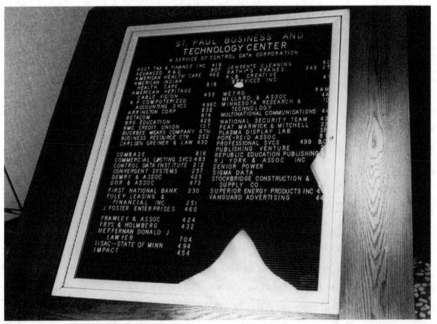

The company directory at the first Business and Technology Center in St. Paul, Minnesota. (Photo courtesy of the Charles Babbage Institute.)

This chain, called the Business and Technology Centers (BTC), were start-up development incubators. They combined everything Control Data had created and developed throughout the years. Small business entrepreneurs could essentially "shop" all of Control Data's products, services, and technology in one location, leveraging the pieces they needed to build their new businesses. The majority of the ventures the Business and Technology Centers supported were technology-focused client companies, as Control Data obviously had the most expertise and background in supporting these types of startup ventures.

The Business and Technology Centers were first and foremost created to accommodate the physical facilities a technology start-up required to develop its operations. Each center contained a large amount of office space which the small businesses could rent a portion as their base of operations. Then, as Control Data described in its promotional material, "these centers provide small, technically orientated tenant companies with many of the same resources available to large corporations." Each center had a drafting facility where engineers could draw and refine their product designs. The Business and Technology Center also contained a clean room where sensitive equipment and materials could be stored and maintained. A flexible laboratory space was present where the tenant ventures could share to develop and test their products.

If the technology the start-up venture needed was not available within the facility, the Business and Technology Center acted as a central library, giving tenant businesses the ability to research and locate the technologies they required to complete their product and/or service line. Likewise, a library of business materials was included at each center, helping the small businesses research market trends and investment information. To round out the physical spaces contained within the center, a state of the art conference room was available. The tenant entrepreneurs could schedule use of the room, often to deliver presentations to investors and bankers.

Control Data computer and business services were also installed within each Business and Technology Center to provide tenants with the low-cost business support they needed to survive. As an example, fax machines in the early 1980s cost approximately $2,500 apiece, way too expensive for a new business. Each BTC contained a fax machine, giving tenants access to an important technology they normally could not afford. Computer printers and word processors were also available through the mainframe network to answer each business venture's soft copy and hard copy document needs. Naturally, the latest Control Data mainframe computer system was also installed at each center. The tenant ventures could use the data services provided through the mainframe terminal to handle their daily business needs—purchasing and selling cycles, payroll processing, and general accounting. The tenants could then save their data on the storage media connected to these mainframe computers. These connected terminals also became the communication tools for yet another early online community. The tenant entrepreneurs could send electronic messages (they were not called email at this time) to other entrepreneurs on the network, sharing ideas, asking for advice on how to handle laws, and making business propositions. Another important service was that each Business and Technology Center had a central receptionist and switchboard; the person at this switchboard would answer each line using the company name of that line. This helped give each tenant company a professional image.

Education was a major component within each Business and Technology Center. The most common subject taught was how to create complete business plans. For many beginning entrepreneurs, business plans are the most difficult part of the process. Control Data trainers held seminars on how to draw up thorough business plans. They also connected these entrepreneurs with individuals in the same or related fields to help them understand the marketplace they were trying to enter. These connections, in turn, helped the entrepreneurs draw up better business plans. These plans could then be submitted to potential investors and bankers to help the new business gain much needed capital. The Business and Technology Centers also arranged a number of seminars led by small business investors and loan officers, explaining the investment and small loan process to the tenant entrepreneurs. Frequently, meetings were also more support-oriented, as various professionals would either call in or meet with the tenant entrepreneurs to find out the current issues and concerns they were facing. In effect, they served as a quasi boards of directors. Control Data Business Advisors had a presence in these facilities as well, making its business consulting, human resources, personnel recruiting, and business education services available. Because PLATO terminals were present at each Business and Technology Center, these small business entrepreneurs could leverage the courses CDBAI had developed as needed.

Other key services rounded out the small business resources. Each Business and Technology Center housed a marketing service so tenant organizations could run their promotional campaigns. A legal representative was also present so the tenants could access legal counsel to draw up business contracts, complete internal legal documents, and even handle lawsuits.

Through this combination of physical space and support services, the Business and Technology Centers contained a complete set of tools each new small business needed to grow and mature into a vibrant, independent company. Eventually these small businesses would outgrow the facilities available and move into their own buildings. Before that happened, Control Data would gain income from the rent it received from the tenants and payment for the services the company offered. Because most of these ventures were technology-oriented, Control Data would also have a direct relationship with new, cutting edge technology companies with whom CDC could perhaps partner or even potentially acquire. If nothing else, Control Data would have a finger placed directly on the pulse of new, cutting edge technology.

The Business and Technology Centers were started concurrently with Control Data Business Advisors to complete the small business support venture. The early centers were direct Control Data investments, and they were staffed by Control Data employees. The first center was built in St. Paul in 1979, and others were soon built domestically in Minneapolis, Toledo, Bemidji (Minnesota), Charleston, Baltimore, Champagne (Illinois), and Philadelphia. An international Business and Technology Center was built in Amsterdam. Like the poverty-area plants, each Business and Technology Center was built in a job-deficient area to stimulate employment growth and entrepreneurialism in these communities. As an article written in *Ebony* magazine in 1982 describes, "The pioneer project, located in St. Paul, houses fifty-nine small businesses and has created 287 new jobs." By creating these facilities, Control Data Corporation supported the development of new businesses that would in turn help the overall economy in their local communities. Each Business and Technology Center also served as a bridge out to the community. Just like the entrepreneurs needed help with business planning, many community leaders also needed education on how to evaluate business plans. Through this service, the Business and Technology Centers were able to join entrepreneurs with community leaders and better support the growth of new companies and jobs within these communities.

As the 1980s went on, Control Data licensed the concept to state, city, and community economic development agencies. The licensed facilities followed the Control Data model and were all linked electronically through Control Data's BTC mainframe network. The staff members at these facilities were initially trained by Control Data consultants to keep the offerings consistent among the licensed centers. To make sure staff at the Control Data and licensed centers were current on the latest technology and business trends, the Business and Technology Centers held regular conferences. Smaller conferences were held every six months, and a large conference was assembled once a year. These three-day conventions were filled with seminars, and keynote speakers were part of the itinerary as well. Walter Mondale, the former vice president of the United States and presidential candidate, spoke at the 1988 convention. As Wilbur French, the vice president of Business and Technology Centers (1982-1988) recalls, "He came to talk about politics in state and federal government, and how to work with government to create jobs." These conventions served to directly communicate with and educate staff members at all Business and Technology Centers simultaneously. The BTC staff members then returned to their centers with additional knowledge to help their tenant entrepreneurs develop their business concepts.

Perhaps symbolically, the Business and Technology Centers completed the circle of Control Data Corporation's development as a company. CDC had started out as a small business at 501 Park Avenue. Now during the early 1980s, at the height of the company's prosperity, Bill Norris and his management team were embarking on a venture to stimulate the creativity and innovations needed to create new companies and drive capitalism to further economic heights. Such new economic heights were needed, as the U.S. economy was suffering through a stagnant period. By creating an incubator for small businesses and by leveraging the expertise and knowledge available within Control Data, the company would promote the creation of new, groundbreaking businesses. These small businesses would then grow to create new jobs within their communities, improving the social and economic well-being of as many individuals as possible. The underprivileged and the uneducated could become the employees of these new businesses, spurring sustainable economic growth for these communities.

These centers fit directly into Bill Norris's approach to business, but the Business and Technology Centers were controversial for many of Control Data's shareholders. They did not feel these centers added to the company's bottom line of developing computer technology. Norris was characteristically unapologetic about the BTCs, saying, "We all live in the same communities, not on a charitable basis, but on an actual fundamental basis." The Business and Technology Centers satisfied a major concern Norris had about the poverty-area plants. Eventually each of those manufacturing facilities would become obsolete and forced to close. However, the Business and Technology Centers could continue, empowering fledging entrepreneurs with the tools and resources they needed to build the next generation of businesses within their communities. For Norris, the Business and Technology Centers were a strategic long-term initiative that would sustain Control Data into the future.

The Business and Technology Centers succeeded in doing everything they set out to do—except make money for Control Data. For the small businesses, this incubator environment proved ideal. The BTCs significantly increased the likelihood of the tenant entrepreneurial ventures surviving and becoming stable businesses. The percentage of new businesses able to grow and move out of the BTCs was impressive. Unfortunately, that successful outcome was also the major problem—the tenants moved out. What typically occurred was a one or two person operation would initially rent office space in the BTC. As the small business grew, these tenants would rent out larger blocks of space within the center. Then, just as the business was paying its largest amount of rent, it would outgrow the Business and Technology Center and move out.

Suddenly Control Data had a large vacancy which was no longer generating income. As Jack Baloga, a former executive of Control Data Properties, Inc. (the function that administered the BTCs) describes, "It is very difficult to build a successful business when the concept is to have your customers go away." Because most of the costs associated with the Business and Technology Centers were fixed costs, these large vacancies meant the centers frequently lost money. Another problem occurred when the federal government passed the Tax Reform Act of 1986. Through this legislation, companies could no longer write off passive losses and depreciation life cycles were extended dramatically. Because of these tax changes, it was no longer possible to syndicate the Business and Technology Centers with investment partners. Starting in 1986, some of the Business and Technology Centers were sold to help Control Data's cash flow problems. Then in 1989, the strategic direction for the remaining Business and Technology Centers changed drastically. Instead of providing a nurturing business environment, these facilities were converted into more traditional commercial rental properties. The last of these converted Business and Technology Centers was sold off in 1991.

The concept itself, though, has not faded. Control Data's original Business and Technology Center model continues to be emulated, as several examples of similar institutions exist today. The Mid-America Manufacturing Center, or MAMTC, located in Kansas, provides, as it states on its website, "manufacturing expertise to companies throughout Kansas to improve productivity, profitability and overall business performance." Likewise in New York City, the Audubon Business and Technology Center works to facilitate development of the biotechnology industry to "ensure improved health care, while contributing to economic growth through the creation of private sector research collaborations and the generation of new bio-medically related business." The Raleigh Business and Technology Center in North Carolina follows an identical business incubation concept by gathering small businesses inside one facility and providing them with the technology and services these small businesses need. As this organization describes on its website, these small businesses ". . . work near other entrepreneurs—people with similar goals and problems, forming a community of like-minded professionals that combines its experience and ingenuity to create and multiply success."

The concept behind the Business and Technology Centers has become a standard way to foster entrepreneurial ventures throughout the United States. The new companies that have emerged and continue to emerge from these facilities are a major force behind America's entrepreneurial spirit, a spirit continually needed in order to search for new ways to improve the human condition.

Chapter Six

The Human Resources Legacy

"People work their whole lives and wonder what it was all about. Well, we left our footprints on the business landscape, and that was what it was all about."
—Gene L. Baker

WHILE ULTIMATELY THE CONTROL DATA brand was lost from the global marketplace, many of Control Data's original business units, products, and services are present to this day in some form—whether as actual products and services still in use today or as ancestral items from which current products/services are built. William Norris's entrepreneurial approach caused the company to support a nearly never ending variety of business concepts and start-up ventures. Because of this seemingly shotgun strategy, he was frequently criticized for investing capital and resources into disparate and often risky concepts. However, as described in previous chapters, many of these businesses were service-based, technology-related ventures Norris felt would ensure the long term viability of Control Data. The company's "hothouse of innovation" culture resulted in major advances in the use of computer technology. When the company began in 1957, computers were primarily used for military or scientific research purposes. When the Control Data name disappeared thirty-five years later, in 1992, there were more computers in the United States than typewriters. The rapid and wide acceptance of computer technology is significantly due to the company's persistent exploration of new applications for its electronic hardware and software.

Norris was constantly trying to find ways he could get Control Data off the one-legged stool of computer hardware development, encouraging employees to come up with new businesses that would give the company a broader and hopefully longer term, stable financial base. While it is true William Norris did not always see by what exact technological means the innovation would come about (PLATO technology is an example of the right concept on an unsustainable hardware platform), he could stunningly perceive what would eventually happen through the application of computer technology. Even if the resulting business wasn't profitable or his timeframe was ahead of the curve, something was very intriguing about the idea. Other entrepreneurs would purchase the CDC product, service, or business unit and find a way to make the resulting company succeed—frequently through using the same business and employee relations ethics championed by Control Data. While the parent company is long gone, its legacy is not. The entrepreneurial spirit of Control Data Corporation is alive and well throughout many sectors of corporate America.

This chapter contains brief histories about organizations either launched through the human resources function or directly influenced by Control Data's HR approach to employee relations. Many more successful and dynamic child companies emerged from Control Data, but they are not described here. The amazing range of child companies which have all or part of their roots in Control Data Corporation is a testament to the pioneering, innovative culture of the parent organization. Documenting all of these companies would be the subject for another book.

Ceridian Corporation

CONTROL DATA CORPORATION WAS RESTRUCTURED and renamed as Ceridian Corporation in 1992. Simultaneously, the legacy mainframe computer business for which the company was best known was separated and spun off into a separate, publicly traded company called Control Data Systems, Ltd. Following that transaction, the three remaining businesses comprising Ceridian were Human Resources Services, Arbitron Inc., and Computing Devices, Ltd. This outcome was the culmination of an effective and controversial restructuring strategy orchestrated in a bid to save the company, headed by Lawrence Perlman, Control Data's last CEO. The restructuring plan was viewed as a great success by many investors, as Ceridian Corporation emerged from the transformation as a financially stable, focused organization. However, while the transformation certainly achieved its objectives, many observers and former Control Data employees still feel this restructuring plan went too far to please Wall Street investors. During the company's transformation process, several businesses, products, and services were liquidated at a level far below what they were worth. For example, in the case of the VTC product line, the entire multi-million dollar business was sold to former employee Larry Jodsaas and investor Gregory Peterson for assumption of debt, and the resulting company became very profitable in a relatively short period of time. For former Control Data employees who built the original company, seeing these businesses being sold off and spun away was an extremely painful, bitter experience.

Perhaps worst of all to some, renaming the company Ceridian Corporation removed the venerable Control Data brand from the public eye. This gave some the impression that CDC had completely imploded—when in reality the organization survived as a smaller company which owes some of its major services to the same social business ventures that had been vehemently castigated earlier by investors and business commentators. Critics argue the name change had more to do with Perlman's desire to reshape the company as his own organization rather than serve an actual business purpose of repositioning the company in the marketplace. Former Control Data employees frequently have to explain the company isn't gone, but continues as Ceridian Corporation. The result of selling or spinning off major pieces of Control Data and then renaming the organization had the long-term effect of severing Bill Norris's legacy with the company. Critics of Perlman's tenure wonder if less drastic approaches would have worked equally well and not diminished the parent organization and its cultural history.

However, other viewpoints support Perlman's nearly total transformation of the company. The sales and divestures resulted in a much more focused organization. This approach matched the "stick to your knitting" principle strongly advocated by many business analysts, that companies should focus their resources on what they do best. This principle had gained popularity in the 1980s, and it certainly factored into the decisions made by the company's leadership during the last years of Control Data's operations. And it can also be equally argued these decisions were the right ones, as Ceridian Corporation continues as a thriving, growing organization today.

The smaller company that emerged focused on information services for businesses, combining several of the human resource initiatives like Employee Advisory Resource and the HR consulting services concept with Control Data's electronic payroll, general ledger, and accounts payable processing services. Control Data acquired the original pieces of this payroll service line through the anti-trust lawsuit IBM settled with Control Data in 1973. As a result of the settlement, CDC acquired the Service Bureau Corporation (SBC). Because the SBC organization remained a major piece of the reshaped company, Ceridian Corporation also cites Service Bureau Corporation, founded in 1932, as another source organization for the configuration of the current company.

This combination of payroll data processing and human resource support services positioned Ceridian Corporation to become a major human resource solution provider, helping client companies better manage their employees—reducing their costs and improving their internal HR initiatives. Because Ceridian Corporation contained a complete slate of human resource offerings, the revamped organization emerged as a profitable company. Many of Ceridian's products and services are clearly the descendents of SBC services and the cutting edge initiatives launched by Control Data's HR function. As of this writing, the following HR business services are available through Ceridian:

- Multinational payroll services—This payroll service supports organizations based in the United States, Canada, and the United Kingdom who have employees in other countries. Ceridian provides global pricing, local compliance, and global reporting through its payroll administration services. Their service system integrates with many ERP systems that have a centralized human resources database. Ceridian currently provides payroll services for employees who work in nearly fifty countries.
- Tax filing and payment solutions—Another central piece of Ceridian's HR/payroll outsourcing business, this service handles tax payments and form filing in over 6,000 taxing jurisdictions across the United States.

- Benefit administration—This service manages the employee benefits and billing needs of client organizations. The service administers FSA/HSA flexible spending accounts, HIPAA and COBRA administration, and Dependant Verification services.
- Health and productivity—Ceridian continues the original services provided by Employee Advisory Resource through its employee assistance program. This 24/7 assistance program supports many thousands of employees and military personal around the world. In addition to their employee assistance program, this service group provides health assessment and consultations, onsite health services, outreach and engagement, and health care incentives.

Client organizations purchase whatever service segments they wish to outsource to Ceridian. In addition to the payroll services based in the United States, the company has two other payroll organizations, Ceridian Canada and Ceridian UK, which handles international payroll needs for organizations based respectively in Canada and the United Kingdom.

The employee assistance program is a massive business for Ceridian, handling over 75,000 calls every month. One major client is the Department of Defense, so Ceridian assists members of the armed services returning from one or multiple deployments in the Iraq and Afghanistan wars. The assistance program helps these individuals readjust to life outside the war zone. A number of commercial clients also purchase these services to support their employees. Ceridian has large call centers that receive these calls, and a professional staff of counselors is ready to assist these individuals. The concepts established by Employee Advisory Resource continue on, giving distressed individuals tools and support to weather difficult times while reducing healthcare and other costs for client companies and the various branches of the armed forces.

Through strategic acquisitions, Ceridian has also added two other significant areas of business. The company's Comdata subsidiary provides payment solutions to firms, like trucking companies, which manage vehicle fleets. Comdata administrates fleet cards drivers use for purchasing gas and repairs for their vehicles. This service also has a gas discounting program in partnership with over 30,000 locations across the United States. Customers for this fleet card service include FedEx, UPS, Swift, JB Hunt, and other fleet-based organizations. Another major business run by a subsidiary is gift card processing. Through the company's Stored Value Solutions (SVS) subsidiary, retailers outsource the management of their gift card programs to SVS. Stored Value Solutions provides the plastic gift cards and administers the electronic purchases customers make with these cards. Client customers for this service include Lowes, Barnes and Noble, JCPenny, Toys"R"Us, WHSmith, and H&M.

Today, Ceridian is a private company co-owned by Thomas H. Lee Partners and Fidelity National Financial. These partner investment firms acquired Ceridian in 2007. The company currently has over 7,000 employees worldwide, including major offices in the United States,

Canada, United Kingdom, and Mauritius. Ceridian's world headquarters is located in Bloomington, Minnesota, in a building just across the street from the original Control Data headquarters. Ceridian moved into this new facility in 2000. Ceridian's current CEO is Stuart Harvey, who joined the company in August 2010. Like Ceridian's previous CEOs, Harvey is dedicated to making the organization an innovative workplace that explores potential uses for new technologies and maintains a dedicated group of talented employees. As Norb Berg describes, "It is especially pleasingly to see the continuation of the corporation's historical, caring attitude towards their employees." The company continues to grow; during the 2009 fiscal year Ceridian enjoyed revenues of $1.5 billion.

What is perhaps most interesting about Ceridian is that, in many ways, this company personifies the services direction William Norris and Robert Price envisioned for Control Data. While the mainframe computers developed in the 1960s-1980s are now obsolete pieces of technological history, several of the human resources services Norris championed during their early development at Control Data remain relevant, vital businesses. Of all directions the restructured organization could have followed, the company's leadership decided to focus on human resources as a growth area for CDC, and this investment paid off in Cerdian's continuation of these products and services. Ceridian Corporations is an important testament to the entrepreneurial spirit CDC fostered within the human resource function.

StayWell

DURING THE TRANSFORMATION of the company in the late 1980s, the StayWell health program was sold to a group of former Control Data employees. CDC employee alumni David Anderson and G.L. "Bud" Anderson teamed up with John Tarbuck, an entrepreneur, to purchase StayWell through a management buyout. This purchase was made in 1989. The StayWell service was renamed StayWell Health Management Systems, and began operations as an independent business. The resulting organization started out small, with only twelve employees. Over the next couple years, the company functioned much like a start-up organization. As Susan Willette, a former national sales representative for the organization describes, "The tone was set by Bud, John, and David. We were a flat organization—everybody did everything in those days. We did what we had to do." The company grew into one of the industry leaders of integrated health management solution providers, solutions that, as described on their website, "center on healthy behavior change and creating a culture of health in the workplace." StayWell Health Management clients include companies large, small, and every size in between.

The company continued to follow the approach to the business Control Data had used, discovering ways to leverage technology to improve employee health. In 1992, the company created a telephone-based health coaching and information technology system. This targeted program responded to an employee's needs through a health assessment tool, delivering this information over the phone based on health risk status, the individual's willingness to change, and other individual factors. Then in 1999, StayWell truly advanced Control Data's goal of integrating computer technology into wellness by creating StayWell Online®. This service provides Internet access to each individual's health assessment results, linking together personalized information and behavior change tools that fit the individual logged into the web system. The online service extended the reach of StayWell's programs, as it made much of the programming and health information available to employees worldwide, at any hour of the day or night. During this time period, StayWell Health Management also released the HERO Study. This large-scale study demonstrated a direct link between employee health risks and the rising costs of health care. The study then demonstrated the positive effect health management programs have on reducing these costs by training employees to lead healthier lives.

At the start of the new century, MediMedia USA, Incorporated, acquired StayWell Health Management, but the company still maintains its name, continuing to operate as a subsidiary of MediMedia. StayWell's services continue to deliver impressive results. In 2007, the Pepsi Bottling Group became the ninth StayWell client to receive the C. Everett Koop National Health Award, and in 2009, Alliance Data became the tenth StayWell client to receive this award. The C. Everett Koop National Health Awards are given out each year to companies who improve health care and decrease medical costs for their employees. Considered the most prestigious awards in the health management field, ten companies assisted by StayWell have received this award, a powerful indicator about the StayWell approach to health management. During 2009, StayWell also acquired LifeMasters Supported Self Care, Inc., a disease management firm. Both StayWell and LifeMasters are accredited by the National Committee for Quality Assurance (NCQA), a non-profit organization dedicated to improving health care quality.

As of this writing, StayWell programs and publications reach more than fifty million people each year. The healthcare reform act (Patient Protection and Affordable Care Act, or ACA) signed into law in 2010 validates the early vision Control Data had for their original wellness initiative. The ACA legislation attempts a major overhaul of the healthcare system, shifting focus from diagnosis and treatment to prevention and wellness. This legislation includes a provision for employers and other health plan sponsors to offer financial incentives to their employees or members tied to achieving an objectively measured, wellness-related health standard. These incentives amount to thirty percent of the total cost of health care coverage. While parts of the ACA remain controversial, the wellness incentive and several other provisions encouraging wellness have strong bipartisan support. Passage of the ACA has clearly brought wellness into the mainstream of the U.S. healthcare system. This signals a bright future for StayWell and other organizations who anticipated this transformation. StayWell's original objectives remain the same: to improve the health of employees, and ultimately the corporation, through its wellness plans, courses, and counseling. Founding members John Tarbuck and David Anderson are still a part of the company's senior managers, maintaining a CDC stamp on the service-focused organization.

Gantz Wiley Research

ONE OF THE KEY PERFORMANCE TOOLS Control Data's HR function developed was its employee surveys. These surveys measured specific factors within various Control Data business units, assessing everything from job satisfaction to organizational structure and efficiency, using the resulting data to measure employee productivity. This tool helped the HR function locate troubled business units within Control Data, correcting employment problems before they became even more difficult. These surveys became one of the offerings sold to outside customers through Control Data Business Advisors, under the auspices of the Survey Research Unit group. The Survey Research Unit was managed by Gail Gantz (previously Bergsven) and Jack Wiley. Gail Gantz was the vice president responsible for marketing and sales, operations, and product development within the organization. Jack Wiley was the director of organization research at Control Data. The HR employee surveys were a service sold externally and were one of the major profit centers within Control Data Business Advisors.

When Control Data began divesting itself from some pieces within Control Data Business Advisors in 1986, Gail Gantz and Jack Wiley purchased the Survey Research Unit with financial assistance from Control Data. Together they saw an opportunity to create a new business whicih would combine scientific research and survey methods with an understanding of the key factors that create positive business performance. Using their employee opinion and customer satisfaction surveys, they could then assess the performance of client companies to help them become more profitable. The services would identify ways these companies could improve their performance. With their business plan in place, the partners renamed the Survey Research Unit as Gantz Wiley Research, and the new business venture began assisting and evaluating client companies. Their first day of business was on December 1, 1986, and they had six employees— two of whom were part-time.

During the company's first full year of operation in 1987, Gantz Wiley Research's primary client was Control Data. Over the next few years, the company's clients grew to include Chevron, Proctor and Gamble, LensCrafters, and Harris Trust. With the expanded sales, Gantz Wiley Research was able to completely pay back Control Data's investment. Gail Gantz left the organization in 1990 to form Gail Gantz and Associates, a company that provides consulting services on organization development, executive training, and management training. Jack Wiley became the sole owner of Gantz Wiley Research. Throughout the 1990s, the company achieved steady growth year after year.

Gantz Wiley Research improved its analysis tools, developing the High Performance Model. This unique strategic model identifies the ways leadership practices, employee satisfaction, and customer satisfaction impact the financial performance of an organization. Through this scientific model, Gantz Wiley Research was able to specialize in helping client organizations understand how their employees and customers impact the productivity of their businesses. By measuring, through research, the attitudes of employees and customers towards the client company, Gantz Wiley Research developed a series of actions these companies could pursue to improve corporate performance and ultimately, corporate profitability. The employee surveys, customer surveys, and the High Performance Model helped fuel the growth of the organization, expanding it globally through an office in Melbourne, Australia, an additional domestic office in San Francisco, and a clientele base in locations around the world. Jack Wiley continued to serve as the president and CEO of the organization.

Then in 2006, Kenexa, a provider of talent acquisition and retention solutions, acquired Gantz Wiley Research. Kenexa began as a provider of recruitment services to a spectrum of industries. This company was looking for strategic acquisitions to improve its human capital management services and integrate them with its on-demand software applications. Because of the company's senior consulting staff, strategic locations, and stable client base, Gantz Wiley was a strategic attraction. The company wanted to include employee research as part of its business, so Gantz Wiley Research was a great fit for the Kenexa organization. Currently Jack Wiley continues his career as an executive director at Kenexa. The publicly traded company expanded rapidly throughout 2008-2009, increasing to more than thirty offices and locations around the world. Then in 2012, IBM acquired Kenexa to help their clients better leverage social business technologies. The IBM acquisition has helped the company expand its customer base. Kenexa combines science, technology, business processes, and consulting. As the company states on its mission, "When people are in jobs they love, and are in environments that maximize their potential, they are not only more productive employees, they are better parents, friends, partners, and neighbors. Our work is to make this happen for everyone." Their mission shares the same spirit as Control Data's HR function, representing another piece of CDC's legacy on improving employee relations in corporate culture.

VTC

VTC WAS A CHILD COMPANY that leveraged key facets of Control Data's approach to employee relations. This company began when Control Data entered into a collaborative venture with Fairchild Computer to design and produce new semi-conductor technologies. To build these technologies, Control Data and Fairchild Computers built a new state of the art manufacturing facility for the VTC venture. Design and manufacture of disk drive component technologies began. However, by 1988, this business was in difficult shape and Control Data decided to completely take over the venture. Larry Jodsaas, a long-term Control Data executive, was selected to lead the restructured VTC organization. Jodsaas started his career as an electronics engineer for Control Data in the early 1960s, but then discovered that "he liked working with engineers better than being one." Over the years, he ran several computer businesses for CDC, focusing on opening up new markets for Control Data technology. During the years 1980-1983, he worked in the Peripherals products group. Now he was responsible for restoring the business. Within about a year, the VTC organization became profitable.

When Control Data divested its remaining hardware manufacturing units during its transformation into Ceridian, VTC was a business unit that no longer fit Control Data's strategic direction. Larry Jodsaas found an investing partner, Gregory Peterson, and together they acquired the former Control Data business unit in 1990. This sale was unique, as they purchased the company for the total price of one dollar and assumed all the debt, $50 million, held at that time by the business unit. Larry Jodsaas became this company's chairman and CEO. The one-dollar purchase price seemed like a good deal, but the technology sector went into a recession in 1991, and VTC found itself immediately struggling to survive. However, the demand for disk drive technology recovered quickly and the company began a nearly decade-long expansion, going from $18 million in sales in 1992 to a massive $180 million in sales in 1999.

The main technology VTC designed and manufactured was a pre-amplifier circuit for disk drives. This circuit sends out a signal to the disk drive head that causes the reading (accessing data) and writing (saving data) that occurs when a computer interacts with a disk. Every disk drive needs to have a pre-amplifier circuit. As sales of personal computers ballooned during the 1990s, VTC assumed sixty-five percent of the market share for pre-amplifier technology. The company had one of the best technologies on the market throughout the boom years of the 1990s.

During these profitable times, Jodsaas decided to share these profits with VTC employees. For every quarter the company was profitable, VTC would distribute fifteen percent of the quarterly profit among the work force. The company enjoyed a profitable seven-year run from 1992-1999, and so each quarter employees received a significant piece of the company profit. This policy proved to be strategically brilliant. Because the employees received extra income every quarter, very few employees left the organization. Thus VTC was able to create and maintain an experienced, stable, and loyal workforce. Jodsaas explains the only turnover the company experienced was when new employees did not like the clean room environment. If new employees were able to handle this aspect of the work, they usually became long-term employees.

When increasing competition hit VTC in 2000, Jodsaas was no longer able to maintain the profit-sharing plan. Despite the hard times, most employees continued to stay with on with VTC, knowing when good times returned, they would share in the company's fortunes. The company thus remained a strong organization, as the employees were an experienced workforce. As Jodsaas describes, "If you don't have your employees when you recover, you will never recover because you won't be ready to take on the market."

In order to keep the business going, VTC sold the pre-amplifier technology to Lucent Technologies in 2000. As a result of this sale, Lucent acquired the semiconductor component products, marketing, and sales teams from VTC. The acquisition now positioned Lucent to produce a complete line of disk drive technology within the growing storage market of the early 2000s. The acquired company could provide hard disk manufacturers with a complete series of chips needed for many hard drive devices, and the merger proved strategically viable for Lucent Technologies.

However, while Lucent bought the technology, the company did not purchase the manufacturing assets of the business. Once again, Larry Jodsaas and his partner, Gregory Peterson, created a new manufacturing-focused organization from these remaining assets. The new organization would continue to fabricate wafers, a piece of disk drive hardware that provides the circuits to link various disk drive systems to a computer. The company could then sell these wafers back to Lucent. This new company was named PolarFab. Because most of the original production employees stayed, the organization made a smooth transition into the new business. Eventually PolarFab began selling wafers to other customers besides Lucent, manufacturing wafers to forty-five customers worldwide. The culture within PolarFab remained intact, and the company continued to be a positive place to work.

Unfortunately, the market during the years 2002-2005 was difficult, and PolarFab was unable to continue the profit-sharing policy that had worked so well for VTC. Then in 2005, PolarFab became a subsidiary of Sanken Electronic Company of Japan. Rather than keep all the income from the sale, Jodsaas decided to give half the amount back to the PolarFab employees. This dollar amount totaled eight million, and each employee received a piece of this income as a thank you for all their hard work maintaining the organization over the years. The PolarFab facility continues manufacturing wafers to this day. According to their website, the PolarFab subsidiary processes more than 4,000 wafers a week with a workforce of 525 employees. This manufacturing facility is located in Bloomington, Minnesota, not far from Control Data's former headquarters.

Many VTC and PolarFab employees credit Larry Jodsaas with making these companies positive, exciting places to work. Larry Perlman, the former CEO of Ceridian Corporation relates, ". . . you'll hear about the corporate culture he . . . worked to create: about rewarding people for their hard work and loyalty with everything from profit-sharing to roasted turkeys delivered to their doors at Thanksgiving. He helped define what a Minnesota company can be: profitable as well as a great place to work." That description sounds very similar to Control Data's business philosophy. While the parent company was gone, the child company continued to follow the Control Data approach to human resources that had worked so well. Jodsaas reflects that one of the company's major accomplishments was many people had better lives because of VTC. He really enjoyed creating the work environment that made this possible.

Larry Jodsaas also followed another philosophy advocated so strongly at Control Data—giving back. He funded the Jodsaas Center for Engineering Leadership at the University of North Dakota, his alma mater, a center devoted to fostering both the entrepreneurial spirit and a better trained, high-tech workforce. He also provided major funding for the Jodsaas Sciences Building at Normandale Community College. Besides supporting science, technology, and engineering in these schools, Jodsaas carried on the Control Data torch in another significant way: he has served on the board of directors and contributed significant funding and personal time to the Alzeimer's Association, the organization launched by Hilda Pridgeon through the paid sabbatical she received from Control Data.

Business and Technology Centers

THE BUSINESS AND TECHNOLOGY CENTERS built by Control Data were a major piece of the parent organization's assets. These centers were sold to Dan Pennie, a former employee who had served for many years as Control Data's general counsel and secretary. During the financial turmoil of 1985, he ran many of the legal procedures needed to keep the corporation afloat, leading a team that created the legal documents required to receive loans from banks. When the total restructuring of the organization became a reality, Control Data decided to sell their remaining Business and Technology Centers. Dan Pennie acquired these facilities, renaming the resulting organization BTC Management, Incorporated. BTC Management turned these assets into more standard commercial rental properties.

Pennie eventually sold BTC Management and became a general partner of Bluestem Holding, L.P., a private investment company. This organization finances a number of unique organizations. Through his role as a part of Bluestem Holding, Dan Pennie serves on the board of directors on some of the organizations the investment company supports. One of these organizations, Adventium Labs, is a non-profit organization "dedicated to performing and publishing scientific research and to the creation, maturation, and commercialization of intellectual property." The lab works with universities, technology partners, and government organizations to develop these properties. The lab is also a strategic partner with a for-profit organization, Adventium Enterprises. As it describes on its web site, "Adventium Enterprises is dedicated to the maturation and commercialization of leading edge technologies in the areas of information technology, cyber security, automated reasoning, and systems engineering." These two organizations resemble start-up technology ventures financed by Control Data.

Dan Pennie also serves on the board of directors for Pathways Health Crisis Resource Center, an organization that supports innovative, new ways for people to treat and recover from a major illness. The organization teaches participants how to treat their illnesses through holistic means by providing classes, special events, and individual sessions. Both organizations focus on innovation and creativity as a means to discovering new solutions to human needs.

NJK Holding Corporation

NASSER J. KAZEMINY WAS BORN in Iran and educated in England—beginning his career by designing a worldwide logistics and management information system to handle inventory for Honeywell Corporation. Control Data needed such a system as well, and Nasser Kazeminy was recruited away from Honeywell to work for CDC. Kazeminy vividly described his recruitment experience. At the time, he and his young family lived in London, and Kazeminy was enjoying a successful career. He planned on making London a long-term home, as he had just bought a house and a new car. When Control Data made the job offer, Nasser Kazeminy did not believe the company was offering a serious commitment. He had not heard of the company before, and they were making an offer so large it seemed unbelievable. The HR recruiters said if he accepted the position, Control Data would help him sell his car and his house—plus they would raise his salary.

Still thinking this was too good an opportunity to be true, Nasser Kazeminy said he would need to speak to the chairman of the board before he would accept the offer. Within two weeks, Control Data set up a meeting between Kazeminy and Jerry Smith, a vice president in the Peripheral Products business, as well as General Manager Fred Kaeppel. Both men backed up everything the HR recruiter had told him. To close the deal, they asked him to resign from Honeywell the next day. Kazeminy did. Control Data also paid for his family to visit Iran before they moved to the United States. Everything went smoothly until he applied for a visa to work in the United States. Nasser Kazeminy's overly enthusiastic answers to some questions raised the suspicions of an immigration clerk at the American Embassy in Tehran, who believed Kazeminy would try to stay illegally in America. His visa was denied. Suddenly, the great opportunity looked like a great big mistake. Consummately tenacious, Nasser Kazeminy refused to leave the embassy until he could speak to the general counsel for the U.S. Embassy. After pointedly describing the Control Data position awaiting him in America, the embassy finally approved his visa. Kazeminy and his family moved to the United States in 1969.

While adjusting to life in America and Minneapolis, he began to design and implement a world logistics and management information system for Control Data. Kazeminy was put in charge of the logistics system design group, creating a dynamic inventory system that gave Control Data a means to find and track spare parts, equipment usage, and equipment requirements for every CDC location around the world. Nasser was a great fit for Control Data's entrepreneurial culture. He relished that company leaders encouraged employees to think about innovative ways they could help the company come up with new business opportunities. He moved to positions in other areas of the organization.

While working within Peripheral Products in the 1970s, Nasser Kazeminy discovered a unique business opportunity. Control Data was not leasing their peripheral equipment to customers. He felt there was potentially a large market for low cost, tax-leveraged leases for this CDC product line. He presented this business concept to Control Data executives, and they agreed this idea held promise. Recognizing his entrepreneurial spirit, a number of these executives encouraged Kazeminy to pursue this business opportunity. First he needed backing from Wall Street investors to launch the business—a startup investment of $35 million.

The story of how Nasser Kazeminy's leasing company began illustrates the ethical way Control Data conducted business. Kazeminy went to Wall Street and got a group of investment bankers interested in meeting with both him and Control Data. The investment meeting was going very well as Norb Berg and other Control Data executives assured the investors the company would support the leasing business. At one point Kazeminy briefly left the meeting. When he returned, everyone was quiet. The next incident solidified Nasser Kazeminy's admiration for Control Data. Berg explained the bankers had just tried to do an "end run" around him; they proposed Control Data deal directly with their investment bank and start the business venture without Kazeminy. Berg stated Control Data conducted business with integrity and the company would not be a party to any cutthroat deal making. If the bankers did not work directly with Kazeminy, he could take his proposal to another investment bank willing to work with him. Instead of giving Nasser Kazeminy $35 million, this investment bank gave him $50 million.

Nasser Kazeminy's new company grew to become the largest privately held computer leasing company within the United States. Although he had officially left Control Data, he maintained a strong relationship with the organization. His business expanded rapidly, providing leases to customers who normally could not afford Control Data's peripheral technology. Eventually he bought another leasing company, DPF, and merged it with his own company. After the merger was complete, he decided to sell the entire organization. Using this sale amount as a financial base, Kazeminy then launched NJK Holding Corporation in 1986—an investment organization he still runs today.

Through this investment company, Kazeminy either started or acquired several privately held businesses. These businesses were then merged with similar organizations, sold to public organizations, or remained within NJK Holding Corporation as part of the company's portfolio. Many of these companies were spin-off business units from Control Data which the company sold him during the restructuring efforts of the mid-1980s. These companies include XP Systems Corporation, Quorum Group, Inc., CENTRA Benefit Services, and Drake ProMetric. Nasser Kazeminy was considered a favored buyer for these Control Data business units, as he did his best to maintain the CDC culture and was committed to keeping the employees in place within these organizations. His holding company has helped create thousands of jobs in numerous industries worldwide.

Nasser Kazeminy represents an example of how talent and ambition transcended all boundaries within Control Data's culture. Not only did he, as an immigrant, rapidly rise to leadership positions within the organization, Control Data gave Nasser Kazeminy the support and guidance he needed to develop a new business concept—and they even stood up for him against a cutthroat proposal that would have scuttled his leasing company. Likewise, his leasing company opened up new markets for CDC peripheral products, so Control Data benefited immensely from this strategic partnership. Then as Control Data divested itself of various businesses, Kazeminy had the capital to purchase these organizations, guiding them into sustainable profitability while at the same time maintaining good relationships with the employees in these organizations. Nasser Kazeminy credits Control Data for these core employment principles:

- Give your employees good leadership.
- Recognize that employees' families come first, the company comes second.
- Trust your employees by giving them responsibility and authority over their areas of the business.
- Create job opportunities.
- Recognize that employees are a company's greatest asset. Do well by them and they will do well by you.
- Do good for the community.

The company continues to purchase companies and nurture their development. Kazeminy also acknowledges his success was due to surrounding himself with experienced, talented executives like Jim McGuire, president of NJK Holding Corporation, and Dan Erickson, chief financial officer, both of whom had worked in executive positions at Control Data. Likewise, several executives who ran the operating companies contributed greatly to the leadership and profitability of his business ventures. These executives include Control Data alumni such as Bruce Aho, Jon Lineweaver, Clarke Porter, John Hudgens, and Michael Eleftheriou. Nasser Kazeminy is a true Control Data success story and an important part of the organization's legacy.

Plato Learning, Inc.

WHILE THE PLATO MAINFRAME and terminal systems were eventually rendered obsolete by personal computer technology, the computer-based education expertise and courseware developed for PLATO was a valuable commodity. Starting in 1986, PLATO courseware became available for distribution through Local Area Networks on personal computers, opening up the market for courseware to any organization that ran these smaller computer networks. As part of the downsizing and capital raising initiatives that occurred in 1989, Control Data sold its PLATO courseware to The Roach Organization, Inc. (TRO), a company led by William R. Roach. Soon the company was publicly traded and changed its name to TRO Learning, Incorporated, to reflect the purpose of the business. The company maintained the PLATO brand, and as time went on the company decided, in 2000, to rename itself Plato Learning, Incorporated, as the company was more recognized for its PLATO courseware. Plato Learning cites its expertise in computer-based education as begining in 1963, when Control Data and the University of Illinois used a grant from the National Science Foundation to develop a computer-assisted instructional system.

Plato Learning has made many strategic acquisitions over the years, including Learning Elements, a software developer who created the FOCUS™ Reading and Language program for emerging kindergarten to third grade readers; Lightspan, Inc., a leading provider of elementary and post-secondary educational software; and New Media (Holdings) Limited, a leading publisher of science simulation software. The company's product line reflects the courseware Control Data developed through many of its educational initiatives. As the company's website states, "Plato Learning is a leading provider of education technology solutions for K-adult learners, offering curricula for reading, writing, mathematics, science, social studies, and life and job skills." The courseware utilizes many innovations developed through the original PLATO system, including just-in-time online assessments to identify student needs, used to identify a course of study for each student. A description of the company's purpose sounds very similar to FAIRBREAK's original purpose: "Most importantly, we make a difference in the lives of learners—as they upgrade their skills, increase their self-esteem, discover successful employment, and become better, more self-sufficient students and employees." Control Data's influence on this successful company is very evident.

Plato Learning has three families of courseware:

- PLATO®—The PLATO courseware is designed to help struggling students master basic skills in order to gain academic success in the regular classroom. This offering builds on the PLATO courseware originally developed by Control Data.
- Straight Curve®—This courseware family teaches the major concepts each student is required to learn through federal and state mandates. These teacher-facilitated courses are designed to use technology to make these required concepts easier to learn and understand.
- Academic Systems®—This set of software teaches various post-secondary education to students who can take the classes through a flexible schedule, creating an interactive learning environment that balances their needs and lives.

The company states it is committed to keeping up with current technologies, constantly updating its courseware to utilize new innovations. Plato Learning describes its technologies as flexible and scalable, so these technologies change with the evolving needs of the students and teachers who use their courseware. The courseware also has multiple implementation scenarios—from a single classroom to a district-wide series of classrooms. Plato Learning handles all the implementation and technological issues clients may experience to help reduce the cost of the courseware, and the company also works hard to stay aware about each customer's needs and wishes. To do this, the company provides courseware compatible with the Internet in order to provide the anytime/anywhere access students need.

Plato Learning's mission and values statement, available on the company's website, also reflects the company's history with Control Data:

'

- We respect each other. We value the diversity of experience, background, and culture that we each bring to the company. We approach every interaction believing we share a loyalty to the company and its success. We discuss issues, concerns, and suggestions to reach a decision that focuses on improving processes rather than fixing people. We behave in a professional manner at all times, working diligently to communicate effectively.
- We value our customers. We operate the company in an efficient, effective, and profitable manner—in the best interest of our customers and ourselves. We establish reasonable expectations through candid and honest communication with our customers. We work diligently to deliver quality products and services with the appropriate specifications, at the right price, on the agreed-upon schedule—every time.
- We expect financial success. We are earnest about our obligations to financial objectives. We recognize that our employees, customers, and shareholders share the financial benefits of a well-managed business that achieves predictable growth and profitability, greater than the market.
- We embrace change. We energetically adapt our products, services, practices, and processes to new opportunities and methods of doing business. We assure that changes in the market drive changes in the company.
- We are dedicated to excellence. We are individually and collectively committed to exceptional performance. We plan, prepare, and execute in a manner that leads to extraordinary results.
- We value education. We believe that education is a life-long process that contributes to productive citizenship. We strive to add quality and innovation to the learning process through our inspired solutions.

Were he alive today, William Norris would be very pleased the PLATO education system he championed for so long has become an accepted, welcome, standardized method for delivering education to students of all ages and needs. Plato Learning Systems continues to empower students to master the knowledge they need to become educated and gainfully employed.

Last Thoughts and Observations

ANY DISCUSSION ABOUT CONTROL DATA CORPORATION often invokes an extreme response. Depending on the interview, news article, or other information source, Control Data Corporation was either a groundbreaking, cutting edge organization that dared to do good for employees and at-risk communities, or it was an increasingly diffuse organization that squandered its energy or capital on failed "do-gooder" social programs. The decline and transformation of Control

Data is a difficult part of the company's legacy. Everyone involved with Control Data struggles with this part of the narrative—regardless of whether they are for or against the approach Norris followed. As work on this book began, Jim Morris, an executive with both Employee Advisory Resource and Control Data Business Advisors, described this aspect of the company as "the elephant in the room" for which this project would have to respond to in some way. While this book has primarily focused on the successful social business ventures developed by Control Data's HR function, it has also tried to document those ventures and outcomes which did not turn out as well. The approach was to present the initial concept of each social business venture or concept, describe the history about how CDC developed it, and then document the outcome—whether good, bad, or somewhere between.

A common assessment of the company is Control Data missed its chance to enter the personal computer market and invested too many resources on unprofitable social programs. This assessment is voiced by various individuals—from people who casually know about the company to business commentators of the time to former employees who disliked how Norris guided the organization. As the members who hold this viewpoint state, the company placed more and more public emphasis on correcting social ills, ignoring the growing personal computer behemoth that eventually trampled over their mainframe computer products. These individuals typically assert the social business ventures were well-intentioned experiments that did help a few people, but overall were unprofitable businesses and too insignificant to really make any long-term changes. Control Data should have focused on its strengths as a technological innovator, but it squandered too many resources on noble experiments that eventually led to the financial problems in the mid-1980s. Following this argument, by the time the right leadership was in place to correct the company's direction, it was too late to stop the dissolution.

In contrast, Robert Price asserts Control Data was very aware of personal computer technology, but the company made a strategic choice not to develop a personal computer product line. As Price describes, Control Data instead made a studied decision to continue development of its mainframe computers, exploring the services these products could provide—and eventually spun off hardware manufacturing as this market space became a low-cost commodity. Both Norbert Berg and Frank Dawe also assert the amount of money invested in the social responsibility ventures was far less than the company would have donated had it followed the typical charitable giving patterns of other corporations. Plus the benefit Control Data gained from employee pride and support helped motivate and recruit a large population of dedicated workers for many years.

As to the reasons why the company dispersed into smaller entities, Berg is more reflective, saying, "I'm not so sure I could come up with the simple answer as to why Control Data faltered financially. I have heard many different versions about why Control Data transformed, but at the end of the day the various versions are in conflict and nobody that I know was adequately connected and blessed with the needed objectivity (including myself) to accurately say these were the key three reasons' or 'this was the reason.'" Hopefully though, this book success-fully makes the argument that the social business ventures should not be the main target of blame. In 1980, the organization had a peak employment of 60,000 employees and over $4 billion in assets, and Control Data's total investment in the social business ventures was an insignificant fraction of these resources. Most of the capital for these ventures came from money other cor-porations would typically set aside as as social responsibility money for corporate, charitable, and community donations—so Control Data would typically have donated that money to charity anyway. While Control Data did donate some funds, primarily this capital was used to start new businesses. Some of these businesses could be considered research and development expenditures, initiatives that explored new ways to use computer services. Even if this entire budget would have been lost, it would never have been large enough to sap the resources of the organization.

However, this misconception about the size of Control Data's investment in social business ventures has become part of the company's epitaph. Interestingly, nearly all the numbers that describe these investment costs are consistently too high—and one of the numbers frequently cited is $200 million. The actual source for this amount originates from William Norris himself. During the late 1970s and early 1980s, Norris heavily promoted computer-based education through the company's newly acquired PLATO technology. Norris used this number, $200 mil-lion, to describe the total cost spent on PLATO's development from the early 1960s to the mid-1970s from the University of Illinois, government grants, Control Data Corporation, and other investors. Norris' point was Control Data now completely owned this substantial technology, and it would take a similar level of investment for competitors to enter this market. Norris wanted to discourage competitors from trying to get into the business, emphasizing that the cost of entry would be too high. However, because PLATO was leveraged heavily in FAIRBREAK, HOMEWORK, and a number of other social ventures, this number became associated as the actual total cost of these ventures instead.

Part of the motivation behind the social business ventures was to promote Control Data as an innovative company seeking new ways technology could be leveraged. For example, toward the end of the 1970s, Control Data placed a massive advertisement in *The Wall Street Journal*, em-phasizing the company was now much more than a mainframe computer and peripheral manu-facturer. The advertisement featured a mix of technology innovations and social business innovations through a series of full-page advertisements, each page focused on a specific business. Showcased near a full-page layout advertising Control Data's peripheral equipment was another full-page layout describing Indian Health Management at Rosebud. William Norris heavily advertised these social ventures as a central part of an effort to communicate that the organization was a good cor-porate citizen, but this promotion ended up becoming a double-edged sword. When this uncon-ventional company began to diminish, these ventures were often pointed out as the culprit.

Despite the difficult days of the 1980s, Control Data was very much involved with hardware design, creating peripheral products that would eventually compete with Japanese manufacturing, or creating the ETA supercomputer to maintain a presence in the mainframe market. The turnaround of Peripheral Products into Imprimis Technology was a major breakthrough. When Imprimis was sold to Seagate, it was an equally major shock for those who felt Control Data was financially on track again. However, the Imprimis sale was part of the overall strategy to move the company away from hardware commodity manufacturing into more promising service businesses. Not everyone involved at Control Data understood this services strategy, though, and this led to much confusion over the purpose for theses divestments.

One reason for the company's decline is the mainframe supercomputer market went through tremendous changes in the 1980s. Control Data's major hardware products and services had been stable, profitable businesses for many years. Now these "bread and butter" products and services were in rapid decline. During this financial crisis, it would have been very difficult to retool the company into a personal computer manufacturer. A key reason why Control Data did not embrace personal computer manufacturing was simply because the organization did not have the facilities and the expertise to manufacture a line of personal computers. Mainframe computers were built slowly, meticulously by a group of highly trained workers, and only a few hundred mainframe computers were ever available for sale at any given time. Personal computer manufacturing was significantly different. The manufacturing process resembles typewriter assembly or other mass production processes. Control Data would have needed the foresight to invest heavily into personal computer production during the late 1970s and early 1980s, during a period when the company was enjoying its most profitable years. It would have been hard to imagine just what a huge technological shift the personal computer would represent. "If it ain't broke, don't fix it," was most likely a spoken or unspoken mantra in company discussions at the time. So when Control Data experienced significant losses in 1985, the company was no longer truly able to invest in PC manufacturing without a huge amount of capital and new expertise—both resources the corporation now sorely lacked.

It is difficult to imagine how hard this financial downturn must have been for the organization. Gary Nelson, the executive vice president, general counsel and corporate secretary for Ceridian Corporation, vividly describes this period. At the time, he was a lawyer for Oppenheimer, Wolff, and Donnelly. Dan Pennie, Control Data's general counsel, asked him to help work with the banks. As Nelson describes in an online interview with General Counsel Consulting,

> The Company lost in excess of $500 million, was in default with its banks, and was trying to restructure debt and restore credibility. It was intense and traumatic. I ended up working on an offering to raise money so we could pay the banks. We worked on that offering from November to July, seven days a week. The bankers would come in Monday morning, we'd negotiate through the week, and then I'd draft over the weekend: one of the business writers at the local newspaper read the prospectus and described it as 'more than 200 pages long, and dry as hell.' It needed to be."

A number of seismic changes happened within the company because of this crisis, and probably the most significant was William Norris's retirement. Instead of retiring at a major milestone in his career, he had to leave amid the chaos. Despite all his success, the unfortunate timing of his exit tainted his legacy. He spent the last years of his life defending many of the choices he made. But the major investment Norris made into ETA Systems was ironically perhaps the choice that may have decided Control Data's fate. By heavily investing once again in mainframe technology, a move many investors initially applauded, Control Data spent away a major piece of its financial foundation.

Control Data's transformation into Ceridian is still hotly debated and controversial. The central question is whether the extreme actions taken had really been necessary. Several people interviewed for this book question why Larry Perlman's team needed to spin off or sell so many dynamic, profitable Control Data businesses. The histories of the companies described here showcase that the overall organization did not really collapse and fail—it primarily split apart into smaller companies. Larry Perlman's reasoning was to focus the company and restore the confidence of investors. Since Ceridian exists today, the strategy worked, but was the price too high? Some feel strongly the spin-off businesses were sold for too little return and the company name should not have been sacrificed. By far the most passionate reaction in several interviews relates to the company name. Why did Perlman change it? Was it purely about Wall Street? Was the name change also about the ego of the leaders at the time, recasting the organization in a completely new image? Or was it also about distancing the remaining organization from the legacy of William Norris? The ire raised against Perlman's choices is still very real for many who admired Control Data. In hindsight, perhaps the transformation had been too extreme, given that many of the child companies are still active and profitable. What probably stings most of all, however, is the name change unfairly reinforces the viewpoint that Control Data failed.

The above thoughts are a combination of theories and viewpoints—yet another perspective about the "elephant in the room" that is part of Control Data's legacy. The outcome of the choices Control Data's leaders made is what remains today. As this chapter illustrates, the organization split apart into many businesses that, for the most part, thrived and prospered. The impact these organizations have on the United States and world economy is impossible to assess. And besides these businesses, the ethical principles followed by Control Data remain an admired piece of the company's legacy. In a Minneapolis *StarTribune* article about the fiftieth anniversary of the company, the article describes four main legacies of Control Data:

- CDC pushed the idea of software unbundling—selling software separately from the sale of computers. Microsoft owes its existence to unbundling.
- Innovative business practices, such as providing work for people who have handicaps, allowing people to work from home and helping employees deal with their personal problems.

- Fostering entrepreneurship through spin-off companies and opening technology center incubators that provided small businesses with services they need.
- Collaborating with government to help society through projects such as inner-city manufacturing plants, remedial education for prison inmates and child care for women employees.

What has perhaps been the most interesting, common reaction to William Norris is his approach to business reflects a liberal, social justice agenda. In both articles and interviews, Norris is often referred to as a liberal "do-gooder" or "welfare capitalist" that put his social justice agenda ahead of the prosperity of his company. This viewpoint reflects the political dichotomies that define what it means to be liberal and conservative in the current political climate than the more blended business strategy Norris followed. While it is certainly true that Norris guided his company into finding ways to address social injustice, for the most part he did this by leveraging the tools of private enterprise instead of the public sector.

Norris believed, and much research backs up his viewpoint, that the remediation of the social ills related to unemployment is eventually picked up by the taxpayer through increased costs related to crime prevention, homelessness, welfare, drug addition, spousal and child abuse, and lost productivity. William Norris felt that Control Data, as a major taxpayer, had a vested interest into finding ways to reduce unemployment, as reducing unemployment would reduce the public demand for government services that address these ills—which in turn would reduce taxes and shrink the size of government. One of the primary reasons Control Data built plants in poverty-area communities was to reduce the costs of welfare in these communities, thus reducing the rate of taxes. So was Control Data a liberal or a conservative company? The definitions of either ideological extreme break down quickly, as Control Data really embraced both philosophies. Perhaps Control Data's history is a place where both liberals and conservatives can find common ground—and maybe even a way forward.

Another theme that emerged throughout interviews for this book was that several former Control Data employees were surprised other corporations didn't follow Control Data's example and pursue social justice initiatives of their own. What would America be like if the private and public sector were not always seemingly at odds, but instead working together to come up with ways to improve the lives of all Americans? Norris's ideas about corporate social responsibility feel more relevant today than they probably were at the time. In recent history, the United States has been shook by the corporate crimes of WorldCom and Enron. Ponzi schemes by corrupt business leaders, such as Bernie Madoff and Tom Petters, have drained the life savings of thousands of individuals. The Great Recession of 2008 caused by subprime mortgage lending is, as of this writing, still negatively affecting the American economy, causing depressed home values and a large unemployment rate. At the same time, local, state, and federal government budgets continue to grow at an alarming, probably unsustainable rate—charged with maintaining the national defense, the country's infrastructure, and the welfare of the poor and unfortunate. The past three decades have been an era of deregulation and corporate freedom that for much of this time generated immense prosperity, so it is not impossible to speculate that greed and unscrupulous business practices have squandered a golden opportunity to maintain that prosperity through social investment from the private sector.

What if more corporate leaders had followed at least some of the ideas championed by William Norris? Corporations serve people—customers, employees, and stockholders—but what if they also directly served their surrounding communities? Combine that observation with the cultural reality that today, many employees consider corporations as a place to work for a short time until a better position can be found at another company. From an HR perspective articulated by the professionals interviewed for this book, this fluidity reduces the stability of organizations to such an extent their productivity is also diminished. So it is worthwhile exploring what William Norris and the others who shared in his vision tried to do, and in several cases succeeded in doing, at Control Data Corporation.

William Norris was interviewed in an article for Inc. magazine in February, 1989. His words are eerily prophetic:

> . . . As I look across the land today, I see an education system that has gone to hell, bulging prisons, homeless people, millions of Americans without health insurance, and a widening gap between the haves and have-nots. It is clear that the current lean-and-mean corporate mentality will assure further deterioration of our society. Corporations must address our unmet or poorly met needs as long range, profitable business opportunities, in cooperation with government and other sectors. That is the only way that we will achieve a fair measure of social justice for all Americans.

William Norris showed us the pathway. All we need to do is follow it.

Appendix A

Control Data Corporation Organizational Charts

THIS APPENDIX CONTAINS A SERIES of organizational charts. These charts show a snapshot of the organizational structure of the company during each decade. Several of the following organizational charts are reprinted, with permission, from *The Eye for Innovation* by Robert M. Price.

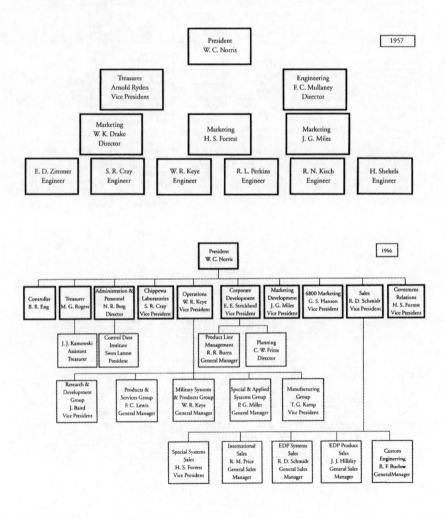

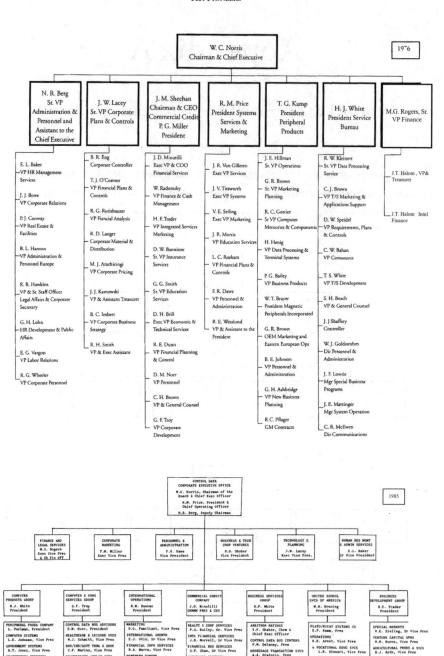

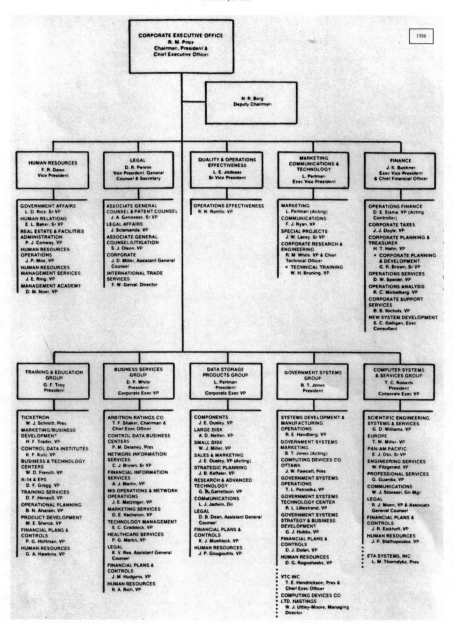

Appendix B

St. Paul *Pioneer Press* Editorial

THE FOLLOWING EDITORIAL WAS PRINTED in the St. Paul *Pioneer Press* on June 2, 1992. The editorial is a perceptive assessment of Control Data's transformation and the moment it marked in corporate history.

Control Data's Story Bears Moral for All

LAST WEEK'S BREAKUP of Control Data Corp. is, we trust, a sound business decision. We wish all success to the new Ceridian Corp., consisting of CDC's computer services operations, and to the new Control Data Systems, Inc. which will continue with the systems-design segment of the business.

The sharpened focus each company will enjoy encourages Wall Street analysts and promises a brighter, more secure future for the corporation's remaining 12,000 employees (more than 3,000 in Minnesota).

Yet we can't help feeling a measure of sadness at this final dismembering of a once-great Minnesota company. A decade ago, Control Data was a cutting-edge colossus with 60,000 worldwide employees and some $4.5 billion in sales. It was a visionary giant, too, committed to a unique scheme to address social problems through corporate strategies—inner-city manufacturing plants, small business support systems, health care initiatives for rural areas, aid to paroled felons and a great deal more.

Sometimes far-fetched, almost always grandiose, Control Data's lofty aspirations at minimum seemed the product of a sound and self-confident business. It was possible to hope the firm's success might inspire imitation of its social programs. Few foresaw the steady withering of the company that has marked the past ten years.

What happened? Well, first off, it wasn't starry-eyed altruism that did CDC in. The social focus was at most a minor distraction. Control Data simply missed the stunning personal computer revolution and otherwise failed to adapt to intensifying competition, foreign and domestic. The company became a casualty—hardly the only one—of the ferocious computer-industry shakeout of the '80s.

There are lessons to be learned from the story, including a simple and ancient one: "Pride goeth before a fall." A more contemporary moral for all American businesses and America

265

itself is this: No one is invincible anymore. In the white-hot competitive atmosphere of the age, it takes but a few mistakes and a trace of complacency to send the mightiest entities tumbling. Ask General Motors.

Control Data, of course, has by no means disappeared, and through many thousands of workers it has trained and seasoned, through scores of successful spin-off companies it has spawned, and through a legacy of responsible and imaginative corporate citizenship, its contributions to the Twin Cities community remain gigantic.

But CDC's less than happy recent history should put us all on alert. In these times, eternal vigilance is the price not just of freedom but of competitiveness too—for companies, for individuals in their careers, for nations.

Bibliography

"About Arbitron—Home." Web. 28 July 2010. <http://www.arbitron.com/about/home.htm>.

Adventium Enterprises. Web. 25 Sept. 2010. <http://www.adventiumenterprises.com/>.

"The Arbitron Company—Company History." *Connecting Angel Investors and Entrepreneurs.* Web. 28 July 2010. <http://www.fundinguniverse.com/company-histories/The-Arbitron-Company-Company-History.html>.

AGPROS—Ag Producers Accounting System. Lubbock, Texas: Agro System Corporation.

"Artesyn Technologies Inc.: Information from Answers.com." Answers.com: *Wiki Q&A Combined with Free Online Dictionary, Thesaurus, and Encyclopedias.* Web. 28 July 2010. <http://www.answers.com/topic/artesyn-technologies-inc>.

Baker, E. L., and R. D. Conner. *Historical Information on CDC Human Services.* Rep. Bloomington, MN: Human Resources Function, Control Data Corporation, July 11, 1980. Print.

Baker, Eugene L. "EAR 10th Anniversary Speech." 2 Aug. 1984. Speech.

———Personal interview. 29 Dec. 2007.

———Telephone interview. 1 Jan. 2011.

Baloga, Jack. Telephone interview. 11 Feb. 2011.

Basic Skill Learning System Productization Plan. Strategic Plan. CBI Research, 1977. Print. Learning Center Courses.

Benson, Chris. "Getting Down to Business: Control Data Corp. Programs Provide Jobs with Dignity." *Ebony* June 1982. Web.

Berg, Norbert R. "Letter to James D. Hodgson." Letter to James D. Hodgson, Secretary of Labor. 4 May 1972. MS.

———"San Antonio Speech." San Antonio, Texas. 2 Mar. 1981. Speech.

———"Speech to the Personnel Department." Aug. 1960. Speech.

———Telephone interview. 17 May 2009.

———Telephone interview. 29 May 2009.

Berg, Norbert, Gene Baker, Frank Dawe, and Jim Morris. Personal interview. 2 Sept. 2008.

Berg, Norbert R., and John P. Moe. "Assistance For Troubled Employees." *PAIR Policy and Program Management.* Washington, D.C.: Bureau of National Affairs, 1978. Print.

"Bill English." Personal interview. 17 June 2009.

"Board of Directors | Adayana." *Adayana | Adayana.* Web. 28 July 2010. <http://www.adayana.com/aboutus/board_of_directors>.

Bowe, James J. "Control Data: One Company's Approach to Productivity Through Improving Work Life." 1982. Web.

"Bowe Talk to PENN." Consumer Conference. 20 May 1980.

"Bruce Aho Joins Legal Research Center's Board of Directors | Business Wire | Find Articles at BNET." *Find Articles at BNET | News Articles, Magazine Back Issues & Reference Articles on All Topics.* 4 Mar. 1999. Web. 24 Sept. 2010. <http://findarticles.com/p/articles/mi_m0EIN/is_1999_March_4/ai_54009693/>.

"Carrier Fleet Management | About PeopleNet Carrier Fleet Communications Systems." *Maximizing Truck Fleet Performance | Truck Fleet Mobile Communications from PeopleNet.* Web. 25 Sept. 2010. <http://www.peoplenetonline.com/company>.

"CDC 6600." *Wikipedia, the Free Encyclopedia.* Web. 27 July 2010. <http://en.wikipedia.org/wiki/CDC_6600>.

"CDC 7600." *Wikipedia, the Free Encyclopedia.* Web. 27 July 2010. <http://en.wikipedia.org/wiki/CDC_7600>.

"CDC 8600" *Wikipedia, the Free Encyclopedia.* Web. 27 July 2010. <http://it.wikipedia.org/wiki/CDC_8600>.

CDC History—Interoffice Memo. Rep. Bloomington, MN: Control Data Corporation. Print.

"CDC Interoffice Memorandum." Letter. 25 July 1988. MS.

A Celebration of the Legacy of Control Data. 12 Oct. 2007. DVD.

"Citi's—Citi's History." Citi—Home. Web. 28 July 2010. <http://www.citigroup.com/citi/corporate/history/>.

"CIVISnet to Help Saint Thomas Academy Build Web-Based Community.—Free Online Library." *Free News, Magazines, Newspapers, Journals, Reference Articles and Classic Books—Free Online Library.* Web. 25 Sept. 2010. <http://www.thefreelibrary.com/CIVISnet to Help Saint Thomas Academy Build Web-Based Community.-a063287349>.

Cluttabeck, David. "Making Social Responsibility Pay." *International Management.* Web.

"Company Milestones | Seagate." *Hard Drives | Seagate.* Web. 28 July 2010. <http://www.seagate.com/www/en-us/about/corporate_information/company_milestones/>.

"Computer Firm Attacked Problems to Humans." *Minneapolis Tribune* [Minneapolis, MN] 2 Feb. 1975. Print.

Conner, R. D. "Fair Break Plan." 1977. MS. Control Data Corporation, Minneapolis.

———*Fair Break Flow Chart.* 1977. Rep. Print.

———Telephone interview. 12 Jan. 2011.

Conte, Alision. *Business Advocate Publicity Plan.* Strategc Plan. 1981. Print.

Control Data: Addressing Society's Major Needs as Profitable Business Opportunities. Bloomington, MN: Control Data Corporation. Print.

"Control Data and the North Side." *Minneapolis Tribune* 28 Nov. 1967. Print.

"Control Data Announces Plan to Build Plant to Train Unskilled." *Minneapolis Star* [Minneapolis, MN] 27 Nov. 1967. Print.

"Control Data Commentary." *Pioneer Press* [St. Paul, MN] 6 Apr. 1989. Print.

Control Data Corporation. "Bright Ideas So Successful, It Will Continue in '83." *Contact* (Jan.-Feb. 1983). Print.

———"Bright Ideas Update." *Management Current* (12 Dec. 1982). Print.

———"Keep Those Bright Ideas Coming." *Contact* (Jan.-Feb. 1984). Print.

———"Perspective." *Management Current* (8 Oct. 1982). Print.

———Simple to Complex, Bright Ideas Save Money, Improve Productivity." *Contact* (Apr.-May 1983). Print.

———"Thirty-Two Days of Bright Ideas." *Management Current* (26 Nov. 1982). Print.

———"Twenty-Five Years of Bright Ideas." *Management Current* (22 Oct. 1982). Print.

———"Twenty-Two Days of Bright Ideas." *Management Current* (12 Nov. 1982). Print.

———"Your Bright Idea Can Win You Extra Vacation." *Contact* (Sept.-Oct. 1982). Print.

"Control Data Corporation." *Wikipedia, the Free Encyclopedia.* Web. 27 July 2010. <http://en.wikipedia.org/wiki/Control_Data_Corporation>.

Control Data Corporation Annual Report. Rep. Bloomington, MN: Control Data Corporation, 1968. Print.

Control Data Corporation Annual Report. Rep. Bloomington, MN: Control Data Corporation, 1970. Print.

Control Data Corporation Annual Report. Rep. Bloomington, MN: Control Data Corporation, 1973. Print.

Control Data Corporation Annual Report. Rep. Bloomington, MN: Control Data Corporation, 1978. Print.

Control Data Corporation Annual Report. Rep. Bloomington, MN: Control Data Corporation, 1980. Print.

Control Data Corporation Annual Report. Rep. Bloomington, MN: Control Data Corporation, 1981. Print.

Control Data Corporation Employee Benefits. Publication. Bloomington, MN: Personnel Department, Control Data Corporation, 1965. Print.

Control Data Corporation History. Rep. J.M. Dain and Company, Feb. 26, 1962. Print.

Control Data Education Company. FairBreak: A Creative Program Addressing Inner City Youth Unemployment. Control Data Corporation, 1977. Print.

"Control Data Spin-Offs and Start-Ups." *The Eye For Innovation.* Web. 27 July 2010. <http://eye4 innovation.typepad.com/eye4innovation/control-data-legacy-trees.html>.

"Control Data Systems, Inc.—Company History." *Connecting Angel Investors and Entrepreneurs.* Web. 28 July 2010. <http://www.fundinguniverse.com/company-histories/Control-Data-Systems-Inc-Company-History.html>.

"Control Data's story bears moral for all." *Pioneer Press* 2 June 1992. Print.

Convergys, A Leader in Relationship Management, Customer Management Solutions, BSS Solutions, and HR BPO Solutions. Web. 28 July 2010. <http://www.convergys.com/company/company-overview.php>.

Conway, Pat. Telephone interview. 13 Nov. 2009.

"The Corporate Psyche and Social Reform." *St. John's Magazine* Fall 1969. Web.

Cox, Meg. "Control Data Puts Its Computers to Work Helping Farmers Make It on Small Plots." *Wall Street Journal* 14 Oct. 1980. Print.

"Cray Inc., The Supercomputer Company—About Cray—History." *Cray Inc., The Supercomputer Company.* Web. 28 July 2010. <http://www.cray.com/About/History.aspx>.

"Cripple Creek Miners' Strike of 1894." *Wikipedia, the Free Encyclopedia.* Web. 5 Sept. 2010. <http://en.wikipedia.org/wiki/Cripple_Creek_miners'_strike_of_1894>.

Cronin, J. P. *Human Resource Center and Handicapped Awareness Course.* Project Update. 1980. Print.

"DARPA | About DARPA." *DARPA | Home.* Web. 1 Jan. 2011. <http://www.darpa.mil/about.html>.

Dawe, Frank R. "International Personnel Manager's Meeting." 3 June 1980. Speech.

———"Personnel Challenges in the Fair Exchange Era." 17 Sept. 1981. Speech.

———"Remarks—International Personnel Conference." 10 June 1982. Speech.

———Personal interview. 12 June 2008.

———Personal interview. 23 Oct. 2009.

———Personal interview. 24 Jan. 2009.

———Telephone l interview. 27 Nov. 2010.

———"Washington Trip—October 18, 1983." Memo. Bloomington, MN: Control Data Corporation, 1983. Print.

"Deal Radar 2009: Adayana." *Sramana Mitra on Strategy.* Web. 28 July 2010. <http://www.sramanamitra.com/2009/02/10/deal-radar-2009-adayana/>.

Desilver, Drew. "Stuckey Eyes Overseas Market—Minneapolis / St. Paul Business Journal." *Business News | Bizjournals.* Web. 28 July 2010. <http://www.bizjournals.com/twincities/stories/1997/06/16/focus2.html?page=2>.

"DigitalThink." *Wikipedia, the Free Encyclopedia.* Web. 28 July 2010. <http://en.wikipedia.org/wiki/DigitalThink>.

"Ed Harris, Chief Executive Officer, Catalyst International, Inc. | Spoke." Spoke.com - Business Directory, Lead Generation, Find People, Business to Business, Business List, Sales Leads, Company Research, B2B, Professional Networking, Social Networking, Find Connections | Spoke. Web. 24 Sept. 2010. <http://www.spoke.com/info/p6JgSqq/EdHarris>.

Eisele, Albert. "MinnPost—Albert Eisele." *William Norris Saw This Coming: In Business, Greed Isn't Always Good.* 20 June 2009. Web. 27 July 2010. <http://www.minnpost.com/alberteisele/>.

"Elearnity - Corporate Learning Analysts." Elearnity - Corporate Learning Analyst. Web. 28 July 2010. <http://www.elearnity.com/EKCLoad.htm?load=ByKey/SHOE53EFMU>.

"Elton Mayo." *Wikipedia, the Free Encyclopedia.* Web. 5 Sept. 2010. <http://en.wikipedia.org/wiki/George_Elton_Mayo>.

"Email from Bob Jones." 11 Sept. 2007. E-mail.

Employee Advisory Resource Intro Piece. Control Data Corporation. Print.

Enberg, Jennifer. Personal interview. 24 Jan. 2009.

Evaluation of Control Data EAR Program: Employee Usage and Cost Impact. Rep. Bloomington, MN: Human Resources Function, Control Data Corporation, July 9, 1987. Print.

Exceptional Care Giving Recognitions. Award Report. Control Data Corporation, April 27th, 1988. Print.

"FAIRBREAK Program." 1978. MS. Control Data Corporation, Minneapolis.

Financial Statement. Rep. Bloomington, MN: Control Data Corporation, 1982. Print.

Financial Statement. Rep. Bloomington, MN: Control Data Corporation, 1983. Print.

Fleck, Helen. "Homework Pilot Program Letter." Letter. 10 July 1978. MS.

Fossum, John A. *Personnel Research Report #10-69* "Rainbow Female Assembler Tenure Study. Rep. Bloomington, MN: Personnel Department Control Data Corporation, 1969. Print.

———Personal interview. 13 Sept. 2008.

———*Personal Research Report #13-69.* Rep. Bloomington, MN: Personnel Department Control Data Corporation, 1969. Print.

———*Personnel Research Report #6-69.* Rep. Bloomington, MN: Personnel Department Control Data Corporation, 1969. Print.

French, Wilbur. Telephone interview. 2 Jan. 2011.

The Functions and Responsibilities of the Personnel Department in the Computer Division. Personnel Department, Control Data Corporation. Print.

"Gone, but Not Forgotten." *Star Tribune* [Minneapolis, MN] 12 Oct. 2007. Print.

Governor's Workforce Development Council. Web. 28 July 2010. <http://www.gwdc.org/member-s/Jack_Wiley.htm>.

Griffith, Cary. "Gary Nelson, In-House General Counsel, Ceridian Corporation, General Counsel Consulting." *In-*

House Attorney Placement, Attorney Resources, General Counsel Jobs, In-House Jobs Search, Attorney Search Placement—General Counsel Consulting. Web. 25 Sept. 2010. <http://www.gcconsulting.com/articles/120044/65/Gary-Nelson-Executive-Vice-President-General-Counsel-Corporate-Secretary-Ceridian-Corporation>.

"A Guide for Managing Cooperative Ventures." 1985. TS. Control Data Business Advisors, Minneapolis.

Guide to Soliciting Venture Capital. 1982. MS. Control Data Business Advisors, Inc.

Handicapped Awareness Course. Strategic Plan. Print. Project MLDC - Minnesota Learning Disabilities Consortium.

Harvey, Stuart. Personal interview. 19 May 2011.

"HealthPlan Services Announces Acquisition Of Controlling Interest In CENTRA Benefit Services - Free Online Library." *Free News, Magazines, Newspapers, Journals, Reference Articles and Classic Books—Free Online Library.* Web. 25 Sept. 2010. <http://www.thefreelibrary.com/HealthPlan Services Announces Acquisition Of Controlling Interest In...-a020807180>.

"Henry Ford." *Wikipedia, the Free Encyclopedia.* Web. 5 Sept. 2010. <http://en.wikipedia.org/wiki/Henry_Ford>.

Henry Ford: America's Greatest History Attraction Home Page. Web. 4 Sept. 2010. <http://www.hfmgv.org/exhibits/fmc/battle.asp>.

"History 1." *Contact* 15 July 1976. Web.

Hobsen, Edwin L., and Richard M. Morrison. "How Do Corporate Start-Up Ventures Fare?" *Strategic Planning Institute.* Print.

Holistic Health Classes, Events and Community : Health Crisis Resource Center : Pathways Minneapolis, Inc. Web. 25 Sept. 2010. <http://www.pathwaysminneapolis.org/page/home>.

HOMEWORK: A Program for Long-Term Disabled Employees of Control Data Corporation. Control Data Corporation. Print.

HOMEWORK Evaluation. Rep. Bloomington, MN: Control Data Business Advisors, October 1985. Print.

HOMEWORK Intro Sheet. Bloomington, MN: Control Data Corporation, 1979. Print.

"How to Black Ban the Unions." *The Weekend Australian* 6-7 Mar. 1982.

Human Resource Management Services "Resource". TS. Control Data Business Advisors.

Humphrey, Hubert H. "Telegram from Hubert H. Humphrey." Letter to Control Data Corporation. 27 Nov. 1967. MS.

"Industry Moves to the Ghetto." *Minneapolis Star* 28 Nov. 1967. Print.

"Internet Society (ISOC) All About The Internet: History of the Internet." *Internet Society (ISOC).* Web. 01 Jan. 2011. <http://www.isoc.org/internet/history/brief.shtml>.

Inter-Office Memorandum. Memo. Bloomington, MN: Control Data Corporation, Aug 26, 1975. Print.

"Inventor Henry Ford Biography." *The Great Idea Finder—Celebrating the Spirit of Innovation.* Web. 5 Sept. 2010. <http://www.ideafinder.com/history/inventors/ford.htm>.

"Jack Wiley, Executive Director, Kenexa Research Institute." *HR People & Strategy.* Web. 3 Jan. 2011. <http://www.hrps.org/?page=Jack_Wiley_bio>.

"Jacobs Wind." *Wikipedia, the Free Encyclopedia.* Web. 28 July 2010. <http://en.wikipedia.org/wiki/Jacobs_Wind>.

Jodsaas, Larry. Telephone interview. 22 Jan. 2011.

———*Minnesota Science and Technology Hall of Fame.* Web. 28 July 2010. <http://www.msthalloffame.org/larry_jodsaas.htm>.

Jones, C. Robert. "Problems at Work." Web. 15 Sept. 1975.

Kaemnerr, William, and Lori Robertson. *Results of the Formative Evaluation of the HOMEWORK Program.* Rep. April 1981. Print.

Kamp, Thomas G. *Management Operating Philosophy.* Memo. 1976. Print.

Klaus, George. Telephone interview. 16 Mar. 2010.

Lacy, Sarah. *BusinessWeek—Business News, Stock Market & Financial Advice.* Web. 28 July 2010. <http://www.businessweek.com/technology/content/jul2006/tc20060720_501134.htm>.

"Leftover Restaurant Food Goes to Needy." *Star Tribune* 5 Dec. 1984. Print.

"The Legacy of William C. Norris." *Ethikos* January/February (1988). Print.

Lemann, Nicholas. "The Question Is: Will He Deliver?" *Washington Post* 16 Dec. 1979. Print.

LePage, D. H. *Basic Skills Project Status.* Issue brief. Control Data Corporation, 1977. Print. Media Development Department.

Liebig, James B. "Business Ethics: Profiles in Civic Virtue." Web.

Liebig, James E. *Control Data Corporation History.* MS.

Lineback, J. Robert. "Remnants of VTC Will Become Analog Chip Foundry." Web. 27 July 2010. <http://www.ee-times.com/electronics-news/4107953/Remnants-of-VTC-will-become-analog-chip-foundry-item-2>.

Lohn, G. H., and J. A. Fossum. Personnel Research Report 12-69 Northside Assembler Tenure Study. Rep. Minneapolis, MN: Control Data Corporation Personnel Department, August 18, 1969. Print.

"Making Social Responsibility Pay." *Contact* Aug. 1977. Web. "Reprinted by special permission from the July 1977 issue of *International Management*"

Management Current 5, #16 (19 Mar. 1979). Print.

Management, StayWell Health. "Total Health Management History—StayWell Health Management—Health Management History." Home_slideshow. Web. 28 July 2010. <http://www.staywellhealthmanagement.com/Company/History.aspx>.

Magnetic Data Technologies Corporation. Web. 25 Sept. 2010. <http://www.mdtglobal.com/Welcome/>.

Marquart, M.D., Clark, and Robert (Sunny) Waln. *Control Data Business Advisors Indian Health Management, Inc.: A Study of Its Development and Services.* Rep. Bloomington, MN: Control Data Business Advisors, April 1984. Print.

"Mary Parker Follett." *Wikipedia, the Free Encyclopedia.* Web. 5 Sept. 2010. <http://en.wikipedia.org/wiki/Mary_Parker_Follett>.

"MDL:MICRO:October 97:Special Report (p.47)." *Chip Shots.* Web. 27 July 2010. <http://www.micromagazine.com/archive/97/10/specrpt.html>.

"Measuring Start-Up Business Performance." 1983. TS. Control Data Business Advisors, Minneapolis.

Medallion Capital, Inc. Web. 27 July 2010. <http://www.medallioncapital.com/>.

"Mel Stuckey." *Fundamental Capital: Financial Expertise, Operating Advice, Guidance, and Growth Capital for Buyouts, Recapitalizations, Mergers and Acquisitions.* Web. 28 July 2010. <http://www.fundamentalcapital.com/team/mel.htm>.

"Memo—N.R. Berg Accomplishments." Letter. 27 Nov. 1985. MS.

Memo to Distribution A and Personnel Managers. Memo. Bloomington, MN: Control Data Corporation, August 29, 1986. Print.

Memo from the 2007 Committee. Memo. Bloomington, MN: Control Data Corporation, Aug. 12, 1986. Print.

Memo from the 2007 Committee. Memo. Bloomington, MN: Control Data Corporation, June 16, 1986. Print.

Morris, Jim. "Email Bullet Points." 10 Sept. 2007. E-mail.

———Personal interview. 15 Jan. 2009.

———Personal interview. 15 Oct. 2007.

———Personal interview. 18 Mar. 2009.

———Personal interview. 19 Sept. 2007.

———"Retirement Letter." Letter to Norbert Berg. 11 July 1988. MS.

"Nasser J. Kazeminy." *Neco.org.* Web. 28 July 2010. <http://www.neco.org/awards/recipients/nasserjkazeminy.html>.

———Personal interview. 25 April 2011.

———Telephone interview. 21 Sept. 2010.

"NetBackup." *Wikipedia, the Free Encyclopedia.* Web. 28 July 2010. <http://en.wikipedia.org/wiki/NetBackup>.

"Network Systems Corporation." *Wikipedia, the Free Encyclopedia.* Web. 28 July 2010. <http://en.wikipedia.org/wiki/Network_Systems_Corporation>.

"New Day at Rosebud." *Contact* Oct. 1974. Web.

Noer, David M. "Agony and Ecstasy: One Company's Experience in Transforming the Human Resource Function to a Line Organization." Control Data Business Advisors. Speech.

———"Chapter 10 Lessons in Converting Staff Units into Profit Centers." *Internal Markets Bringing the Power of Free Enterprise inside Your Organization.* New York: J. Wiley, 1993. Print.

———"Managing for Entrepreneurism—A Three Pronged Approach." Executive MBA Alumni Workshop. University of Illinois. 19 May 1984. Speech.

———"Speech Utah State University." Utah State University. 23 Jan. 1985. Speech.

———Telephone interview. 22 Nov. 2009.

"Norbert Berg, CDC Exec, Is Retiring after 29 Years." *The Wall Street Journal* [New York, NY] 8 June 1988. Print.

Norris, William. "Back to the Countryside Via Technology." National Agri-Marketing Outlook Conference. Kansas City, MO. 8 Nov. 1977. Speech.

———*Control Data Corporation Annual Report (Introduction).* Rep. 1964. Print.

———"A New Opportunity to Improve America's Prisons." (29 Dec. 1983). Print.

———*President's Newsletter No. 44* (14 Dec. 1967). Print.

N.R. Berg Accomplishments. Memo. Bloomington, MN: Control Data Corporation, 1985. Print.

O'Connell, James. Telephone interview. 19 May 2009.

O'Fahey, S. M., and T. M. MiddenDorf. *The East Central Minnesota Small Family Farm Proposal. Proposal.* 1980. Print.

Olsen, Fred C. "How Peer Review Works." *Harvard Business Review* Nov.-Dec. 1984. Web.

"Operation Inner Dale "An Operation Plan for Installing and Operating FAIRBREAK Center in the Selby/Dale District of St. Paul." 1977. MS. Control Data Corporation, Minneapolis.

"Operational Planning Workbook." 1982. TS. Control Data Business Advisors, Inc., Minneapolis.

Paris, M.L., R.A. Rich, J.E. Ring, and M.H. Vacura. *Ties That Bind.* Ethics Statement. Bloomington, MN: Human Resources Function, Control Data Corporation, July 1988. Print.

"Sandy Weill: Information from Answers.com." *Answers.com: Wiki Q&A Combined with Free Online Dictionary, Thesaurus, and Encyclopedias.* Web. 28 July 2010. <http://www.answers.com/topic/sandy-weill>.

People Management Principles. Ethics Statement. Bloomington, MN: Human Resources Function, Control Data Corporation, March 10, 1987. Print.

Personnel Department, Control Data Corporation. "Control Data Corporation—Highlights and Organization Talk Before College Grad New Hires." June 1967. Speech.

Personnel Hiring Philosophy. Ethics Statement. Minneapolis, MN: Personnel Function, Control Data Corporation, 1961. Print.

Phillips, Scott. Memo: *HOMEWORK Background.* Rep. Bloomington, MN: Control Data Corporation, Feb 4, 1986. Print.

"PLATO (computer System)." *Wikipedia, the Free Encyclopedia.* Web. 27 July 2010. <http://en.wikipedia.org/wiki/PLATO_(computer_system)>.

"Plato Learning—Our History." Web. 27 July 2010. <http://www.plato.com/index.asp>.

Polar Semiconductor, Inc—A Sanken Company. Web. 28 July 2010. <http://www.polarfab.com/>.

Price, Robert M. "Change: Innovation in the Corporate DNA." *Quality and Participation Magazine* Summer 2006. Web.

———"Computer Systems Strategic Threats and Responses." 14 Mar. 1985. Speech.

———"Sowing the Seeds of Innovation." Hesolbim and Co Winter (2007). Print.

———*The Eye for Innovation: Recognizing Possibilities and Managing the Creative Enterprise.* New Haven [Conn.: Yale] UP, 2005. Print.

———Telephone interview. 24 Nov. 2009.

———Telephone interview. 31 Mar. 2010.

———Telephone interview. 20 Nov. 2010.

Pobtilla, Laural. *Personal Research Report 13-69: The Effect of the College Recruitment Program on the Termination and Prevention Rates.* Rep. Bloomington, MN: Personnel Department, Control Data Corporation, 1970. Print.

Prometric Services: Testing and Assessment. Web. 22 Sept. 2010. <https://www.prometric.com/Services/company/default.htm>.

Radsack, E.R. *Basic Skills.* Inter-Office Memo. Text Development, 1977. Print.

Reid, R.C., and S. J. Busch. *Chronology of Key Events in Control Data's History.* Rep. Bloomington, MN: Control Data Corporation. Print.

Reilly, Mark. "Adayana Deal Expands Reach in Defense—Minneapolis/St. Paul Business Journal." *Business News | Bizjournals.* Web. 28 July 2010. <http://www.bizjournals.com/twincities/stories/2006/09/04/newscolumn1.html>.

Reflections and Expectations: 25 Years of Personnel at Control Data. Decathlon Club, Minneapolis, MN. 13 May 1982. Speech.

Rich, Ruth A. "Employee Relations at Control Data: A Review and a Preview." 1981. Speech.

———Telephone interview. 1 Mar. 2009.

———Telephone interview. 8 Feb. 2009.

Risking Credibility—A History of Control Data's First Inner City Plants. 1982. MS.

Rizza, P. J. *Schedule for Basic Skills.* Progress Update. 1977. Print.

Rolfes, Nicholas A. *Farm Management Plan.* Rep. no. Strategic Plan. Print.

"Rosebud Brings Health Care Home." *Contact* Oct. 1977. Web.

Rosenberg, Jennifer. "Henry Ford—Biography of Henry Ford." *20th Century History.* Web. 5 Sept. 2010. <http://history1900s.about.com/od/1920s/p/henryford.htm>.

Rudack, E. R. "Memo." Letter to P.J. Rizza. 20 Oct. 1977. MS.

Rural Venture—Comprehensive Economic and Human Development in Small Towns and Rural Areas. Rural Venture. Print.

Ryan, Frank. "Norbert R. Berg—Deputy Chairman of the Board to Retire from CDC." *Star Tribune* 8 June 1988. Print.

Schoenbohm, William. "Courage Center Letter." Letter to William Norris. 16 Feb. 1981. MS. Courage Center.

"Seymour Cray." *Wikipedia, the Free Encyclopedia.* Web. 27 July 2010. <http://en.wikipedia.org/wiki/Seymour_Cray>.

"Specific Plan: A Fair Break in Rural Minnesota." Web. 21 Dec. 1976.

Sullivan, Beth. *Chapter 1 Project Overview.* Publication. Minnesota Department of Education, 1979. Print.

"Syntegra (USA) Inc. Company Profile—Yahoo! Finance." *Top News Archive—Yahoo! Finance.* Web. 28 July 2010. <http://biz.yahoo.com/ic/11/11174.html>.

"Ticketron." *Wikipedia, the Free Encyclopedia.* Web. 28 July 2010. <http://en.wikipedia.org/wiki/Ticketron>.

"Ticketron—Get Great Deals for Ticketron on EBay!" *EBay—Find Popular Products on EBay!* Web. 28 July 2010. <http://popular.ebay.com/entertainment-collectibles/ticketron.htm>.

Twelve Baskets—Food Rescue Program. St. Paul, MN, 2008. Print.

"Various Forms of Conducting Business." 1983. TS. Control Data Business Advisors, Inc., Minneapolis.

Varley, Tom. Telephone interview. 25 Jan. 2011.

Walter-Hunter, P. *Basic Skills Council.* Rep. 1978. Print.

Watson, Jr., T.J. *IBM Memorandum.* Memo. IBM Corporation, August 18, 1963. Print.

Welcome to Adventium Labs | Adventium Labs. Web. 25 Sept. 2010. <http://www.adventiumlabs.org>.

Welltimes—"A Health Newsmagazine for Control Data Employees and Their Families" Vol. 1, No. 3, (1981). Print.

Worthy, James C. "The Business Philosophy of William C. Norris Founder of Control Data Corporation." *Barcelona International Academy of Management* (1987). Print.

———*William C. Norris: Portrait of a Maverick.* Cambridge, MA: Ballinger Pub., 1987. Print.

Willette, Susan. Telephone interview. 2 Mar. 2009.

"Winland Electronics, Inc.—2000 Annual Report." Corporate Information, *Winland Electronics, Inc.* Web. 25 Sept. 2010. <http://www.winland.com/corporate/annual00/part3.html>.

"WTIC Profile." *Wind Turbine Industries.* Web. 28 July 2010. <http://www.windturbine.net/about.htm>.

Youngblood, Dick. "Control Data Commentary." *Star Tribune* 10 Apr. 1989. Print.

Index